The House of the Seven Gables

Salem Witchcraft and Hawthorne's House of the Seven Gables

Enders A. Robinson

HERITAGE BOOKS, INC.

Published 1992 By
HERITAGE BOOKS, INC.
1540E Pointer Ridge Place, Bowie, MD 20716
(301)–390–7709

ISBN   1-55613-515-7

Library of Congress Catalog Card Number: 91–78137

Library of Congress Cataloging-in-Publication Data
Robinson, Enders A., 1930-
   Salem Witchcraft and Hawthorne's House of the Seven Gables/
Enders A. Robinson
   p.   cm.
   Includes bibliographical references and index.
   1. Trials - (Witchcraft) - Massachusetts - Salem. 2. Witchcraft -
Massachusetts - Salem - History. 3. Hawthorne, Nathaniel, 1804-1864. 4.
New England - History - Colonial period, ca 1600-1775. I. Robinson,
Enders A. II. Title: Salem Witchcraft and Hawthorne's House of the
Seven Gables

Cover design: Elizabeth Brewster Rocchia
Imagesetting by Custom Printing & Design, Leominster, MA 01453
Printed in the United States of America

In memory of

Sarah Wardwell and her daughters
Sarah Hawkes, Mercy Wardwell, and Rebecca Wardwell
imprisoned in Salem in 1692

"I am not aweary, mother," replied the little girl. "But you may sit down, if you will tell me a story meanwhile."

"A story, child!" said Hester. "And about what?"

"Oh, a story about the Black Man," answered Pearl, taking hold of her mother's gown, and looking up, half earnestly, half mischievously, into her face. "How he haunts this forest, and carries a book with him—a big, heavy book, with iron clasps—and how this ugly Black Man offers his book and an iron pen to everybody that meets him here among the trees; and they are to write their names with their own blood. And then he sets his mark on their bosoms! Didst thou ever meet the Black Man, mother?"

"And who told you this story, Pearl?" asked her mother, recognizing a common superstition of the period.

Nathaniel Hawthorne
The Scarlet Letter

TABLE OF CONTENTS

PREFACE

M ILLIONS OF AMERICANS are descendants of the Puritans who first settled New England. In researching their genealogies, more than a few people with names like Johnson and Jackson are astonished to find that their families were involved in the Salem witchcraft affair of 1692. To discover that one's forebears include a witch—or two—among the usual mix of farmers, tradesmen, and goodwives is indeed a rude shock.

As a young man, my father made an extensive collection of the family lore that had been handed down over generations. Because his great-great-great-great-great grandparents, Samuel and Sarah Wardwell, were both convicted of witchcraft, and Samuel was hanged in Salem on September 22, 1692, my father (1872–1952) always believed that his mother's side of the family, the Wardwells, had been placed in permanent disgrace and shame. Although he saved all the collected records, letters, and other written accounts, he consigned them to oblivion in the attic of our house in Marshfield, Massachusetts. The attic became a morass filled indiscriminately with everything from valuable antiques to worthless junk. Ancient military commissions of the Barker family, and bibles, books, and framed portraits of Wardwell ancestors were piled with scrap wood left over from some carpenter job. Old willow-ware china was mixed with decoys, canvas, oar locks, and fishing equipment.

Many heirlooms throughout the house—old rope beds and other furniture, many books, and written material in notebooks and folders—originally belonging to my Wardwell and Barker ancestors in the town of Andover, Massachusetts, came to us by way of my father's aunt, Hanna Wardwell (1857–1950). Because the unorganized and unprotected materials of history easily are dispersed and lost, it seemed appropriate to gather those pieces which formed a readable narrative. Starting out on this journey, I soon felt an irresistible urge to learn more, even to find, perhaps, some possible explanation for the Andover phase of the Salem witch hunt.

The accused Salem witches came not only from the township of Salem but from nearly all the towns of Essex County. In fact more people were arrested in Andover than in Salem Village. Much information on Andover's role in the witch hunt can be found in records deposited in archives in the towns of Andover and North Andover. Andover today represents the southern part of the original seventeenth-century Andover township, and North Andover represents the northern part.

The most valuable source for the present book proved to be the published and unpublished work of Charlotte Helen Abbott (1844–1921). Abbott was born in Andover, a descendant of an early Andover family which was intimately linked with the witchcraft tragedy. She taught school and was a dressmaker. A naturalist of the Thoreau tradition, she spent many hours walking the Andover countryside. She wrote articles on astronomy and the rare trees and flowers of Andover. She was one of the first women in Andover to register when women finally gained their right to vote in 1921. She knew everybody in town, and enjoyed collecting their family stories handed down through generations. Starting as a hobby, genealogy soon became her profession. Her extensive knowledge of the families of old Andover was published in her numerous articles in the *Andover Townsman* and the *Boston Transcript*. A popular contributor to the *Andover Townsman* for more than twenty-five years, her final column appeared only a few days before her death. Abbott was a fine writer and an accomplished and authoritative genealogist.

In addition to her published work, Charlotte Helen Abbott left thousands of pages of hand-written documents, largely genealogies and the materials upon which they were based. During the 1930s the Andover Historical Society obtained a government grant for a WPA typist to transcribe many of her manuscript genealogies into typescript, an enormous task, carefully and conscientiously done. Five years ago I spent weeks poring over her work. At first, the job of trying to piece together the roles of all the Andover people involved in the Salem witchcraft tragedy seemed overwhelming. Gradually, however,

PREFACE

an underlying structure became evident which helped to explain many of the Andover events of 1692. That structure forms the basis for this book.

I am especially indebted to Helen M. Bowdoin who contributed numerous passages to the book. In addition she edited the manuscript with patience and skill, and offered unfailing support throughout the entire project.,

Grateful thanks are given to Robert Dean Clark of the Society of Exploration Geophysicists; Alison C. D'Amario and Tina Jordan of the Salem Witch Museum; Alice Bowdoin Goodfellow of Washington College; Professor David D. Hall of Harvard University; Martha Hamilton, former director of the North Andover Historical Society; Michael Hays, assistant vice-president of Prentice Hall Inc.; Gratia Mahony, president of the Andover Historical Society; Professor Daniel Marder of the University of Tulsa; Rufus M. Perkins; and Barbara Thibault, director of education of the Andover Historical Society.

Special thanks go to Marjorie Wardwell Otten, my cousin, for her many contributions of genealogical and historical material and for her long-standing support of this project.

I want to express my sincere thanks to Karen Ackermann and Lyn Cannon of Heritage Books for their help in the preparation of the manuscript.

It is with deep appreciation that I acknowledge my gratitude to Anne Farnam, president of the Essex Institute in Salem from 1984 until shortly before her death in 1991. Her interest in the book gave valued encouragement. Her rare grace and her courage offered an inspiring example to be treasured for years to come by all who knew her.

Enders A. Robinson
Lincoln, Massachusetts 01773
November 1991

EXPLANATIONS AND ABBREVIATIONS

The letters mnu stand for "maiden name unknown."

In the genealogical charts, an equal sign between a man and woman indicates marriage. The two married people can be either on the same horizontal level or they can be one above the other, depending upon the space available in the construction of the chart. A solid vertical line and tree diagram leads to their children underneath. In case a stepchild or a nephew is shown under a married couple, a dashed line is used instead and the relationship is indicated in parentheses.

In the charts, accused witches are shown in boldface. The conspirators and the afflicted are shown in italics.

The Andover touch test was an event held on September 7, 1692 and is treated in Chapter 14.

This book makes use of genealogical information available at the Andover Historical Society, the North Andover Historical Society, and the New England Historic Genealogical Society, in particular the works of Charlotte Helen Abbott and Marjorie Wardwell Otten. More detailed information, including the tracing of the seventeenth-century families to more recent generations, can be found in their works.

1

THE CRIME OF WITCHCRAFT

S TORIES AND CHRONICLES OF THE PAST, whether happy or sad, form the common heritage of all civilizations. History is overburdened, however, with grim events. Of the countless stories of suffering and injustice, most are cast aside, replaced by an unending supply of new ones. Yet tempting as it is to discard and sometimes even to deny old stories, we do so at our peril. These accounts are often our only reminders of the past; they are valuable for what they can teach. A story may be lost for many years, only to be found and retold. This book gives an account of the Salem Village witch hunt. It also tells the almost forgotten story of the fifty people of Andover, Massachusetts, who were imprisoned for witchcraft in Salem in 1692.

Nathaniel Hawthorne was and remains the foremost author writing about early New England life. His place in American literature, one could argue, approaches that of Shakespeare in English literature. Suppose that information about the life of Shakespeare's great-great-grandfather had been preserved, even including many verbatim transcripts of his dialogue, his very words. Suppose further that Shakespeare claimed that much of his own work was inspired by his ancestor. Would it not be worthwhile to place the fiction of Shakespeare and the actual expressions of his ancestor in one volume as point and counterpoint? Although such a situation, of course, does not hold for Shakespeare, it does hold for Nathaniel Hawthorne.

1

Nathaniel Hawthorne's great-great-grandfather, John Hathorne, was the chief witch hunter during the Salem witchcraft affair of 1692. Nathaniel Hawthorne wrote about the sentiments and passions of the people involved in these events. Because of what he regarded as the "persecuting spirit" of his Puritan forebears, Hawthorne wrote, "I, as their representative, hereby take shame upon myself for their sakes, and pray that any curse incurred by them may now and henceforth be removed."[1] The writing of his classic romance, *The House of the Seven Gables*, served as an expiation of the guilt he felt for the misdeeds of his ancestors, a catharsis of his own feelings.

Extant legal and family documents cannot reveal people's innermost thoughts and aspirations. Nathaniel Hawthorne's ancestry and genius uniquely equipped him to look into the past, to delve into the minds of the early Puritan forebears and bring to light their hidden feelings. Even as a book is enriched by old prints and drawings, the same book can be enhanced by the words of a perceptive writer. For this reason a few score passages from the fiction of Nathaniel Hawthorne, identified by footnotes, have been included in this volume. These Hawthorne excerpts are intended as illustrations, nothing more. Like a picture of an old house, the fictional passages here convey no factual information about the story, but help to illuminate seventeenth-century New England life and its people.

Hawthorne's fiction stands in sharp contrast to the pronouncements made by his ancestor. When magistrate John Hathorne examined Mary Lacey, Jr. in 1692, he asked the questions, "Did you at any time use to ride upon a stick? Do you not anoint yourself before you fly?"[2] Nathaniel Hawthorne answered the questions when he wrote, "But—would your worship believe it?—my broomstick hath strangely disappeared, stolen, I suspect, by that unhanged witch, Goody Corey, and that, too, when I am all anointed with the juice of smallage and cinque-foil and wolf's bane—"[3]

---

1   Hawthorne, *The Custom-House.*
2   Essex Institute, *Witchcraft Collection,* "Examinations."
3   Hawthorne, *Young Goodman Brown.*

To the grandmother of Mary Lacey, Jr., Goody Foster, who denied the allegations, John Hathorne cried, "But as for you, old woman, though you have shown something of relenting, yet you retain a lie in the mouth."[4]   Of the same grandmother, Nathaniel Hawthorne in fiction wrote, "There hobbles Goody Foster, a sour and bitter old bedlam, looking as if she went to curse, and not to pray, and whom many of her neighbors suspect of taking an occasional airing on a broomstick."[5]

To the modern reader, the real words of his ancestor seem like fiction, whereas the fictional words of Nathaniel Hawthorne ring true. Two representatives of the same family, living in different centuries, were able to capture the essence of the Puritan age, yet in widely divergent, nearly opposite ways.

Throughout history, witch hunts or their counterparts have occurred periodically. Accusations of people as witches or agents of the Devil are commonplace. But a witch hunt can take place only when the government provides police action to arrest the accused, and legal authority to prosecute on the basis of the imaginary crime of covenanting with the Devil. Witch hunts feed upon fear. Their primary causes are envy, avarice, and pride in one or more of their many disguises. All witch hunts that have been carefully studied are shown to be impostures; the accusations spring from conspiracies sanctioned by governing authorities.

Historically witchcraft represented the various types of nature religions emphasizing healing arts by magical means. Witchcraft also included varieties of magic and sorcery practiced in Asia, Africa, and Latin America. The traditional European viewpoint held that witchcraft was a type of harmful sorcery associated with worship of the Devil. This diabolical interpretation of witchcraft was formulated in the late Middle Ages. Many of the beliefs about witches were based on delusion but some were claimed to be based on reality. The punishment of supposed witches by the death penalty first became common in the fifteenth century.

---

4   Essex Institute, *Witchcraft Collection*, "Examinations."
5   Hawthorne, *Main-Street*.

The doctrine of witches and familiar spirits has been current from ancient times. Scripture depicted the witch's character, warned of its blighting influence, and enacted heavy penalties against employing its agency. The biblical authority was Exodus xxii, 18: "Thou shalt not suffer a witch to live." Leviticus, xx. 27, states, "A man also or a woman that hath a familiar spirit, or that is a wizard, shall surely be put to death: they shall stone them with stones: their blood shall be upon them." Deuteronomy, xviii. 9-12, says, "When thou art come into the land which the Lord thy God giveth thee, thou shalt not learn to do after the abominations of those nations. There shall not be found among you any one that maketh his son or his daughter to pass through the fire, or that useth divination, or any observer of times, or any enchanter, or a witch, or a charmer, or a consulter with familiar spirits, or a wizard, or a necromancer; for all that do these things are an abomination unto the Lord."

Witchcraft as a force in European life was manifested chiefly during the fifteenth, sixteenth, and seventeenth centuries. During prior centuries, when faith was universal and doubt almost unknown, the Devil was regarded with something like contempt. Usually depicted as an insignificant imp, the Devil could have his malignity rendered harmless by the repetition of a prayer or by making the sign of the cross. However with the onset of skepticism and heresy, the church began to picture the Devil as more dangerous and to concern itself with his direct relations with human beings. It was in the thirteenth century that theologians worked out their theory of witchcraft, and in the fourteenth century the church drew all witchcraft cases into its own jurisdiction. The end of the sixteenth century, and the beginning of the seventeenth century, a period of religious conflict and chaos, mark the height of the witchcraft persecutions in Europe.

The first major witch hunt occurred in Switzerland in 1427, and the first important book on the subject, the *Malleus Maleficarum* (Hammer of Sorceresses), appeared in Germany in 1486. Persecution of alleged witches reached its height between 1580 and 1660, when witch trials raged throughout western Europe. Geographically, the center of witch persecutions lay in Germany, Austria, and Switzerland, but few areas were left untouched. The total number of victims is unknown. In southwestern Germany alone, however, it is said that more than 3,000 witches were executed between 1560 and 1680.

"It is astonishing that there should still be found today people who do not believe that there are witches. For my part I suspect that the truth is that such people really believe it in their hearts, but will not admit it. They are refuted by Canon and Civil Laws; Holy Scripture gives them the lie; and repeated confessions of witches prove them wrong." With these words, Henri Boguet justified his actions as one of the judges involved in the trials, torture, and burning of many alleged witches in Burgundy at the end of the sixteenth century.[6]

Not all witch trials ended in conviction and death. In England, where many forms of torture were prohibited, only about twenty percent of the accused witches were executed (by hanging); in Scotland, where torture was used, nearly half of all those put on trial were burned at the stake. Almost three times as many witches were executed in Scotland as in England. Some countries held fewer trials than others. In the Dutch republic, no witches were executed after about 1600, and none were tried after 1610. Accusations of witchcraft in Spain and Italy were handled by the Inquisition, and although torture was legal, only a dozen witches were burned out of 5,000 put on trial. Ireland apparently escaped witch trials altogether. [Significantly, many witch trials were provoked, not by hysterical authorities or fanatical clergy, but by village quarrels among neighbors.]

About three-quarters of all accused witches were women. Traditional theology assumed women to be weaker than men and thus more likely to succumb to the Devil. Woman, having been formed from a bent rib, was supposedly an imperfect being and considered a deceiver. It may in fact be true that having few legal rights, women were more apt than men to settle quarrels by resorting to magic rather than law. However, blatant misogyny was always evident.

All these aspects of witchcraft crossed over to the Americas with the European colonists. In the Spanish and French territories, cases of witchcraft were under the jurisdiction of

---

6   Boguet, *An Examen of Witches*, Introduction.

church courts and no one suffered death on this charge. In the English colonies about 40 people were executed for witchcraft between 1650 and 1692, half of them in the infamous Salem witch trials of 1692. Witch trials declined in most parts of Europe after 1680; in England the death penalty for witchcraft was abolished in 1736. The last legal execution of a witch occurred in Switzerland in 1782.

In many places the superstition lingers even to today. Beginning in the 1920s, witchcraft was revived in Europe and America by groups that considered it a survival of pre-Christian religious practices. This phenomenon was partly inspired by such books as Margaret Murray's *The Witch Cult in Western Europe* (1921). So deeply rooted are these beliefs that the passage of centuries has not removed them. Some forms of modern witchcraft follow the traditions of medieval herbalists and lay healers. Nowadays the term witch hunt is commonly used to describe a drive to punish political dissidents without regard for the normal legal safeguards.

To most Americans, witchcraft suggests a specific isolated historical event, the Salem witchcraft affair of 1692. However the Salem witch hunt may be considered in conjunction with the many European witchcraft crazes in the sixteenth and seventeenth centuries. From this viewpoint Salem was not a unique event. What is unique about Salem is that it occurred after the great European witchcraft epidemics had ceased. By 1692 most learned people knew, or should have known, better. No major witch hunt took place after Salem, although isolated events occurred for nearly another one hundred years.

Educated men gave the Western concept of witchcraft its most disturbing characteristic, the connection of sorcery with heresy. In non-Western cultures, a so-called witch was one who performed magic. The magic could be evil, but it was not viewed as an effort to destroy religion. The Europeans, however, created a demonic image of the witch by associating harmful magic with religious dissent. In European culture a witch came to be regarded as an agent of Satan and an enemy of God. In the invisible world run by the Devil, a witch would attend black sabbats, worship Satan, and reject Christianity. The result of these beliefs was the witchcraft trials which swept Europe and America reaching their culmination at Salem.

In Puritan New England, Satan was a vivid reality. The clergy preached that the Devil was constantly using his ingenuity to defeat the divine will and employing his hellish agents to plague and tempt the select of God. All the conditions favoring a witch hunt had been fermenting in Massachusetts from its earliest settlement.

It may seem surprising that witch hunts simultaneously developed with the great cultural movements of the sixteenth and seventeenth centuries. The renaissance in art and literature, the reformation and the counter reformation, overseas explorations, and the rise of modern science provide an unlikely backdrop for witchcraft persecutions. A closer look, however, shows that witch hunting was a means for the educated elite to impose its values and standards of behavior on the lower classes. Elite groups—lawyers, judges, theologians, physicians, large landowners, and political rulers—were the very ones who most vigorously asserted the reality of cults devoted to the Devil. By promoting and transmitting superstitions and fears to the uneducated majority, they were able to divide and rule. Rival religious groups were labeled heretic and satanic in origin, and so-called undesirable people could be driven out simply by branding them Devil worshippers and witches. The witch hunts were the inevitable consequence of the elite's hunger to gain more power.

The foremost literary work representing the official point of view in the Salem trials is Cotton Mather's book *The Wonders of the Invisible World*, published in October 1692. In fact, Cotton Mather and some other Harvard-educated clergy, notably Samuel Parris, Nicholas Noyes, John Hale, and Thomas Barnard, provided the theological impetus for the witch hunt. Nathaniel Hawthorne wrote, "In the rear of the procession rode a figure on horseback, so darkly conspicuous, so sternly triumphant, that my hearers mistook him for the visible presence of the fiend himself; but it was only his good friend, Cotton Mather, proud of his well won dignity, as the representative of all the hateful features of his time; the one blood-thirsty man, in whom were concentrated those vices of spirit and errors of opinion, that sufficed to madden the whole surrounding multitude."[7]

Rational people did speak out at Salem, but their words were not heeded until the witchcraft mania had claimed many victims. Boston merchants Thomas Brattle and Robert Calef were the two most powerful voices. Brattle's opposition was expressed in his letter of October 8, 1692 and Calef's was documented in his book *More Wonders of the Invisible World*, composed and distributed during and after the witch hunt, but not published until 1700. In his poem *Calef in Boston*, John Greenleaf Whittier (1807-1892) contrasts Calef, the tradesman, and Cotton Mather, the preacher.

> In the solemn days of old,
>   Two men met in Boston town,
> One a tradesman frank and bold,
>   One a preacher of renown.
>   ...
> In the ancient burying-ground,
>   Side by side the twain now lie;
> One with humble grassy mound,
>   One with marbles pale and high.
>
> But the Lord has blessed the seed
>   Which that tradesman scattered then,
> And the preacher's spectral creed
>   Chills no more the blood of men.[8]

---

7   Hawthorne, *Alice Doane's Appeal.*
8   Whittier, *Complete Poetical Works.*

2

PURITAN DOGMA

IN THE EARLY PART OF THE SEVENTEENTH CENTURY, the Puritan settlers of New England worked to create a very different world from the one they had left behind. The Puritan settlers devoutly believed that their colony represented the nation described in I Peter 2: 9,10, "But ye are a chosen generation, a royal priesthood, a holy nation, a peculiar people; that ye should show forth the praises of him who hath called you out of darkness into his marvelous light." They devised an entirely new legal structure for their Puritan commonwealth. At its base was a dogma which drew from the militancy of the Old Testament in combination with English law and its traditional safeguards. These elements did not mesh well together. More than this, the structure was fundamentally flawed.[9] The history of New England was marked by continuing controversy over the role of civil laws in a religious community.

It is not easy for present day Americans to visualize life in England in 1630. England at that time was in the process of emerging from the medieval system in which people generally had been divided into two classes. The great majority, those of the lower class, were expected to do the manual work required to keep the society functioning. A small aristocracy represented the upper class. The oldest aristocratic son inherited his father's estate to become the new lord of the manor. The younger sons of the aristocracy usually entered the church, military service, or universities, and under their guidance the system was perpetuated.

---

9   Nowhere would this become more apparent than in the Salem witchcraft proceedings of 1692.

Under the medieval system, the sons of the workers would generally follow in the footsteps of their fathers with little opportunity for advancement or change. However, by the 1600s, a new group was springing up at the forefront of a technological revolution. This group had acquired technical skills which enabled them to earn money on their own rather than be dependent on the landed aristocracy. This was the beginning of the middle class.

The middle class formed the backbone of the Calvinistic movement. In England, Calvinists generally came to be known as Puritans. They organized their churches under the congregational principle. The Puritans stood in opposition to the religious establishment of England, which was under the control of the aristocracy. The established Church of England was an authoritarian church, pyramidally organized from the peak of earthly authority (the King of England) downward through archbishops, bishops, and priests to the lowly communicant.

The Puritans, or at least the extremists, renounced the Church of England entirely, declaring it false and counterfeit. The Puritan leaders then went about establishing separatist congregations, voluntarily covenanting together to live as a people of God under ministers of their own choosing (rather than ministers set over them by a bishop). Moreover, the congregations were free to discipline their own membership and to admit only those who, so far as they could judge, were sanctified and entitled to the promises of salvation and eternal life.

Of course, such an extreme position put forth publicly in England could subject a Puritan minister to persecution. Normally, the dissenting ministers remained within the national church as nonconformists, all the while hoping for an ultimate reformation. Meanwhile, the new world beckoned.

In 1630, John Winthrop, a wealthy gentleman of Groton in Suffolk, England, led a small group of Puritans to New England. En route across the Atlantic on the *Arbella*, the flagship, Winthrop delivered a sermon which he summed up with the vow, "We shall be as a City upon a Hill."[10] The community

---

10   Winthrop, *Journal, 1630-1649*.

would become the center and the seat of the church. Beyond would be fields which the people would cultivate and on which they would graze cattle. In a larger sense, the community would be a city of God, a society where ideas of Christian brotherhood and right conduct would be expounded from every pulpit. The new American city was founded at a place called Shawmut by the Indians. Soon the name of this new town was changed to Boston, after the Boston in Lincolnshire, England.

But why should these events, which took place so many centuries ago and involved only a handful of people, be of interest today? The Puritan heritage is deeply rooted in American culture. On one hand, bitter criticism is often directed against America's Puritan mentality. On the other hand, lavish praise is just as often heaped upon America's Puritan ethics. Everything concerning Puritanism seems painted as either good or bad; seldom is there a middle ground.

The American Puritans were avid disciplinarians. The congregations were supposedly voluntary associations of the brethren, but actually they gave rise to a collectivist discipline marked by tense watchfulness. Despite what is said about Puritan individualism, in the seventeenth century there was never respect for the privacy of the individual. The Puritans believed that they were living in a world of chaos and crime, and directed their efforts to constantly guard against sin. They routinely enforced their concept of moral discipline to unreasonable degrees. The following is a partial list of offenses that merited criminal punishment in New England.

Crimes against the church (disturbing the congregation, contempt of the ministry, absence from service).

Contempt of authority (criticism of the government, berating public officials, seditious speeches).

Disturbing the peace (disorderly conduct, drunkenness, card playing, dancing and other vanities).

Fornication and sexual adventure (including offenses charged against married parents whose first child came too soon after the wedding).

Crimes against persons (assault, slander, defamation).

Crimes against property (theft, borrowing and not returning, sloth in business, wagering).

In each congregation a type of local terrorism was maintained by the "godly" elders to enforce this discipline. According to the eminent British Puritan Richard Baxter, the enforcement of the new moral order was made possible "by the zeal and diligence of the godly people who thirsted after the salvation of their neighbors."[11] In each town informers spied on their neighbors and reported suspicious behavior to the clergy and the magistrates.

Any deviant behavior was criminal. The Puritans did not take into account the myriad shadings between various forms of misbehavior; everything not white was black. No distinction was made between persons who flatly violated the law and those who infringed on the prescribed customs. The court took instant notice of anyone who drank too much, who dressed in inappropriate clothes or indulged some other form of scandalous behavior, who let their hair grow too long, who talked too much or played frivolous games. The word of God governed everything and was to be protected with all the state's machinery. Punishments were severe: the stocks, banishment, whippings, and executions.

Hawthorne evoked such a scene: "In close vicinity to the sacred edifice appeared the sacred engine of Puritan authority, the whipping-post—with the soil around it well trodden by the feet of evil doers, who had there been disciplined. At one corner of the meeting house was the pillory, and at the other end the stocks. Side by side, on the meetinghouse steps, stood a male and female figure. The man was a tall, lean, haggard personification of fanaticism, bearing on his breast this label—A WANTON GOSPELLER—which betokened that he had dared to give interpretations of the Holy Writ, unsanctioned by the infallible judgment of civil and religious rulers. The woman wore a cleft stick on her tongue, in appropriate retribution for having wagged that unruly member against the elders of the church. Among the crowd were several whose punishment would be life-long; some whose ears had been cropped; others, whose cheeks had been

11   Sylvester, M., ed., *Reliquiae Baxterianae*, 87.

branded with the initials of their misdemeanors; one, with his nostrils slit and seared; and another, with a halter about his neck, which he was forbidden ever to take off. There was likewise a young woman, with no mean share of beauty, whose doom it was to wear the letter A on the breast of her gown, in the eyes of the whole world and her own children."[12]

The court ordered that "no person shall spend his time idly or unprofitably, under pain of such punishment as the court shall think meet to inflict; and for this end it is ordered that the constable of every place shall use special care and diligence to take knowledge of offenders of this kind."[13] The community as a whole was expected to bring any deviants to the court's attention. Each citizen was expected to guard the public moral code as carefully as that of his own household. He had license to spy on his neighbors and to disrupt their privacy. Nathaniel Hawthorne described New England as a place where it was policy to search out and expose even the most secret sins.

The obligation of a citizen included the duty of reporting even members of his own family who deviated from the strict Puritanical code. Governor John Winthrop, in his explanation of this responsibility, wrote, "A godly minister, upon conscience of his oath and care of the commonwealth, reported to the magistrates some seditious speeches of his own son, delivered in private to himself."[14] In the tightly disciplined Puritan community, people were familiar with each other's affairs and willing to interfere at the slightest hint of sin or scandal. The towns were small and compact; everyone was ready to report the movements of neighbors to the magistrates. A woman who had lost her temper when the cow kicked over the milk pail would be brought trembling into court. Happy in the belief that they were doing their duty, her accusers would cite her delinquencies into the public record so she could be punished as a criminal. In 1692, she would be hanged as a witch.

---

12   Hawthorne, *Endicott and the Red Cross.*

13   Essex County, Massachusetts, *Court Records*, 1:109.

14   Winthrop, *Journal, 1630-1649.* 1:126.

Many scholars seem to connect the spiritual roots of the Puritans with a sense of guilt. The writings of New England divines offer a reliable transcription of the dark ideas that tortured the Puritan conscience. Their works provide insight into the principles of good and evil that they passed down to their congregations in their sermons. The Puritan ministers subscribed to a moral code of great simplicity. The forces of good, all stemming from God, were pitted against the evil powers of Satan. God and the Devil pursued their own ends in antagonism to each other. Moreover, each had the same ultimate goal, the conquest of man's spiritual kingdom. John Milton's great epic poem *Paradise Lost* represents the classic expression of Puritan thought.

Because salvation through the love of God was the central doctrine of their religion, it followed that subordination of present pleasures to future good was a primary tenet in the conduct of social and religious life. The clergy always feared that their parishioners would be seduced by illusory pleasures of earthly existence. A most insidious temptation was the sensuous appeal of the beautiful. To the Puritans, the religious art of the Catholics, not only the rich vestments and beguiling liturgical music, but also the paintings and statues, fostered a Devilish iconolatry. The Puritan clergy believed that beauty seduced the hearts of men away from God.

Not only did the Puritan ministers dread the temptations of earthly pleasures, but they also harbored a deep fear of intellectual curiosity. They were alarmed by the scientific revolution currently taking place. To them any endeavor to look into the mysteries of the universe that went beyond the revelations of scripture was anathema. Such an undertaking was regarded as something done in league with the Devil to gain forbidden knowledge.

The sincerity of Puritan belief in the possibility of personal communion with the Devil was unequivocal. The Devil relied upon temptation as his chief weapon. Since man was tainted by original sin, his soul was in constant jeopardy. Consciously or unconsciously, he could establish a fatal pact with the Devil and become a witch. Although a witch might gain transitory pleasures, it would lose eternal salvation. To the clergy witchcraft was the most shocking example of depravity and the most abhorrent sin imaginable. Its worst feature was the witch's arrogant rejection of God. Any outbreak of witchcraft could seriously menace the security of Christendom. Consequently the Puritan clergy had to stand guard, ready to put down incipient evil wherever it appeared.

The early leaders of New England dedicated themselves to the task of establishing the Kingdom of God in the new world. Members of the ruling class set themselves up as "visible saints," and required everyone to live as they believed God intended. Drawing their authority from holy scripture, the Puritan leaders regulated their society according to its rigid code. Quickly they imposed rigorous controls on the personal behavior on all citizens, Puritans and non-Puritans alike. Swearing, drunkenness, and any other licentious behaviors were severely penalized. The law and government were in effect derived from the sermons about hell-fire and burning brimstone that were delivered from the pulpits. The Puritan leadership no more believed in democracy and the political rights of individuals than in religious toleration, and they denounced both with equal vehemence.

The intolerance inherent in Puritan thinking permitted the old guard to become despotic in their rule; the Puritan elite were, after all, the "elect," God's representatives on Earth. To the devout Puritan, New England resulted from God's plan to plant His kingdom. Conflict between the Puritans and the Indians was continuous over land and power, but it also extended into the supernatural realm. The Puritan clergy preached that Indians were like devils from hell and that their rituals were diabolic. The clergy dismissed the Indian shamans and medicine men as witch doctors, open practitioners of magic and witchcraft.

Although the intention was to build a heaven on earth, the fate of New England was, predictably, far different. The Puritan founding fathers had decreed such a fanatical code of conduct that, after the first great wave of immigration during the 1630s, many new settlers shunned New England like a plague. By the late 1650s it was common knowledge that Quakers coming into New England suffered terribly from Puritan despotism. As time went on the Puritan old guard turned its wrath even more harshly against its own citizens. The stocks, whipping posts, and gallows were in constant use in New England, all for the preservation of God's kingdom. Anyone who offended the scruples of Puritan morality had a great price to pay.

Misogyny was rampant throughout New England from its earliest settlement. Underlying distrust of women first came to a head in Massachusetts in the trial of the Puritan woman Anne Hutchinson in November 1637. The pretext was that the religious leaders were merely protecting their cherished religious tenets. In actuality it was an action against a woman who exceeded her assigned place in a society absolutely dominated by an elite group of men. "Mrs. Hutchinson was a woman of extraordinary talent and strong imagination," wrote Nathaniel Hawthorne.[15]

What were the feelings of Anne Hutchinson as she faced her accusers in court? The magistrates compelled her to stand until her "countenance discovered some bodily infirmity." Governor John Winthrop pointed out that the magistrates were the fathers of the Commonwealth of Massachusetts, and thus in criticizing their conduct she was disobeying God's command to honor her father and mother. Winthrop concluded, "Your course is not to be suffered for, besides that we find such a course as this greatly prejudicial to the state."[16] With these words, Winthrop lent authority to the continuing series of attacks against women that would culminate in the Salem witchcraft trials of 1692.

Anne Hutchinson was banished from Massachusetts. She first went to Rhode Island and then finally settled in New Amsterdam at a place which is now New Rochelle, New York. There Anne and her children were killed in an Indian assault, except for an infant daughter who was carried away into captivity. The river which flowed by her homesite was named the Hutchinson River in her honor.

It was an offense in Massachusetts to walk the streets on a Sunday other than to church. A young couple in Connecticut were arrested for sitting under an apple tree on a beautiful Sunday afternoon. Not only were all people required to attend both

---

15   Hawthorne, *Mrs. Hutchinson.*
16   Styles, *A Report on the Trial of Mrs. Anne Hutchinson.*

morning and afternoon services on Sundays, but also long services called lectures on Thursday afternoons.

"It is Thursday Lecture; an institution bearing relations to both the spiritual and ordinary life, and bringing each acquainted with the other. The tokens of its observance are of rather questionable cast. It is, in one sense, a day of public shame; the day on which transgressors, who have made themselves liable to the minor severities of the Puritan law, receive their reward of ignominy. At this very moment, the constable has bound an idle fellow to the whipping-post, and is giving him his deserts with a cat-o'-nine-tails. Ever since sunrise, Daniel Fairfield has been standing in the steps of the meetinghouse, with a halter about his neck, which he is condemned to wear visibly throughout his lifetime; Dorothy Talby is chained to a post at the corner of Prison Lane, with the hot sun blazing on her matronly face, and all for no other offense than lifting her hand against her husband; while, through the bars of that great wooden cage, we discern either a human being or a wild beast. Such are the profitable sights that serve the good people to while away the earlier part of lecture-day."[17]

Charles Francis Adams, the eminent scholar and descendant of American presidents, wrote, "The mania of 1691-92 in Massachusetts was no isolated or inexplicable manifestation; on the contrary, it was the most noticeable instance of the operation of law—given John Winthrop's journal in 1630-1640, Salem witchcraft at a somewhat later period might with safety be predicted. The community was predisposed to the epidemic."[18] Adams goes on to say that the Puritan leaders in waging their vigorous struggle for self-government and a church free from English control unwittingly indoctrinated New Englanders with the seeds of democratic thinking, a far cry from their professed beliefs.

---

17   Hawthorne, *Main-Street*.
18   Adams, *Massachusetts, Its Historians and Its History*, 85-86.

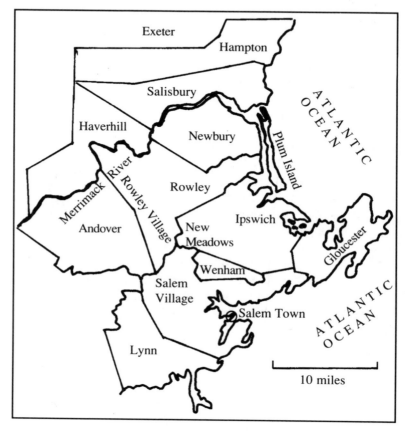

Essex County and the towns of Hampton and Exeter in 1643.

3

SALEM AND ANDOVER

S ALEM, MASSACHUSETTS, WAS FIRST SETTLED IN 1626, only six years after the arrival of the *Mayflower* at Plymouth. Except for a few little coastal settlements, the whole of New England was an undisturbed wilderness inhabited by Indians.

The Algonquin Indians of New England were less warlike and less nomadic than generally perceived. Primarily an agricultural people, they remained within the general area where they cultivated the soil. The tribes that lived in Essex County in Massachusetts each possessed certain acknowledged territory. The region north of the Merrimack River belonged to the Pentucket tribe. The remainder of the present county of Essex was divided by a line from North Andover to Salem Bay. East of the line was the territory of the Agawam tribe. West of the line was the land of the Naumkeag Indians, who constituted a part of the great Massachusetts tribe.

The Indians had a village at the site of Salem before the white man's arrival. They lived in wigwams and had cleared a considerable piece of ground, on which they cultivated corn. These Indians were friendly, a quiet and peaceful people. They welcomed Roger Conant and his little band of settlers when they first came to this locality to make it their home. Conant described the place as a fruitful neck of land, projecting into the sea, with grass growing thick and long and very high. There were strawberries everywhere, raspberries, plums, grapes, and other wild fruits in profusion. Brilliant wild flowers, scented herbs, and wild roses made the place seem like a paradise.

Tradition says that the main thoroughfare, Main Street (now called Essex Street), was originally an Indian path. Near the

19

corner of present-day Essex and Washington Streets, the settlers erected the first meetinghouse. "There stands the meetinghouse, a small structure, low-roofed, without a spire, and built of rough timber, newly hewn, with the sap still in the logs, and here and there a strip of bark adhering to them. Their house of worship, like their ceremonial, was naked, simple, and severe. But the zeal of a recovered faith burning like a lamp within their hearts, enriching every thing around them with its radiance; making of these new walls, and this narrow compass, its own cathedral," wrote Nathaniel Hawthorne. He then continued, "All so well, so long as their lamps were freshly kindled to the heavenly flame. After a while, however, whether in their time or their children's, these lamps began to burn more dimly, or with a less genuine luster; and then it might seem, how hard, cold, and confined, was their system—how like an iron cage was that which they called Liberty."[19]

In 1628 John Endicott arrived with many new settlers, and the community became a substantial and permanent settlement. Shortly afterward a flood tide of immigration converged on New England, and Salem turned into a flourishing and prosperous town. The catching and curing of fish for shipment to Europe became a major occupation. Ship-building was an important industry and sea trade opened up with distant ports. The thriving young town of Salem became wealthy, aristocratic, and influential.

Salem's crown of glory was always her shipping and her commerce. At one time, the name of Salem was known in the Far East—China, Japan, Sumatra, and Java—as well as in other ports as far away as the Cape of Good Hope. Yet the birth of Nathaniel Hawthorne in Salem marks the town to the world more than perhaps all else that has happened before or since. No great author is as closely associated with Puritan New England as Nathaniel Hawthorne. The ties handed down from his ancestors were literal and spiritual, and neither strayed far from his awareness. His ancestors had won prominence and wealth in New England's early history. Yet from them he had inherited a curse, or so he believed. The ancestral curse sprang

---

19   Hawthorne, *Main-Street.*

from the role his ancestors played during the Quaker persecutions in the 1650s and the 1660s, and the Salem witchcraft affair of 1692.

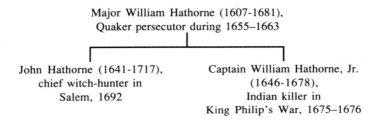

Major William Hathorne (1607-1681),
Quaker persecutor during 1655–1663

John Hathorne (1641-1717), chief witch-hunter in Salem, 1692

Captain William Hathorne, Jr. (1646-1678), Indian killer in King Philip's War, 1675–1676

Nathaniel Hawthorne was born in Salem on July 4, 1804. At the time his name was spelled Hathorne, but later he added a "w," changing the name back to its ancient spelling, Hawthorne. (The pronunciation is the same, whichever way it is spelled.)

The lineage of Nathaniel Hawthorne is as follows. His American ancestor was Major William Hathorne (1607-1681), the forebear of the line of the family in Salem, Massachusetts. The Major's son was magistrate John Hathorne (1641-1717); his son was sea-captain Joseph Hathorne (1691-1762); his son was sea-captain Daniel Hathorne (1731-1796); his son was sea-captain Nathaniel Hathorne (1775-1808); and his son was Nathaniel Hawthorne (1804-1864), the author. Major William Hathorne (1607-1681) had a brother John Hathorne (1605-1676) who was the forebear of the line of the family in Lynn, Massachusetts.

When Nathaniel Hawthorne was only four years old, his father, sea-captain Nathaniel Hathorne, died on a sea voyage. The death was attributed to the ancestral curse of the Hathornes. In 1809 the Nathaniel Hawthorne's widowed mother moved with him and his two sisters into the house of her relatives, the Mannings. It soon became apparent that the family had lost its independence. As time went on, his mother's mourning gradually became lifelong seclusion.

Although Nathaniel was a sailor's son, and came from an ancestry of sailors, he was taken in charge by a landsman, his Uncle Manning. From 1821 to 1825, Nathaniel attended Bowdoin College in Brunswick, Maine, where Henry Wadsworth

Longfellow and Franklin Pierce (later to become the fourteenth president of the United States) were his classmates and friends.

In 1825 Nathaniel returned to his mother's house in Salem and spent a dozen years in relative seclusion. His mother and sisters were very reclusive in their habits. Each lived alone in her own room. There was no family meal, no family circle. Rarely did they go visiting, and visitors seldom came to them. Nathaniel quickly fell into the same habits. He stayed in his room most of the day, and his meals were usually left at his locked door. When he did go out it was typically for a solitary walk to the seaside, usually early in the morning or after dark. The few people aware of his existence looked upon him as an aimless idler.

During these years Hawthorne was working to establish himself as an author. He read and wrote, instead of entering a profession or trade as expected of him. But his efforts attracted no attention and earned him no money. He grew discouraged, and portrayed his despair in *The Devil in Manuscript* and *The Journal of a Solitary Man*. In 1828 he anonymously published *Fanshawe*, a story that drew heavily on his experiences at Bowdoin College. He also began writing tales and sketches that appeared in newspapers and magazines.

In 1839 Nathaniel Hawthorne emerged from his seclusion to court Sophia Peabody. They became engaged to marry. In 1839 and 1840 he worked in the Boston Custom House, writing very little. In 1841 he joined the Brook Farm Community at West Roxbury, Massachusetts, where he had hoped to provide a home and a living for Sophia, but he withdrew before the end of the year.[20] On July 9, 1842 he and Sophia married in Boston, and from 1842 to 1845 they lived in the Old Manse in Concord, where their neighbors were Emerson, Thoreau, and Alcott. There he wrote more sketches and tales, and in 1846 published *Mosses from an*

---

20   Brook Farm was founded as an experiment in transcendentalism "to insure a more natural union between intellect and manual labor" and "to prepare a society of liberal, intelligent and cultivated persons." The commune also attracted Ralph Waldo Emerson, feminist Margaret Fuller, newspaper editor Charles Dana, and abolitionist Bronson Alcott, the father of writer Louisa May Alcott.

Nathaniel Hawthorne
1804-1864

Sophia Hawthorne
1809-1871

Old Manse. From 1846 to 1849 he worked in the Salem Custom House. His mother died while he was writing *The Scarlet Letter.* This book, which won him his first fame, was published in 1849. From 1851 to 1852 Hawthorne lived in Lenox, Massachusetts, where Herman Melville was his neighbor and friend. In 1851 he published *The House of the Seven Gables.* Hawthorne then entered into his mature stage of writing which lasted to his death on May 19, 1864.

Nathaniel Hawthorne wanted to restore his family's good name through his writing. Much of his work was drawn from his knowledge of his forebears and their roles in the seventeenth-century events in New England. He steeped himself in the lore of Essex County, using places there as scenes for many of his stories. He wrote historical sketches, and allegorical tales dealing with moral conflicts in colonial New England. These stories of guilt and secrecy reveal Hawthorne's near constant preoccupation with the effects of Puritanism in New England. Hawthorne's marriage to Sophia Peabody profoundly influenced his life. Their very happy marriage was founded on mutual love and understanding. Sophia not only encouraged his writing but also opened his imagination to the beauty and strength of womanhood. The nobility of Hester Prynne in his romance *The Scarlet Letter* is almost wholly due to the example and influence of Sophia.

Typical of seventeenth-century New England towns was Andover, 25 miles north of Boston. The township of Andover originally included the present towns of Andover and North Andover and that part of the city of Lawrence which lies south of the Merrimack River. The territory was called Cochichawick by the Indians, and was part of the territory of the Naumkeag, which was within the Indian domain ruled by the Massachusetts tribe. The sagamore (that is, subordinate chief) of the Massachusetts when Andover was settled was Cutshamache, who lived near Dorchester (now a section of the city of Boston). In 1642 he asked the colonial authorities to give him a coat. He was one of five Indians who on March 8, 1644 placed themselves under the authority of the government of the Massachusetts Bay Colony. The legal document drawn up by the Puritan leaders states that these Indians "put ourselves, our subjects, lands and estates under the government and jurisdiction of the Massachusetts."[21] The European concept of property rights was unknown to the Indians; they could not have possessed the least understanding of the consequences of such a deed.

The Puritans went one step further. They found it necessary to examine these Indians as to their religious beliefs and moral attitudes. To the requirement "to worship the only one true God," the Indian response was, "We do desire to reverence the God of the English, and to speak well of him, because we see he doth better to the English than other gods do to others." To the requirement "not to swear falsely," the Indian answer was, "They say they know not what swearing is among them." To the requirement "to commit no unclean lust, or fornication, adultery, incest, rape, sodomy, buggery, or bestiality," the Indian answer was, "Though sometimes some of them do it, yet they count that naught, and do not allow it." The document concludes, "The authorities were satisfied with the result of the examination and accepted their allegiance. The General Court ordered the colonial treasurer to give each of the Indians a coat of red cloth, two yards of material in each, and a potful of wine. The Indians presented the members of the court with twenty-six fathom of wampum."[22] The result of this exchange was that the five Indians surrendered all the land in Massachusetts to the colonists.

In 1644 the General Court in Boston granted the ownership of the entire Andover township to a group of men under the leadership of Simon Bradstreet. These men, known as the first settlers or proprietors, numbered twenty-three on the first extant list. The village center of Andover was established in the northeastern section of the township. Two roughly parallel streets were laid out, separated by open land, and house lots were assigned to these men. Each owner of a house lot also received a meadow, tillage, and a woodlot on the outskirts. According to their plan, all of them would live in the relatively compact village center, and would farm the land that surrounded the center, but in some cases lay quite distant.

---

21 Perley, *Indian Land Titles of Essex County*, 35-35.
22 Ibid.

A church was formed in Andover on October 24, 1645 with the installation of the Rev. John Woodbridge as pastor.[23] In 1646, on behalf of the town, he purchased from the sagamore Cutshamache all the land in the township. The amount paid was £6, which was handed over by the Rev. Woodbridge and Edmond Faulkner. As part of the consideration, a coat was also given to Cutshamache. The local Indians also received a consideration, namely, Roger, the Indian, and his company, were given the liberty to take alewives in the river for their own consumption, but that privilege would cease if the Indians spoiled or stole any corn or other fruit belonging to the English inhabitants. Further, it was granted that Roger should continue to enjoy the four acres of ground that he then cultivated. The mass of the Indians had retreated to the lands north of the Merrimack River. Yet they were close enough that Andover was considered the frontier of the wilderness.

Because the first settlers could not sustain a self-contained community without additional support, it was necessary for them to attract others to live in their town. The plan was that the proprietors would take a certain amount of land for themselves, leaving the bulk of the land in common to be distributed one way or another to newcomers as well as to themselves as the need arose. However the first settlers in making their decisions took care to ensure that they would retain political control of the town.

In any new community, distribution of land is of fundamental importance. In Andover the first settlers were responsible for deciding how to divide the abundant land. Every inch of land in the entire town had been given to them by the General Court. The cumulative effects of their decisions regarding the

---

23   John Woodbridge, born in England in 1613, attended Oxford before emigrating to Newbury, Massachusetts in 1634. He entered Harvard College and was its first graduate. He then became master of the Boston Latin School. In 1638 he married Mercy Dudley, born in 1621, the daughter of Thomas Dudley. Mercy was the sister of Simon Bradstreet's wife Anne. John Woodbridge, ordained in 1644, became the first minister of the Andover church. Resigning the post in 1647 he returned to England and became minister at Andover in England. Ejected at the Restoration, he came back to Newbury, Massachusetts.

allotments of land were decisive in determining their positions of power. From the beginning, there was a hierarchy of rank and wealth among Andover families rather than equality.

The earliest book of Andover town records still existing lists of "the names of all the freeholders in order as they came to town."[24] In fact, the order in the table reflects more accurately the rank of the first settlers than their date of arrival. By the witchcraft epidemic of 1692, these original settlers were in old age or dead. But, except in a few instances, their families were prosperous and held political control of the town government. These Andover proprietors were:

Mr. Simon Bradstreet (first on the list by his rank)
John Osgood, Sr. (second on the list by his rank)
Joseph Parker (brother of Nathan Parker)
Richard Barker
John Stevens
Nicholas Holt
Benjamin Woodbridge
John Frye, Sr.
Edmond Faulkner
Robert Barnard (no relation to the Rev. Thomas Barnard)
Daniel Poor
Nathan Parker (brother of Joseph Parker)
Henry Jacques
John Aslet
Richard Blake
William Ballard
John Lovejoy
Thomas Poor
George Abbot, Sr.
John Russ
Andrew Allen
Andrew Foster
Thomas Chandler

---

24   Bailey, *Historical Sketches of Andover*, 11.

Simon Bradstreet, the town's leader, was a magistrate and an assistant to the governor.[25] His wife, Anne (Dudley) Bradstreet, was the first woman poet in America. The original minister in Andover, the Rev. Woodbridge, served from the town's first settlement in 1643 to 1647, when he returned to England with his brother, proprietor Benjamin Woodbridge. The next minister of Andover was the Rev. Francis Dane, who served for 49 years, from 1648 to his death in 1697.

The land distribution scheme provided the first families with holdings on a scale impossible for most of them to have anticipated possessing either in England or in the towns in which they had first settled in the New England. Nathan Parker, who had arrived in 1638 as a young indentured servant, received more than 213 acres from the town. At his death in 1685 he left an estate of more than 225 acres to his widow Ann (mnu) Foster.[26] Daniel Poor, also originally a servant, received the same amount of land. Others, like George Abbot, Sr., who settled as landless young men, received at least 122 acres. Men such as Nicholas Holt and John Osgood, Sr., both of whom had owned land in Newbury before settling in Andover, increased their landholdings appreciably, Holt from 110 acres in Newbury to at least 457 in Andover, and Osgood from 163 acres in Newbury to 610 in Andover.[27]

By 1663 the big chunks of the land, for all practical purposes, had been distributed. The first formative twenty years of the town's history, 1643–1663, were over. The division of land made in those years served to establish for many generations the basis for family life in this essentially agricultural community. The first settlers' economic futures in Andover were secure.

---

25 On this list Bradstreet was the only one given the honorific title of Mr. The titles Mr. and Mrs. were only used by the upper classes. Ordinary men were addressed with the title Goodman, and their wives with the title Goodwife, shortened to Goody in familiar speech.

26 Often the maiden name of a married woman helps clarify relationships. In such cases the maiden name is inserted in parentheses after the first name. In case her maiden name is unknown, the abbreviation mnu for "maiden name unknown" is used.

27 Greven, *Four Generation: Population, Land and Family in Colonial Andover*, Chapter 3.

Henceforth, the families of the first settlers would control most of the land in the community, with far-reaching consequences for everyone. Those who arrived after 1663 were to discover why it paid to be among the pioneers.

The first settlers ensured their economic and social status after 1663 by decisively altering the method of granting land to prospective Andover settlers, whether to their own children or newcomers from outside. Previously, only five second-generation sons of early settlers had been granted estates comparable to those of first-generation inhabitants. Although such ample grants might have been continued, the first settlers decided to institute a new policy.

By the late 1660s, no more large divisions of common land were granted. The town thus drastically reduced the amount of land available to individuals seeking land. However, the town did sell twenty-acre plots of land to any acceptable person wishing to settle in Andover. The price of the twenty-acre lots was not great. The purchasers were to pay the town forever the sum of ten shillings a year, half in wheat and half in Indian corn.

By the early 1660s, the structure of Andover began to change. Many of the townsmen with sizable parcels of land at a considerable distance from the village center preferred to live there instead of in the village center. By about 1680, nearly half the inhabitants of Andover had moved to the south part of the town, an area remote from the village center, which was in the north part. The dispersion of so many people to their distant farming lands radically altered the character of Andover, transforming it into a scattered collection of farms among which communication was no longer easy and constant.

The first families still formed a small closely-knit group, most of whom were interrelated by marriage. Four or five selectmen were elected each year to run the town. (In New England, a town was governed not by a mayor but by a group of selectmen who were elected at the town meeting.) For the twenty-three-year period from 1670 to 1692, these selectmen positions were filled by just 24 men. With one exception, these few men represented the first families. John Marston, Sr., who settled in Andover in 1664, was the only outsider ever to penetrate this exclusive group.

Over the years the dispersal of the first families weakened and diminished the cohesive structure that they had enjoyed when living together in the village center. The scattering of the first families made them more vulnerable to the charges which would be brought against them in 1692.

The Barkers are representative of the first families of Andover. Richard and his wife Joanna settled in Andover in 1643 and had nine children. Richard was adept at land investments. Buying additional property with ponds and mill streams, he eventually owned land down to the Merrimack River. Richard Barker was a surveyor and was road commissioner as early as 1653. His name appears as witness on most of the wills of the period and he signed petitions and acted as a town selectman up to his last days. By 1692, he was infirm. The power of the family had shifted to his children; his oldest son, Lieutenant John Barker, took a leading role in town affairs. Richard Barker died in 1693. The small group of the first-settler families dominated the political and economic life of the community to the near exclusion of newcomers and those of lesser status.

A few farms were already in place in Andover before 1643. Job Tyler, born in England about 1619, was one of these early farmers. About 1640 Job married a woman named Mary and squatted in Andover near the present-day Boxford line. The couple had six children. Four of their children enter this story: Moses born about 1642, Mary about 1643, Hopestill about 1645, and John about 1653. In 1643 Job and his growing family were forced out of Andover by the new settlers, the proprietors. He moved, with burning resentment, across the border into the adjacent Rowley Village (named Boxford in 1685).[28] But in 1644 he was able to buy back a small portion of his former land from the proprietors and thereby become an admitted inhabitant of

---

28 Over the years the original township of Rowley, founded in 1639, was cut up into separate towns. The southwestern section, first known as Rowley Village, was incorporated as a separate town in 1685 and named Boxford. The northwestern section, first known as Rowley Village by the Merrimack, was named Bradford in 1675 and was annexed in 1897 by the city of Haverhill. The eastern section is the present-day town of Rowley.

Andover. Deeply in debt because of this transaction, he had to mortgage his house, land, and cows in Andover to John Godfrey.

In 1658, Job Tyler apprenticed his son Hopestill Tyler to Thomas Chandler, an original proprietor and the blacksmith of Andover. As part of the ruling class, Chandler treated the young Hopestill with the disdain appropriate for the lower classes. Hopestill and his father had many disagreements with Chandler. Turning to litigation to obtain a settlement, Job Tyler instigated a number of lawsuits against Chandler, but to little or no avail.

Job Tyler regularly felt pinched in his dealings with the blacksmith Thomas Chandler, who nonetheless permitted Hopestill Tyler to complete his apprenticeship. "The blacksmith sat in his elbow chair, among those who had been keeping festival at his board. Being the central figure of the domestic circle, the fire threw its strongest light on his massive and sturdy frame, reddening his rough visage, so that it looked like the head of an iron statue, all a-glow from his own forge, and with its features rudely fashioned on his own anvil. The only other person at the fireside was [Hopestill Tyler], formerly an apprentice of the blacksmith, but now his journeyman."[29]

John Godfrey, described as "a most active patron of county courts and a stirrer up of strife,"[30] was a man who knew how to make effective use of the law suit. In a series of disputes over the mortgage and other things, Job Tyler and Godfrey instigated law suits against each other. Still frustrated, Job Tyler discovered an effective means that made the establishment sit up and take notice. Job Tyler accused Godfrey of witchcraft in 1659. Although never convicted on this count, Godfrey was discredited and his standing weakened. Job Tyler realized that a witchcraft allegation acted as powerful medicine for his otherwise failing causes.

A sample of Job Tyler's use of a witchcraft accusation is the following record of 1659. "The deposition of Job Tyler, aged about 40 years, Mary, his wife, and Moses Tyler, his son, aged betwixt 17 and 18 years, and Mary Tyler [his daughter], about 15 years

29   Hawthorne, *John Inglefield's Thanksgiving.*
30   C. H. Abbott, *The Andover Townsman,* October 2, 1896.

old. These deponents witness that they saw a thing like a bird to come in at the door of their house with John Godfrey in the night, about the bigness of a blackbird or rather bigger, to wit, as big as a pigeon, and did fly about, John Godfrey laboring to catch it, and the bird vanished, as they conceived, through the chink of a jointed board; and being asked by the man of the house wherefore it came, he answered, it came to suck your wife. This was, as they remember, about 5 or 6 years since. Taken upon oath of the 4 above mentioned parties, this 27th day, 4th month, 1659, before me, Simon Bradstreet."[31]

In 1661 Godfrey initiated a complicated suit against Job Tyler who countersued, and Job's oldest child, Moses Tyler then 19, testified. Moses, a loyal son, supported his father. Job appeared in 17 court cases overall against his nemesis John Godfrey, 7 as defendant and 10 as plaintiff. The final result of these suits and countersuits was that the Tyler family lost most of their land in Andover for a second time. To add to their troubles, their house burned down while Job was away looking for work. In 1661, Job Tyler, destitute and beaten down from fighting Andover's tight-knit establishment moved again to Rowley Village (named Boxford in 1685). Godfrey inflicted a parting blow on Job Tyler in a suit for wheat, worth £5, that Job had not paid for. Defeated, Job sold on June 11, 1662 his four acre house lot in the center of Andover, with two acres on the west side next to John Frye's land. These two acres held a house, barn, orchard, and rights to more common land not laid out. The buyer was George Abbot, "the tailor," who paid £29.[32] Last of all, in November 1662, Job alienated his remaining estates in Andover, including forty acres in the common lands, to his opponent John Godfrey. In 1665, in one last futile attempt, Job Tyler brought a suit against Thomas Chandler and John Godfrey to right old wrongs. Reduced to groveling for a living, Job Tyler continued to aggravate the establishment. In 1665 Job, considered a trespasser, was actually sued by a farmer for removing Indian graves from his property.

---

31 Bailey, *Historical Sketches of Andover*, 196; Drake, *Annals of Witchcraft*, 52.

32 Essex County, Massachusetts, *Court Records*, Deeds, 2:58.

The question of the rights of the buried Indians was never an issue.

In 1671 with little more than the clothes on their backs, Job and his family moved west to the new town of Mendon, a land of apple trees and wild cranberries. They settled beyond the last garrison houses, the only places of safety during Indian raids. There, up the Blackstone River, Job Tyler helped to establish the new settlement. His blacksmith son, Hopestill, was attracted by the iron ore found in the swamps. His daughter Mary, now married to widower John Post, went with the family.

In 1676 an Indian raid on Mendon destroyed the town, yet again leaving the besieged family with nothing, except the pewter plates and brass kettles that they had managed to bury in time in the swamp. John Post was killed by the Indians. His wife Mary (Tyler) Post and their young daughters, Mary Post and Hannah Post, survived, as well as his daughter, Susannah Post, by his previous marriage. In 1678, Hopestill Tyler married Mary Lovett, daughter of Mendon neighbor Richard Lovett. In the next year Hopestill and his new wife loaded their precious feather bed and settled in the south part of Andover, where he took up his trade as blacksmith. Hopestill's sister, Mary (Tyler) Post, now remarried to blacksmith John Bridges, settled in the north part of Andover. Mary (Tyler) Post Bridges and Mary (Lovett) Tyler, both wives of Andover blacksmiths, would be arrested for witchcraft in 1692. The original Andover blacksmith, Thomas Chandler, aged 65, was on the side of the accusers.

By 1680 Job Tyler and his sons, Moses Tyler and John Tyler, managed to make their way back to their original safe haven, Rowley Village, and settled there permanently. As before, they tried to avoid the taxes of both Rowley Village (named Boxford in 1685) and Andover by settling in an area between the two centers. However, Job Tyler and his son Moses were duly inspected to see if they attended church services, with the result that they were assigned to pay rates to the Andover church. In this sense, they were more citizens of Andover than Boxford. Job died in 1700 and was buried in Andover.[33]

---

33 In the old North Andover burying ground, a stone bears the tablet, "In memoriam. Job Tyler, immigrant. First Andover settler, about 1640,

Job's son Moses Tyler learned and retained one important lesson from his father's experiences; witchcraft accusations represented a powerful weapon to use against enemies. After the death of Moses' wife in 1689, Moses married the widow of Phineas Sprague. Her daughter, Martha Sprague, aged 13 in 1689, provided the ideal means for Moses Tyler to make witchcraft accusations in 1692. Martha became the leader of the Andover circle of afflicted girls. "She was naturally a girl of quick and tender sensibilities, gladsome in her general mood, but with a bewitching pathos interfused among her merriest words and deeds. It was remarked of her, too, that she had a faculty, even from childhood, of throwing her own feelings like a spell over her companions."[34]

The exclusionary town policies practiced so long by the first proprietors created deep resentment and anger in some Andover residents. That this repressed hostility would eventually erupt was inevitable. One-half of the first families had members accused of witchcraft in 1692. Of the 23 first proprietors of Andover, the families of the following twelve were targets of witchcraft accusations in 1692.

Simon Bradstreet
John Osgood, Sr.
Joseph Parker
Richard Barker
John Stevens
John Frye, Sr.
Edmond Faulkner
Nathan Parker
John Aslet
Richard Blake
Andrew Allen
Andrew Foster

born 1619, died about 1700. Dedicated by the whole clan, Sept. 4, 1901."
34   Hawthorne, *John Inglefield's Thanksgiving.*

In brief this was the sequence. The family of Andrew Allen was brutally attacked with witchcraft accusations. His daughters Mary (Allen) Toothaker and Martha (Allen) Carrier were both arrested on May 28, 1692. Mary's husband, Dr. Roger Toothaker, had already been arrested on May 18, 1692. He died in prison in Boston on June 16, and Martha (Allen) Carrier was hanged on August 19, 1692 in Salem. Two daughters of Mary (Allen) Toothaker and four children of Martha (Allen) Carrier were also arrested and imprisoned.

First settler Andrew Foster had died in 1685. His widow Ann Foster, aged about 72 in 1692, was an easy target. She was arrested on July 15, 1692, and condemned on September 17. Her daughter Mary (Foster) Lacey was also condemned on September 17. Ann's granddaughter Mary Lacey, Jr., imprisoned as a witch, was brought from her jail cell to the courtroom several times to act as an afflicted person. Several other girls and young women of Andover also suffered the anguish of both worlds; in the eyes of the law they were not only witches but also victims of witches.

At the beginning of August 1692, Rebecca (Blake) Eames, aged 51, of Boxford was imprisoned. She was condemned on September 17. Rebecca was the daughter of George Blake of Gloucester, who was related to first settler Richard Blake of Andover.

On August 10, Elizabeth Johnson, Jr. was arrested. On August 30, her mother, Elizabeth (Dane) Johnson, and her sister, Abigail Johnson, were arrested, and a couple of days later her brother, Stephen Johnson, was arrested. The mother, Elizabeth (Dane) Johnson, was a daughter of the Rev. Francis Dane. In January 1693, Elizabeth Johnson, Jr. was sentenced to death.

On August 11, 1692, Abigail (Dane) Faulkner was arrested and imprisoned. She was sentenced to death on September 17, 1692. One of the highest ranking women in Andover, she was also a daughter of the Rev. Francis Dane. Her husband was Francis Faulkner, the son of the first settler Edmond Faulkner. Their daughters Dorothy Faulkner, aged 12, and Abigail Faulkner Jr., aged 9, were imprisoned on September 7.

About August 15, 1692, Sarah Parker, aged 22, was arrested. She was the daughter of first settler Nathan Parker, who died in 1685. She lived with her widowed mother, Mary (Ayer) Parker, and her brother, Joseph. The widow Mary (Ayer) Parker was imprisoned on September 1 and hanged in Salem on September 22. First settlers Nathan Parker and Joseph Parker were brothers.

On August 29, 1692, William Barker, Sr., aged 46, and Mary Barker, aged 13, were imprisoned. William Barker, Sr. was the second son of first settler Richard Barker, and Mary Barker was a daughter of Lieut. John Barker, oldest son of Richard Barker. Mary Barker's mother (wife of Lieut. John Barker) was Mary (Stevens) Barker, daughter of first settler John Stevens. On September 1, William Barker, Jr. aged 14, the son of William Barker, Sr., was imprisoned. On September 7, 1692, Abigail (Wheeler) Barker, aged 36, was imprisoned. She was the wife of Ebenezer Barker, the third son of Richard Barker.

The only outsider admitted to the elite group of men from the first-settler families who ruled Andover was John Marston, Sr. His son's wife, Mary (Osgood) Marston, was imprisoned for witchcraft on August 29, 1692.

First settler John Osgood, Sr. (1595-1651) was second only in rank to Simon Bradstreet in Andover. His eldest son, John Osgood (1630-1693) was a captain in the Andover militia. On September 7, 1692, the captain's wife, Mary (Clement) Osgood, was arrested at the Andover touch test.[35] Also arrested at the same time and place were Eunice (Potter) Frye and Rebecca (Aslet) Johnson. Eunice was the wife of Deacon John Frye, son of first settler John Frye, Sr. Rebecca, a widow, was the daughter of first settler John Aslet. Rebecca's daughter, Rebecca Johnson, Jr. was arrested with her.

Ephraim Stevens was a son of first settler John Stevens. Dudley Bradstreet was a son of first settler Simon Bradstreet. In 1692 Dudley was the justice of the peace in Andover and a captain in the Andover militia. About the second week of September 1692, Ephraim Stevens as well as Dudley Bradstreet and his wife were cried out upon as witches. They managed to flee to avoid arrest.

Simon Bradstreet (1603–1697), born in England, was still a boy in grammar school at the time of his father's death. The death postponed his entry into college. Bradstreet matriculated

---

35   The Andover touch test is treated in Chapter 14.

at Cambridge, receiving a bachelor's degree, and later a master's degree.

Thomas Dudley, a Puritan who was steward to the Earl of Lincoln, became Bradstreet's patron. Dudley possessed such executive ability that he had rescued the Earl's estate from insolvency. From his patron, Bradstreet learned the business of stewardship. When Dudley moved to Boston, England, Bradstreet succeeded him in his office as steward and was later called into the service of the Countess of Warwick. Living close to the families of the Countess of Lincoln and the Countess of Warwick, he was thoroughly familiar with the ways of the upper class.

In 1628 Bradstreet married Anne Dudley (1612-1672), the daughter of Thomas Dudley. She wrote of herself, "But as I grew up to be about fourteen or fifteen, I found my heart more carnal and sitting loose from God, vanity and the follies of youth take hold of me. About sixteen the Lord laid his hand sore upon me and smote me with the smallpox. When I was in my affliction, I besought the Lord, and confessed my pride and vanity and He was entreated of me, and again restored me."[36] For a time the disease deformed her countenance. Whether smallpox left a permanent mark on the features of Anne Dudley is unknown, but her illness apparently did not trouble Simon. They were married as soon as she had regained her strength. She was sixteen. The first two years of their married life were spent in England.

Thomas Dudley and other eminent Puritans decided to immigrate to New England. Simon Bradstreet threw in his lot with the Puritan adventurers. He and his wife Anne, then eighteen, embarked with Gov. John Winthrop in the early spring of 1630. Their ship, the *Eagle*, was renamed *Arbella* in honor of Lady Arbella, daughter of the Earl of Lincoln. She and her husband, Mr. Isaac Johnson, were on board. The Bradstreets joined the select group who dined with Lady Arbella in the great cabin. The ship carried, besides the crew, about thirty passengers. Seaborn Cotton, son of the Rev. John Cotton, was born during the voyage across the ocean and aptly named. Seaborn would grow up to become a minister and marry Anne (Dudley) and

---

36   Bradstreet, *The Works of Anne Bradstreet in Prose and Verse.*

Simon Bradstreet's daughter, Dorothy Bradstreet, on June 25, 1654.

On June 12, 1630, the *Arbella* anchored in Salem Harbor. The newcomers found Salem in a sorry condition. More than eighty of the residents had died the winter before and the survivors were weak and sick. Their remaining provisions were hardly sufficient to feed them for a few weeks. Discouraged by the prospects in Salem, the Dudleys and the Bradstreets quickly moved on and settled in Cambridge. Thomas Dudley was elected deputy governor of the colony and Simon Bradstreet was elected a magistrate, an assistant to the governor. The Board of Assistants was the ruling council in the Massachusetts government, much like the board of directors in a corporation today. Bradstreet held this position for forty-nine years, from 1630 to 1679. In 1679 he was elected governor of the colony.

After the territory known as Agawam was taken from the Indians, it was laid out as the town of Ipswich and opened up for settlement. Thomas Dudley and Simon Bradstreet moved to Ipswich in 1635, becoming the most prominent citizens. Simon Bradstreet looked westward from Ipswich and contemplated a plantation on the south bank of the Merrimack River. This was the beginning of Andover. Among the original proprietors, Bradstreet held by far the most wealth and property. Most of the first settlers took up residence Andover around 1643; Simon and Anne Bradstreet moved there in 1644.

The life of the Bradstreets was not only scholarly but poetic. Anne, the first poet in the English colonies, qualifies as the first significant woman poet in the English language.[37] Of her devotion to her husband she wrote:

> If ever two were one then surely we,
> If ever man were loved by wife, then thee;
> If ever wife was happy in a man,

---

37   Anne's brother-in-law, John Woodbridge, the first minister of Andover who had left his post and returned to England in 1647, carried a manuscript containing the verses Anne had copied out for family circulation. He had them published in London in 1650 under the title, *The Tenth Muse, Lately Sprung Up in America*.

> Compare with me ye women if you can.
> I prize thy love more than whole mines of gold,
> Or all the riches that the East doth hold.

In a poem dated June 23, 1659 she wrote about her eight children, four boys and four girls:[38]

> I had eight birds hatcht in one nest,
> Four cocks there were, and hens the rest;
> I nurst them up with pain and care,
> Nor cost, nor labor did I spare,
> Till at the last they felt their wing,
> Mounted the trees, and learn'd to sing.

In the same poem Anne wrote about her daughter Dorothy with the words:

> My second bird did take her flight,
> And with her mate flew out of sight;
> Southward they both their course did bend,
> And seasons twain they there did spend,
> Till after blown by southern gales,
> They norward steered with filled sails.
> A prettier bird was nowhere seen,
> Along the beach among the treen.

The beach refers to the beautiful white-sand beach at Hampton. As indicated in Chapter 4, Dorothy (Bradstreet) Cotton, like her mother, may have struggled with a heart that was "carnal and sitting loose from God." Of her son Dudley, Anne wrote:

---

38   At the time, five of her children had left home: Samuel was in England; Dorothy and her husband Seaborn Cotton had been two years in Connecticut before settling in the sea-coast town of Hampton, New Hampshire, where Seaborn was appointed minister; Sarah and her husband Richard Hubbard were living in Ipswich; Simon, Jr. was at Harvard; and Dudley, the fifth to leave home although he was the seventh child (born in 1648), was at school in Ipswich. The three still at home were Hannah, born 1642, Mercy, born 1646, and the youngest, John, born in 1652.

SEVERAL

POEMS

Compiled with great variety of Wit and
Learning, full of Delight;
Wherein efpecially is contained a compleat
Difcourfe, and Defcription of

The Four { ELEMENTS.
CONSTITUTIONS,
AGES of Man,
SEASONS of the Year.

Together with an exact Epitome of
the three firft *Monarchyes*

Viz. The { *ASSYRIAN,*
PERSIAN,
GRECIAN.

And beginning of the Romane Common-wealth
to the end of their laft King :

With diverfe other pleafant & ferious *Poems,*

By a Gentlewoman in *New-England.*

The fecond Edition, Corrected by the Author'
and enlarged by an Addition of feveral other
Poems found amongft her Papers
after her Death.

Bofton, Printed by *John Fofter,* 1678.

Title page of the American edition of Anne Bradstreet's book of
poetry published in 1678.

The residence of Simon Bradstreet in Salem from
1676 to his death in 1697

My fifth, whose down is yet scarce gone,
Is 'mongst the shrubs and bushes flown,
And his wings increase in strength,
On higher boughs he'll perch at length.

As mentioned earlier, Dudley Bradstreet in 1692 was cried out upon as a wizard. Accused of killing nine persons by witchcraft, he found escape from Andover his safest course. Anne's youngest child, John, would also flee in 1692; he was said to have bewitched a dog so that his specter could ride upon the animal. Did Anne anticipate these events when she wrote:

Alas, my birds, you wisdom want,
Of perils you are ignorant;
O to your safety have an eye,
So happy you may live or die.[39]

People of education and refinement, the Bradstreets collected a library of some eight hundred volumes in their fine Andover house. A fire in 1666 tragically destroyed these books together with family portraits, heirlooms, and furniture brought from England. After forty-four years of married life, Anne Bradstreet died in Andover in 1672. Four years after her death, at the age of seventy-three, Simon married the widow of Captain Joseph Gardner of Salem, whose husband had been killed in the attack on the Narragansett fort during King Philip's War.[40] After his marriage to Mrs. Gardner, Bradstreet lived until his death in a house which stood on Main Street, Salem. It had belonged to Emmanuel Downing and was the property of Bradstreet's new wife, the daughter of Emmanuel Downing and a sister of Sir George Downing. Simon Bradstreet was elected governor in 1679 and held that post until 1686 when a royal governor was appointed by the king. When Massachusetts overthrew the royal governor in 1689, Bradstreet was again elected governor and

---

39 Bradstreet, *The Works of Anne Bradstreet in Prose and Verse.*
40 Captain Gardner had been the guardian of John Hathorne's child bride.

held the post until May 14, 1692, when a new royal governor, Sir William Phipps, took office.

In each of the three sorriest episodes in Massachusetts colonial history, Simon Bradstreet took part: the banishment of Anne Hutchinson, the mistreatment of the Quakers, and the witchcraft persecutions. Bradstreet was a member of the Court that tried and banished Anne Hutchinson. Bradstreet supported the persecution of Quakers carried out in Massachusetts from 1656 to 1663, but he was the only Massachusetts ruler to oppose the death penalty for Quakers returning to New England after banishment.

In 1680, while Bradstreet was governor, Elizabeth Morse was sentenced to death for witchcraft. The governor did not allow the sentence to be executed. But the governor's leniency was not due to the fact that he did not believe that witches existed. There was authority for this belief in the Scriptures and in the laws of all civilized nations which at the time recognized witchcraft as a crime. The governor's difficulty lay in proof of the offense. He could not discern what kind of evidence was competent, relevant, and material. The fundamental problem, of course, lay not in types of evidence but in the mistaken belief that witches existed in the first place.

4

PERSECUTION OF THE QUAKERS

N ATHANIEL HAWTHORNE'S FIRST AMERICAN ANCESTOR
was William Hathorne (1607-1681). William Hathorne
came from England to Massachusetts sometime before 1633 and
settled in Dorchester, then a town just south of Boston and now a
part of Boston. In 1636 he moved to Salem where he worked his
way up in government. An influential figure during the entire
period (1656-1663) of the so-called Quaker invasion, William
Hathorne earned a reputation as the most ardent of the Quaker
persecutors.

In his essay *The Custom House*, Nathaniel Hawthorne
described his Puritan ancestors with a mixture of pleasure and
pain. He was convinced that as he walked the streets of his
native Salem, with which he had a love-hate relationship most
of his life, he breathed in the dust of these early Puritans who
"have mingled their earthly substance with the soil, until no
small portion of it must necessarily be akin to the mortal frame
wherewith, for a little while, I walk the streets." Not only did
he inhale the dust of his ancestors, but he also spoke of the
"moral quality" that haunted him.[41] His accounts of his ancestry
(on the Hathorne side) continue the ambivalence, describing the
shame he felt for their cruelties coupled with his pride in their
influence.

Hawthorne wrote, "The figure of that first ancestor [Major
William Hathorne] invested by family tradition with a dim and
dusky grandeur, was present to my boyish imagination, as far
back as I can remember. It still haunts me, and induces a sort of
home-feeling with the past. I seem to have a stronger claim to a

---

41   Hawthorne, *The Custom-House*.

residence here on account of this grave, bearded, sable-cloaked and steeple-crowned progenitor—who came so early, with his Bible and his sword. He was a soldier, legislator, judge; he was a ruler in the Church; he had all the Puritanical traits, both good and evil. He was likewise a bitter persecutor, as witness the Quakers, who have remembered him in their histories, and relate an incident of his hard severity towards a woman of their sect."[42]

William Hathorne rose to prominence because of his capacity for administering the stern and unforgiving Puritanical rule. "After long waiting, coming to be a magistrate, what a bloody persecutor has he been of the truth!"[43] His acts in the name of authority led to worldly goods and advancement in government, and these in turn gave him respectability. But, as Nathaniel Hawthorne stated in the previous passage, history forgets the trappings of success and remembers his misdeeds.

As long as he lived in Salem, until 1655, John Endicott was chief Essex County magistrate. William Hathorne was one of several deputy magistrates, serving thirteen years in this capacity, twice as long as any other. Of all the colony's civil officials, Hathorne was the most experienced, the most zealous, and the most dreaded. He grew more and more exacting in his efforts to compel people to adhere to the Puritan code. His informers were forever on the lookout for critics of church or government. Case after case was heard by Hathorne, and his punishments to men and women were unfailingly severe. For so-called unseemly speeches, a Salem woman was ordered to sit in the stocks and suffer a severe whipping. Another, because of a chance remark, according to the testimony of the informer Robert Cotty, was sentenced to be tied to the whipping post with a slit stick in her tongue. For any more serious crime, hanging was the rule and Hathorne sent many to their deaths at the gallows.

Upon Endicott's transfer to Boston in 1655 to become governor, William Hathorne moved up to Endicott's place. In his splendid clothes, with his magistrate's staff in hand, Hathorne made his way to the meetinghouse. Inside waited his family, including

---

42   Ibid.
43   Bishop, *New England Judged*, 279.

his fourteen year old son, John. Every eye was upon the new chief magistrate as he strode to the bench of honor and for the first time took the seat which until then had been reserved for Endicott.

The Quakers represented one of several religious movements with origins in the seventeenth century. George Fox (1624-1691) founded the Society of Friends (known as the Quakers) in England in 1652. Fox's conviction was that every individual was endowed with a measure of the Divine Spirit which he called the inner light. Most of his early followers were young people. Indeed, the Quakers represented the youth movement of those times. Quakers wore their hair long and kept their hats on in public assemblies. Almost immediately their persecution in England began, authorized under the austere rule of Oliver Cromwell.

In July 1656, two Quaker women, Mary Fisher and Ann Austin, landed in Boston. They were promptly arrested, put in jail, and their Bibles burned. They were caused "to be stripped stark naked and to be searched and misused, as is a shame to modesty to name."[44] Eight more Quakers arrived and were treated equally harshly. Their unwelcome appearance in New England marked the beginning of the Quaker invasion, which took place from 1656 to 1663. These first comers were all forced to leave, with stern admonitions not to return. The Puritans had established themselves in New England to enjoy their religious convictions undisturbed. This required the exclusion of all other religions; the idea of tolerance was unknown to them. They regarded the Quakers as dangerous persons threatening public authority.

Yet the Quakers continued to come to New England and began to make converts. The Massachusetts authorities, urged on by their Puritan ministers, resolved to strangle this new heresy in its infancy and attacked the Quakers with venom. That these peaceful and inoffensive people who did so much to promote the welfare of other colonies were treated so badly in Massachusetts is a travesty. Fears and prejudices against them were engendered intentionally by the writings and sermons of the Puritan

---

44   Bishop, *New England Judged*, 15-16.

ministers. The democratic tendency and peculiarities of social conduct of the Quakers were extremely offensive to the Puritan leaders, who regarded themselves as an aristocracy of the Saints of God. The treatment of Quakers in New England became an international scandal even while it was taking place. Fortunately, the Quakers understood that the pen is more powerful than the sword. The atrocities against the Quakers were recorded contemporaneously by George Bishop and appeared in his book *New England judged by the Spirit of the Lord*, published in London in the 1660s. The wide circulation and strong impact of this book would mark the beginning of the end of Puritan theocracy in New England.

The General Court took action in 1657. A law was passed providing special punishment for any Quakers found in the colony of Massachusetts Bay. The law imposed severe penalties such as scourgings, brandings, cropped ears, prison, and banishment. Although rigidly enforced, it was soon found inadequate as the number of Quakers continued to grow. A law decreeing death to any Quaker who should presume to return after banishment was enacted. The persecution intensified until, in the year 1659, the government of Massachusetts hanged two members of the Quaker sect, William Robinson and Marmaduke Stevenson. The following year they hanged a Quaker woman, Mary Dyer. The victims' crimes were that they dared return to Boston after banishment.

Among the Quaker converts who came to Boston were Lawrence and Cassandra Southwick. On the day they were sentenced to banishment, they heard that the court had authorized the sale of their twenty-two-year-old son Daniel and their eighteen-year-old daughter Provided into servitude. The children were to be sold into slavery because, having no visible estates, they could not pay an accumulated fine of £10. What was the horrible crime that warranted such a heavy penalty? They had not attended Puritan church services. The order that the children pay the fine with their freedom, perhaps because of its extreme inhumanity, was never executed. "Edmond Butter, a wicked and cruel man, sought out for a passage to Barbados to send them there for sale, as men sell goods, to fill his purse, he being your [the government's] treasurer. But the man to whom he

New-England Judged,

BY THE
Spirit of the Lord.

In Two Parts.

First, Containing a Brief Relation of the Sufferings of the People call'd Quakers in *New-England*, from the Time of their first Arrival there, in the Year 1656, to the Year 1660. Wherein their Merciless Whippings, Chainings, Finings, Imprisonings, Starvings, Burning in the Hand, Cutting off Ears, and Putting to Death, with divers other Cruelties, inflicted upon the Bodies of Innocent Men and Women, only for Conscience-sake, are briefly described. In Answer to the Declaration of their Persecutors Apologizing for the same, MDCLIX.

Second Part, Being a farther Relation of the Cruel and Bloody Sufferings of the People call'd Quakers in *New-England*, Continued from *anno* 1660, to *anno* 1665. Beginning with the Sufferings of *William Leddra*, whom they put to Death.

Formerly Published by **George Bishop**, and now somewhat Abreviated.

With an Appendix,

Containing the Writings of several of the Sufferers; with some Notes, shewing the Accomplishment of their Prophecies; and a Postscript of the Judgments of God, that have befallen divers of their Persecutors.
ALSO,
An Answer to *Cotton Mather*'s Abuses of the said People, in his late History of *New-England*, Printed *anno* 1702. The whole being at this time Published in the said Peoples Vindication, as a Reply to all his Slanderous Calumnies.

And they overcame by the Blood of the Lamb, and by the Word of their Testimony; and they loved not their Lives unto the Death, Rev. 12. 11.

LONDON, Printed and Sold by *T. Sowle*, in *White-Hart-Court* in *Gracious-Street*, 1703.

Title page of *New England Judged* by George Bishop

spoke, would not carry them on that account—a thing so horrible! Said the ship-master, 'Will ye offer to make slaves of so harmless creatures?'"[45]

Concerned that a Quaker man would fail to pay the stiff fine imposed for not attending Puritan services, William Hathorne, then deputy magistrate, advised, "That if he had not, or would not pay, they must send him to Barbados and sell him, to pay for it." The ambitious Hathorne "turned from the tenderness that was once in him to get an employment whereby to live; and having got it, thus turned against his tender principles and his friends, to sell them for slaves, as he did in other particulars."[46]

Still the number of Quaker converts in Salem grew, and from time to time new strangers, in pairs or in groups, came to meet with them. William Hathorne pursued all "like a bloodhound, and had his will on them, in person and estate." In an order to a constable he wrote, "You are required, by virtue hereof, to search in all suspicious houses for private meetings; and, if they refuse to open the doors, you are to break open the door upon them, and return the names of all ye find to Ipswich Court."[47]

When the Quaker Wenlock Christison stood trial for his life, in 1661, Catharine Chatham made an unusual protest. "But look yonder! A Quaker woman, clad in sackcloth, and with ashes on her head, has mounted the steps of the meetinghouse. She addresses the people in a wild and shrill voice—wild and shrill it must be, to suit such a figure—which makes them tremble and turn pale."[48] For this offense the Puritans "put her in prison, out of which you would give no deliverance, until you drove her with sword and club into the wilderness."[49]

Following the death of Cromwell in 1658 and the restoration of the monarch King Charles II of England in 1660, a wave of reaction against Puritans and Puritanism set in. While the Massachusetts Bay leaders vigorously were pressing the

---

45   Bishop, *New England Judged*, 88-93.
46   Ibid.
47   Ibid.
48   Hawthorne, *Main-Street*.
49   Bishop, *New England Judged*, 273.

persecution of the Quakers, they suddenly were faced with an act of King Charles II, dated September 9, 1661, stating that any case involving a Quaker held in Massachusetts Bay on a capital charge must be transferred to courts of law in England. The royal decree finally put in check the hangings, the cutting off men's ears, the boring of holes through women's tongues with red hot irons, and the starving of the imprisoned in Boston. Even whippings and fines were to be exacted only after careful deliberation on the part of the magistrates.

William Hathorne was not pleased with these changes. In 1661 he was promoted to the rank of major. In 1662 Major Hathorne was elevated to the position of a full-fledged magistrate, that is, an assistant to the governor. He now had the prestige of membership on the Board of Assistants, the governing council of the colony. His new status served to make him all the more vindictive and all the more dreaded. An examination of the Essex County, Massachusetts, *Court Records* shows that whippings of thirty stripes and fines running into pounds were common penalties after 1662.

Thomas Wardwell was a Puritan and a freeman of the Massachusetts colony. His oldest son, Eliakim, was born in Boston in 1634 and his daughter Martha in 1637. Thomas was a follower of Anne Hutchinson and her brother-in-law, the Rev. John Wheelwright. After the Puritan old guard had convicted Wheelwright of sedition for a sermon that he had delivered, he was disfranchised and banished. In 1638, with twenty of his sympathizers, including Thomas Wardwell, Wheelwright fled north and founded Exeter, New Hampshire. Thomas' son Benjamin was born in Exeter in 1639 and his son Samuel in 1643. After Massachusetts annexed Exeter in 1643, Wheelwright moved to Wells, Maine. A few years later the Rev. Wheelwright confessed himself misled by Satan's temptations and his own passions. Allowed to return to Massachusetts, he became an assistant to the pastor at Hampton in 1647. Hampton granted Wheelwright not only a town house but also a farm south of Taylor River.

The seacoast town of Hampton then was under Massachusetts jurisdiction, but is now in the state of New Hampshire. Hampton lies on the strip of seacoast between the mouths of the Merrimack and Piscataqua rivers. The coast is a long sweep of hard sand beach, washed by the ebb and flow of the Atlantic Ocean. The beach line is broken occasionally by the outlet of a tidal river or shallow creek, or where some bold promontory, like Boar's Head, rises far out from shore. Perfectly protected by these beaches, long expanses of yellow salt marshes stretch inland toward the green hills.

Thomas Wardwell, who had stayed in Exeter, died in December 1646, at aged 44. Four months later his widow, Elizabeth Wardwell, and her four children, Eliakim, Martha, Benjamin, and Samuel, moved to Hampton. Wheelwright let them live on his farm where Eliakim, aged 13, took on the responsibility for the farming. Ten years later, in 1657, Wheelwright left America and returned to England.

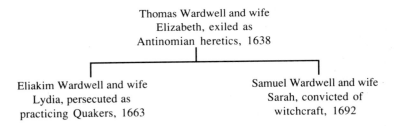

Thomas Wardwell and wife
Elizabeth, exiled as
Antinomian heretics, 1638

Eliakim Wardwell and wife
Lydia, persecuted as
practicing Quakers, 1663

Samuel Wardwell and wife
Sarah, convicted of
witchcraft, 1692

When the Quakers first came to Massachusetts in 1656, Eliakim Wardwell was 22 years old. Three years later, in 1659, he married Lydia Perkins in Hampton. As young people drawn to the new movement, Eliakim and Lydia (Perkins) Wardwell became Quaker converts. In violation of the law, they stopped going to Puritan church services. As atrocities against Quakers escalated, the activities of Eliakim and Lydia quickened pace. Both were active in the work of Quaker missionaries in the colony. On April 8, 1662, Eliakim was fined for absence from church for twenty-six Sundays.

In Dover, New Hampshire, in December 1662, at the instigation of the Rev. Rayner, three Quaker women were arrested. Richard Waldron, deputy magistrate of Dover, issued the warrant, "To the constables of Dover, Hampton, Salisbury, Newbury, Rowley, Ipswich, Wenham, Lynn, Boston, Roxbury,

Dedham, and until those vagabond Quakers are carried out of this jurisdiction. You are required to take these vagabond Quakers, Ann Coleman, Mary Tompkins, Alice Ambrose, and make them fast to the cart's tail, and driving the cart through your several towns, to whip them upon their backs, not exceeding ten stripes apiece on each of them, in each town. Dated December 22, 1662."[50]

Although the execution of such punishment, ten stripes in eleven towns, one hundred ten in all, would result in their certain deaths, it was nonetheless undertaken. In Dover on Christmas day, a holiday not celebrated by the Puritans, the three Quaker women were stripped naked to the waist and tied to a cart. The constable, Thomas Roberts, brutally whipped them. As a fellow Quaker and an ally of the women, Eliakim Wardwell was present. While the flogging was taking place, the Rev. Rayner "stood and looked on, and laughed at it."[51] Deeply offended, Eliakim Wardwell reproved the minister, providing the Puritans with yet another piece of insolence to add to their list of Quaker outrages. For this offense, Waldron sentenced Eliakim to the stocks.

Roberts then marched the three women to Hampton. The constable there, William Field, "spake to a woman to take off their clothes; the woman said she would not do it for all the world; and other women also refused to do it. Then he said, 'I profess I will do it myself.' So he stripped them, and then stood, with the whip in his hand, trembling as a condemned man, and did the execution as a man in that condition. One Anthony Stanyel hastened up for the work, having a great desire himself to do the execution on the women, but he was disappointed, for it was done ere he came."[52] Eliakim's wife, Lydia Wardwell, watched the proceedings in silence.

Next the three Quaker women were taken "through the dirt and snow, half-way the leg deep, to Salisbury, the constable forcing them after the cart's tail, at which he whipped them." Though they now were on the verge of death from pain, shock,

---

50   Bishop, *New England Judged*, 231-238.
51   Ibid.
52   Ibid.

and loss of blood, the persecutors showed no mercy. Among the spectators was Edward Wharton, who accosted Thomas Bradbury, clerk of the court at Salisbury, and said, "I am here to see your wickedness and cruelty, that so if you kill them, I may be able to declare how you murdered them."[53] The Rev. John Wheelwright advised the constable that his safest alternative was to drive on. But the constable appointed Walter Barefoot as a deputy, who then set the three women free. Earlier that year Wheelwright had come back to America from England to become pastor of the church at Salisbury.

In time the three Quaker women returned to Dover. The constable, Thomas Roberts, and his brother, John Roberts, "laid hands on Alice Ambrose, as she was in prayer, and taking her, the one by the one arm, and the other by the other arm, they unmercifully dragged her out of doors, with her face toward the snow, which was knee-deep, over the stumps and old trees near a mile, in the way of which, when they had wearied themselves, they commanded two others to help them, and so laid her up a prisoner in the house of T. Canny, a very wicked man. They made haste to fetch Mary Tompkins, whom they also dragged along, with her face toward the snow. T. Roberts, the poor father of these two wicked constables, followed after, lamenting and crying, 'Woe, that ever he was the father to such wicked children.'"[54]

They also made a prisoner of the third woman, Ann Coleman. "In the morning, it being exceedingly cold they got a canoe. They furiously took Mary Tompkins by the arms, and dragged her on her back, over the stumps of trees, down a very steep hill to the water-side. Alice Ambrose they plucked violently in the water, and kept her swimming by the canoe. And they put Ann Coleman in great danger of her life also. But on a sudden a great tempest arose, and they had them back to the house again, and kept them prisoners till near midnight, and then they cruelly turned them out of doors in the frost and snow. These are the fruits of the minister of Dover, the gall and vinegar that he pours into the

---

53   Ibid. In 1692, Thomas Bradbury's wife, Mary (Perkins) Bradbury, was arrested for witchcraft and sentenced to death.
54   Ibid.

wounds of those whom his cruelty had torn; these are some of the fountains of wickedness which flow in the land through the cruel influences of the heads and rulers thereof."[55]

Anyone who provided a meal or harbored a Quaker even for a single night was guilty of breaking the law and liable to heavy penalty. Undaunted, Eliakim Wardwell welcomed his friend Wenlock Christison as a visitor to his house. The authorities took immediate notice. The minister at Hampton was the Rev. Seaborn Cotton, old John Cotton's son. With truncheon in hand, the pastor headed a party of order-loving citizens and marched from his house to the Wardwell house, two miles away. Christison opened the door, and asked the pastor, "what he did with that club in hand?" The minister replied, "I come to keep the wolves from my sheep."[56] Christison was then seized and taken away to jail. The wolf having been secured, Eliakim, one of the sheep, was taken to court and fined.

Eliakim did not have cash enough to pay the excessive fine. In lieu, the court confiscated his saddle horse, worth about fourteen pounds. Since the value of the horse was greater than the fine, the court owed Eliakim the difference. Instead of paying him, the court officers seized a vessel of green ginger from an old man named William Marston. Their justification for this theft was that Marston himself owed a fine. As compensation to Eliakim, the officers placed the green ginger in Eliakim's house. Eliakim refused to touch it. But the green ginger soon went the way of the horse, as the court again fined Eliakim for his and his wife's absence from church. The fine was ten shillings for each absence.

Towns in New England did not pay their ministers. Instead a town allocated to each citizen a portion of the minister's salary to be paid directly. The minister in Hampton, the Rev. Seaborn Cotton, had married Dorothy Bradstreet in Andover in 1654. Dorothy's father was magistrate Simon Bradstreet, the leading resident of Andover.

---

55   Ibid.
56   Ibid.

Because Eliakim refused to pay his allocation, Seaborn Cotton offered to sell his claim on Eliakim to a man called Nathaniel Boulter. This man was essentially a bill collector who bought bad debts at a tremendous discount and then used fair or foul means to try to collect them. To check if this were a good investment, Boulter first went to Eliakim's house on the pretext of borrowing a little corn. The honest Eliakim willingly led Boulter into the barn and lent him the corn. Boulter saw the large supply stored there. Judas-like, he returned and bought the bad debt from Seaborn Cotton. Boulter then returned to Eliakim's barn with the constable and carted off as much corn as he could manage.

Eliakim's debt to the Rev. Seaborn Cotton continued to build. Seaborn Cotton wanted a calf that Eliakim owned. The minister simply directed his servant to steal the calf from Eliakim's pasture. The intent of the minister and the town officials was to leave Eliakim penniless by repeated seizures of his property. Again, Eliakim was taken to court and fined. To satisfy the fine, they took most of his marsh and meadow lands. Hay from these fields kept his cattle alive in winter. Eliakim's young wife Lydia continued to suffer in silence.

The town of Newbury lies south of Hampton, on the south side of the Merrimack River outlet. South of Newbury, on the coast, is the town of Ipswich and further south is Salem. Between Ipswich and Newbury were rocky pastures and hills covered with cedar trees, and on the sea side the flat Rowley marshes. Newbury sits on a ridge of high land on the bank of the Merrimack. The crude bell tower of the Newbury meetinghouse thrust through the tops of the trees that hid the village. In this meetinghouse, on a Sunday morning in May 1663, an unforgettable event was to take place.

It was a bright spring morning; the sea was azure and calm. In the distance the hills seemed to rise abruptly from the flatness of the ocean. The sun filtered through the foliage as the Newbury meetinghouse opened its doors to the usual throng of worshippers. Among them was Nicholas Noyes, an aspiring young Puritan who would later become the assistant minister of the Salem church.[57]

When the congregation had assembled, a beautiful young woman, tall, with a slim figure and golden hair, walked into the service. She was Lydia Wardwell. Everyone knew her; she was a member of the church, a high honor which only a few of the congregation were able to attain. The elders had repeatedly sent for Lydia to explain her separation from the church. At last she had come and in an instant she riveted the eyes of everyone present, men and women, the worthy and the less worthy. Lydia appeared as "a woman to whom her own beauty was the sole and sufficient garment."[58] She was naked.

Lydia Wardwell, described as an "honest young woman," went to church on that glorious spring morning as an act of protest against the vicious abuse that the Puritan church was inflicting on Quakers.[59] Her membership in the Puritan church affirmed that she had been highly respected, a woman of rank in a class-bound society. A person of unusual courage, she wanted to protest the coarseness and brutality of the Puritans in stripping women of their clothing, whipping them, and making them tramp the streets tied naked to a cart. With her own eyes she had seen the anguish and torment of her women friends who were so treated. Moreover the officials had stripped her husband and herself of all their worldly possessions, leaving them, in this sense, naked in the world. These officials, who believed that they were carrying out the word of God, failed to understand that they themselves were blinded by bigotry and intolerance.

Unlike Puritans, the Quakers refused to resort to violence in any form, for any reason. Lydia resorted to a protest that was simultaneously desperate and peaceful, a uniquely powerful act, one she knew would not soon be forgotten. "As a sign to them, she went in naked amongst them, though it was exceeding hard to her

---

57   In 1692 Noyes would prove himself a leader in the fight against the Devil and the witches engaged in the hellish design of bewitching and ruining New England. When Lydia's brother-in-law Samuel Wardwell and seven other convicted witches were hanged, Noyes call them eight firebrands of hell.

58   Hawthorne, *The House of the Seven Gables*, Chapter 13.

59   Bishop, *New England Judged*, 238–241.

modest and shamefaced disposition."[60] The authorities were enraged; they arrested her for appearance at the next Court at Ipswich.

The Court was held in a tavern, its customary meeting place. There the magistrates would sit and pronounce sentences while eating, drinking, and listening to music. Sometimes the Rev. Cobbet would sing. Although there was no statute against what Lydia had done, the magistrates ordered that she be tied to the fence-post of the tavern. While they served "their ears with music, and their bellies with wine and gluttony," they watched her "tied, stripped from the waist upwards, with her naked breasts to the splinters of the post, and there sorely lashed, with twenty or thirty cruel stripes."[61]

Her body miserably torn and bleeding, Lydia had the fortitude to endure the torture, "to the shame and confusion of these unreasonable men, whose name shall rot, and their memory perish." Such was the discipline of the Puritan church, whose "weapons are cruel whips and torturing of the body, instead of reaching to the spirit. This is their religion, and their usage of the handmaid of the Lord, who, in a great cross to her natural temper, thus came in among them—a sign, indeed, significant enough to them and to their state, who, under the mask of religion, were thus blinded into cruel persecution."[62]

Still the persecution of the Wardwells was not over. The court at Hampton met to fine Eliakim and Lydia for not attending church services. The judges were Simon Bradstreet, Thomas Wiggins, Thomas Bradbury, Robert Pike, and Bryan Pembleton. Lydia did not honor the summons. In her absence, Simon Bradstreet took occasion to upbraid her for appearing in such a fashion at the Newbury church service, neglecting to mention the lashings she subsequently had received. Incensed, Eliakim no longer could hold his tongue. Bradstreet, he said, was

---

60   Ibid. In the 1703 edition, attached to the phrase "naked amongst them," the following appeared as a footnote. "As a sign of their [the Puritans'] wretchedness and inhumanity, in stripping and whipping others, even women, in such an immodest and shameless manner as they did."

61   Ibid.

62   Ibid.

maliciously reproaching his wife, a virtuous woman. He reminded Bradstreet that, although Lydia had broken no law, she had been brutally beaten. Unable to stop, Eliakim in a final burst of temper then talked of "that report that went abroad of the known dishonesty of Bradstreet's daughter."[63] The daughter, Dorothy, was the wife of the Rev. Seaborn Cotton.

On hearing this, it was Simon Bradstreet's turn to lose his temper. He announced to the other judges, "If such fellows are suffered to speak so in the court, I will sit there no more." With that, the court sentenced Eliakim to be stripped to his waist, to be bound to an oak tree near the meetinghouse, and to be whipped fifteen lashes. Before they executed the punishment, Bradstreet called the Rev. Seaborn Cotton, Bradstreet's son-in-law, to come and watch. The Rev. Cotton, eager at the prospect, hastened out. When Eliakim was stripped and tied to the tree, old Thomas Wiggins, magistrate of Dover, New Hampshire and one of the judges, declared, "I pity thee for thy father's sake." To the whipper he said, "Whip him a good!" The beating was performed with cords nearly as big as a man's little finger. When they untied him, the Rev. Seaborn Cotton was standing close by. Eliakim, bleeding badly, found his voice and within everyone's hearing asked the minister, "Seaborn, has my pied heifer calved yet?"[64] The Rev. Cotton stole off, thief that he was.

Despite Lydia's astonishing protest, the Puritan authorities, undeterred, continued to strip Quaker women in public. "And there a woman—it is Ann Coleman—naked from the waist upward, and bound to the tail of a cart, while the constable follows with a whip of knotted cords. He loves his business, faithful officer that he is, and puts his soul into every stroke, zealous to fulfill the injunction of Major Hathorne's warrant, in the spirit and the letter. There came down a stroke that has drawn blood!"[65]

These abuses occurred in the summer of 1663. Ann Coleman was the same woman who had suffered before under the warrant of Richard Waldron in Dover, New Hampshire. Now she and

63   Ibid.
64   Ibid.
65   Hawthorne, *Main-Street*.

three other Quakers—a woman and two men—had been arrested by magistrate William Hathorne. They were "by the said Hathorne's warrant, apprehended and so cruelly whipped through Salem, Boston, and Dedham, that [Ann] was near death, being well-nigh murdered. She was a little woman, and her back was crooked, and your executioner had her fast in a cart at Dedham; Bellingham, your deputy, having seen Hathorne's warrant, bidding them, 'Go on,' and saying, 'The warrant was firm;' and so encouraging the matter, he so unmercifully laid her on, that, with the knots of the whip, he split the nipple of her breast, which so tortured her, that it had almost cost her life."[66]

In one of his tirades against the Quakers, Cotton Mather, nephew of the Rev. Seaborn Cotton, wrote that during the Quaker invasion two women of their sect came stark naked into the public assemblies, and they were sentenced to the whipping post. Expanding on this theme, Puritan apologists have claimed more recently that it was not the Puritans, but the Quaker women who were the offenders, often parading the streets and entering the churches completely naked. The apologists maintain that the Puritan authorities, thus goaded, were forced to resort to barbarous treatment to curb such wild and provocative actions.

This argument is mistaken. The truth is that the Puritans first stripped two Quaker women naked in 1656, and then instituted a policy of public disrobing, exhibition, and torture of Quaker women. The women themselves made no response until November 1662 when Deborah Wilson appeared naked in the streets of Salem. This was six years after the initial mistreatments. In May 1663, Lydia Wardwell entered the Newbury church service naked. These two were the only such instances; both were calculated acts of protest.

Some may dismiss Lydia Wardwell's choice of protest as nothing more than a bizarre form of indecency. Others may consider it outlandish and outrageous. But what recourse was available to a Quaker woman in a closed Puritan community? No official channels existed, civil or clerical, through which a verbal protest could fairly be heard. For Quakers, the use of any form of violence was out of the question.

---

66   Bishop, *New England Judged*, 279-280.

Lydia had watched powerless as her husband's estate was confiscated; she had watched as her women friends were beaten and brutalized in the streets. Finally, she was compelled to act. Her strength might lie in simple and sudden confrontation—to shock and shame the Puritan church into a realization of their misdeeds. Strange as it was, her protest may have helped. By the following year the persecution of Quakers in New England had stopped.

5

SAMUEL WARDWELL, CARPENTER

I N 1664 A FRESH OPPORTUNITY presented itself to the
Quakers. The English had taken New Amsterdam from the
Dutch, thereby opening land in New Jersey for settlement.
Eliakim and Lydia Wardwell and their three young children
wisely decided to leave New England forever. They settled in
New Jersey, taking with them Eliakim's widowed mother
Elizabeth. In New Jersey Eliakim became a Quaker leader.

Eliakim's two younger brothers remained in Massachusetts.
Samuel Wardwell, aged 21, had nearly finished his
apprenticeship as a carpenter. Benjamin Wardwell, aged 24, was
already living in Salem, having become a sailor before the mast.
Because of the thriving commercial shipping business in Salem,
there was a great need for seamen. This was the period when
Salem was starting to feel prosperity from its growing mercantile
trade with England and the West Indies.

Samuel Wardwell moved to Salem and took up his
occupation as carpenter. During these years of rapid growth,
there was ample work; old houses were being enlarged and many
new homes were being built. In 1668 John Turner had an elegant
house constructed on a splendid site overlooking the harbor. "So
faithfully had this contract been fulfilled, that now, as the
carpenter approached the house, his practiced eye could detect
nothing to criticize its condition. The peaks of the seven gables
rose up sharply; the shingled roof looked thoroughly watertight;
and the glittering plasterwork entirely covered the exterior
walls, and sparkled in the October sun."[67] This was the House of
the Seven Gables, the foremost relic of Salem's past. Today the

---

67   Hawthorne, *The House of the Seven Gables*, Chapter 13.

house has been beautifully restored. With its almost human-like visage it still looks proudly out to the sea in calm and in storm, just as it did in the days of witchcraft.

The young carpenter married and the couple soon had a son Thomas, named after Samuel's father, Thomas Wardwell. Sadly, Samuel Wardwell's wife died in 1671. The town of Andover needed skilled workers and was enticing them to move there by offering 20-acre plots for a nominal price. Samuel's occupation as a carpenter made him eligible. Yet, while he wanted to make a fresh start, he must have had some misgivings, because the chief resident in Andover was Simon Bradstreet, the same magistrate who had so harshly treated his brother Eliakim. In 1665 Samuel's first cousin, Elihu Wardwell, a resident of Ipswich, had married Elizabeth Wade, daughter of Jonathan Wade, the richest man in Ipswich. Elizabeth (Wade) Wardwell's brother, Nathaniel Wade, was the drinking companion of Dudley Bradstreet, son of Simon Bradstreet of Andover. Nathaniel started courting Dudley's sister Mercy Bradstreet, and they were married on October 31, 1672 in Andover.[68] This family association with the Bradstreets may have lessened Samuel's reluctance to settle in Andover.

In 1672 Samuel made his fatal decision and moved to Andover with his young son to begin a new life. But was the conflict that Samuel's brother had with Bradstreet and the Rev. Seaborn Cotton forgotten, or did the grudges live on? Recall that in 1663 Eliakim in a spurt of anger had told magistrate Simon Bradstreet that his daughter Dorothy had the reputation of a "dishonest woman." To say the least, this accusation had not pleased the magistrate. Nor could it have pleased Seaborn Cotton who was married to Dorothy. Seaborn was the uncle of a nine-year-old prodigy, Cotton Mather, who in a couple of years

---

68   As was customary the two fathers, Simon Bradstreet and Jonathan Wade, met to decide the marriage settlement. At first there was a fairly serious financial disagreement between them, but it was finally settled amicably, so the young persons might proceed in marriage with both of their consents. A few weeks before the marriage, Mercy's mother, Anne Bradstreet, the poet, died on September 16, 1672 in Andover, aged 60.

would become the youngest person ever admitted to Harvard College, before or since.

When Samuel moved to Andover, the Barker family was already firmly established. First settler Richard Barker was a town official. His beautiful daughter Sarah Barker, aged 25 in 1672, was unmarried. Samuel Wardwell and Sarah Barker fell in love. But Sarah's father, Richard Barker, turned down the prospective marriage because Samuel was not one of the established elite. It seemed next to impossible for Samuel to improve his position under the rigid Puritan rule.

Samuel often amused himself by telling fortunes and acting as an amateur magician. Twenty years later, in his witchcraft confession, he described his situation as it appeared to him in 1672. "When I was a young man I could make all my cattle come round about me when I pleased. I was sensible I was in the snare of the Devil. I used to be much discontented that I could get no more work done. And I had been foolishly led along with telling of fortunes, which sometimes came to pass. Also when any creature came into my field, I used to utter, 'The Devil take it.' And it may be the Devil took advantage of me by that.

"Being once in a discontented frame I saw some cats, together with the appearance of a man who called himself a prince of the air and he promised me I should live comfortably and be a captain. And he required me to honor him, which I promised to do. And it was about twenty years ago [that is, about 1672]. The reason for my discontent then was because I was in love with a maid named [Sarah] Barker who slighted my love. And the first appearance of the cat then was behind Captain [Simon] Bradstreet's house. About a week after that, a black man appeared in the daytime at the same place, and called himself prince and lord. And told me I must worship and believe him, and he promised as above, with this addition that I should never want for anything. But the black man has never performed anything. And further when I went to prayer with my family, the Devil would begin to be angry.

"At the time when the Devil appeared and told me that he was prince of the air, then I signed his book by making a mark like a square with a black pen. And the Devil brought me the pen and ink. I covenanted with the Devil until I should arrive to the age of 60 years, and I am now about the age of 49 years. And at that time the Devil promised on his part, as I just expressed."[69]

The indictment, written in 1692, reads, "Samuel Wardwell, of Andover, carpenter, about twenty years ago in the Town of Andover, wickedly and feloniously, with the Evil Spirit, the Devil, a covenant did make, wherein he promised to honor, worship and believe the Devil, contrary to the Statute of King James the First, and against the peace of the Sovereign Lord and Lady, the King and Queen, their crown and dignity."[70]

Wardwell's neighbor, Ephraim Foster, living in the north part of Andover, believed in Wardwell's ability to prophesy. When Ephraim, aged 20, married Hannah Eames, aged 16, in 1677, Wardwell predicted that they would have five daughters before a son should be born to them. This had proven true. Their oldest child, daughter Rose Foster, was born in 1678. Their next two daughters died young, in Ephraim's mind possibly from witchcraft. Then daughters Hannah and Jemina were born. Their first boy, their sixth child, was born in 1688. In 1692 eldest daughter Rose was ill, believed to be afflicted by witchcraft.

Ephraim Foster had often seen Wardwell tell fortunes and observed that in so doing Wardwell always "looked first into the hand of the person, and then cast his eyes down on the ground before he told anything."[71] To Ephraim this indicated that Wardwell was in league with Satan, master of the underworld.

In 1692 Thomas Chandler, an original proprietor and blacksmith of Andover, said, "I have often heard Samuel Wardwell of Andover tell young persons their fortune. He was much addicted to that, and made sport of it." Abigail Martin, Jr., aged sixteen, added, "I testify that some time last winter Samuel Wardwell was at my father's house with John Farnum. I heard John Farnum ask Wardwell his fortune, which he did. Wardwell told him that he was in love with a girl, but he would be crossed, and should go to the southward, which Farnum

---

69   Woodward, *Records of Salem Witchcraft*, 2:146-152.
70   Ibid.
71   Ibid.

admitted to be his thought. Wardwell further told Bridges he had like to be shot with a gun, and should have a fall off from his horse. Farnum afterwards admitted that Wardwell told right. And further I heard him tell James Bridges his fortune. Wardwell said that he loved a girl fourteen years old, which Bridges admitted to be the truth. But he could not imagine how said Wardwell knew; for he never spoke of it. John Bridges, father of James Bridges, said he heard James say, 'I wonder how Wardwell could tell so true.'"[72]

Andover historian Sarah Loring Bailey wrote in 1880, that, in Samuel Wardwell, "we see one of those odd geniuses, or wonder-loving characters, of whom every community has some always, who deal in the marvelous, tell great stories, dupe the credulous to the amusement of the crowd, and who, in an age of superstition, were apt to claim a knowledge of future events, and who, perhaps, believed in a measure in their own supernatural gifts."[73]

Sarah Hooper was born on December 7, 1650. From a well-to-do family, Sarah was tall and beautiful with dark hair and even features. Sarah's father took care to introduce her to the elite of Salem, the Corwins, the Hathornes, the Gedneys. When Sarah was 19 her father made his decision and arranged, against her wishes, her marriage to Adam Hawkes, a rich widower 65 years old. In June 1670, the elderly Hawkes, in failing health, married the vibrant Sarah Hooper.

A baby, Sarah Hawkes, was born to the young wife one year after her marriage, on June 1, 1671. Only eight months later, on March 13, 1672, her husband, Adam Hawkes, died. Adam left no will, unusual in Puritan times for someone of his age and wealth. It was especially strange because he made no written provision for his young wife and baby. Possibly the old man was displeased with them. Adam had two children from his first marriage, twins John Hawkes and Susanna (Hawkes) Cogswell, now aged 38. An agreement was reached whereby the young widow, aged 21, was awarded one-third of Adam's land and

---

72   Ibid.
73   Bailey, *Historical Sketches of Andover*, 211.

property.[74] However the usual provision that the widow could remain in her present dwelling place was omitted, so Sarah and her baby had to leave their home. The baby, Sarah Hawkes, was awarded £90, of which £5 was to be paid every two years until £40 was paid, and then £50 at age or marriage. The sizable inheritance of the attractive young widow caught the attention of all, and many a swain vied for the position of courting her.

In 1672, after the rejection of his marriage proposal to Sarah Barker, Samuel Wardwell turned his own attentions to the widow Sarah. "It is wonderful how many absurdities were promulgated in reference to the young man. He was fabled, for example, to have the strange power of getting into people's dreams, and regulating matters there to his own fancy. There was a great deal of talk among the neighbors, particularly the petticoated ones, about what they called the witchcraft of his eye." To everyone's amazement, the wealthy and aristocratic Sarah (Hooper) Hawkes soon chose to marry the penniless Samuel Wardwell. The date was January 9, 1673; she was 22 and he was 29. Tongues must have wagged; here was a real piece of gossip. "That low carpenter man. He no business so much as to look at her a great way off!" Imagine the impudence, the audacity of this young man of his "station and habits" daring to marry so far out of his class. Equally surprising was that Major William Hathorne, the Salem magistrate who had been a leading Quaker persecutor, made the trip from Salem to Andover on horseback to perform the wedding ceremony. This was the only time that Major William Hathorne ever came to Andover to celebrate a marriage. Certainly he did not come because of "the mesmerizing carpenter."[75] What interest could the major have taken in Sarah or her daughter?

With Samuel's hard work as a carpenter and with the advantages of his new wife's inheritance, the young family prospered. By 1692, they owned a large farm in the south part of Andover, the holdings stretching over to Prospect Hill, to Ducktail Swamp, back up the Boston road to the north part of Andover, with land over on the Merrimack fields near the widow

---

74   Essex County, Massachusetts. *Court Records*, Probate, 12:899.
75   Hawthorne, *The House of the Seven Gables*, Chapters 13-14.

Parker. They also owned a great deal of land in Lynn, Sarah's third of Adam Hawkes' property. This was an extensive estate for a carpenter who only twenty years before had owned practically nothing. Samuel and Sarah Wardwell's children, three girls and three boys, were all born in Andover. Their first child, a daughter, Mercy Wardwell, was born in 1673. Their youngest child, a girl named Rebecca, was born on September 18, 1691.

The family of Samuel Wardwell had found security and happiness. Then in March 1692 the witch hunt started in Salem Village. In early July Samuel Wardwell prophesied his own fate. The blow struck on Monday, August 15, 1692. At age 49, Samuel Wardwell was arrested for witchcraft and imprisoned in Salem. The magistrate who tracked him down was John Hathorne, son of Major William Hathorne. About two weeks later, Samuel's wife Sarah Wardwell, 41; her daughter Sarah Hawkes, 21; and their daughter Mercy Wardwell, 18, were arrested and also imprisoned in Salem. Sarah Wardwell carried her baby, Rebecca, with her to prison. The mother and three daughters survived imprisonment. When the heavily timbered oaken door of the jail was finally flung open, Sarah Wardwell "bore in her arms a child, a baby who winked and turned aside its little face from the too vivid light of day."[76]

---

76 Hawthorne, *The Scarlet Letter*, Chapter 2. The similarity between Sarah Wardwell leaving prison with her baby daughter, Rebecca, and Hawthorne's fictional Hester Prynne leaving prison with her baby daughter, Pearl, is striking.

6

JOHN HATHORNE, MAGISTRATE

W ILLIAM HATHORNE MADE FULL use of his position as magistrate to obtain wealth. During the Quaker persecution the authorities took a yoke of oxen from the Quaker John Small to settle a fine. Small's wife came to court and asked the magistrates William Hathorne and Daniel Denison, "If her husband and the Friends were such an accursed people, how then did they meddle with their goods, for they must be accursed also?" Denison turned to the woman and said, "Woman, we have none of it, for we give it to the poor." As she was speaking, John Gedney, the rich Salem innkeeper in whose tavern the court was held, entered the room. "Is this man the poor you give it to? For it is this man that had my husband's oxen," she cried. "Woman," replied Hathorne, "would you have us starve, while we sit about your business?"[77] In 1692, John Hathorne, son of the magistrate, and Bartholomew Gedney, son of the innkeeper, would sit together as justices on the witchcraft court.

William Hathorne (1607-1681) had four sons, Eleazer Hathorne, born in 1636, Nathaniel Hathorne, born in 1639, John Hathorne, born in 1641, and William Hathorne, Jr., born in 1646. Nathaniel Hathorne died as a young man. As noted earlier, William Hathorne became a major in 1661, and became a magistrate, an assistant to the governor, in 1662. That year, John became twenty-one and his father gave him a portion of Mill Pond Farm on the outskirts of Salem Town. His father retained about sixty acres. John was employed in Salem Town to keep accounts for merchants. In 1668 Major William Hathorne turned

---

77   Bishop, *New England Judged*, 245.

over his downtown house on Main Street in Salem Town to his oldest son Eleazer, and returned to live permanently in his house on Mill Pond Farm.[78]

In March 1675, at age 33, John Hathorne married Ruth Gardner. The bride was only 14. She had been born when the Quaker persecution was at its height. Her mother was an open convert and her father was a sympathizer. Her parents were fined mercilessly for absence from Puritan church services, and persistently molested in other ways. Finally in 1673 her parents moved to Connecticut. But they left behind in Salem their daughter Ruth in the household of her childless uncle, Captain Joseph Gardner and his wife. John Hathorne received permission from the Gardners to court Ruth which led to their marriage.

In 1675 King Philip's War commenced, the only Indian war that nearly succeeded in driving the white man from New England. Throughout the war John Hathorne took advantage of the excellent opportunities it afforded for war profiteering. He entrenched himself in business, purchased a wharf, and secured a license to sell strong liquors. It was an auspicious time to build his permanent family seat.

John Hathorne wished to erect a mansion, framed in heavy oak timbers and designed to endure for many generations. He built his house in the center of Salem Town, on the west side of School Lane near South River. John and his child-bride moved into the new mansion as soon as it was finished, at the end of 1675. But what would be the fate of this grand house and the Hathorne descendants destined to live in it? "What we call real estate—the solid ground to build a house on—is the broad foundation on which nearly all the guilt of this world rests. A

---

78 Major William Hathorne had a brother, John Hathorne, who ran a tavern in Lynn and died in 1676. In 1652 this John Hathorne was charged with forgery and confessed himself guilty. In 1657, the peninsula of Nahant was purchased from an Indian sagamore for a suit of clothes; John Hathorne, Adam Hawkes, and a few others laid out the land for division. In 1663 John Hathorne complained that two residents of Lynn had given false testimony. They accused him of slander; he was found guilty and had to pay a fine and make a public acknowledgment in the meetinghouse. John Hathorne died in 1676 in Lynn, leaving sons and daughters.

man will commit almost any wrong—he will heap up an immense pile of wickedness, as hard as granite, and which will weigh as heavily upon his soul to eternal ages—only to build a great, gloomy, dark-chambered mansion, for himself to die in, and for his posterity to be miserable in."[79]

The first portent of disaster came quickly, December 1675. Captain Joseph Gardner, the uncle and guardian of John Hathorne's new bride, was killed in King Philip's War. "Here it comes, out of the same house whence we saw brave Captain Gardner go forth to the wars. What! A coffin, borne on men's shoulders, and six aged gentlemen as pall-bearers, and a long train of mourners, with black gloves and black hatbands, and everything black, save a white handkerchief in each mourner's hand, to wipe away the tears withal. Now, my kind patrons, you are angry with me. You were bidden to a bridal-dance, and find yourselves walking in a funeral procession."[80]

John Hathorne's younger brother, William Hathorne, Jr., was the lieutenant in Captain Gardner's company. When Gardner was killed in battle, his lieutenant succeeded him. William Hathorne, Jr., only 29 years old, attained the high military rank of captain. William Hathorne, Jr., one of the most dashing and one of the most ruthless officers in the army, was obsessed with fame. In 1676 he returned to Salem and married Sarah Ruck, daughter of John Ruck. In August 1676, Captain Hathorne was ordered with his company north to kill hostile Indians.

At Dover, New Hampshire, the captain met Richard Waldron, deputy magistrate of Dover. Waldron was the same man who, fourteen years earlier, had sentenced the three Quaker women to be stripped of their clothes and whipped in the snow on Christmas day. Together Hathorne and Waldron devised a plan. They would lead friendly neighborhood Indians into a trap by lying to them. The plan was neatly executed in September 1676, and by his treachery Captain Hathorne took four hundred captives. The strongest two hundred men were loaded into two waiting sloops and sold as slaves in Bermuda. Waldron was an old hand at the slave trade, and this transaction, the result of

---

79   Hawthorne, *The House of the Seven Gables*, Chapter 17.
80   Hawthorne, *Main-Street*.

betrayal of the Indians' trust, brought great wealth to him and the young captain. All this was done with the approval of the Puritan leaders, the old guard. Cotton Mather later described the details in his history of King Philip's War, calling the devious affair "the stunningest wound of all given to the Indians."[81] Puritan teaching maintained that the Indians were the Devil's children.

Two years later, in 1678, Captain William Hathorne, Jr., only 32 years old, died a mysterious death. Unsure of the cause of the captain's death, people blamed an old Indian wound. Some whispered that the wound was aggravated by the Devil because of the captain's treachery to his children, the Indians. Did the charms of some sorcerer carry out the Devil's will and cause a festering wound to inflict hideous torture? William's death dealt a major blow to his brother, John Hathorne. "The reserved and stately gentleman forgot his dignity; the gold-embroidered waistcoat flickered and glistened in the firelight with the convulsion of rage, terror, and sorrow of the human heart that was beating under it."[82]

In 1680 disaster struck the family again. Major William Hathorne's oldest son, Eleazer Hathorne, who had married a sister of Jonathan Corwin, died suddenly in Maine at age forty-three. His death was equally mysterious. The following year, 1681, Major William Hathorne died. John inherited his father's property at Mill Pond Farm. The future of the Hathorne family now rested in the hands of the only surviving son, John Hathorne.

In 1683, John Hathorne was elected to represent Salem as a deputy, and the following year as a magistrate, an assistant to the governor. At age 42, John Hathorne found himself a member of the Board of Assistants, and a full inheritor of his father's privileges. He became a tireless judge who over the years adjudicated an endless number of cases in the Essex County Court.

As a young man, John Hathorne had entered into land speculation in Maine. He soon became obsessed with acquiring and owning land. At times he was obliged to go to sea in

---

81   Cotton Mather, *Magnalia Christi Americana.*
82   Hawthorne, *The House of the Seven Gables,* Chapter 13

connection with his work; on one sea voyage he landed at a small settlement on the Maine coast. There for a few gold guineas he bought from a sagamore Indian called Robin Hood a vast and as yet unexplored and unmeasured tract. This Maine property, known to the Hathornes as the eastern land, embraced woods, lakes, and rivers. Apparently Robin Hood was aptly named, for he continued to sell the same land to other speculators. John Hathorne would spend a lifetime trying to track down these purchasers to buy back their deeds and give himself clear title. To later generations of Hathornes the eastern land offered dreams of great wealth. "When the pathless forest that still covered this wild principality should give place—as it inevitably must, though not perhaps till ages hence—to the golden fertility of human culture, it would be the source of incalculable wealth." In point of fact, it would bring nothing but bitter disappointment. "This impalpable claim, resulted in nothing more solid than to cherish, from generation to generation, an absurd delusion of family importance," wrote Nathaniel Hawthorne.[83]

In 1684 the English monarch, King Charles II, annulled the charter of the Massachusetts Bay Company under which the Puritans ruled. However the king's decree was blithely ignored in Boston, and things went on as before. With the death of King Charles II and the accession of King James II in 1685, the new king dismissed Simon Bradstreet as governor and appointed a temporary council to rule Massachusetts. Next the king named Sir Edmond Andros as the royal governor. On December 19, 1686, Andros landed in Boston and proclaimed himself captain general and governor-in-chief. With the complete abrogation of the old Massachusetts Bay charter, the colonists feared that the crown would demand ownership of all the land in the colony. They were all too familiar with the situation in England where the crown and the aristocracy owned the soil, and the common people were merely tenants. The colonists legitimately feared that the same feudal system might be imposed upon them.

---

83   Hawthorne, *The House of the Seven Gables*, Chapter 1. Although most people today regard the state of Maine as being north of Boston, the colonists regarded it as being east of Boston. Actually it is northeast.

The large landowners in New England had carefully used all possible means to substantiate their claims to the soil. Specifically they had implemented a scheme of persuading the descendants of the sagamores who had ruled New England to convey land deeds to them. This was an outlandish course of action; it was known that the crown held no regard for signatures of Indians. However, the colonists thought that the deeds signed by the Indians might embarrass the new royal governor just enough to prevent him from executing the king's plan. When Andros asked the senior minister of Salem, the Rev. John Higginson, Sr. whether New England was king's territory, Higginson replied that it belonged to the colonists because they held it by just occupation and purchase from the Indians.

Action taken by Salem to safeguard its vested interests resulted in a deed dated October 11, 1686. The grantees were John Ruck, John Higginson, Sr., Timothy Lindall, William Hirst, and Israel Porter, selectmen and trustees for the township of Salem.[84] The deed was signed, sealed and delivered by David Nonnuphanohow, Cicely Petaghuncksq, and eight other Indians. The consideration of release was £20 in current money. The Salem magistrate Bartholomew Gedney was present and the deed was acknowledged before him. The deed was written on parchment, a document of remarkable beauty and elaborateness of execution.[85]

The deed for Lynn, which includes the present city of Lynn and towns of Saugus, Lynnfield, Nahant, Swampscott, and a portion of Reading, was granted by David Kunkshamooshaw, who by credible intelligence was grandson to old sagamore George No Nose, so-called, alias Wenepawweekine, and by four other Indians. The land was obtained for a consideration of the sum of £16 of current sterling money of silver in hand paid to the Indians claiming, viz. David Kunkshamooshaw &c. The deed was executed on May 31, 1687. It was witnessed by John Hawkes and

---

84   John Ruck was the father of Sarah (Ruck) Hathorne Burroughs. She was the widow of the deceased Captain William Hathorne, Jr. She married the Rev. George Burroughs in Salem Village in 1682 and she died in Maine in 1690. John Higginson, Sr. was the senior minister of Salem and Israel Porter was the brother-in-law of John Hathorne.

85   Perley, *Indian Land Titles of Essex County*, 64-87.

three other residents of Lynn and by Samuel Wardwell of
Andover.   The deed was acknowledged before Bartholomew
Gedney, magistrate of Salem.[86]

The extensive and valuable Lynn land of the deceased Adam
Hawkes was owned by his son, John Hawkes, and by his widow,
Sarah (Hooper) Hawkes Wardwell.   The value of Sarah's
holdings was not lost on Bartholomew Gedney, aged 46, the
magistrate acknowledging the deed.   Gedney had become a
magistrate, an assistant to the governor, in 1680.   He was a
captain in the militia at the time, and soon would be promoted to
major.   This crafty man was the son of John Gedney, the wealthy
Salem innkeeper.   Bartholomew Gedney lived all his life in
Salem and owned a shipyard there.   He is best known in history
for his land speculations.

Bartholomew Gedney and his friend, John Hathorne, were
two of the witchcraft judges who condemned the carpenter,
Samuel Wardwell.   This "pestilent wizard" was hanged and
buried on Gallows Hill on September 22, 1692.   In January 1693,
Samuel's wife, Sarah Wardwell, was sentenced to death.   Her
grave was dug, but the governor, Sir William Phipps, reprieved
her at the last minute.   Yet the attainder—the loss of all civil
rights legally consequent to a death sentence—remained in place
and she could neither own nor pass down property.   Her lands in
Lynn were confiscated, falling into the hands of the assignees of
Bartholomew Gedney, John Hathorne, John Corwin, and the
others who divided the plunder of the witch hunt.   They took
"possession of the ill-gotten spoil—with the black stain of blood
sunken deep into it.   The wizard had been foully wronged out of
his homestead, if not out of his life," wrote Nathaniel
Hawthorne.[87]

John Hathorne was the most active and the most diligent
government official in searching out and arresting those people
accused of witchcraft in 1692.   He rightly deserves the title of
chief witch-hunter.   "He is a determined and relentless man,
with the genuine character of an inquisitor."[88]   In *The Custom*

---

86   Ibid.
87   Hawthorne, *The House of the Seven Gables*, Chapter 1.
88   Hawthorne, *The House of the Seven Gables*, Chapter 14.

House, Nathaniel Hawthorne wrote that John Hathorne "inherited the persecuting spirit, and made himself so conspicuous in the martyrdom of the witches, that their blood may fairly be said to have left a stain upon him. So deep a stain, indeed, that his old dry bones, in the Charter Street burial-ground, must still retain it." Again Hawthorne, with his ancestor, John Hathorne, in mind, wrote, "We shall only add, therefore, that the Puritan—so, at least, says chimney-corner tradition, which often preserves traits of character with marvelous fidelity—was bold, imperious, relentless, crafty; laying his purposes deep, and following them out with an inveteracy of pursuit that knew neither rest or conscience; trampling on the weak, and, when essential to his ends, doing the utmost to beat down the strong."[89]

Joseph Hathorne, a younger son of John Hathorne, inherited his father's house on Mill Pond Farm. The rocky outcrop of Gallows Hill, standing less than a couple of thousand feet from the house, shed an ominous shadow across the door. "It is not the less certain, however, that awe and terror brooded over the memories of those who died for this horrible crime of witchcraft. Their graves, in the crevices of the rocks, were supposed to be incapable of retaining the occupants who had been so hastily thrust into them."[90] Joseph, a small boy in 1692, had been too young to understand his father's prominent role in the witchcraft hangings. By the time of Joseph's death, however, the house had vanished. Had it burned to the ground? Or had Joseph ordered it torn down? Joseph's great-grandson would later write, "There is no such unwholesome atmosphere as that of an old home, rendered poisonous by one's defunct forefathers and relatives. It were a relief to me if that house could be torn down, and so the earth be rid of it, and grass be sown abundantly over its foundation."[91]

Nathaniel Hawthorne's *The House of the Seven Gables* is based upon the Salem witchcraft tragedy. The novel explores

---

89   Hawthorne, *The House of the Seven Gables*, Chapter 8.
90   Hawthorne, *The House of the Seven Gables*, Chapter 13.
91   Hawthorne, *The House of the Seven Gables*, Chapter 17.

the question of inherited guilt. Hawthorne lays great emphasis upon a definite moral purpose at which he directs his work. He is obsessed with "the truth, namely, that the wrongdoing of one generation lives into the successive ones, and, divesting itself of every temporary advantage, becomes a pure and uncontrollable mischief."[92] The wrongdoing to which Hawthorne alludes in the novel refers to the crime perpetrated against the fictional Matthew Maule by the fictional Colonel Pyncheon during the Salem witchcraft affair. In 1692 the Puritan colonel accuses Matthew Maule of witchcraft. Before Maule is put to death, however, he curses the colonel. The colonel easily obtains the land of the dead wizard and builds the House of the Seven Gables on it. The carpenter who does the construction is Thomas Maule, none other than the dead wizard's son. As soon as the house is finished, however, the colonel meets with an untimely, mysterious death in it. The successive generations of the Pyncheon family who live in the seven-gabled house believe that their fortunes are blighted by the wizard's curse.

Many generations later, in 1850, the Pyncheon family has been reduced to only a few living members. Judge Pyncheon, a direct descendant of the Puritan colonel, is his "very image, in mind and body." Phoebe Pyncheon, a young cousin of the Judge, is "very pretty, as graceful as a bird, as pleasant about the house as a gleam of sunshine." Holgrave, a boarder in the house, is an artist, "a young man with so much faith in himself, and with so fair an appearance of admirable powers." Unknown to the Pyncheons, Holgrave is a descendant of the condemned Matthew Maule and inherited some of his magical powers. Judge Pyncheon meets his death in the house in the same manner as his seventeen-century ancestor, the colonel. The ancestral curse is finally lifted, however, when the young Phoebe Pyncheon falls in love with and agrees to marry Holgrave, who refused to exploit his magical powers over her.[93]

Despite Hawthorne's artistic license, some of the characters and events in his narrative may be linked to actual historical counterparts. In creating the fictional Pyncheon family,

Hawthorne freely drew upon his knowledge of his own Hathorne ancestors. Literary critics generally accept that Hawthorne modelled the fictional seventeenth-century Colonel Pyncheon after his own great, great grandfather, John Hathorne. In turn, the nineteenth-century Judge Pyncheon embodies all of his ancestor's characteristics; "the Colonel Pyncheon of two centuries ago steps forward as the Judge of the passing moment!" Thus Hawthorne produced not one, but two fictional characters, Colonel Pyncheon and Judge Pyncheon, based upon the personal attributes of magistrate John Hathorne.[94]

"The similarity, intellectually and moral, between the Judge and his ancestor, appears to have been at least as strong as the resemblance of mien and feature would afford reason to anticipate. In old Colonel Pyncheon's funeral discourse, the clergyman absolutely canonized his deceased parishioner. So also, as regards the Judge Pyncheon of today, neither clergyman, nor legal critic, would venture a word against this eminent person's sincerity as a Christian, or respectability as a man, or integrity as a judge."[95]

The Salem witchcraft affair was sanctioned by the Puritan old guard: the most respectable magistrates and the most esteemed ministers in the colony. One was Hawthorne's ancestor, magistrate John Hathorne. In *The House of the Seven Gables*, Hawthorne's purpose was not merely to chronicle his ancestor's misdeeds, but to investigate the overriding question of why the witch hunt had occurred. What were the characteristics that permitted John Hathorne to condemn to death so many innocent people, and to escape with near total impunity? Hawthorne's explanation has been excerpted as follows (abbreviated with italics added for emphasis). In it he profiles his great, great grandfather with vivid immediacy as representative of the Puritan old guard who so eagerly propelled the witch hunt. Nathaniel Hawthorne supplies the strongest and most compelling answer offered before or since to the question which lies at the crux of the matter: Why was the witch hunt allowed to take place?

---

94   John Hathorne was both a colonel and a judge.
95   Hawthorne, *The House of the Seven Gables*, Chapter 8.

Like his fictional counterparts, magistrate John Hathorne was "a man of eminent respectability. The church acknowledged it; the state acknowledged it. It was denied by nobody. His conscience bore an accordant testimony with the world's laudatory voice. And yet, strong as this evidence may seem, we should hesitate to peril our own conscience on the assertion that the Judge and the consenting world were right. Hidden from mankind there may have lurked some evil or unsightly thing.

"Men of strong minds, great force of character, and a hard texture of sensibilities are very capable of falling into mistakes. They are ordinary men to whom forms are of paramount importance. They possess vast ability in grasping, and arranging, and appropriating to themselves the big, heavy, solid unrealities, such as gold, landed estate, offices of trust and emolument, and public honors. With these materials, and with deeds of goodly aspects, an individual of his class builds up, as it were, a tall and stately edifice, which in the view of other people is no other than the man's character, or the man himself. Behold, therefore, a palace! Its splendid halls are floored with a mosaic of costly marbles. Ah, but in some low and obscure nook—beneath the marble pavement, in a stagnant water puddle—may lie a corpse, half decayed, and still decaying, and diffusing its death scent all through the palace! *The inhabitant will not be conscious of it, for it has long been his daily breath! Neither will the visitors, for they smell only the rich odors which the master sedulously scatters through the palace.* Here then, we are to seek the true emblem of the man's character, and of the deed that gives whatever reality it possesses to his life. And beneath the show of the marble palace, that pool of stagnant water, foul with many impurities, and, perhaps, tinged with blood, is this man's miserable soul.

"The purity of his judicial character, while on the bench; the faithfulness of his public service; his remarkable zeal as president of Bible society; the cleanliness of his moral deportment; his prayers at morning and eventide; the studied propriety of his dress and equipment—what room could possibly be found for darker traits in a portrait made up of lineaments like these?

"A hard, cold man seldom or never looking inward, and resolutely taking his idea of himself from what purports to be his image as reflected in the mirror of public opinion, can scarcely arrive at true self-knowledge."[96] But Nathaniel Hawthorne withholds his most scathing indictment until the close of the book when he refers to the Judge as a man of "inward criminality."[97]

Hawthorne further probed the central issue when he asked "whether judges, clergymen, and other characters of that eminent stamp and respectability could really be otherwise than just and honorable men." His answer was that "a wider scope of view, and a deeper insight, may see rank, dignity, and station all proved illusory, so far as regards their claim to human reverence."[98]

---

96   Hawthorne, *The House of the Seven Gables*, Chapter 15.
97   Hawthorne, *The House of the Seven Gables*, Chapter 21.
98   Hawthorne, *The House of the Seven Gables*, Chapter 8.

7

COTTON MATHER, CLERGYMAN

B ECAUSE NEW ENGLAND WAS A THEOCRACY, the Puritan
clergy had a significant hand in the government, and
together with the politicians, they formed the elite ruling class.
As a result of a heavy ministry tax, the clergy were very well
paid. The Cotton and Mather families provide the most eminent
representatives of the Puritan clergy. The activities of these two
families are intertwined in the unfolding of New England
history.

John Cotton (1584–1652) was a renowned English minister
who emigrated to America in 1633. Many of his congregation in
England followed him to New England, where he became
minister of the First Church in Boston. Richard Mather (1596–
1669) came to Massachusetts in 1635. He settled in Dorchester (a
town just south of Boston then, and now a part of Boston) and
preached there for nearly thirty-four years. Two of John Cotton's
sons and four of Richard Mather's graduated from Harvard
College and entered the ministry. Both John Cotton and Richard
Mather were Moses-like figures, leaders and law givers of
immense influence on American Puritans.

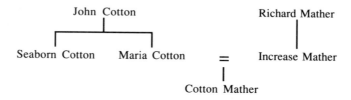

The two sons who play a role in this story are John Cotton's
son, Seaborn Cotton, and Richard Mather's son, Increase Mather

(1639-1723). The critical link between the two families comes by way of John Cotton's daughter, Maria Cotton, who married Increase Mather. Their son, Cotton Mather, was named so as to perpetuate the bond between the two families.

Increase Mather became the minister of the North Church in Boston. He married Maria Cotton in 1662 and on February 12, 1663, the couple's first child, Cotton Mather, was born. In the fall of 1674, Cotton Mather entered Harvard College at the age of eleven and a half, the youngest student admitted to the college in its history. The General Court had founded the college in 1636 as a training ground for the future leaders of New England, both spiritual and secular. The normal time spent for the bachelor degree was three years. By present day standards the number of students was small. While Cotton Mather attended, the total enrollment at Harvard was never more than 20 students. Most ranged in age from about 15 to 18. There were three buildings, located close to the entrance to Harvard yard today—the president's house, a small brick school building, and the college hall. The last was a two-story wooden edifice which contained the recitation hall, study, library, and dormitory.

As an eleven year old boy with a stutter, Cotton Mather was immediately unhappy at Harvard. He was threatened by some students who thought he was tattling to his father about their misbehavior. In little more than a month he left college and returned home. He re-entered the next fall, 1675, and graduated three years later in the class of 1678. After graduation he spent a brief time studying medicine. He then turned his attention to the ministry and became assistant minister in his father's church, the North Church in Boston.

Two of Cotton Mather's college-mates, both named Thomas, enter the witchcraft story in a significant way. Thomas Barnard, class of 1679, became a close personal friend of Cotton Mather while at Harvard. Barnard became a minister and used his eloquence to bring to the people the rigid doctrine espoused by Cotton Mather. In 1692 Barnard was instrumental in prolonging the witchcraft epidemic. Thomas Brattle, class of 1676, never was congenial with Cotton Mather at college. Brattle, an eminent opponent of the Puritan theocracy, saw through the prejudice, egotism, and vanity of Cotton Mather. In 1692 Brattle made use of his keen judicial mind to oppose and discredit the witch hunt. The powerful arguments that he used in his letter dated October 8, 1692, helped bring the affair to an end.[99]

With age the Rev. Francis Dane of Andover had mellowed from strict adherence to Puritan doctrine. Dane was "a clergyman, enthusiastic in his profession, and apparently of the genuine dynasty of those old Puritans whose faith in their calling, and stern exercise of it, had placed them among the mighty of the earth. But, yielding to the speculative tendency of the age, he had gone astray from the firm foundation of an ancient faith, and wandered into a cloud region, where everything was misty and deceptive. His instinct and early training demanded something steadfast; but, looking forward, he beheld vapors piled upon vapors, and, behind him, an impassable gulf between the man of yesterday and today."[100]

Members of the Andover church, unhappy with the Rev. Dane's preaching, decided that he was infirm and in need of a young colleague. In January 1682 they invited Cotton Mather's good friend, Thomas Barnard, to give a sermon. "The eloquent voice, on which the souls of the listening audience had been born aloft, as on the swelling waves of the sea, at length came to a pause. There was a momentary silence, profound as what should follow the utterance of oracles. Then ensued a murmur and half-hushed tumult; as if the auditors, released from the high spell that had transported them into the region of another's mind, were returning into themselves, with all the awe and wonder still heavy on them. Now that there was an end, they needed another breath, more fit to support the gross and earthly life into which they relapsed, than the atmosphere which the preacher had converted into words of flame."[101]

The sermon was a key instrument of education and entertainment for the Puritan settlers; there were few books, no newspapers, and no theater. Impressed by Barnard's sermon, the elders of the Andover church wanted him as their minister.

---

99   Brattle, "Letter of October 8, 1692," in Burr, *Narratives*, 169-190.
100   Hawthorne, *The Christmas Banquet*.
101   Hawthorne, *The Scarlet Letter*, Chapter 23.

Claiming that Mr. Dane was in comfortable circumstances, they decided that he could subsist without any salary. Unwilling to support the older pastor but still expecting him to carry on his work, they chose to give all the ministerial pay to Barnard.

Dane was not one to accept this injustice, and he took Barnard to court. After a bitter legal battle, the Court partially supported Dane's claim, much to the aggravation of the young Barnard. The General Court, in consideration of the fact that Dane "had for a long time been an officer among them" told the Andover church to pay him £30 per year, one-half his former salary. The court then admonished Dane, advising him to "improve his almost diligence to carry on the public worship of God," and to "forget all former disgusts."[102]   The elders, meanwhile, voted to pay Barnard only £50 a year, a bitter disappointment as he had expected at least £60. But there was a provision that the low remuneration should continue only as long as Mr. Dane "should carry on part of the work." The bright side was that as soon as Dane should cease to aid him, Barnard would have his pay increased to £80 per year. In other words, once Dane was gone, Barnard could add Dane's pay of £30 to his low pay of £50, reaching the impressive figure of £80 a year.[103]

In his protracted struggle with the elder Dane, Barnard turned to the one person he could trust, his old college-mate Cotton Mather. The two fanatical young ministers determined to expose what they believed were the short-comings in Dane's ministry; their opportunity was not to come for ten years, the fateful year 1692. Thomas Barnard would direct the witch hunt in Andover along the lines dictated by Cotton Mather. The long-standing relationship between these two men reveals the underlying explanation of why more witches were arrested in Andover in 1692 than any other town including Salem Village.

---

102 Bailey, *Historical Sketches of Andover*, 422-423.

103 The value of £1 then was equivalent to at least $1000 now. For example, the price of an ocean-going vessel bought in Salem or Boston would be in the range from about £50 for a small sloop to about £200 or £300 for a larger vessel. The Rev. Peter Thatcher of Milton, Massachusetts bought an Indian woman in 1674 for £5 down and £5 more at the end of the year—a high-priced slave for the times.

The New England colonies started introducing laws against witchcraft as early as 1641. Aspirations and achievements of women were held in check by a steady trickle of witchcraft accusations and trials. On May 14, 1656 Governor John Endicott, about to engage in his battle with the Quaker invaders, pronounced the death sentence on Ann Hibbens. She was hanged on Boston Common. Ann Hibbens was no Quaker; she was the wealthy widow of William Hibbens, a merchant, a magistrate, an assistant to the governor. William had been a member of the elite ruling Board of Assistants. The execution of Ann Hibbens as a witch on June 19, 1656 surprised few citizens. Her doubts and subsequent defiance of the establishment had been documented in 1640 when she suffered admonition and then excommunication from the Puritan church. Following her husband's death in 1654, her days were numbered.

In the decade before the trial of Ann Hibbens, at least sixteen women were tried for witchcraft, about eight of whom were executed. In the following decades dozens more women were accused and tried for witchcraft. Even though many were executed, some were able to put up a defense that allowed them to escape the hangman. Yet not until 1692 did the ever-lurking witchcraft accusations reach the intensity of mass persecution. More than one hundred seventy people were arrested, mostly women, and every person tried for witchcraft in that year was found guilty.[104] Some trigger was required to transform the ever present misogyny into an open and raging witch hunt. History has laid blame on the Rev. Cotton Mather.

Massachusetts was a theocracy ruled by the old guard. These political and clerical leaders, all hard-line Puritans, detested dissent in any form. Disagreement with or rejection of the doctrines of the established Puritan church was a most serious crime, punishable by extreme measures. In the colony's early stages, the general public acquiesced to the persecution of heretics like Anne Hutchinson and the Quakers, as well as the

---

104 However, from January 1693 to May 1693 only three women out of the many prisoners brought to trial were found guilty. Soon after the May trials Governor Phipps ordered the release of all remaining witchcraft prisoners, bringing the affair to an end.

hanging of an occasional witch. But by the 1680s many citizens no longer supported the repressive measures used to stifle dissent. Instead thoughtful people of all classes sought greater individual freedom. Anxious about this democratic trend, the old guard looked for an effective strategy to return people to the old ways. Cotton Mather sensed that the root of the trouble lay not with outside agitators, whose presence was altogether real, but with increasing discontent within the Puritan community itself. The public no longer exhibited the same devotion and unquestioned loyalty as had their fathers and grandfathers.

Cotton Mather attacked the growing trend head-on. In sermons and pamphlets he used various tactics in his quest for effective ways to control and browbeat. The religious leaders required people to accept every word in the Bible as fact. The existence of witchcraft had long been a required belief of the church. Puritan beliefs were rooted in contrasts. Since there was good, there must be evil. Since there was a God, there had to be a Devil. As there were visible saints chosen to do God's work on Earth, there must be witches who were instruments of the Devil. By this perverted logic it followed that if one denied the existence of witches, one did not believe in God. A disbelief in witches thus translated into the ultimate heresy.

As the colony's leading young clergyman, Cotton Mather undertook the task of exposing and unmasking the dangers of witchcraft to glorify the Lord Jesus Christ. In his sermon *A Discourse on Witchcraft* in 1688, he wrote, "Witchcraft is a most monstrous and horrid evil. Witchcraft is a renouncing of God, and advancing a filthy Devil into the throne of the most high. Witchcraft is a renouncing of Christ, and preferring the communion of a loathsome lying Devil before all the salvation of the Lord redeemer. Witchcraft is a siding with Hell against Heaven and Earth; and therefore a witch is not to be endured in either of them. 'Tis a capital crime. Friend, believest thou the Scriptures? Christian, there are Devils, and so many of them too, that sometimes a legion of them are spared for the vexation of one man. Since there are witches and Devils, we may conclude that there are immortal souls."[105]

---

105 Cotton Mather, *A Discourse on Witchcraft*.

In 1689 Cotton Mather published *Memorable Providences, Relating to Witchcraft and Possessions*. Its major thrust was to demonstrate the effectiveness of witchcraft accusations as a means to bring down perceived enemies of the church and state. The book was a compendium of slander and fabrications against Mary Glover, a Roman Catholic woman executed for witchcraft in Boston in 1688. The chief justice in her trial was William Stoughton, an admirer of Cotton Mather. Mary Glover, like Anne Hutchinson, Ann Hibbens, and the Quaker women, were targeted as symbolic enemies. Cotton Mather devoted himself to persuading one and all that the Devil was at work in assaulting the righteous through the instrumentality of witches. The zealous young minister claimed that covens of witches were ready to destroy New England. In vague terms, he let it be known who these witches might be. Typical is his sermon in 1688, in which he used 1 Sam. 15:23, *Rebellion is as the sin of witchcraft*, as the text. He preached, "Let not a course of rebellion be followed. Consider what you are doing. You have been doing of iniquity. There is a sort of witchcraft charged on you."[106] His message was picked up and broadcast by other ministers. The average person, knowing far too well the punishment for religious or political dissent, quietly accepted these pronouncements, however absurd or false.

After the publication of his book *Memorable Providences*, Cotton Mather stepped up his discourse against Devils and witches. He demanded to know, "How many doleful wretches have been decoyed into witchcraft itself, by the opportunities which their discontent has given to the Devil to visit them and seduce them?"[107] He preached, "The Devils are stark mad that the House of the Lord our God has come into these remote corners of the world; and they fume; they fret prodigiously."[108] His efforts succeeded. He transmitted his apparent paranoia, undiminished, to the civil authorities who proceeded to take legal action against these imagined enemies of the state in the witchcraft persecutions of 1692. Cotton Mather's scholarship

---

106 Ibid.
107 Cotton Mather, *Fair Weather*, 50.
108 Cotton Mather, *The Present State of New England*, 38.

wielded enormous influence among the Puritan old guard. His friends in high government circles listened carefully to his congenial arguments. In effect he was marketing a philosophy of fear. The political leaders were not only pleased with his message, but actively encouraged its promulgation. They, too, saw it as a method to ensure their control.

The old guard stood willing to take any action to destroy its ideological enemies in order to prevent disunity. The Salem witch hunt of 1692 was the starkest manifestation of this covert policy. More than one hundred seventy people were accused as witches and imprisoned. Although much of the political vengeance was ultimately intended for men, most of the immediate victims were women. Women were the most vulnerable members of a targeted family. In those cases when the authorities did arrest a man, they usually would take several women from his family for good measure.

In the witch hunt of 1692 Cotton Mather became obsessed by the spell of his own dogma. Described as a man of overweening vanity, he was unflinching in the search for witches, always haranguing others to take stronger actions. He had an inexhaustible inventory of epithets to apply to accused women; on various occasions he used such expressions as ignorant and scandalous hags, crazed in their intellects, blasphemous, railing, grossly lying, the most impudent, scurrilous, wicked creatures of the world. Always mindful of future political implications, the old guard wanted no responsibility laid directly at their hands. From the beginning they took care to dodge all accountability. They hid behind a carefully crafted facade. Their strategy was to make the witch hunt appear as if it were carried out in response to popular demand to protect a long-suffering public from the witches in its midst. Official records were written to give credibility to the existence of witches; every effort was made to make it appear as if the witch hunt resulted from an intrinsic belief by the people in the dangers of witchcraft. Little did the public know that the witch hunt was created and implemented from the start by small conspiracies sanctioned by the ruling Puritan old guard seeking to perpetuate its own wealth and power.

Essex County and the towns of Hampton and Exeter in 1692.

8

SALEM VILLAGE WITCH HUNT

B Y 1692 THE IRON-HANDED RULE imposed on Massachusetts by the Puritan old guard was in serious jeopardy. The common people, in a quest for democracy, had begun to question the very basis of theocratic government. Only the elect, about four or five percent of the people, were allowed to vote and participate in the colonial government. These visible saints of the Puritan church were those who had obtained the high honor of church membership. Everyone else was still required to pay ministry taxes, attend services, and adhere to the strict Puritan code. An undercurrent of dissent was growing, not only among the disenfranchised, but also among liberal church members who favored a plural society. Leading merchants, such as Thomas Brattle of Boston and Philip English of Salem, joined in expressing these viewpoints.

The township of Salem had three main parts, Salem Town (now the city of Salem), Salem Farms (now the city of Peabody), and Salem Village (now the town of Danvers). Most of the people lived in Salem Town, a thriving seaport, simply referred to as Salem. Salem Farms was west of the town and Salem Village was north of Salem Farms. Each was a community of only a few hundred residents living on scattered farms. The people of Salem Farms generally identified with Salem Town, whereas the people of Salem Village had shown a bit of independence over the years. Salem Village had its own center, about five miles northwest of the center of Salem Town. In the village center were a meetinghouse, a parsonage, a tavern, and a few private houses. The meetinghouse was used both as church building and municipal building. Because the meeting house was damp and unheated, the large public room of the tavern, warmed by a great fireplace, was often used as the courtroom. The Rev. Samuel Parris was the village parson and Nathaniel Ingersoll owned the tavern.

Nathaniel Ingersoll, who lived in the private rooms of his tavern, was a man of industry and thrift. As a licensed innkeeper, he could sell liquor by the quart even on Sunday. He was a lieutenant of the Salem Village militia company and a deacon in the church. A close neighbor was his nephew, Jonathan Walcott, the captain of the company and also a deacon. A couple of miles away lived Thomas Putnam, the sergeant of the company and the parish clerk.

The witch hunt started as innocent play in the parsonage of the Rev. Samuel Parris. In his household were two slaves whom Parris had brought from Barbados, John Indian and his wife, Tituba. Tituba was long familiar with magic, fortune-telling, incantations, and necromancy (or spirit communication with the dead) from her native West Indies. Such lore was a fascination to the neighborhood children, and during the winter of 1691-1692 a small circle of girls got in the habit of meeting with Tituba and pretended to practice the black art. The group included Parris' daughter Elizabeth Parris, aged 9, and his niece Abigail Williams, aged 11. The others, all neighborhood girls, were Sergeant Thomas Putnam's daughter Ann Putnam, Jr., aged 12, and his servant, Mercy Lewis, aged 17; Captain Jonathan Walcott's daughter, Mary Walcott, aged 17; and Dr. William Griggs' maid, Elizabeth Hubbard, aged 17. Fascination soon turned to enchantment. By February 1692 the girls began acting in strange and bizarre manners. They went into so-called fits in which they seemed to lose touch with the real world. They uttered foolish and nonsensical speeches. They made odd gestures and contorted themselves into freakish postures. In fact, these afflicted girls acted in much the same way as the bewitched children described in graphic detail by Cotton Mather in his book *Memorable Providences Relating to Witchcraft and Possessions*, published in 1689.

Dr. William Griggs, the local physician, quickly rendered his services. Upon examining the girls, he found no physical cause for their afflictions. He concluded that the girls were bewitched. To display his knowledge of witchcraft, the Rev. Parris, in the fashion of Cotton Mather and other ambitious ministers, called in other clergy and elders to hold days of fasting and prayer. The Rev. John Hale, minister in the neighboring town of Beverly and the Rev. Nicholas Noyes, assistant minister in Salem Town, enthusiastically joined in. The result of these sessions was to whip up witchcraft fears among the populace.

John Indian tried an experiment to discover who were the witches causing the afflictions. He made a cake of rye meal with the children's urine, and baked it in the ashes. When he gave it to a dog to eat, the afflicted children went into their fits. They fell into strange positions, appearing convulsed and distorted. The girls now claimed to see into the invisible world ruled by the Devil. The inhabitants of this forbidding domain were specters and ghosts. With their newly-found spectral sight, the girls could see the specters of some of the witches who were causing their afflictions.

In the invisible world, the witch's specter was pinching, pricking and tormenting the girls. At the same time, in the real world, the witch herself commonly appeared quite harmless and innocent. The girls identified some of the witches whose specters were afflicting them. Because the girls claimed to be in excruciating pain, they would cry out upon these witches. Their pitiful screams could be heard far and wide. The first named was Tituba herself. Note that since the girls alone had the required spectral sight, only they could provide the damning spectral evidence against a witch.

The clergy confirmed that the girls, though afflicted, were blessed with the gift of spectral sight. Some claimed that this spectral sight was not a blessing, but rather a deception by the Devil. These dissenters said that the specter was, in fact, the Devil himself appearing in the shape of an innocent woman, who would then be mistaken for a witch. But the Rev. John Hale rushed in to defend the use of spectral evidence. He asserted that the Devil could not appear in the shape of an innocent person. Thus the specter seen by the girls was not that of the Devil, but that of a *bona fide* witch.   The authorities accepted his viewpoint; in their eyes spectral evidence was valid.

The number of afflicted persons began to grow. Although most of the newly afflicted were girls, there were also a few women as well as a boy or two. Notable was Ann (Carr) Putnam, the sergeant's wife, a well-educated woman of 30, whose fits were even more intense than those of the girls. She was deeply engaged in the village quarrels, and she acted as an adult role model supporting her daughter, Ann Putnam, Jr. and the other afflicted girls in their accusations.

The original afflicted girls—Elizabeth Parris, Abigail Williams, Ann Putnam, Jr., Mercy Lewis, Mary Walcott, and Elizabeth Hubbard made up the inner circle of the afflicted of Salem Village. Their fathers and guardians—the Rev. Samuel Parris, Sergeant Thomas Putnam, Captain Jonathan Walcott, and Dr. William Griggs—formed a conspiracy. The brother, two uncles, and two male cousins of Sergeant Thomas Putnam joined the conspiracy. The final member was Captain Walcott's uncle, Lieutenant Nathaniel Ingersoll. Members of this conspiracy filed the written legal complaints against all but two of the seventy-four people arrested in the first phase, known as the Salem Village witch hunt, of the 1692 tragedy.

Four young women, Elizabeth Booth and Susannah Sheldon, each 18, and Mary Warren and Sarah Churchill, each 20, made up the outer circle of the Salem Village afflicted. Like the inner circle, the outer circle was under the control of the conspiracy. The afflicted girls in both the inner and outer circles received deferential treatment from the magistrates.

In their fits the afflicted girls continued to cry out upon witches whose specters were tormenting them. In addition to Tituba, the afflicted cried out upon two other woman, Sarah Good, aged 38, and Sarah Osborne, aged 50. Sarah Good was poor and homeless, and Sarah Osborne was bed-ridden. Both had already been slandered by vicious gossip so that the accusations would be more readily accepted. Each of the three accused persons was depicted by their accusers as fitting the prevailing stereotype of a witch.

On March 1, 1692, the Salem magistrates John Hathorne and Jonathan Corwin issued warrants for the arrest of the three women, Tituba, Sarah Osborne, and Sarah Good, accusing them of witchcraft. The two magistrates, in their impressive magisterial clothing and the insignia of official station, rode on horseback for the five-mile journey from Salem Town to Salem Village. The attending constables and marshals, bearing long staffs, wore the bright red coats that were the official dress of men charged with the enforcement of law. The entrance of this colorful and august troop provided the tiny village with a moment of high drama. The examinations were to be held in Ingersoll's tavern, but the crowd was so great that they were moved to the meetinghouse instead.

The chief accusations against Sarah Good were that she had spoken angrily to some neighbors and soon after some of their cattle sickened and died; that she threw the children into fits; and that she tried to persuade Ann Putnam, Jr. to sign the Devil's book. It was believed that the Devil's servants, the witches, went about with the infernal book soliciting signatures; each signature was equivalent to a deed surrendering the signer's soul to the Devil. Similar accusations were made against the other two women. During each examination the afflicted girls ranted and raved. At the indignant denials by Sarah Good and Sarah Osborne, their din grew all the louder. When Tituba was questioned, she claimed that she had been taught about witchcraft in her own country in the Caribbean. Soon she confessed. She said that the Devil urged her to sign his book, and told her to work mischief on the children. When she admitted that it was she who enchanted the girls, their symptoms vanished and perfect calm ensued.

Much later Tituba gave the account that the Rev. Parris beat her and abused her in other ways to force her to confess and accuse her sister witches. She stated that her confession and her accusations of others were a result of his treatment. When Tituba was searched, they found the marks of the Devil upon her body. Quite likely the marks were the result of Parris' beatings.

After their examinations, the three women were committed to prison and put in chains. Sarah Osborne survived in jail only a little while, dying there on May 10, 1692. Sarah Good was destined to die on the gallows that summer. Tituba was allowed to become an accuser instead of a prosecuted witch. She stayed in prison for more than a year and finally was sold in slavery to a new owner for payment of her prison fees.

The next women accused were Martha Corey and Rebecca Nurse, both church members. Because they were highly respected women of good character, the community was thunderstruck.

On March 21, 1692, Martha Corey was examined before the magistrates at the meeting house in Salem Village. A throng of spectators watched in fascination. The Rev. Nicholas Noyes, the assistant minister at Salem, opened with prayer. Next the prisoner was called in to answer the allegations against her. Martha said that she too desired to pray. Magistrate John Hathorne retorted that he did not come to hear her pray, but to examine her.

The afflicted children threw their customary fits throughout the examination. They accused Martha Corey of afflicting them by biting, pinching, and strangling. And they said that in their fits they saw her specter coming to them and bringing a book for them to sign. Hathorne asked her, "Why do you afflict those children?" She responded, "I do not afflict them." He asked, "Who does then?" She answered sensibly, "I do not know, how should I know? They are poor distracted creatures, and no heed to be given to what they say." Hathorne replied, "It is the judgment of all that are present, that they are bewitched, and only you say they are distracted."[109] Wrote Hathorne's great, great grandson, "Here we have the man, sly, subtle, hard, imperious, and, withal, as cold as ice. Look at that eye! Would you like to be at its mercy?"[110]

With their spectral sight the afflicted girls saw the Black Man whispering into Martha's ear while the examination was taking place. They said that her familiar, a yellow bird, was sucking between her fingers. When Martha made any motion of her body, hands or mouth, the afflicted would cry out. When

---

109 Essex Institute, *Witchcraft Collection*, "Examinations."
110 Hawthorne, *The House of the Seven Gables*, Chapter 6.

Martha bit her lip, they screamed that they were being bitten. If she grasped one hand with the other, they complained of being pinched by her, and showed the marks. For other motions of her body, they complained of being pressed. When she stirred her feet, they stamped and cried out in pain. Martha Corey still refused to confess. Hathorne committed her to prison.

What had begun as a game of fascination and fantasy for the afflicted girls quickly became the darkest of nightmares—for the girls as well as the women and men they accused. The girls' faith in their elders, the men of the conspiracy, was implicit and fixed. The girls were obedient in following their directions to the end of the witch hunt. (Had their submission wavered, fear of the consequences would have dissuaded them from rebellion.) These men transformed their children's game into a macabre theatrical routine with the names of the accused scripted in. With each repetition of their act, another person fell victim to the delusion.

Topsfield, previously called Ipswich New Meadows, was the town just north of Salem Village.[111] On March 24, 1692, Rebecca Nurse, aged 70, of Salem Village was brought before magistrates Hathorne and Corwin in the Salem Village meetinghouse. Rebecca Nurse was one of three sisters, daughters of William Towne. Her sisters, Sarah Cloyce of Salem Village and Mary Easty of Topsfield, were arrested soon after her. The three sisters and their husbands were all highly respected. However, they were sympathetic to Topsfield in a fierce land dispute between that town and Salem Village. This feud had engendered bitter feelings between them and the Putnam family of Salem Village. Out of revenge the Putnams accused the three sisters of witchcraft. Adding to their troubles, Rebecca Nurse and her husband had opposed the Rev. Samuel Parris in church disputes.

The Rev. John Hale, minister of Beverly, began the examination with prayer, after which Rebecca Nurse was accused of much the same crimes as Martha Corey. Rebecca made similar responses, asserting her own innocence. The afflicted were the familiar circle of Salem Village girls with the

---

111 Ipswich New Meadows, the western section of the original township of
     Ipswich, was incorporated in 1650 as a separate town named Topsfield.

addition of Sergeant Thomas Putnam's wife, Ann (Carr) Putnam. Shrieking loudly enough for the whole neighborhood to hear, Mrs. Putnam charged that the specter of Rebecca Nurse was tormenting her in the courtroom. Rebecca Nurse, in fragile health, was committed to prison.

Now comes one of the lowest points in Salem witchcraft affair. Dorcas Good, Sarah Good's four-year-old child, was apprehended on March 23, 1692. The afflicted girls said the specter of this small girl bit them, and they showed marks upon their arms like those from a small set of teeth. A mere glance from Dorcas would send the afflicted girls into intense spasms as they rolled and writhed on the floor in apparent pain. Dorcas Good was committed to prison, but this was not enough. The afflicted girls demanded that Dorcas be put in irons, saying that only constraint could keep her specter from tormenting them. Because the tiny wrists and ankles of this small girl slipped out of the ordinary manacles and fetters, special small ones had to be made for her.

The Rev. Deodat Lawson, a former minister at Salem Village, wrote, "On the 26th of March, Mr. Hathorne, Mr. Corwin, and Mr. Higginson were at the prison-keeper's house, to examine the child. It told them there, it had a little snake that used to suck on the lowest joint of its forefinger; and when they inquired where, pointing to other places, it told them, not there, but there, pointing on the lowest point of forefinger; where they observed a deep red spot, about the bigness of a flea-bite. They asked who gave it that snake, whether it was the great Black Man. It said no, its mother gave it."[112] The Rev. Cotton Mather gloated, "Among the ghastly instances of the success which these bloody witches have had, we have seen some instances of their own children, so dedicated unto the Devil, that in their infancy, it is found, the imps have sucked them, and rendered them venomous to a prodigy."[113]

Dorcas' mother, Sarah Good, was executed on July 19, 1692. Dorcas's father, William Good, reported in 1710 that in 1692

---

112 Lawson, *A Brief and True Narrative*, in Burr, *Narratives*, 160.
113 Cotton Mather, *Wonders*, 83.

Dorcas had been chained in the dungeon for eight months and, abused beyond all endurance, she had never recovered her full senses.

On Sunday, April 3, 1692, Sarah Cloyce, sister of Rebecca Nurse, was prevailed upon to be present at the church service. Sarah knew that the Rev. Parris had stood by while Rebecca Nurse, a devoted church member, had been committed to jail for witchcraft. Sarah Cloyce may have suspected that he was, in fact, conspiring with the Putnam family in making witchcraft accusations. Upon entering the building, she heard the Rev. Parris name as his text, John vi. 70-71: "Jesus answered them, Have not I chosen you Twelve, and one of you is a Devil. He spake of Judas Iscariot, the son of Simon; for he it was that should betray him, being one of the twelve." As Parris began his sermon, "Christ knows how many Devils there are in His church, and who they are," Sarah decided she had heard enough.[114] She rose and went out; the wind slammed the door shut behind her. The next morning, April 4, 1692, Sarah Cloyce was complained of and arrested.

Arrested on the same day as Sarah Cloyce was Elizabeth Proctor, a midwife. A week earlier, on March 28, 1692, at Ingersoll's tavern, Elizabeth Hubbard, an afflicted girl and the maid of Dr. William Griggs, had cried out, "There is Goody Proctor. There is Goody Proctor. I'll see her hang!" When Goodwife Ingersoll sharply reproved the afflicted girls, "they seemed to make a joke of it."[115] Dr. Griggs was instrumental in having Elizabeth Proctor arrested for witchcraft; she had been dispensing medicine which proved more effective than his own. Testimony against Elizabeth Proctor claimed that she was responsible for a man's death because Dr. Griggs had not been sent for to give him medicine.

On April 11, 1692, Sarah Cloyce and Elizabeth Proctor, were examined in the large meetinghouse in Salem Town. On this occasion, the Massachusetts government took formal charge of the witch hunt. Simon Bradstreet, who in 1663 had seen to the

114 Lawson, *A Brief and True Narrative*, in Burr, *Narratives*, 161.
115 Woodward, *Records of Salem Witchcraft*, 1:109-110.

whipping of Eliakim Wardwell, was now governor. Bradstreet had won thirteen annual elections. The electorate did not include all citizens as in a democracy, but was restricted to the freemen, the male church members, who made up less than five percent of the population. In 1692 at age 89, Simon Bradstreet was the grand old man of his time. Aged and ill, he did not attend the examination. Some of the most influential magistrates of the Puritan old guard carried out the examination: Thomas Danforth (the lieutenant governor), Isaac Addington of Boston (the secretary of the province), Major Samuel Appleton of Ipswich, James Russell of Charlestown, Capt. Samuel Sewall of Boston, Jonathan Corwin, and, of course, John Hathorne.[116]   The examinations were officially described as taking place at a Council held at Salem. In addition to the magistrates, several ministers were present.

The afflicted girls exhibited their contortions and writhings, and screeched their lungs out for the benefit of the high dignitaries present. The two women were committed to prison. Elizabeth Proctor's husband, John Proctor, came to support her. The afflicted cried out against him too, and with such energy that he was also committed.

This examination firmly established the complicity of the ruling old guard in the actions of the witch hunt. The presence of these officials, their lines of questioning, and their verdicts make abundantly clear that the highest levels of government as well as the church sanctioned the witch hunt. In concurring with the methods used up to that time, the old guard gave its seal of approval to the further pursuit of the witch hunt.

Increase Mather, Cotton Mather's father, the minister of North Church, had been in England for the past four years. A new royal charter for New England had been signed by the King in October 1691. On Increase Mather's suggestions, the King appointed Sir William Phipps as the new royal governor, and William Stoughton as the new royal lieutenant governor, of the

---

116 Appleton, Russell, Corwin, and Hathorne were related by marriage. Corwin and Hathorne had conducted all the previous examinations at Salem Village.

Province of Massachusetts.[117] Increase Mather was also allowed to name the new Council members.[118] Phipps was in England at the time. On May 14, 1692, the frigate *Nonesuch* from England arrived in Boston. On it was Sir William Phipps, ready to take up his duties. Phipps carried with him the new charter with which to govern New England. Increase Mather sailed home from his four year sojourn in England on the same ship. At this point, the Mathers, father and son, in their drive to influence government to their way of thinking, had reached the pinnacle of power. Cotton Mather wrote, "All the councilors of the Province are of my father's nomination. The governor of the province is not my enemy, but one whom I baptized, namely Sir William Phipps, and one of my own flock, and one of my dearest friends."[119]

The aged governor, Simon Bradstreet, was immediately replaced by Sir William Phipps. The newly appointed lieutenant governor, William Stoughton superseded Thomas Danforth. New England was in dire straits as the colonists waged both an external war with the French and Indians and an internal war with the Devil's agents, the witches. Phipps, a former military commander, naturally gravitated toward dealing with the real-world war, whereas Stoughton, with his clerical training, preferred to face the invisible-world war. William Stoughton's views on the elimination of witchcraft were in full sympathy with those of Cotton Mather; if anything, they were even harsher.

---

117 William Phipps, born in Maine in 1651 of simple origins, became a ship captain. In the West Indies he retrieved sunken Spanish treasure for the English crown, and was rewarded with a knighthood in 1687. Sir William Phipps came under the tutelage of Cotton Mather and became his convert. Cotton Mather baptized him in 1690 and received him into membership of the North Church. William Stoughton was born in 1631, became a minister, and on occasion had preached in company with Increase Mather. He gave up the ministry, and became a magistrate, an assistant to the governor, in 1671. He lived in Dorchester, the first town south of Boston.

118 The Council appointed under the new charter occupied the same position as the old Board of Assistants, each being the upper chamber of the General Court, which was both a legislative and a judicial body.

119 Cotton Mather, "Diary," May 1692.

Sir William Phipps was told that the prisons in Essex and Suffolk counties were crowded with accused witches and wizards. The witchcraft affair had become so formidable and public infatuation so intense, that Phipps had difficulty in determining what ought to be done. In his dilemma he yielded to the direction of the religious fathers, especially the Mathers. His new government did not interfere with the witch hunt in progress. The number of accusations increased every day, and examinations and imprisonments went on unabated.

Whenever an accused woman was imprisoned, the afflicted girls would stop crying out against her and be restored to health. But often, sometime later, the afflicted girls would renew their cries against her, claiming that she would send her specter from the prison to torment them. Continual complaints were made to Sir William Phipps that the afflicted girls were being hurt in this way by the imprisoned witches. The afflicted suggested that irons on the prisoners' legs and arms would hold back their specters. Sir William gave the order to put irons on all the imprisoned.   The girls' torments immediately vanished. Unknown to the girls, prison-keepers soon removed the irons from some of the prisoners. Yet the girls did not renew the cry against those that were unshackled. For this and other reasons Lady Mary Phipps, the wife of Sir William, was skeptical about the validity of the accusations. Nevertheless Cotton Mather and William Stoughton represented the matter to Sir William Phipps as genuine.

With so many accused people in prison, plans had to be made for their trials. Instead of going through normal legal channels, Phipps yielded to the views of the leading men in the Council and, in particular, his lieutenant governor, William Stoughton. On May 25, 1692, on their recommendation, Phipps instituted a special court to try the accused witches. This court, the Court of Oyer and Terminer, was illegal from the outset because the approval of the lower legislative body, the House of Representatives, was not obtained for its creation. William Stoughton was named the chief justice. The other justices chosen were Nathaniel Saltonstall, John Richards, Wait Still Winthrop, Samuel Sewall, Peter Sergeant, John Hathorne,

Jonathan Corwin, and Bartholomew Gedney.[120] The Court could sit with any five members present. All the members of the Court were full-fledged magistrates, that is, assistants to the governor or, as they were called under the new charter, council members. Phipps had been persuaded to rely upon the Court as the right method of proceeding in the witchcraft cases.[121] The Court started the first trial on June 2, just 19 days after the Phipps' arrival in Boston.

The town of Salem had three full-fledged magistrates: John Hathorne, Jonathan Corwin, and Bartholomew Gedney. They were related by marriage.[122] It is worth noting that all three were on the Court of Oyer and Terminer. The examination of Sarah Cloyce and Elizabeth Proctor on April 11, 1692, had been a special event; it was in the nature of a Council meeting with many high dignitaries of the colony present and it was presided over by the then lieutenant governor, Thomas Danforth. (Both John Hathorne and Jonathan Corwin were present at the April 11 meeting as magistrates.) Except for the April 11 meeting, the three Salem magistrates, alone or together and sometimes with the help of other magistrates and justices of the peace, presided over the preliminary examinations for the entire witch hunt, both the Salem Village and the Andover phases. At first, the preliminary examinations had been carried out by Hathorne and Corwin; later Gedney joined in. Magistrate John Hathorne did most of the questioning of the accused. Except for one man, Nehemiah Abbot, Jr., every single accused witch was imprisoned on the basis of the preliminary examination. George Corwin, 26,

---

120 Stoughton was from Dorchester; Saltonstall, from Haverhill; Richards, Winthrop, Sewall, and Sergeant were from Boston; and Gedney, Hathorne, and Corwin, from Salem.

121 "The authority by which the court sat may as well be called in question. No authority is given by the Province charter to any powers short of the whole General Court [that is, the Council *and* the House of Representatives] to constitute courts of justice." Manuscript of Thomas Hutchinson (1711-1780), governor of Massachusetts from 1771 to 1774, published in the *New England Historic and Genealogical Register*, 1870.

122 Jonathan Corwin's sister, Abigail, was the widow of John Hathorne's brother, Eleazer. Jonathan Corwin's nephew, George Corwin, was married to Bartholomew Gedney's daughter, Lydia.

was appointed high sheriff of Essex County at the same time that the Court of Oyer and Terminer was established.[123] Sheriff Corwin was in charge of confiscating the property of the convicted witches. He also carried out the executions.

Sir William Phipps was growing aware that the old guard was engaged in a struggle to save the Puritan theocracy and its attendant privileges. He suspected that the accused had been targeted as a means to coerce the colony into continued submission to strict Puritan rule. As apparent from the examinations, most of the accused were intelligent people who thought for themselves. Reason enough for the Puritan authorities to despise them! Yet on an unconscious level the old guard may have envied them. Independent thinking was a luxury that the Puritan rulers could hardly afford. Did something resembling the following events take place?

While Phipps was sitting as governor, his wife came to him, saying, "Have nothing to do with the false accusations against these just people who are accused." But the chief ministers and magistrates, in stirring up the witchcraft fears, had already persuaded the public that they should ask for the lives of these innocent victims. Several times the governor asked, "Why? What evil have they done?" But the ministers and magistrates cried out the more, "Let them be hanged." Phipps saw that he could not prevail, but rather a tumult was rising. He washed his hands of the affair, and directed all his efforts to raising an army to fight the French and Indians. In August he left Boston to command his army in Maine.[124]

---

123 Sheriff George Corwin was Jonathan Corwin's nephew and Bartholomew Gedney's son-in-law.

124 The quotations used in this paragraph are paraphrased from St. Matthew, 27:19-23.

9

PRELUDE TO ANDOVER

I NITIALLY THE SALEM VILLAGE CONSPIRACY accused people living in the environs of Salem Village, but soon it was accusing residents of many other towns. It is useful to trace how the contagion infected the town of Andover.

Roger Toothaker, his wife Mary (Allen) Toothaker, and their children lived in Billerica, a town southwest of Andover. Mary was the daughter of first settler Andrew Allen of Andover. Roger was a physician; his wife, a midwife. Like many of the medical people of his day he believed that some untreatable ailments were due to witchcraft. In fact, Dr. Toothaker spread the story that his daughter had killed a witch. The daughter was 23-year-old Martha (Toothaker) Emerson. Dr. Toothaker said that his daughter had learned the method from him. Martha had wanted to help a person who complained about being afflicted by a witch named Button. Following her father's instructions, Martha put an earthen pot containing the witch's urine into a hot oven. A suitable incantation was made. Remember Shakespeare's *Macbeth*, "Boil thou first in the charmed pot. Double, double, toil and trouble. Fire burn and cauldron bubble. Then the charm is firm and good." According to testimony given later, the witch was found dead the next morning.

But Dr. Toothaker's bragging about his witchcraft prowess led him into a trap. On May 18, 1692, the Salem Village conspiracy of accusers filed a complaint against Dr. Toothaker for afflicting three of the Salem Village circle, Elizabeth Hubbard, Ann Putnam, Jr., and Mary Walcott. He was arrested and imprisoned in Boston. Elizabeth Hubbard was the servant of his Salem Village counterpart and rival, Dr. William Griggs. Dr.

Griggs was a member of the Salem Village conspiracy; through his afflicted seventeen-year old servant he accused many people of witchcraft.

When a doctor failed to cure someone, it was convenient to lay blame on a witch. Doctors feared competition. The medical profession of the day actively persecuted midwives and healers who offered alternative treatments of herbs and natural medicines. Many of these remedies were painless and far more effective than the bleeding, leeching, and purging that were standard medical practices.

On May 28, 1692, ten days after the accusation of Dr. Toothaker, the Salem Village conspiracy filed a complaint against his wife, Mary (Allen) Toothaker, and their nine year old daughter, Margaret. Also arrested on the same complaint was Mary's sister, Martha (Allen) Carrier of Andover and Elizabeth (Jackson) Howe of Ipswich Farms. The arrests took place on May 31. Martha Carrier was the first resident of Andover to be arrested. The two Allen sisters, namely Mary (Allen) Toothaker and Martha (Allen) Carrier, were related by marriage to Elizabeth (Jackson) Howe through an intermediary, the Rev. Francis Dane of Andover. Thus two sisters, Mary Toothaker and Martha Carrier, and their cousin-in-law, Elizabeth Howe, were arrested together. Their arrests form the prelude to the Andover witch hunt.

After his arrest on May 18, 1692, Dr. Toothaker's life was short. He died in Boston prison less than one month later, on June 16. His death was not a natural one; most likely, it was murder by a non-violent torture. The authorities took great care to cover themselves. They summoned twenty-four able and sufficient men to view the body and attest that he came to his end by natural causes. One of the men was the Rev. Thomas Barnard, assistant minister of Andover.

Mary Toothaker, now a widow, was examined before John Hathorne on July 30, 1692. She said that in May "she was under great discontentedness & troubled with fear about the Indians, and used often to dream of fighting with them." Her fear was so intense that she imagined that "the Devil appeared to her in the shape of a tawny man and promised to keep her from the Indians and she should have happy days with her son." When magistrate John Hathorne asked if she was to serve the Devil, she answered, "Yes, for he said he was able to deliver her from the Indians, and it was the fear of the Indians that put her upon it."[125] Having made this confession, she was returned to jail.

The widow Toothaker's dread of the Indians was well founded, indeed prophetic. On August 1, two days following her examination, the Indians raided Billerica and killed a number of people. They burned the empty Toothaker farm to the ground. Mary and her younger daughter, Margaret Toothaker, were left to languish in prison before being released at the end of January 1693. In the middle of winter, they returned to their burned-out home.

Dr. Toothaker was dead; his widow, the midwife, carried on. "By that indissoluble bond she had gained a home in every sick chamber, and nowhere else; there were her brethren and sisters; thither her husband summoned her, with that voice which had seemed to issue from the grave of Toothaker. At length she recognized her destiny. There is hardly a more difficult exercise of fancy, than, while gazing at a figure of melancholy age, to re-create its youth, and, without entirely obliterating the identity of form and features, to restore those graces which time has snatched away.   Such profit might be derived, by a skillful observer, from my much-respected friend, the Widow Toothaker, a nurse of great repute."[126]

Her career was short lived. On August 5, 1695, Mary (Allen) Toothaker was killed by the Indians she so feared, and her younger daughter, Margaret Toothaker, by now 12 years old, was taken captive, never to be seen again. The descendants of Roger and Mary Toothaker were to die out. The last of the family, two Toothaker brothers, fought for the American cause at the battle of Bunker Hill in 1775. One brother was mortally wounded; the other in trying to save his brother's life was also killed. In compensation, the government gave the family of each American soldier who died at Bunker Hill a coat and a blanket. No one stepped forward to claim theirs.

---

125 Suffolk County, *Court Records*, case 2713, page 50.
126 Hawthorne, *Edward Fane's Rosebud.*

The real name of Martha Carrier's husband, Thomas Carrier, Sr., was Thomas Morgan. Born in Wales, he served in the bodyguard of King Charles I. In 1649, during the English civil war, the victorious Puritans captured King Charles I and sentenced him to death. The regular executioner, fearing what might happen to one who killed an anointed king, refused to behead him. Thomas Morgan had no such fears; he volunteered and became the substitute executioner. It was he who wielded the axe that sent the whole kingdom of England into initial misgivings and subsequent terror. The king went to his death with courage, "as full of valor as of royal blood. Both have I spilt; O! would the deed were good; for now the Devil, that told me I did well, says that this deed is chronicled in hell."[127]

In 1660, after the dark years of Puritan rule, the people of England restored the monarchy and crowned King Charles II their new sovereign. Thomas Morgan wisely took a hasty leave of England; he did not wish to suffer the vengeance of the new king. As a refugee, he fled to America and changed his name to Thomas Carrier.[128] He married Martha Allen and raised a family in Billerica. In 1685, the family moved to Andover.

In late 1689 tragedy struck. Smallpox ravaged the Carrier family, and it was rumored that they spread the epidemic to other Andover residents. Martha Carrier's brother, Andrew Allen, died of smallpox on September 26, 1690, and his son, Thomas Allen, died on December 18. Martha Carrier's brother, John Allen, died of smallpox on November 26, 1690, and his wife, Mercy (Peters) Allen, died of smallpox one month later on Christmas day, 1690. Martha (Allen) Carrier's sister, Hannah, was married to James Holt. He died of smallpox on December 13, 1690.

Instead of showing compassion for the troubles of Martha (Allen) Carrier, many of the townspeople resented and feared her presence. "What a history might she record of the great sicknesses, in which she had gone hand in hand with the

---

127 Shakespeare, *King Richard II*, Act 5, Sc. 4.
128 Other Puritan soldiers who fled to New England in 1660 were Robert Russell of Andover, John Marshall of Billerica, and Thomas Farnum and Captain Thomas Marshall of Lynn.

exterminating angel! She remembers when the smallpox hoisted a red-banner on almost every house along the street. Where would be Death's triumph, if none lived to weep!"[129]   The selectmen of the town of Andover took note that Martha Carrier and some of her children were "smitten with that contagious disease, the smallpox," and that they are to "take care that they do not spread the distemper with wicked carelessness, which we are afraid they have already done."[130]   This extract from the town records was dated October 14, 1690.

After the arrest of Martha (Allen) Carrier on May 31, 1692, the authorities rounded up about a dozen people willing to testify against her.   Suspicion that she had spread the smallpox epidemic in Andover had antagonized them; she was blamed for all sorts of troubles.   John Rogers, aged 50, of Billerica testified that, about seven years ago, "Martha Carrier, being a neighbor, there happening some difference betwixt us, she gave forth several threatening words.   In a short time after, this deponent had two large lusty sows that were lost & the same summer, to the best of my remembrance, I had a cow which used to give a good mess of milk twice a day & of a sudden she would give none. I did in my conscience believe that Martha Carrier was the occasion of those ill accidents by means of witchcraft."[131]   Most damaging to Martha was the resentment caused by the intelligence and wit she used to protect her family and lands. "Martha Carrier was a woman of a disposition not unlikely to make enemies: plain and outspoken in speech, of remarkable strength of mind, a keen sense of justice, and a sharp tongue."[132] Some of her choice words are preserved to this day.

Land had been granted to Benjamin Abbot, aged 30, in the south part of Andover close to the Carrier farm.[133]   Abbot saw no harm in indulging in a little encroachment on Martha's land,

129   Hawthorne, *Edward Fane's Rosebud.*

130   Bailey, *Historical Sketches of Andover,* 202.

131   Woodward, *Records of Salem Witchcraft,* 2:61-62.   John Rogers was "slain by the Indian enemy in Billerica, August 5, 1695."   In the same raid Martha Carrier's sister, the widow Mary Toothaker, was killed.

132   Bailey, *Historical Sketches of Andover,* 203.

133   Benjamin Abbot was the son of Hannah (Chandler) and George Abbot, Sr., an original proprietor of Andover.

thinking that if he put up his stone walls soon enough there would be nothing the Carriers could do about it. Martha, however, was not so easily fooled and set about putting an end to his mischief. In an angry confrontation she warned, "I will stick as close to you, Benjamin Abbot, as the bark sticks to a tree. You will repent of this before seven years comes to an end." She added, "I will hold your nose as close to the grindstone as ever it was held since your name was Benjamin Abbot."[134] Benjamin Abbot was glad to present this as evidence against her in his deposition of August 3, 1692.

Remember that Elizabeth (Jackson) Howe was arrested on the same day, May 31, 1692 as Martha (Allen) Carrier and Mary (Allen) Toothaker. Elizabeth (Jackson) Howe was married to James Howe, Jr. They lived in Ipswich Farms close to the Topsfield border. Her husband was blind and in need of her constant care. After her arrest, the witchcraft evidence brought against her was comprised of the usual slander. Mary Cummings, about 60, testified that "we had used no brimstone nor oil nor no combustibles to give to our mare, because there was a report that Howe's wife had said we had given the mare brimstone and oil and the like." Samuel Perley, about 52, testified that he had a falling out with James Howe, Jr. and his wife. Perley claimed that afterwards his ten year-old daughter told him that "it was James Howe, Jr.'s wife that afflicted her both night and day, sometimes complaining of being pricked with pins and sometimes falling down into dreadful fits."[135]

Many people, however, stepped forward to testify in favor of Elizabeth (Jackson) Howe. Among them were the two ministers of the town of Rowley, Samuel Phillips and Edward Payson. They had visited Samuel Perley's house in Ipswich "to see his young daughter who was visited with strange fits. When we were in the house the child had one of her fits, but made no mention of Goodwife Howe. When the fit was over, Goodwife Howe went to the child and took her by the hand & asked her whether she had ever done her any hurt. And she answered no,

---

134 Woodward, *Records of Salem Witchcraft*, 2:59-60.
135 M. V. B. Perley, *Salem Village Witchcraft Trials*, 37-48.

never."[136]   Later the two ministers overheard the little girl's brother tell her to say Goodwife Howe was a witch.   The ministers rebuked the brother for stirring up his sister to accuse Goodwife Howe.   They testified that it was not surprising that the child mentioned Goodwife Howe in her fits, when the child's nearest relations constantly were expressing their allegations in the child's hearing.   The Rev. Payson added that the afflicted daughter fell into one of her strange fits after her mother spoke angrily to her, and during her fit she did not mention Elizabeth Howe.   Although the testimony of the two ministers discredited Perley's claims, the court disregarded it together with all the other favorable testimony.

Both Martha Carrier and Elizabeth Howe were hanged. Martha Carrier's house still stands in Andover.   By her witchcraft, according to Cotton Mather, "the poor people were so tortured that every one expected their death upon the very spot." Elizabeth Howe's house in Ipswich Farms met a different fate. According to Cotton Mather her house was "visited with apparitions of ghosts, and the ghosts affirmed that this Howe had murdered them."[137]   After Elizabeth's death at the gallows, her two unmarried daughters, Mary Howe and Abigail Howe, continued to live in the house and take care of their blind father. First the father died and then Abigail; Mary stayed on, living secluded and alone in the front chamber.   This lonely room "resembled nothing so much as the old maid's heart, for there was neither sunshine nor household fire, and save for ghosts and ghostly reminiscences, not a guest, for many years gone by, had entered the heart or the chamber."   With Mary's death, the old house fell into ruin and decay.   It was "untenanted so long—except for spiders, and mice, and rats, and ghosts—that it was all overgrown with the desolation which watches to obliterate every trace of man's happier hours."[138]   Eventually the foundation of the ancient structure, known as Mary's cellar, was all that remained.   By the nineteenth century, the stones had fallen in and the depression was called Mary's hole.   Today even

---

136 Ibid.
137 Cotton Mather, *Wonders*, 154, 149-150.
138 Hawthorne, *The House of the Seven Gables*, Chapter 5.

that has gone. Not the slightest sign remains of the house of
Elizabeth Howe, who, according to Cotton Mather, was baptized
by the Devil in the river at Newbury Falls.

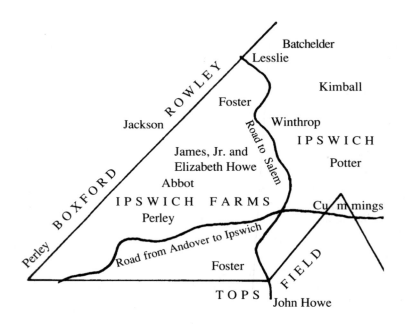

Map of the section of Ipswich known as Ipswich Farms
showing landowners in 1692.

10

FIRST AND SECOND TRIALS, JUNE 2 AND 30, 1692

B Y THE END OF MAY 1692 the authorities had imprisoned about seventy-five people, all of whom awaited trial. Only four in this group confessed; Tituba, on March 2, 1692; Abigail Hobbs, on April 19; Deliverance Hobbs, on April 22; and Margaret Jacobs, on May 11. Mary Warren, an afflicted girl from Salem Village arrested and temporarily imprisoned, also made a confession of sorts. At her examination on April 19, Mary "fell into a violent fit, & cried out, 'Oh Lord, help me! Oh, good Lord, save me!' And then afterwards cried again, 'I will tell! I will tell,' & then fell into a dreadful fit again." She was "called in afterwards in private, before magistrates and ministers. She said, 'I shall not speak a word; but I will, I will speak, Satan. Avoid, Satan, for the name of God, avoid!' and then fell into fits again." While she writhed on the floor, trying to fend off Satan, magistrate John Hathorne, ever curious, could not resist asking, "Tell us, how far have you yielded?"[139] Between June 1, 1692, and October 15, 1692, about one hundred more people were imprisoned. Of these about fifty confessed. Hathorne devoted most of his time in the summer and early autumn of 1692 to holding preliminary examinations, as he had done since March 1.

The first meeting of the Court of Oyer and Terminer opened in Salem on June 2, 1692. Seven justices were sitting for this session: chief justice, Stoughton, and associate justices Nathaniel Saltonstall, John Richards, Bartholomew Gedney, Wait Still Winthrop, Samuel Sewall, and Peter Sergeant. Four were

---

139 Woodward, *Records of Salem Witchcraft*, 1:119.

intimate associates of Cotton Mather, namely Stoughton, Richards, Winthrop, and Sewall.

Only one of the imprisoned, Bridget Bishop, was brought to trial at this session. Bishop had been arrested on April 19, 1692. This first trial was a test case, and a large number of accusers and accusations were brought against her. She was charged with such things as losses her neighbors suffered in their cattle and poultry or with overturning their carts. Testimony against her included spectral evidence given by John Louder of Salem, aged 32. He stated that on waking in the dead of night he did clearly see Bridget Bishop, or her likeness, sitting on his stomach. Two workman testified that they found puppets in her cellar. The puppets were made of hog bristles and rags, and stuck with headless pins. Upon search a witchmark, or "tet," was found upon her body. Cotton Mather wrote, "There was little occasion to prove the witchcraft, it being evident and notorious to all beholders."[140] The jury found her guilty, and she was sentenced to die. To the end she did not make the slightest confession of anything relating to witchcraft. The court adjourned to June 30.

In Salem prison whispered voices passed the word; Bridget was going to hang. A terrible shudder went through the inmates; the prison walls seemed to reel around them. The few chained in view of the narrow slot-like windows could glimpse a little patch of sky; the rest were shrouded in gloom. The night before the execution, an ominous silence fell. With the hangman close at hand, the prisoners "passed a miserable night, so full of ugly sights, of ghastly dreams."[141] In the morning, June 10, 1692, the sheriff entered the prison and took Bridget away. Her legs made lame by the fetters, she stumbled painfully through the prison door into the open air.

Sheriff George Corwin pushed her into a horse-drawn cart and forced her to stand so the hundreds of spectators could see her better. A company of Salem militia marched to the fife and drum. John Hathorne, on horseback, was a prominent figure in the procession which followed her to the place of execution. As the cart passed the Salem meetinghouse, Bridget looked in that

---

140 Cotton Mather, *Wonders*, 129.
141 Shakespeare, *King Richard III*, Act. 1, Sc. 4.

direction. The Rev. Cotton Mather later wrote that a board on the inside of the building broke from the heavy nails which held it and flew to the opposite wall with a crash that could be heard throughout Salem.[142] He intended his words to record for all time the power of her witchcraft.

Outside town the cart turned from the main street into a narrow track that led up to a rocky mound. This was Gallows Hill. With three fathoms of hemp rope, Bridget Bishop was hanged. Her body was cut down and thrown into a shallow, unmarked grave which had been dug among the rocks close by. Out of her grave, tradition has it, grew a wild red rose.

The insane proceedings of the Court proved too much for justice Nathaniel Saltonstall of Haverhill. Unable to prevail against the furious tide, Saltonstall resigned from the Court after its first meeting. Returning to his home in Haverhill, Saltonstall spoke out so strongly against the witch hunt that in time the afflicted girls started to cry out against him. They had seen his specter at several witch meetings, they said. The courageous Saltonstall, undeterred, continued to oppose the proceedings, and his arguments and tenacity eventually convinced others to take similar stands.

The use of spectral evidence to obtain the conviction of Bridget Bishop alarmed some ministers who questioned its validity. All the evidence provided by the afflicted girls was spectral. If this type of evidence were not admitted, it would be much more difficult to convict any of the imprisoned except those few who had confessed witchcraft. The Rev. Cotton Mather realized that his witchcraft war might be curtailed or even brought to a screeching halt. Cotton Mather intensified his efforts to have the magistrates use any means, fair or foul, to obtain additional confessions, both from those already imprisoned and from the newly arrested. Soon he would find help from his friend, the Rev. Thomas Barnard.

---

142 Cotton Mather, *Wonders*, 138.

As an immediate remedy Cotton Mather jumped in and drew up a document entitled *The Return of Several Ministers*.[143] By design the document was equivocal, worded in a double sense. It affirmed the reality of the witchcraft epidemic, "the afflicted state of our poor neighbors, that are now suffering the molestations of the invisible world." It acknowledged "the success of our honorable rulers to detect the abominable witchcrafts which have been committed, humbly praying that the discovery of these mysterious and mischievous wickednesses may be perfected." To please those questioning the validity of spectral evidence, the document stated that, "Convictions ought certainly be more considerable than barely the accused person being represented by a specter unto the afflicted, inasmuch as 'tis an undoubted and a notorious thing, that a demon may, by God's permission, appear even to ill purposes, in the shape of an innocent, yea, and a virtuous man." The document concluded by recommending "unto the government, the speedy and vigorous prosecution of such as have rendered themselves obnoxious, according to the direction given in the laws of God, and the wholesome statutes of the English nation, for the detection of witchcrafts."[144]

The afflicted girls claimed to have the gift of spectral sight whereby they could see the specter of a witch in plain daylight hurting its victim and causing mischief. In fact, the afflicted girls claimed that they were tormented by the specters of the accused witches right in the courtroom in front of the magistrates. In contrast, a witness for the prosecution brought into the courtroom to provide slander to be used as evidence against the accused never claimed to have the gift of spectral sight. At best the witness would claim that he could remember seeing a shape, often many years past, usually when he was awakened during the night. He would identify the shape as the apparition of the accused person, thereby establishing to the satisfaction of the court that the accused person was a witch. Although this slander

---

143 Cotton Mather, in his *Life of Sir William Phipps*, states that the *The Return of Several Ministers* was "drawn up at their desire by Mr. Mather, the Younger," that is, by himself.

144 Cotton Mather, *The Return of Several Ministers, June 15, 1692.*

was obviously spectral in nature, the court did not judge it as such, but instead classified it as "human testimony against such as were condemned and undoubted proof of their being witches."[145] Some of the prosecution witnesses never claimed even to see a shape; instead they testified to things like accidents that happened to them following an altercation with the accused person. The inference was that the accident was caused by the specter of the accused person, thus proving that the person was a witch. Cotton Mather and the other learned gentlemen regarded such human testimony as valid evidence of witchcraft. With the use of human testimony and confessions, the court would not have to base convictions on only the spectral evidence of the afflicted girls. This was the essential point of *The Return of Several Ministers* as brought out by the statement, "Convictions ought certainly be more considerable than barely the accused person being represented by a specter unto the afflicted."

Nowhere did the document recommend that spectral evidence be disallowed. The intention of the document was to encourage the Court to proceed in the same way as it had done in the trial of Bridget Bishop. In her trial the Court had indeed obeyed the injunctions as put forth by Cotton Mather in the document. The justices had not relied exclusively on the spectral evidence of the afflicted girls, but additionally had admitted a tremendous amount of slander against Bridget. This personal evidence was typified by William Stacy's statement, "Being then gone about six rods from her [Bridget Bishop], with a small load in his cart, suddenly the off-wheel stumped, and sank down into a hole, upon plain ground, so that the deponent was forced to get help for the recovering of the wheel. But stepping back to look for the hole, which might give him this disaster, there was none at all to be found. Some time after, he was waked in the night, but it seemed as light as day; and he perfectly saw the shape of this Bishop in the room troubling of him, but upon her going out, all was dark again. He charged Bishop afterwards with it, and she denied it, but was very angry."[146]

---

145 Phipps, "Letter dated at Boston, February 21, 1693," in Burr, *Narratives*, 199.

146 Cotton Mather, *Wonders*, 136.

Cotton Mather's document was presented to the Council on June 15, 1692. They were in full accord with its tenets; they agreed that the spectral evidence of the afflicted girls should always be supplemented by human testimony and when possible by confessions. The prosecutions continued more vigorously than ever. The incident reveals the devious nature of Cotton Mather. Intent on carrying out his witchcraft plan, he succeeded in paving the way for the court to bypass growing dissent toward the use of spectral evidence. Thus did Cotton Mather manage "to keep the word of promise to our ear, but break it to our hope."[147]

The second trial was held again at Salem, June 30, 1692. Five women were brought to trial: Sarah Good and Rebecca Nurse, of Salem Village; Susannah Martin of Amesbury; Elizabeth Howe of Ipswich Farms; and Sarah Wildes of Topsfield. None would confess. All were condemned and hastily executed on July 19, 1692.

Recall that Sarah Good was one of the first three women imprisoned. Of the other two, Sarah Osborne had already died in prison on May 10, and the slave Tituba was being held as a potential witness. The suckling child of Sarah Good, taken to prison with her, had died before its mother was executed. To compound her tragedy, this poor mother had to leave her four-year-old girl, little Dorcas Good, chained in the dark jail. Although Sarah Good suffered from melancholy, her spirit would not break. While she stood on the executioner's ladder, the Rev. Nicholas Noyes told her, "You are a witch, and you know you are a witch." But it was Sarah's last words that held the ring of truth. "You are a liar. I am no more a witch than you are a wizard, and if you take away my life, God will give you blood to drink."[148] Indeed, according to lasting tradition, Sarah Good's prophecy came true. The Rev. Nicholas Noyes, exceedingly fat, was to die of an internal hemorrhage, bleeding profusely from the mouth.[149]

---

147 Shakespeare, *Macbeth*, Act 5, Sc. 7.
148 Calef, *More Wonders*, 250.
149 Nathaniel Hawthorne preserved Sarah Good's powerful words in his romance, *The House of the Seven Gables*, ascribing them to the fictional

When Rebecca Nurse came to trial, many testimonials about her Christian behavior and her extraordinary loving care for her children were entered in Court. Rebecca had long been a respected church member. The jury returned the verdict not guilty. This outcome took the accusers by surprise. Immediately the afflicted girls in the courtroom burst into a deafening outcry. The jury went out once again. This time they found the seventy-year-old woman guilty. It was Thursday, June 30, 1692; the church would take action the following Sunday.

"It may be mentioned that it was the deliberate conviction of the family of Rebecca Nurse, that Mr. Parris, more than any other persons, was responsible for her execution. Of the prominent part taken by Mr. Noyes in the cruel treatment of this woman, there is no room for doubt. The records of the First Church in Salem are darkened by the following entry: '1692, July 3. After sacrament, the elders propounded to the church, and it was by an unanimous vote, consented to, that our sister Nurse, being a convicted witch by the Court, and condemned to die, should be excommunicated; which was according done in the afternoon, she being present.' The meetinghouse was thronged with a crowd. The sheriff brought in the prisoner, manacled, and the chains clanking from her aged form. She was placed in the broad aisle. Mr. Noyes pronounced the dread sentence."[150]

---

wizard, Matthew Maule. The wizard's persecutor, the fictional Colonel Pyncheon, died "with blood on his ruff, his hoary beard was saturated with it. Thus early had death stepped across the threshold of the House of the Seven Gables."

150 Upham, *Salem Witchcraft*, 2:290.

11

ANDOVER WITCH HUNT

A T THE BEGINNING OF 1692 THE TOWN OF ANDOVER was heading toward reconciliation and prosperity at long last. The bitter and prolonged feuding between the two ministers, Francis Dane and Thomas Barnard, had subsided; the grumblings against the old proprietary families' control of town affairs had quieted. But a foreboding of trouble came suddenly in May when Martha Carrier was arrested for witchcraft. About the same time Joseph Ballard's wife, Elizabeth, came down with a high fever. Joseph Ballard's brother John Ballard was married to Rebecca Hooper. Rebecca was the younger sister of Sarah (Hooper) Hawkes Wardwell, the wife of carpenter Samuel Wardwell. Joseph Ballard later testified to the following exchange, one that touched off the Andover witch hunt.[151]

Sarah and Samuel Wardwell had named their youngest child, Rebecca, after her aunt Rebecca (Hooper) Ballard, wife of John. When the two families visited, Samuel Wardwell and John Ballard liked to talk over the latest news. Quite unexpectedly, Samuel dropped a bombshell, "Your brother Joseph reported that I have bewitched his wife, Elizabeth." John Ballard was thoroughly taken back; witchcraft had never been mentioned to him as a possible cause of Elizabeth's fever. The next day John made a special trip to his brother's house to find Joseph worried and anxious, sitting outside Elizabeth's room. Elizabeth was getting worse. Said John, "Samuel Wardwell told me that you have reported that he has bewitched Elizabeth." Like his brother, Joseph Ballard was completely surprised. It had never occurred to him that Elizabeth's sickness was the

---

151 Woodward, *Records of Salem Witchcraft*, 2:152.

114

result of witchcraft. All that he could blurt out in reply was, "I have no knowledge that my wife is afflicted by witchcraft."

Yet the more Joseph Ballard thought about it, the more he wondered why Samuel Wardwell had raised the subject of witchcraft. Joseph went to the carpenter and told him, "I doubt that you are guilty of hurting my wife. For I have no such thoughts, nor have I spoken any such words of you or any other person." However Samuel did have a reputation for making predictions and prophecies. Elizabeth's disease had baffled the doctors. Joseph, now thinking that her sickness might indeed be due to witchcraft, told the carpenter, "Therefore I do not know whether you are guilty [of witchcraft]." Samuel Wardwell answered equivocally, "I admit that I said that to your brother John."

What strange behavior! Had Samuel Wardwell foreseen that he soon would be charged with witchcraft? Had the carpenter, comprehending that he was a marked man, predicted his own fate?

Elizabeth Ballard's fever did not abate. Witchcraft loomed larger and larger in Joseph Ballard's mind. Desperate, he went to the parsonage. The Rev. Thomas Barnard swiftly returned with Ballard to his house. Barnard confirmed that Satan often worked through the human agency of a witch to cause sickness. As far as Barnard could tell, Elizabeth lay dying under the spell of a witch. Her cure depended upon finding who had bewitched her.

Thomas Barnard turned to his trusted ally, Cotton Mather. Students at Harvard together, the two had been close friends ever since. Cotton Mather had helped support Barnard in his continual squabbles with Dane. Conveniently, Cotton Mather was an acknowledged expert in matters of witchcraft. As the two men talked, the case of Hugh Stone, his wife Hannah, and his mother-in-law Ann Foster quickly came up.

Ann Foster, aged 72 in 1692, was the widow of Andrew Foster. Born in Scotland, he was one of the original proprietors of the town of Andover in 1643. The Fosters had five children born between 1640 and 1655. In 1685, the ancient Andrew Foster died, said to be close to one hundred years old.

Ann Foster's daughter Hannah Foster had married Hugh Stone in 1667. After 22 years of married life, the unthinkable had happened. In 1689 Hannah's husband, in a fit of drunken rage, murdered her. Stone was apprehended and hanged the same year. Barnard was the young assistant minister of Andover. Cotton Mather had quickly obtained every lurid detail from him, and later published the account. "One Hugh Stone upon a quarrel between himself and his wife about selling a piece of land, having some words as they were walking together on a certain evening, very barbarously reached a stroke at her throat with a sharp knife, and by that one stroke fetched away the soul of her who had made him a father of several children, and would have brought yet another to him if she lived a few weeks longer in the world. The wretched man was too soon surprised by his neighbors to be capable of denying that fact and so he pleaded guilty upon his trial. There was a minister [Rev. Thomas Barnard] who walked with him to his execution; and I shall repeat the principal passages of the discourse between them." Cotton Mather recorded the conversation of the Rev. Thomas Barnard with the prisoner on the scaffold, who was allowed to make a final address. Cotton Mather added this brief ending, "After this he was by the prayers of the minister recommended unto the divine mercy."[152] In 1692, even this scant token of respect would be denied to those condemned for the imaginary crime of witchcraft.

Prior to the hanging, Hugh Stone gave the Rev. Thomas Barnard a slanderous account against his mother-in-law, Ann Foster. Now, in the first part of July 1692, the two men, Thomas Barnard and Cotton Mather, remembered this. It seemed apparent to them that Goody Ann Foster must be the very witch that was causing Elizabeth Ballard's fever. The Rev. George Burroughs, arrested May 4, and Martha Carrier, arrested May 31, were in Salem prison. Cotton Mather considered George Burroughs as one who had the promise of being a king in Satan's kingdom and Martha Carrier as the Queen of Hell. Their trials were scheduled for the first week in August. Martha Carrier came from Andover. Cotton Mather realized how useful it could

---

152 Cotton Mather, *Magnalia Christi Americana.*

be if Goody Foster confessed and implicated Martha Carrier as a fellow Andover witch.

Two of the afflicted girls of Salem Village, Ann Putnam, Jr. and Mary Walcott, were taken to Andover to seek out the witch causing Elizabeth Ballard's fever. By now the girls were experts. At the sight of Goody Foster, they fell into their usual fits and a warrant was issued for her arrest. On July 15, 1692, she was conveyed to Salem and thrown into prison.

"We whose names are underwritten, inhabitants of Andover; when as that horrible and tremendous judgment beginning at Salem Village in the year 1692, by some called witchcraft, first breaking forth at Mr. Parris's house, several young persons, being seemingly afflicted, did accuse several persons for afflicting them, and many there believing it so to be, we being informed that, if a person was sick, the afflicted person could tell what or who was the cause of that sickness. Joseph Ballard, of Andover, his wife being sick at the same time, he, either from himself or by the advice of others, fetched two of the persons, called the afflicted persons, from Salem Village to Andover, which was the beginning of that dreadful calamity that befell us in Andover."[153] Such is the description of the beginning of the Andover witch hunt, as written in retrospect by six of the women imprisoned in those hard times.

In his letter of October 8, 1692, Thomas Brattle described the tragic outcome. "The consulting of these afflicted children, about their sick, was the unhappy beginning of the unhappy troubles at poor Andover. Horse and man were sent up to Salem Village, from the said Andover, for some of the said afflicted, and more than one or two of them were carried down to see Ballard's wife, and to tell who it was that did afflict her. I understand that the said Ballard took advice before he took this method, but what pity it was, that he should meet with, and harken to such bad counselors? Poor Andover does now rue the day that ever the said afflicted went among them; they lament their folly, and are an object of great pity and commiseration."[154]

---

153 Calef, *More Wonders*, 271-272.
154 Brattle "Letter of October 8, 1692," in Burr, *Narratives*, 180

The Rev. Barnard set as his objective a confession from Ann Foster. After his experience counseling her son-in-law, a murderer, in the prison cell, Barnard offered to counsel Ann Foster. Following Barnard's lead, other ministers, the Rev. John Hale among them, visited her in prison. Their objective was to make her aware of her sins and lead her to confess witchcraft, always playing upon her fears. After hours of indoctrination by the ministers, Ann Foster became easy play for the magistrates. They obtained what they wanted, a confession signed and owned by Ann Foster. Synopses of four of the examinations, July 15, July 16, July 18, and July 21, have been preserved.[155]

Five years after the event, the Rev. John Hale wrote the following account in a futile attempt to exonerate himself of his cowardly and deceptive actions. "Goody Foster said that she with two others, one of whom acknowledged the same, rode from Andover to the same Village witch meeting upon a stick above ground, and that in the way the stick brake, and gave the said Foster a fall. I happened to be present in the prison when this Foster owned again her former confession to the magistrates. And then I moved that she may be further questioned about some particulars. It was answered that the magistrates had not time to stay longer, but I should have liberty to examine her further by myself, the which thing I did. And I asked her if she rode to the meeting on a stick. She said, yea. I inquired what she did for victuals. She answered that she carried bread and cheese in her pocket. And some time after she told me, she had some trouble on her spirit. And when I inquired what? she said she was in fear that George Burroughs and Martha Carrier would kill her, for they appeared to her in specter (for their persons were kept in other rooms in the prison) and brought a sharp pointed iron like a spindle and threatened to stab her to death with it because she had confessed her witchcraft, and told of them, that they were with her, and that Martha Carrier was the person that made her a witch."[156] The inquisitors had terrified this old woman by leading her to believe that Burroughs and Carrier wanted to attack her as she lay chained in her cell.

---

155 Bailey, *Historical Sketches of Andover*, 214.
156 Hale, *A Modest Enquiry*, in Burr, *Narratives*, 418.

Ann Foster's testimony provided spectral evidence which could be used against Martha Carrier and the Rev. George Burroughs in their upcoming trial. This evidence would supplement nicely that of the afflicted girls. Also extracted from Ann Foster was testimony against "two men besides Mr. Burroughs, the minister, & one of them had gray hair."[157] This man with gray hair was an obvious reference to the Rev. Francis Dane, the senior minister of Andover and the nemesis of the Rev. Barnard.

Ann Foster, the first person delivered from Andover by the Rev. Thomas Barnard, had confessed. Magistrates and ministers were delighted. Cotton Mather was ecstatic. "'More, more!' he cried, with nervous haste in his utterance, as if anxious to retain his grasp of what sought to escape him. 'This is what I need! Give me more!'"[158] The Andover conspiracy was born; its assigned goal was to obtain more confessions. "By these things you see how this matter was carried on, viz. chiefly by the complaints and accusations of the afflicted, bewitched ones, as it was supposed, and then by the confessions of the accused, condemning themselves and others," wrote the Rev. John Hale.[159]

The Salem witchcraft affair may be conveniently divided into two major episodes, the Salem Village witch hunt and the Andover witch hunt. The arrest phase of the Salem Village episode occurred over the four-month time period from March 1, 1692, to July 1, 1692. Essentially all the arrests associated with this episode were made in that interval, from the arrest of Tituba, Sarah Good, and Sarah Osborne on March 1, to the arrest of Margaret Hawkes and Candy on July 1. Only one Andover resident was arrested during that period: Martha Carrier, on May 31, 1692. All the complainants against Martha Carrier came from Salem Village, and she should be classified as a victim of the Salem Village witch hunt.

The arrest phase of the Andover witch hunt began after the arrest phase of the Salem Village witch hunt was over. All the

---

157 Essex County Archives, *Witchcraft*, 2:22.
158 Hawthorne, *The House of the Seven Gables*, Chapter 7.
159 Hale, *A Modest Enquiry*, in Burr, *Narratives*, 421.

arrests made in the Andover episode occurred during the eight-week period from July 15, 1692, to September 7, 1692. The first arrest was that of Ann Foster of Andover on July 15. She was accused by Joseph Ballard, an Andover neighbor. The final arrests of the Andover witch hunt represented a spectacular outburst: eighteen arrests made at the Andover touch test on September 7.

The Salem Village episode has been well documented and exhaustively studied. Because the Andover episode came later, it has been treated as a remnant of Salem Village, and never fully documented in its own right. The Andover witch hunt followed much the same pattern as that of Salem Village. Some elements, however, are more sharply defined in Andover than in Salem Village. The points in common as well as the differences justify a separate investigation. The Salem Village conspiracy was instrumental in launching the Andover conspiracy as an adjunct. Throughout the Andover witch hunt, the Salem Village afflicted girls—Abigail Williams, Ann Putnam, Jr., Mercy Lewis, Mary Walcott, and Mary Warren—worked hand in hand with the Andover afflicted girls. Both conspiracies were sanctioned by the Puritan old guard ruling the colony.

Only in five cases had the Salem Village conspiracy succeeded in obtaining confessions. The first confession was from Tituba, a female slave, on March 1, 1692. The fifth confession was from Candy, also a female slave, on July 4, 1692. Of the more than seventy-five persons arrested in the four-month interval between these two confessions, only three had confessed. Tituba's confession was valuable in launching the Salem Village witch hunt and is part of the folk lore of witchcraft handed down to the present day. (As previously stated, it was revealed later that Tituba's confession resulted not from the spiritual talents of her owner, the Rev. Samuel Parris, but from his physical abuse in beating her.) Parris was the clerical member of the Salem Village conspiracy.

A third female slave, Mary Black, imprisoned on April 22, 1692, had been unshakable at her examination. Magistrate Hathorne said, "Mary, you are accused of sundry acts of witchcraft. Tell me, be you a witch?" She was silent. "But have you been a witch?" he angrily demanded. Finally she replied, "I cannot tell you." "But who does hurt these people?" he asked. She answered, "I do not know." The direct approach proving fruitless, Hathorne turned to the tricks of the afflicted girls. To his question, "Do you prick sticks?" Mary answered, "No, I pin my neck-cloth." Now Hathorne laid his trap, saying, "Well, take out a pin, & pin it again." When she did, the afflicted cried out that they were pricked. "Mary Walcott was pricked in the arm till the blood came. Abigail Williams was pricked in the stomach & Mercy Lewis was pricked in the foot." The minister, the Rev. Samuel Parris, whose task was to induce Mary into confessing, wrote, "Seeing what we did then see together with the charge of the afflicted persons then present, we committed said Mary Black."[160] However, all of Parris' tricks could not make Mary Black confess. Clearly, Cotton Mather needed better clerical talent than Parris could offer.

The other three confessions in that five-month interval came from Abigail Hobbs, aged 22, imprisoned on April 19, 1692; from her mother, Deliverance Hobbs, imprisoned three days later; and from Margaret Jacobs, imprisoned on May 10, 1692. Abigail Hobbs, a rebellious girl, not only confessed on April 19, but became an afflicted person herself. From time to time over the next few months she would be taken from her jail cell to act in the courtroom with the sanctioned afflicted circle. Her mother, Deliverance Hobbs, at first refused to confess. Hathorne cleverly played resentment harbored by her daughter against her. The pressure was too much and Deliverance gave in to his abusive leading questions and made a confession on April 22. Margaret Jacobs, the granddaughter of George Jacobs, Sr. made a confession on May 11, 1692, but retracted it on August 18, the day before her grandfather's execution. "Margaret Jacobs being one who confessed her own guilt, and testified against her grandfather Jacobs, Mr. Burroughs, and John Willard, she the day before execution, came to Mr. Burroughs, acknowledging that she had belied them, and begged Mr. Burroughs' forgiveness, who not only forgave her, but also prayed with her and for her."[161]

160 Massachusetts Archives, *Witchcraft*, 135:20.
161 Calef, *More Wonders*, 258.

Not counting the two slaves, Tituba and Candy, the Rev. Samuel Parris had been successful in obtaining only these three confessions. The remaining seventy-five odd witches imprisoned from March to July had adamantly refused to confess even under pressure. This failure by Parris weakened the credibility of the entire witch hunt. In fact, public sentiment was noticeably turning away from the Puritan church toward the imprisoned. Important ministers in Boston were beginning to question the validity of the spectral evidence provided by the afflicted circle.

Recall that Cotton Mather had drawn up a statement entitled *The Return of Several Ministers* which was presented to the Council on June 15, 1692. To dispel mounting criticism of the prosecution, Cotton Mather acknowledged the need for evidence in addition to the spectral evidence of the girls. Of course, the so-called human testimony, more accurately, the basest type of slander (spectral in nature but not classified as such), could readily be obtained. But in order to insure the credibility of the witch hunt, confessions were needed. Cotton Mather turned his full attention in that direction, believing it essential to obtain a series of confessions. Looking at the confessions of the Hobbs mother and daughter, he guessed that his best strategy was to play generation against generation. He needed another minister who would form a second conspiracy to carry out this task. The Rev. Nicholas Noyes and the Rev. John Hale were helpful, but they preferred to remain apart from the men targeting women and filing legal complaints against them.

The Rev. Cotton Mather instinctively knew that the Rev. Thomas Barnard was the right man for the job. To all appearances these two ministers were very different. Cotton Mather held himself aloof and was not a polished speaker, having stammered as a boy. Barnard was a man of genuine charisma whose sermons were capable of igniting an extreme form of religious fervor. "This vocal organ was itself a rich endowment; insomuch that a listener, comprehending nothing of the language in which the preacher spoke, might still have been swayed to and fro by the mere cadence. Like all other music, it breathed passion and pathos, and emotions high and tender, in a tongue native to the human heart."[162]

In the factual world of today it is difficult, if not impossible, to comprehend the mesmerizing effect of a preacher like Barnard. As a speaker, he could influence the thoughts and actions of people to a degree that Cotton Mather never could. Cotton Mather's sermons spoke to the intellect; Barnard's sermons spoke to the emotions. With his eloquence and the intensity of his discourse, Barnard might well convince a devout and anxious woman that she had fallen into the ways of sin and hence into witchcraft. Even if he did not quite convince her, his charming speech often convinced her Puritanical husband that she had strayed from the narrow path. Barnard's strategy was to offer the hope of redemption as an enticement for an accused woman to confess her witchcraft. Not only did he claim that confession and repentance would save her soul but he suggested that they might save her life.

Barnard was destined to succeed beyond all expectation. The confessions he induced in the Andover witch hunt painted a picture of witchcraft which precisely confirmed Cotton Mather's conception of the Devil's work to take over New England. Cotton Mather wrote, "I believe that never were more satanical devices used for the unsettling of any people under the sun, than what have been employed for the extirpation of the vine which God had here planted. We have been advised of an horrible plot against the country by witchcraft, which if were not seasonably discovered, would probably blow up, and pull down all the churches in the country."[163]

On July 19, 1692, Sarah Good, Rebecca Nurse, Susannah Martin, Elizabeth Howe, and Sarah Wildes, were hanged in Salem. None of them confessed, even to the end. This black day was just four days after Ann Foster's arrest. Joseph Ballard, Ann Foster's accuser, was in Salem and present at the hangings. "Imagine an ancient multitude of people, congregated at the hillside, spreading far below, clustering on the steep old roofs,

---

162 Hawthorne, *The Scarlet Letter*, Chapter 22.
163 Cotton Mather, *Wonders*, 13-14.

and climbing the adjacent heights, wherever a glimpse of this spot might be obtained. I strove to realize and faintly communicate, the deep, unutterable loathing and horror, the indignation, the affrighted wonder, that wrinkled on every brow, and filled the universal heart."[164]

Now was the time to go after the next two generations of the Foster family. Joseph Ballard's wife, Elizabeth had become even sicker; her burning fever could not be treated, and she was on the verge of death.[165] A few hours after the executions, Joseph Ballard, still in Salem, went to the house of Jonathan Corwin and swore out a complaint for the arrest of the daughter and granddaughter of the imprisoned Ann Foster.[166] He accused them of practicing witchcraft on his wife, whom he described as being sorely afflicted with strange pains and pressures for several months. Ballard posted a bond of £100 to prosecute his complaint to the effect that the law directed. The complaint was signed by the three Salem magistrates: John Hathorne, Jonathan Corwin, and Bartholomew Gedney, all members of the Puritan old guard and all justices on the Court of Oyer and Terminer.

The accused daughter of Ann Foster was Mary (Foster) Lacey, 40, who had married Lawrence Lacey in 1673. The Laceys were respected citizens of Andover. The accused granddaughter of Ann Foster was Mary Lacey, Jr., 18, daughter of Lawrence and Mary Lacey. Mother and daughter, both named Mary Lacey, were arrested and imprisoned in Salem. Several ministers visited them in prison, indoctrinating them and urging them to confess.

On July 21 the three Salem magistrates examined the three women: Ann Foster, daughter Mary (Foster) Lacey, and granddaughter, Mary Lacey, Jr. The executions, two days before, were still fresh in people's minds. The magistrates were intent upon getting the two Laceys to confess. Never was there a baser exhibition of trickery and deceit than that displayed by the magistrates during these examinations.

---

164 Hawthorne, *Alice Doane's Appeal.*
165 Elizabeth Ballard died on July 27, 1692.
166 Jonathan Corwin's house, called the Witch House, is open for visitors in Salem today.

The house of Jonathan Corwin, now called the Witch House

SALEM WITCHCRAFT

Salem witch trial in 1692

Without her mother or grandmother present, the adolescent Mary Lacey, Jr., 18, was first examined. As she was led into the courtroom, she looked at some of the Salem Village afflicted girls who were already there. One of them, Mary Warren, 20, was in the midst of a violent fit. Hathorne asked the leading question, "How dare you come in here and bring the Devil with you to afflict these poor creatures?" Mary Lacey, Jr. answered, "I know nothing of it."[167] Lacey was told to lay her hand on Warren's arm, who upon her touch immediately recovered.

Seeing the deferential, almost royal treatment afforded the afflicted girls, Mary Lacey, Jr. soon came to the logical conclusion that she might fare better as an afflicted girl than as a witch. Acting on her hunch, she made a glib confession. To Hathorne's blatant question, "Do you acknowledge now that you are a witch?" she replied, "Yes, the Devil appeared to me in the shape of a horse. He bid me to be afraid of nothing & he would not bring me out, but he has proved a liar from the beginning." When Hathorne asked, "What did he order you to do?" she answered, "He set me to kill a tinker in the town, but I would not." Always interested in the workings of the Devil, Hathorne then asked, "What other shape did he appear in?" Mary answered, "In the shape of a round gray thing." To Hathorne's question, "How many times did the Devil appear to you?" she answered, "Twice & both times in the night. I was in my bed and he awaked me by making a strange noise. He bid me to obey him & he would never bring me out." Hathorne then turned to a strategy of deceit, the offering of false hope. He said, "You may yet be delivered, if God give you repentance. Have you never been molested?"[168]

The examination went on. Mary Lacey, Jr. had a vivid imagination and she played into John Hathorne's hands. She said, "Goody Carrier came to us in her spirit, and to grandmother and would not let her alone till she went with her and afflicted persons." Hathorne asked, "How does she come when she comes in her spirit?" The answer was, "Sometimes in the likeness of a

---

167 Thomas Hutchinson, "The Witchcraft Delusion of 1692," 399-401; Essex Institute, *Witchcraft Collection*, "Examinations."
168 Ibid.

cat; sometimes in the likeness of a bird & tells us it is she." Hathorne then wanted to know, "What color are these cats?" Mary gave the expected answer, "Black." Hathorne next asked, "Where or in what places do those cats suck?" Mary answered circumspectly, saying, "I cannot tell, but believe they do suck her body."

Hathorne, getting down to business, asked the leading question, "Did you hear the 77 witches names called over?" Mary Lacey, Jr., answered, "Yes, the Devil called them. He bid them to obey him and do his commands & it would be better for them & they should obtain crowns in Hell & Goody Carrier told me that the Devil said to her that she should be a Queen in Hell." This is what Hathorne was waiting to hear, and he immediately asked, "Who was to be the King?" The answer was exactly what he wanted, "The minister." So that there would be no ambiguity in the written record, Hathorne then asked, "What kind of man is Mr. Burroughs?" Mary answered, "A pretty little man and he has come to us sometimes in his spirit in the shape of a cat & I think sometimes in his proper shape." Hathorne, seizing upon the opportunity, asked Mary a question with origins going back to the biblical witch of Endor. "Do you hear the Devil hurts in the shape of any person without their consents?" Mary, a professed intimate of "the old serpent," definitively answered the question, saying, "No." This question that had baffled theologians for centuries was finally put to rest by this forthcoming eighteen-year-old New England girl. "After this confession, Mary Warren came and took her by the hand & was no way hurt & she, viz., Mary Lacey, Jr., did earnestly ask Mary Warren's forgiveness for afflicting of her and both fell a weeping together, etc."[169]

The mother, Goody Lacey, was brought in. Hathorne said, "Here is a poor miserable child and a wretched mother!" The reaction was as expected. The daughter, Mary Lacey, Jr., cried, "O mother, why did you give me to the Devil twice or thrice over?" The daughter earnestly bid her mother to repent and call upon God. "O mother, your wishes have now come to pass. For, have you often wished that the Devil would fetch me away

---

169 Ibid.

alive! O my heart will break within me! O that mother should ever have give me to the Devil!" The daughter then wept bitterly, crying out, "O Lord, comfort me and bring out all that are witches!"[170]

The grandmother, Goody Foster, was next brought in. Mary Lacey, Jr. cried, "O, grandmother, why did you give me to the Devil? Why did you persuade me? O, grandmother, do not you deny it, you have been a very bad woman in your time!" Hathorne pointed at Mary Lacey, Jr. and moralized, "Here is an argument of hope for this poor creature that she will be snatched out of the snare of the Devil, because there seems to be something of repentance." Pointing next at the grandmother, he snarled, "But as for you, old woman, though you have shown something of relenting, yet you retain a lie in the mouth. We desire you, therefore, to be free in the presence of God, and tell us the truth in this matter. Will you play with devouring fire, and will not you shun everlasting flames & the society of this devouring lion that has so ensnared thee?"[171]

The elderly grandmother, Goody Foster, held out as best she could. The afflicted Mary Warren said, "Goody Carrier's shape told me that Goody Foster had made her daughter a witch." Goody Foster said, "No! I know no more of my daughter's being a witch than what day I shall die on." Hathorne needled her, "You cannot expect peace and comfort without a free confession." Her daughter, Mary (Foster) Lacey, was less firm, saying "Oh, mother, how do you do? We have left Christ and the Devil hath got hold of us. How shall I get rid of this evil one? I desire God to break my rocky heart that I may get the victory this time." Hathorne turned to Ann Foster and said, "Goody Foster, you cannot get rid of this snare. Your heart and mouth are not open." The old woman answered, "I did not see the Devil. I was praying to the Lord." Hathorne, always thrusting, asked, "What god do witches pray to?" Goody Foster replied, "I cannot tell. The Lord help me." Next Hathorne turned to her daughter, Mary (Foster) Lacey, and brought up one of his favorite topics, transportation. Hathorne asked, "Goody Lacey, had you no discourse with your

170 Ibid.
171 Ibid.

mother while riding?   Who rid foremost on that stick to the village?"   She answered, "I suppose my mother."[172]   If the learned magistrates and ministers believed in witches riding broomsticks, why not she?   The three women were returned to prison.   Their confessions were put in the records, even though Ann Foster, in moments of defiance, had reneged.

Because of her compliance, the magistrates often had Mary Lacey, Jr. taken out of her prison cell and returned to courtroom to act as an afflicted girl.   This eighteen-year old woman was the Andover counterpart of Abigail Hobbs, 22, who was treated in the same way.   The magistrates manipulated these two young women like puppets on a string.   Each young woman was classified both as a witch and as an afflicted person.   They became the prototype confessing witches whose words were used to implicate others.   It is ironic that Abigail Hobbs, after many sterling performances at preliminary examinations, was convicted and sentenced to death by the Court of Oyer and Terminer on September 17, 1692.   Condemned at the same time were the mother, Mary (Foster) Lacey, and grandmother, Ann Foster, of Mary Lacey, Jr.[173]

The successful arrest of Ann Foster, Mary Lacey, and Mary Lacey Jr., three generations of a family of an Andover first settler, opened wide the door to further accusations.   Initially the Andover conspiracy consisted of the Rev. Thomas Barnard and Joseph Ballard.   After the death of his wife on July 27, 1692, Ballard turned his attention away from the witch hunt toward finding a new wife.   Less than four months later, on November 15, he remarried.   Two and one-half weeks after the happy event, the widow Ann Foster, who supposedly had bewitched his first wife to death, died of abusive treatment in Salem prison.   Was this the peace and comfort that Hathorne promised Ann Foster for her confession?

---

172   Ibid.

173   In 1692 the Court of Oyer and Terminer brought no minor children to trial.   However, in 1693 the Superior Court of Judicature did try minors. Mary Lacey, Jr. was tried on January 13, 1693 and found not guilty.

The Rev. Thomas Barnard, assistant minister of the Andover church, never permitted his name to appear on any legal complaint document. It would have been unseemly and, were the conspiracy to fail, unwise. The theme of Barnard's sermons mirrored the teachings of Cotton Mather, "To them that have been seduced into the sin of witchcraft, let them now confess and bewail their own sin in the sight of God."[174] His role was to lead the accused into confessions of witchcraft which would appear to be voluntary and spontaneous. To the degree that he succeeded, it was his own sermons that proved truly dangerous and seductive.

The Andover conspiracy was quickly joined by three brothers: Robert Swan, Jr., 35; Timothy Swan, 29; and John Swan, 24. All residing in the north part of Andover, they were sons of Robert Swan, an influential figure in local and colonial governmental circles. Robert Swan, Jr., was married; Timothy Swan and John Swan were bachelors. The three brothers initially had been recruited by the Salem Village conspiracy to make accusations against Mary Bradbury of Salisbury, whom the brothers knew. Mary Bradbury had been imprisoned on June 29, 1693.

Of all the people caught up in the Salem tragedy, Timothy Swan is one of the most inexplicable. He played a dual role; he was an afflicted man and he was a conspirator. Little else is known about him since all transcripts of his testimony have disappeared. Yet his gravestone still stands in the old burying ground in North Andover, making him the only afflicted person whose resting place is known today. Suffering from an undiagnosed illness, he died on February 1, 1693.

Thomas Chandler was a silent member of the Andover conspiracy, preferring to work through his two sons-in-law, Samuel Phelps and Daniel Bigsby, both active members. Sarah Phelps, Jr. , the daughter of Samuel Phelps and his wife Sarah (Chandler) Phelps, was a member of the Andover afflicted circle. Daniel Bigsby's wife, Hannah (Chandler) Bigsby, on occasion acted with the Andover afflicted circle.

The dominant member of the Andover conspiracy proved to be Moses Tyler, whose son, Joseph Tyler, was also a member. Although Moses Tyler lived in Boxford, he was a member of the

---

174 Cotton Mather, *A Discourse on Witchcraft.*

Andover church. His first wife, Prudence (Blake) Tyler had died in 1689. His second wife was the widow Sarah (Hasey) Sprague. They were married in 1690. Her daughter, Martha Sprague, aged 16 in 1692, was the leader of the Andover afflicted circle. Joseph Tyler was a son of Moses Tyler and his first wife Prudence (Blake) Tyler.

Ephraim Foster was a member of the Andover conspiracy. He and his wife, Hannah (Eames) Foster, aged 31, lived in the north part of Andover where he was constable.[175] His wife Hannah as well as their oldest daughter, Rose Foster, were part of the Andover afflicted circle. Apparently Rose Foster was afflicted by a genuine physical illness, for she died on February 5, 1693.

Samuel Martin was the final member of the Andover conspiracy. He and his wife, Abigail (Norton) Martin, lived in the north part of Andover. Their daughter Abigail Martin, Jr. was one of the afflicted circle.

The circle of afflicted girls of the Andover conspiracy quickly became adept at their calling. They worked in tandem with the Salem Village afflicted girls. When the Andover afflicted girls visited any place where someone was ill, they fell into their fits. When asked who it was that bewitched the sick person, the girls could usually see the specters of two witches. One was sitting on the head, and the other on the feet of the sick person. "When these accusers [the afflicted girls] came into the house of any upon such an account, it was ordinary for other young people to be taken in fits, and to have the same spectral sight."[176] However these "other young people" were never admitted into the privileged afflicted circle of the Andover conspiracy. On the contrary, some were arrested as witches. In their prison cells they were always available to the prosecution. Whenever they were needed, these young people would be taken out of their cells to act as an afflicted in the preliminary examinations.

---

175 Foster was a common name in New England, and Ephraim Foster was not related to Andrew Foster, an original proprietor of Andover and the deceased husband of Ann Foster.

176 Calef, *More Wonders*, 268.

The old guard members most active in the witch hunt were lieutenant governor William Stoughton of Dorchester and the three Salem magistrates, John Hathorne, Jonathan Corwin, and Bartholomew Gedney. If an accused person fled to protect his freedom or was condemned, Sheriff George Corwin would confiscate his property. Philip English, one of Salem's wealthiest residents fled; his property was seized. Confiscated property, both real and personal, was distributed among various old guard members and their friends and relations. After the Salem affair was over, Philip English made a concerted effort to recover his property that had fallen into the hands of the Corwins. After George Corwin died in 1697, English was able to gain a token payment of £60 from Corwin's executors.[177]

Because confessions were needed to confirm the existence of the horrible plot of witchcraft and justify the witch hunt, the old guard sanctioned the work of the Andover conspiracy. John Hathorne was accustomed to dealing with the Salem Village conspiracy, whose members he had known for years and could trust. But he hardly knew the Andover conspirators. As with Salem Village, the old guard indicated only in general terms who was to be accused in Andover. By and large it left the choice to the discretion of the Andover conspiracy. The old guard was unaware that the Andover conspiracy would form its own agenda. The Andover conspiracy had observed that the old guard made no objection to the accusation of Ann Foster, the widow of an Andover first settler. It seemed that the old guard, and in particular the three Salem magistrates, had been blinded by the attractive prospect of obtaining as spoils the extensive lands and property of the Foster family.

The Andover conspiracy set three objectives. In 1692 the families of the original settlers, the proprietors of Andover, still firmly controlled the town. Those conspirators excluded from this privileged group had grown increasingly resentful. The first and fundamental objective of the conspiracy was to break the established power structure of the town. The Andover witch hunt

---

177 Upham, *Salem Witchcraft*, 2:473. After many petitions Philip English finally was awarded £200 from the government in 1718, still only a fraction of his losses.

became primarily an attack against the old proprietary families. The three Salem magistrates were interested in any land or property that could be obtained in the process. Initially the more vulnerable were accused, but in time the most prosperous families of Andover, such as the Barkers and Osgoods, fell victims to the attack. Because of their lethal actions against highly respected people, the Andover conspiracy eventually helped precipitate the end of the witch hunt.

The second objective of the Andover conspiracy was to discredit the Rev. Francis Dane and his family. The younger minister, Thomas Barnard, wanted Dane's position for himself, and to this end Barnard had become locked in a never-ending struggle over salary and doctrine. In the summer of 1692, the conspiracy did not dare accuse Dane directly, but instead accused a large number of his family, both immediate and extended.

The third objective was to use the witchcraft accusations wherever possible as a means of gaining revenge and settling old grudges. The case of Moses Tyler is foremost here. He was even willing to use witchcraft slander to bring down his own siblings.

The madness of the Andover witch hunt took place over a period of about eight weeks from July 15 to September 7, 1692. Nearly fifty residents of Andover were complained of and arrested in that short period. The Andover circle of afflicted girls were as effective as their Salem Village counterparts.

The Rev. Thomas Barnard and Thomas Chandler made no legal complaints. Like the Salem Village witch hunt, the Andover witch hunt was driven not by uncontrolled mass hysteria but by the planned and deliberate actions of a conspiracy. The table lists the Andover conspirators and the members of the afflicted circle.

Conspirator	Afflicted
The Rev. Thomas Barnard, aged 34	
Thomas Chandler, aged 65	
Joseph Ballard, aged 50	Elizabeth (Phelps) Ballard, aged 46
Samuel Phelps, aged 41	Sarah Phelps, Jr., aged 9
Daniel Bigsby, aged 41	Hannah (Chandler) Bigsby, aged 35

Robert Swan, Jr., aged 35 Timothy Swan, aged 29 John Swan, aged 24	Timothy Swan, aged 29
Moses Tyler, aged about 51 Joseph Tyler, aged 21	Martha Sprague, aged 16
Ephraim Foster, aged 35	Hannah (Eames) Foster, aged 31 Rose Foster, aged 14
Samuel Martin, aged 47	Abigail Martin, Jr., aged 16

12

THIRD TRIAL, AUGUST 5, 1692

A T THE THIRD MEETING of the Court of Oyer and Terminer, six more were tried, four men and two women: the Rev. George Burroughs, the minister at Wells, Maine; John Proctor and Elizabeth Proctor, his wife, of Salem Farms; John Willard of Salem Village; George Jacobs, Sr. of Salem; and Martha Carrier of Andover. Not one would confess; all were condemned on August 5, 1692. They were hanged on August 19 with the exception of Proctor's wife who escaped death by pleading for the life of her unborn child.

Burroughs, the minister at Salem Village from 1681 to 1683, had created several enemies there, in particular, the Putnam family. After leaving Salem Village, Burroughs preached at Casco and then at Wells, both towns being in Maine. In his trial he pleaded not guilty. The afflicted girls and some of the confessing witches accused him of being a king in Satan's empire. They claimed that, although he was a small man, he had performed feats beyond the strength of a giant. Burroughs had lost two wives, each by an early death. His second wife had been Sarah (Ruck) Hathorne, widow of the deceased Captain William Hathorne, Jr. The witnesses swore that Sarah had privately complained to the neighbors that their house was haunted by spirits. Cotton Mather claimed that during his trial Burroughs dodged questions and contradicted himself in making his defense. Cotton Mather wrote that Burroughs "was accused by eight of the confessing witches, as being a head actor at some of their hellish rendezvouses, and one who had the promise of being a king in Satan's kingdom, now going to be erected." The "eight of the confessing witches" were Abigail Hobbs, Deliverance Hobbs, Margaret Jacobs, Ann Foster, Mary (Foster)

Lacey, Mary Lacey, Jr., Richard Carrier, and Andrew Carrier. Because of her confession on July 30, Mary Toothaker could also be included in this group.[178]

Tried next was John Proctor, a wealthy innkeeper and landowner. While he and his wife were in prison, sheriff George Corwin[179] came to their house and seized all their possessions. The sheriff sold some of their cattle at half price and killed the rest, sending the cured meat to the West Indies for sale. He even drained the beer from a barrel, and carried away the barrel. He emptied a pot of broth and carried away the pot. Nothing was left in the house, not even food, to support the Proctor children. No part of the property was ever returned to the family. In prison Proctor earnestly requested the Rev. Nicholas Noyes to pray with and for him but Noyes refused, ostensibly because Proctor would not admit to being a witch. Proctor asked for a short respite, saying that he was not fit to die, but that too was denied.

John Willard had refused to act as a deputy to arrest some of the accused. Soon afterward he was accused of causing the demise of Daniel Wilkins, a young man who was bewitched to death. The authorities sent men to hunt down and apprehend Willard, who had escaped to Nashaway, about 40 miles from Salem.

The seizure of the property of a condemned witch for the enrichment of the authorities was standard procedure. When George Jacobs, Sr. was condemned, sheriff George Corwin and officers came and seized all he had. Jacobs' second wife, Mary, had even her wedding ring snatched from her; only after great effort did she eventually recover it. She was forced to buy provisions from the sheriff, things that he had taken, for her own sustenance. Still unable to cope, she was helped by the charity of her neighbors.

Margaret Jacobs, the sixteen-year-old granddaughter of George Jacobs, Sr., had been arrested with him on May 10, 1692.

---

178 Cotton Mather, *Wonders*, 120.
179 Sheriff George Corwin was the nephew of magistrate John Corwin and the son-in-law of magistrate Bartholomew Gedney.

The next day the two were examined separately at Beadles' tavern in Salem Town. An onlooker, Joseph Flint, went into the room where the grandfather was held and told him that his granddaughter had confessed that she was a witch. George Jacobs, Sr. said, "She was charged not to confess." When Flint asked him who charged her, Jacobs reflected and then answered, "If she were innocent, and yet confessed, she would be an accessory to her own death."[180]

George Jacobs, Sr. was condemned on August 5. On August 18, the day before he was executed, Margaret retracted her confession and received forgiveness from both him and the Rev. George Burroughs. She made the following declaration to the court. There is no mistaking that Margaret, 16, was a person of exceptional courage and integrity.

"The humble declaration of Margaret Jacobs unto the honored court now sitting at Salem, showeth: That whereas your poor and humble declarant being closely confined here in Salem jail for the crime of witchcraft, which crime, thanks be to the Lord, I am altogether ignorant of, as will appear at the great day of judgment. May it please the honored court, I was cried out upon by some of the possessed persons, as afflicting of them; whereupon I was brought to my examination, which persons at the sight of me fell down, which did very much startle and affright me. The Lord above knows I knew nothing, in the least measure, how or who afflicted them; they told me, without doubt I did, or else they would not fall down at me; they told me if I would not confess, I should be put down into the dungeon and would be hanged, but if I would confess I should have my life; the which did so affright me, with my own vile wicked heart, to save my life made me make the confession I did, which confession, may it please the honored court, is altogether false and untrue. The very first night after I had made my confession, I was in such horror of conscience that I could not sleep, for fear the Devil should carry me away for telling such horrid lies. I was, may it please the honored court, sworn to my confession, as I understand since, but then, at that time, was ignorant of it, not knowing what an oath did mean. The Lord, I hope, in whom I

---

180 Essex County Archives, *Witchcraft*, 1:90.

trust, out of the abundance of his mercy, will forgive me my false forswearing myself. What I said was altogether false and untrue, against my grandfather, and Mr. Burroughs, which I did to save my life and to have my liberty; but the Lord, charging it to my conscience, made me in so much horror, that I could not contain myself before I had denied my confession, which I did, though I saw nothing but death before me, choosing rather death with a quiet conscience, than to live in such horror, which I could not suffer. Whereupon my denying my confession, I was committed to close prison, where I have enjoyed more felicity in spirit a thousand times than I did before in my enlargement.

"And now, may it please your honors, your poor and humble declarant having, in part, given your honors a description of my condition, do leave it to your honors' pious and judicious discretions to take pity and compassion on my young and tender years; to act and do with me as the Lord above and your honors shall see good, having no friend but the Lord to plead my cause for me; not being guilty in the least measure of the crime of witchcraft, nor any other sin that deserves death from man; and your poor and humble declarant shall forever pray, as she is bound in duty, for your honors' happiness in this life, and eternal felicity in the world to come. So prays your honors' declarant. Margaret Jacobs."[181]

Pity and compassion were unknown to the court; the justices understood only the hysterical and inflammatory outcries of Cotton Mather and his fellow clergy. Livid with rage, the court scheduled Margaret Jacobs for trial at the next meeting in September. But Margaret was not brought to trial because she was so ill with an "impostume" on her head that it was expected that she would die in jail. She survived, however, and when tried in January 1693 by the newly formed Superior Court of Judicature, she was found not guilty.

The court, determined to convict Martha Carrier, would stop at nothing. On July 22, 1692, two weeks before her condemnation on August 5, her sons, Andrew Carrier, 15, and Richard Carrier, 18, were arrested, imprisoned in Salem, and examined. The Rev.

---

181 Thomas Hutchinson, "The Witchcraft Delusion of 1692," 402-403.

Cotton Mather was present at the examination. Despite Cotton Mather's preliminary instructions to the two Carrier boys, they bravely resisted making any confession during the examination. Magistrate John Hathorne, not used to fortitude in teenagers, authorized the use of physical torture on the two Carrier boys. This kind of torture was a departure from the usual methods of non-physical torture (the so-called English torture) used throughout the Salem witchcraft episode. The official record stated: "Richard and Andrew Carrier were carried out to another chamber and their feet and hands bound. A little while after Richard was brought in again." Hathorne said, "Richard, though you have been very obstinate, yet tell us how long ago it is since you were taken in this snare [of the Devil]?" The record then continued, "Under many questions propounded he answers affirmatively as follows." What followed was the required confession.[182]

The next day, July 23, 1692, John Proctor, imprisoned in Salem prison, wrote: "Here are five persons [Ann Foster, Mary (Foster) Lacey, Mary Lacey, Jr., Richard Carrier, and Andrew Carrier] who have lately confessed themselves to be witches, and do accuse some of us of being along with them at a sacrament since we were committed into close prison, which we know to be lies. Two of the five are young men [Richard and Andrew Carrier], who would not confess anything till they tied them neck and heels, till blood was ready to come out of their noses, and it is creditably believed and reported this was the occasion of making them confess what they never did by reason. They said one had been a witch a month, and another five weeks, and that their mother had made them so, who had been confined here this nine weeks. My son, William Proctor, when he was examined, because he would not confess that he was guilty, when he was innocent, they tied him neck and heels till blood gushed out at his nose, and would have kept him so 24 hours, if one more merciful than the rest, had not taken pity on him, and caused him to be unbound."[183]

---

182 Essex Institute, *Witchcraft Collection*, "Examinations."
183 Upham, *Salem Witchcraft*, 2:311.

On August 10, 1692, five days after the condemnation of
Martha Carrier on August 5, her small children, Thomas Carrier,
Jr., 10, and Sarah Carrier, 7, were arrested and imprisoned in
Salem. They were examined the next day, August 11, "by the
magistrate John Hathorne, Esq., and others." The Rev. Cotton
Mather was present at the examination. The examiners asked,
"How long has thou been a witch?" Little Sarah answered,
"Ever since I was six years old. I am near eight years old.
Brother Richard says I shall be eight years old in November
next." Hathorne, with a hard, stern, relentless look on his face,
then exclaimed, "You said you saw a cat once. What did that say
to you?" Sarah, a diminutive child, looked up at the magistrate
sitting upon the bench, and answered. "It said it would tear me to
pieces, if I would not set my hand to the book." Did this small
child mistake her examiners for the black man himself, and
confuse the written confession they wanted her to sign with the
Devil's book? When Hathorne asked whether she went in her
body or in her spirit, she answered, "In spirit. My mother carried
me thither to afflict." He persisted, "How did your mother carry
you while she was in prison?" She responded, "She came like a
black cat." Hathorne then asked, "How did you know that it
was your mother?" Sarah answered, "The cat told me so, that
she was my mother."[184]

The official record demonstrates beyond a shadow of doubt
the falseness of the examiners. The Rev. Cotton Mather and
magistrate John Hathorne were willing to deceive this seven-
year-old child by giving credence to the notion that cats could
talk. Yet not even little Sarah truly believed this fantasy; only
ministers and magistrates purported to believe such nonsense.
She had concocted the whole story to obey their wishes, sensing
what the consequences from the cold, hard minister and the
immitigable magistrate would be if she said otherwise. The
court record portrays one of the most flagrant abuses of authority.
Cotton Mather, defender of New England from the infernal
enemy, and Hathorne, both prosecutor and judge, were pitting
their combined efforts against an imprisoned child who was
allowed no defense counsel. Their behavior offers an example of

184 Upham, *Salem Witchcraft*, 2:209-210.

the severe child abuse practiced by the Puritan authorities. Their verbal abuse of Sarah was at least as damaging as the physical abuse they meted out against her brothers, Richard and Andrew Carrier three weeks before.

Apparently the confessions of the two small children, Sarah Carrier and Thomas Carrier, Jr. were taken only for the purpose of adding to the weight of evidence against their mother, already condemned but not yet executed. The four imprisoned Carrier children were forced to watch their mother's execution on August 19. They did not know whether they would be next. The treatment of the Carrier children represents one of the darkest incidents in the Salem witchcraft affair.

To Cotton Mather the confessions of the Carrier children represented an important symbol. He wrote, "Before the trial of this prisoner, several of her own children had frankly and fully confessed, not only that they were witches themselves, but their mother had made them so. This confession they made with great shows of repentance, and with much demonstration of truth. They related place, time, occasion; they gave an account of journeys, meetings and mischiefs by them performed, and were very credible in what they said. This rampant hag, Martha Carrier, was the person, of whom the confessions of the witches, and her own children among the rest, agreed, that the Devil had promised her, she should be Queen of Hell."[185]

Elizabeth Proctor was reprieved until the birth of her child. On August 19, 1692, the other five condemned were carried in a cart through the streets of Salem to execution. Nathaniel Hawthorne, in *Main-Street*, recaptures the grisly scene.

"Then, here comes the worshipful Captain Corwin, sheriff of Essex, on horseback, at the head of an armed guard, escorting a company of condemned prisoners from the jail to their place of execution on Gallows Hill. The witches! There is no mistaking them! The witches! As they approach up Prison Lane, and turn into the Main-street, let us watch their faces. Listen to what the people say. There is old George Jacobs, Sr., known hereabouts,

---

185 Cotton Mather, *Wonders*, 155-159. The confessing witches were Ann
    Foster, Mary Lacey, Mary Lacey, Jr., Margaret Emerson, and Mary
    Toothaker.

these sixty years, as a man whom we thought upright in all his way of life, quiet, blameless, a good husband before his pious [first] wife was summoned from the evil to come, and a good father to the children whom she left him. There is John Willard too; an honest man we thought him, and so shrewd and active in his business, so practical, so intent on every-day affairs, so constant at his little place of trade, where he bartered English goods for Indian corn and all kinds of country produce! See that aged couple—a sad sight truly—John Proctor, and his wife Elizabeth.[186] If there were two old people in all the County of Essex who seemed to have led a true Christian life, and to be treading hopefully the little remnant of their earthly path, it was this very pair. Behind them comes a woman, with a dark, proud face that has been beautiful, and a figure that is still majestic. Do you know her? It is Martha Carrier. Last of the miserable train comes a man clad in black, of small stature and a dark complexion, with a clerical band about his neck. Many a time, in the years gone by, that face has been uplifted heavenward from the pulpit of the East Meetinghouse [in Wells, Maine], when the Reverend Mr. Burroughs seemed to worship God. What!—he? The holy man!—the learned!—the wise! Yet—to look at him—who, that had not known the proof, could believe him guilty? Who would not say, that over the dusty track of the Main-Street, a Christian saint is now going to a martyr's death."

On Gallows Hill, standing on the ladder with the noose around his neck, Burroughs proclaimed his innocence with such purpose that nearly everyone present was deeply moved. His prayer (which he concluded with the Lord's Prayer) was given with impressive composure and devotion. The scene was so affecting that it seemed for a moment that the spectators would stop the execution. Suddenly the afflicted girls, right on cue, screamed that the Black Man was standing next to him dictating the prayer. Cotton Mather, mounted upon a horse, seized the moment to address the people. Burroughs had never been properly ordained, he declared. To convince them of Burroughs'

---

186 In fact, Elizabeth Proctor was not present with the others, as she had been reprieved until the birth of her child.

guilt, Cotton Mather said that the Devil has often been transformed into an Angel of Light. Cotton Mather's speech did what was needed to distract the people. The executions went on.

Again in *Main-Street* Nathaniel Hawthorne wrote, "Ah! no; for listen to wise Cotton Mather, who as he sits there on his horse speaks comfortably to the perplexed multitude, and tells them that all has been religiously and justly done. Do you see that group of children, and half-grown girls, and among them, an old, hag-like Indian woman, Tituba by name? Those are the Afflicted Ones. Behold, at this very instant, a proof of Satan's power and malice! Betty Parris, the minister's daughter, has been smitten by a flash of Martha Carrier's eye, and falls down in the street, writhing with horrible spasms and foaming at the mouth, like the possessed ones spoken of in Scripture. Hurry on the accused witches to the gallows, ere they do more mischief."

When George Burroughs was cut down, he was dragged by the hangman's noose to a grave about two feet deep between the rocks. His shirt and breeches, the expensive clothes of a minister, were pulled from his body as loot. His body was thrown into the same grave as Willard and Carrier, and one of his hands and his chin were left uncovered.

In one day five good and innocent people had been executed. Nathaniel Hawthorne was a writer of extraordinary sensitivity. To discover the details of his ancestor's central role in this appalling business must have been deeply shaking. The knowledge must have forced an anguished re-examination of his family, of himself, and of his beliefs regarding the nature of good and evil.

13

FURTHER ARRESTS IN ANDOVER

R OBERT CALEF, IN HIS INVESTIGATIONS of the witchcraft
affair, made full use of eyewitness accounts. Regarding the
confessions, he wrote in his *More Wonders of the Invisible World*,
"It may be further added concerning those that did confess, that
besides the powerful argument, of life (and freedom from
hardships and irons not only promised, but also performed to all
that owned their guilt), there are numerous instances of the
tedious examinations before private persons, many hours
together; they all the time urging them to confess (and taking
turns to persuade them) till the accused were wearied out by
being forced to stand so long, or for want of sleep, etc. and so
brought to give an assent to what they said; they then asking
them, Were you at such a witch meeting, or have you signed the
Devil's book, etc. upon their replying, yes, the whole was drawn
into form as their confession." Yet nearly every one of the
seventy-odd people arrested during the Salem Village witch
hunt refused to confess, preferring irons and death. On the other
hand, nearly all those arrested during the Andover witch hunt
quickly confessed.

Calef continued, "That which did mightily further such
confessions, was their nearest and dearest relations urging them
to it. These seeing no other way of escape for them, thought it
the best advice that could be given; hence it was the husbands of
some, by counsel often urging, and utmost earnestness, and
children upon their knees entreating, have at length prevailed
with them, to say they were guilty."[187] Only husbands and
children from Andover did this; none from other towns urged

---

187 Calef, *More Wonders*, 273-274.

their wives and mothers to confess. Rebecca Nurse and the others had gone to their deaths with their husbands' and children's full support in their refusals to confess. The explanation for the Andover confessions can be largely traced to the Rev. Thomas Barnard. With "a word of warm, fragrant, heaven-breathing Gospel truth from his beloved lips,"[188] he convinced Andover men to urge their own wives to fabricate confessions.

It is sometimes stated that during the witch hunt there were instances of children accusing their parents.[189] This statement is misleading and inaccurate. Such accusations were nothing but the usual fabrications scripted by the authorities and placed in the official records. Typical is the examination of Thomas Carrier, Jr., aged 10, which stated, "Thomas Carrier, being accused of witchcraft confesses that he was guilty of witchcraft & that he had been a witch a week & that his mother taught him witchcraft. That a yellow bird appeared to him & spoke to him, which, she being affrighted, his mother appeared to him & spoke to him & brought him a book & bid him set his hand to it, telling him it would do him good if he did so."[190] Such patently absurd and false testimony, the concoction of sadistic magistrates and ministers, was extracted from the child by trickery and intimidation. The frightened child's garbled speech was twisted by the authorities into something they regarded as an accusation of his mother. Today the legal records stand as everlasting accusations not of the accused witches, but of the authorities and their cruel practices.

In 1692 more than one hundred seventy people were accused and imprisoned. None of the accused ever made a formal legal accusation against any family member or, for that matter, against anyone else. All formal accusations came by means of the legal complaint documents filed by the men in the small, close-knit conspiratorial groups, the two principal ones being in Salem Village and Andover. In Salem Village the conspirators'

---

188 Hawthorne, *The Scarlet Letter*, Chapter 20.
189 The conspirators made all of the formal accusations, the legal complaints. The so-called accusations by the children were effected merely to swell the tide of testimony against the accused.
190 Essex Institute, *Witchcraft Collection*, "Examinations."

accusations steered clear of their own family members. Thomas Putnam resented his half-brother Joseph Putnam, but never accused him or his family.

In Andover the situation was very different. The case of the Tyler family is unique and, by all standards, inexplicable. Moses Tyler was a leading member of the conspiracy of accusers in Andover. Using his stepdaughter Martha Sprague as an afflicted girl, Moses Tyler made many accusations. He and his fellow conspirators succeeded in sending a shocking total of eleven members of his siblings' families to prison.

On July 28, 1692, Mary (Tyler) Post Bridges, the wife of Andover blacksmith John Bridges, was accused of afflicting Timothy Swan. She was the sister of Moses Tyler, but he did nothing to prevent her arrest. Bridget Bishop and five other women had already been hanged; he well knew that the same fate could come to his sister. On August 2, Mary Post, his sister's daughter, was arrested and imprisoned for afflicting Timothy Swan. On August 25, in his first overt action against his own family, Moses Tyler filed a complaint against four of his sister Mary's family for afflicting his stepdaughter Martha Sprague. The accused were Susannah Post, Hannah Post, Sarah Bridges, and Mary Bridges, Jr. Sarah Bridges was the daughter of John Bridges by his first wife, Sarah Howe.

The table shows the women and girls of his own family whom Moses Tyler directly or indirectly accused.

Date	Accused
July 28	Mary (Tyler) Post Bridges, 48, (Moses' sister Mary)
Aug. 2	Mary Post, 28, (daughter of Moses' sister Mary)
Aug. 25	Susannah Post, 31 (stepdaughter of Moses' sister Mary)
Aug. 25	Hannah Post, 26, (daughter of Moses' sister Mary)
Aug. 25	Sarah Bridges, 17, (stepdaughter of Moses' sister Mary)
Aug. 25	Mary Bridges, Jr., 13, (daughter of Moses' sister Mary)
Aug. 31	Mary Parker, 55, (mother-in-law of Moses' brother John)
Sept. 7	Mary (Lovett) Tyler, 40, (wife of Moses' brother Hopestill)
Sept. 7	Hannah Tyler, 14, (daughter of Moses' brother Hopestill)
Sept. 7	Joanna Tyler, 11, (daughter of Moses' brother Hopestill)
Sept. 7	Martha Tyler, 11, (daughter of Moses' brother Hopestill)

Mary Parker was the mother of Hannah (Parker) Tyler, the wife of Moses' brother John Tyler. Moses Tyler accused Mary Parker of afflicting his stepdaughter Martha Sprague. Mary Parker was arrested on September 1 and was hanged on Gallows Hill on September 22, 1692.

The action of Moses Tyler against his sister, Mary (Tyler) Post Bridges, and his brothers, Hopestill Tyler and John Tyler, (none of whom took counter action against him) was far more than a hot fit of temper. It started in the summer of 1692; six months later (January 1693) his stepdaughter Martha Sprague was still testifying against his siblings' families in the trials in the Superior Court of Judicature. Moses' niece, Mary Post, was found guilty on January 12, 1693 and sentenced to death.

Moses Tyler must remain an enigma. His "judgment was embittered by one of those family feuds which render hatred the more deadly by the dead and corrupted love that they intermingle with its native poison."[191]   No historical evidence exists, no hints, no rumors to suggest an explanation for his astounding family vendetta. His motivations could have sprung from some twisted form of sibling rivalry, from a paranoid delusional personality, or from a hundred other possibilities. Clearly his character was disordered; here was a man who lacked a conscience, who lacked any sense of guilt. And it is the absence of these very traits which explains how he and his cronies became such cunning and successful witch hunters.

As just seen, the wife, Mary (Tyler) Post Bridges, and five daughters or stepdaughters, of blacksmith John Bridges were imprisoned for witchcraft by August 25, 1692. Apparently John Bridges believed that their witchcraft was real; it seems that he had fallen under a spell himself—the spell of the Rev. Thomas Barnard. "What was it? The complaint of the human heart, sorrow-laden, perchance guilty, to the great heart of mankind; beseeching its sympathy or forgiveness—at every moment—in each accent—and never in vain! It was this profound and

---

191 Hawthorne, *The House of the Seven Gables*, Chapter 8.

continual undertone that gave the clergyman his most appropriate power."[192]

Sarah Bridges, one of the imprisoned daughters of blacksmith John Bridges, was part of the extended Dane family. She was a granddaughter of the Rev. Dane's sister, Elizabeth (Dane) Howe. Two other previously accused witches were part of the same family. One was Nehemiah Abbot, Jr., a grandson of Elizabeth (Dane) Howe. The other was Elizabeth (Jackson) Howe, daughter-in-law of Elizabeth (Dane) Howe.

Nehemiah Abbot, Jr., about 29 years old, lived in Topsfield. The Salem Village conspiracy accused him of witchcraft on April 21, 1692. At his examination, the Salem Village afflicted girls failed to identify him because of a mix-up. As a result, Nehemiah gained the distinction of being the only accused person ever released after a preliminary examination.

Elizabeth (Jackson) Howe had been arrested on May 31, the same day as her cousin-in-law, Martha (Allen) Carrier. Martha was the niece of the Rev. Dane's first wife. Elizabeth (Jackson) Howe was condemned at the second meeting of the Court of Oyer and Terminer on June 30, 1692, and hanged on July 19. Martha (Allen) Carrier was condemned at the third meeting on August 5, and hanged on August 19. The condemnation of these two women demonstrated to the Andover conspirators that the Rev. Dane was indeed vulnerable.

On August 10, 1692, the Andover conspiracy made its first direct strike at the immediate family of the Rev. Francis Dane by charging his granddaughter, Elizabeth Johnson, Jr., with witchcraft. She was accused of afflicting Timothy Swan and Sarah Phelps. The next day the conspiracy struck at another member of the Rev. Dane's immediate family, his daughter, Abigail (Dane) Faulkner. She was accused of afflicting Sarah Phelps. On August 29 conspirators Moses Tyler and Samuel Martin filed a complaint against two more family members: the Rev. Dane's daughter, Elizabeth (Dane) Johnson, and his granddaughter, Abigail Johnson. They were arrested the next

---

192 Hawthorne, *The Scarlet Letter*, Chapter 22.

day, together with Stephen Johnson, his grandson. Three more family members were imprisoned on September 7.

The table shows the eight members of the Rev. Dane's immediate family who were charged and imprisoned:

August 10	his granddaughter Elizabeth Johnson, Jr., 22
August 11	his daughter Abigail (Dane) Faulkner, 40
August 29	his daughter Elizabeth (Dane) Johnson, 51
August 29	his granddaughter Abigail Johnson, 10
August 30	his grandson Stephen Johnson, 13
September 7	his son's wife Deliverance (Haseltine) Dane, 37
September 7	his granddaughter Abigail Faulkner, Jr., 9
September 7	his granddaughter Dorothy Faulkner, 12

More of the Rev. Dane's family, immediate and extended, were attacked than any other family in the entire Salem witchcraft persecution. The execution of the Rev. George Burroughs and the accusations against the Dane family were part of the old guard's plan to make examples of tolerant and liberal Puritan clergymen who were deviating too far from the orthodox line. The persecutors showed no more mercy to clergymen and their families than they did to ordinary citizens. Indeed, their treatment of Burroughs and the Dane family was vicious to an unparalleled degree.

A curious aside on the Tyler case is found in the story of Rebecca (Blake) Eames. Born in 1641, Rebecca Blake married, in 1661, Robert Eames of Rowley Village (named Boxford in 1685). Their daughter, Hannah Eames, born in 1661, married, in 1678, Ephraim Foster, one of the Andover conspirators in 1692.

Five years after Rebecca's marriage, her sister, Prudence Blake, married a man from the same town, Rowley Village (named Boxford in 1685). He was none other than Moses Tyler. Prudence (Blake) Tyler died in 1689 and Moses Tyler soon took a second wife, the widow Sarah (Hasey) Sprague. Her daughter, Martha Sprague, was sixteen in 1692. Using her as an afflicted girl, Moses Tyler made his series of vile accusations in 1692.

At the beginning of August 1692 the Andover conspiracy accused Rebecca (Blake) Eames and she was imprisoned. By

August 9, 1692, (if not earlier) the Andover conspiracy accused her son, Daniel Eames, who was also imprisoned.

On the morning of August 19, 1692, the Rev. George Burroughs, George Jacobs, Sr., John Proctor, John Willard, and Martha (Allen) Carrier were hanged at Salem. As previously noted, all of the executed had scorned confession. The authorities required certain recalcitrant prisoners to watch the executions in an effort to induce confessions. During an examination of Rebecca right after the hangings, "she was asked if she was at the execution? She was at the house below the hill. She saw a few folk. The woman of the house had a pin stuck into her foot, but she said she did not do it." After such intimidation, Rebecca started answering Hathorne's leading questions in the affirmative. To the question, "But have you been a witch 26 years?' she answered. "No, I can remember but 7 years." To the question, "Does not the Devil threaten to tear you in pieces if you do not do what he says?" she answered, "Yes, he threatens to tear me to pieces."[193] Is it surprising that her confession mimicked what the authorities wanted to hear?

Why did Hathorne mention 26 years? An explanation is to be found in her examination on August 31, 1692. "Rebecca Eames further acknowledges & declares that she was baptized about three years ago in Five Mile Pond and that her son Daniel was also then baptized by the Devil, and that her son Daniel has been a wizard about thirteen years. [She] further confirms what she formerly acknowledged, viz., that she has been a witch this 26 years, and the Devil then appeared to her in the likeness of a black man, and she then gave herself, she says, soul and body to the Devil, and that she was then in such horror of conscience, that she took a rope to hang herself, and a razor to cut her throat, by reason of her great sin in committing adultery, & by that the Devil gained her, he promising she should not be brought out or ever discovered."[194] This incident happened in 1665, shortly before Moses Tyler married Rebecca's sister, Prudence Blake. Might the Devil to whom Rebecca gave herself have been Moses Tyler?

---

193 Woodward, *Records of Salem Witchcraft*, 2:143-146.
194 Ibid.

Rebecca's daughter, Hannah (Eames) Foster, supported the activities of her conspirator husband, Ephraim Foster, in the Andover witch hunt. Hannah did so despite the fact that her mother as well as her brother, Daniel Eames, were in prison. Hannah and her daughter, Rose Foster, participated as afflicted persons in the Andover touch test on September 7, which resulted in imprisonment of some of the most respected women in Andover. Ten days later, on September 17, Hannah's mother, Rebecca (Blake) Eames, was condemned to death by the Court of Oyer and Terminer.

On August 15, 1692, the carpenter Samuel Wardwell, 49, was arrested for witchcraft. The year 1692 was a full twenty-nine years after the troubles of Samuel's brother, Eliakim Wardwell, with the Rev. Seaborn Cotton and magistrate Simon Bradstreet in 1663.   Seaborn's wife, Dorothy, was Simon Bradstreet's daughter. Might the long-held grudge be responsible in part for the carpenter's arrest? How much did Cotton Mather know about the Wardwell family from discussions with his uncle, Seaborn Cotton?

Thrown into the Salem dungeon, Wardwell refused to confess. On September 1, 1692, his wife, Sarah (Hooper) Hawkes Wardwell, 41, was arrested. Also arrested were their daughter Mercy Wardwell and Sarah's daughter Sarah Hawkes. One by one, the three women were examined by their formidable opposition, Salem magistrates John Hathorne, Jonathan Corwin, and Bartholomew Gedney. Justice of the peace John Higginson, Jr. was also present. Hathorne, as usual, did most of the questioning. "A red fire kindled in his eyes, and he made a quick pace forward, with something inexpressibly fierce and grim darkening forth, as it were, out of the whole man. To know Judge Pyncheon [Magistrate Hathorne] was to see him at that moment. And it rendered his aspect not the less, but more frightful, that it seemed not to express wrath or hatred, but a certain hot fellness of purpose, which annihilated everything but itself."[195] Samuel Wardwell, fearful of the welfare of his family if he persisted in pleading his innocence, made a confession. All that survives is an

---

195 Hawthorne, *The House of the Seven Gables*, Chapter 8.

account written by John Higginson, Jr. In it the carpenter gave the testimony as to events which supposedly happened when he had come to Andover as a young man twenty years before. "The first appearance of the cat then was behind Captain [Simon] Bradstreet's house. About a week after that a black man appeared in the daytime at the same place, and called himself prince and lord."[196]

It was known to everybody in Andover that Wardwell "told young persons their fortunes, and he was much addicted to that, and made sport of it." When Wardwell told Dorothy Eames her fortune, she said, "After that, I believed Wardwell was a witch or else he could have never told what he did." Constable Ephraim Foster confirmed that Wardwell was a fortune-teller, saying, "This I have both seen and heard several times and about several persons."[197] Foster seemed to believe that Wardwell, who so often had found amusement with magic and fortune-telling, was under the power of supernatural beings.

Following the cruel treatment of Eliakim and Lydia Wardwell by Simon Bradstreet and Seaborn Cotton, Samuel Wardwell might well have carried his own grudge. Wardwell may have fabricated a confession in an effort to save his family from hanging, but he could not resist the temptation of placing the Devil at Bradstreet's back door. Thus he made sport of his own trumped up confession in the same manner that he made sport as the local fortune teller.

On September 13 Samuel Wardwell renounced his confession. Andover historian Sarah Loring Bailey wrote in 1880, "Even in the materialism of the nineteenth century, the mystery is not all solved, of those at least almost preternatural powers which some persons seem to have in certain abnormal conditions. It cannot, therefore, be much wondered at that the simple-minded fortune-teller of the seventeenth century, in old Andover, when his minister and all the most devout magistrates told him he was a witch, should temporarily at least, believe that he was. But it shows that he had, in spite of his odd ways, more strength of character and real principle than might at first be supposed,

---

196 Woodward, *Records of Salem Witchcraft*, 2:148-152.
197 Ibid.

that he did not long remain thus obscured as to his estimate of himself. At the last, although he knew that his only hope of safety was in adhering to his confession, he wholly denied its truth. His mind, once cleared, became strong and steady, and his statements true and consistent."[198]

Wardwell's retraction was, "The written confession was taken from my mouth, and I said it, but I belied myself." He then added, "It is all one. I know I shall die for it whether I admit it or not."[199] Of all the victims he alone made such a statement. Samuel Wardwell knew that he was a marked man. He knew that he was going to hang in either case. He saw that his testimony could not help his family. He preferred to hang for the truth.

The selectmen of Andover petitioned the court at Ipswich "that whereas Samuel Wardwell and his wife were lately apprehended and committed to prison for witchcraft, and have left several small children who are incapable of providing for themselves, and are now in a suffering condition, we have thought it necessary and convenient that they should be disposed of in some families where there may be due care taken of them."[200]

198 Bailey, *Historical Sketches of Andover*, 212-213.
199 Woodward, *Records of Salem Witchcraft*, 2:150.
200 Essex County Archives. *Witchcraft*, 2:45; Bailey, *Historical Sketches of Andover*, 220-221. Baby Rebecca had gone to prison with her mother. Samuel Jr., aged 14, was put into the house of his uncle (by marriage), John Ballard; William, aged 12, was apprenticed to weaver Samuel Frye; Eliakim, aged 5, was bound out to Daniel Poor, one of the Andover selectmen; and Elizabeth, aged 3, was put in the house of John Stevens.

14

ANDOVER TOUCH TEST,
SEPTEMBER 7, 1692

O NE OF THE MOST BIZARRE AND SHOCKING EVENTS in the
entire Salem witchcraft affair was the Andover touch test.
This travesty was carried out by the Rev. Thomas Barnard. It
drew upon the delicate strands linking clergy with congregation,
husband with wife, and parent with child. The New England
Puritans habitually indulged in morbid brooding. Had they
committed an unpardonable sin? Had they scrupulously observed
each ordinance, performed the proper works, experienced the
necessary degree of faith? Because the religion of the Puritans
hinged upon questions of such enormous dimensions, one inevitable
result was an accompanying emotional intensity. In their
religious experience, the manifest theological doctrines were but
the tip of the iceberg. Submerged beneath lay a vast hidden bulk
of unconscious passions—"perpetual remorse of conscience, a
constantly defeated hope, strife among kindred, various misery,
a strange form of death, unspeakable disgrace."[201]

Typically these passions were most intense within families,
affecting the relationships between husband and wife, parents
and children, blood relatives and in-laws. "As there is a
tempting flesh, and a tempting world, which would seduce us
from our obedience to the laws of God, so there is a busy Devil,
who is called the Tempter, because by him, the temptation of the
flesh and the world are managed."[202] The Puritans had to stand

---

201 Hawthorne, *The House of the Seven Gables*, Chapter 12.
202 Cotton Mather, *Wonders*, 172.

on constant guard against sin for the Devil was always lurking in the shadows.

On Wednesday morning, September 7, 1692, the Rev. Thomas Barnard called certain members of his flock to the meetinghouse. Husbands accompanied their wives; some children were also invited. Those summoned were of impeccable standing in the community. Elders of the church came; among them were the most avid of Barnard's supporters: Captain Dudley Bradstreet and his wife Ann; Captain John Osgood and his wife, Mary; Deacon John Frye and his wife, Eunice.[203] Barnard's wife, Elizabeth, came the short distance from the parsonage to the meetinghouse. Elizabeth was the daughter of Dudley Bradstreet's wife, Ann.[204] When the people arrived, they found the Andover circle of afflicted girls already in the meetinghouse. Most of the congregation were absent. The men were working in the fields or at their trades; the women and children were at work in their households.

The Rev. Barnard opened the meeting with prayer. He delivered a short message reminiscent of a recent sermon given by Cotton Mather. "The Devil in his temptations will set the delight of the world before us. There are most hellish blasphemies often buzzed by the temptations of the Devil into the minds of the best men alive. There is witchcraft in those things. To worship the Devil is witchcraft. We are told, *Rebellion is the sin of Witchcraft.*"[205] A husband looked at his wife; he remembered some disobedient remark that she had recently made. A father looked at his daughter; she had resisted his authoritarian pronouncements.

His charismatic force rising to fever pitch, Barnard might have continued with words similar to those of Cotton Mather,

---

203 Dudley Bradstreet, John Osgood, and John Frye were sons of first proprietors of Andover. Dudley Bradstreet, 44, was the son of Ann (Dudley) and Simon Bradstreet. John Osgood, 62, was the son of Sarah (Booth) and John Osgood, Sr. John Frye, 59, was the son of Anne (Stratton) and John Frye, Sr.

204 Dudley Bradstreet's wife, Ann (Woods) Price Bradstreet, had been the widow of Thomas Price. In 1686, the Rev. Thomas Barnard, 28, took Ann's daughter, Elizabeth Price, as his wife.

205 Cotton Mather, *Wonders*, 192-195.

The house of the Rev. Thomas Barnard in North Andover

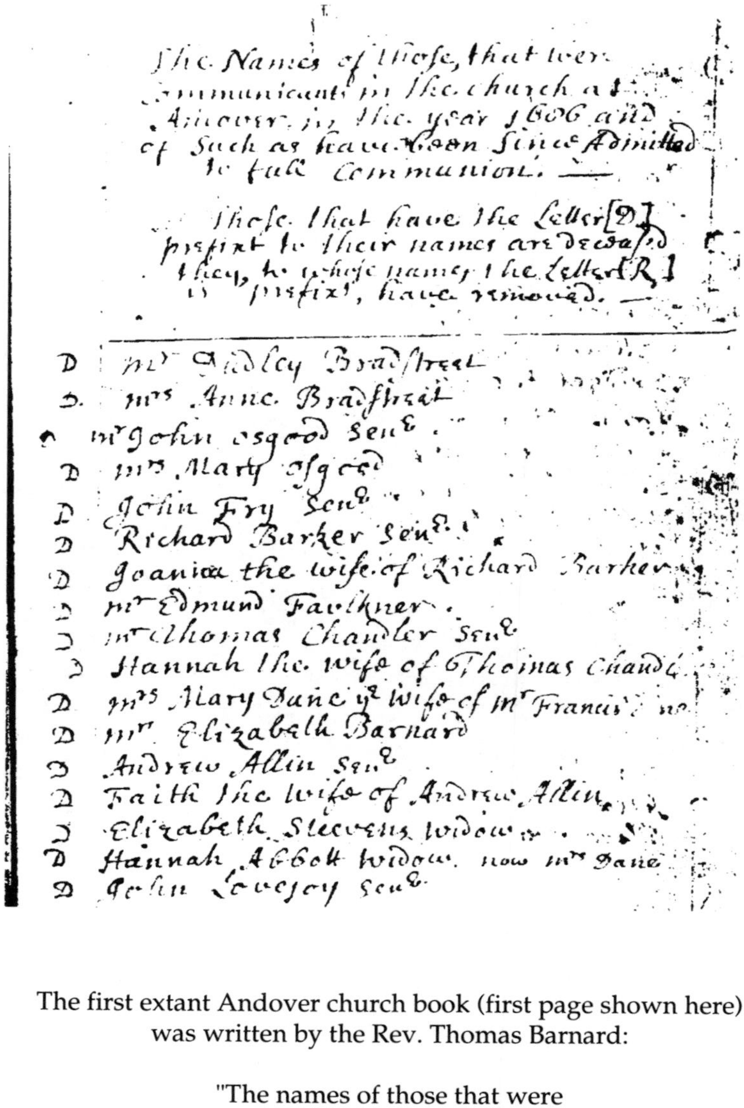

The Names of those, that were
Communicants in the church at
Andover in the year 1686 and
of Such as have been Since Admitted
to full Communion.

Those that have the Letter [D]
prefixt to their names are deceased,
they, to whose names the Letter [R]
is prefixt, have removed.

D   mr Dudley Bradstreet
D   mrs Anne Bradstreet
     mr John Osgood senr
D   mrs Mary Osgood
D   John Fry senr
D   Richard Barker senr
D   Joanna the wife of Richard Barker
D   mr Edmund Faulkner
D   mr Thomas Chandler senr
D   Hannah the wife of Thomas Chandler
D   mrs Mary Dane yr wife of mr Francis
D   mr Elizabeth Barnard
D   Andrew Allin senr
D   Faith the wife of Andrew Allin
D   Elizabeth Stevens widow
D   Hannah Abbot widow now mrs Dane
D   John Lovejoy senr

The first extant Andover church book (first page shown here)
was written by the Rev. Thomas Barnard:

"The names of those that were
Communicants in the church at
Andover in the year 1686 and
of Such as have been since Admitted
to full Communion."

"When the Devil would have us to sin, he would have us to do the things which the forlorn witches do. Perhaps there are few persons, ever allured by the Devil unto an explicit covenant with himself. If any among ourselves be so, my counsel is, that you hunt the Devil from you."[206] The women and children in the audience quaked. In their rebellion had they covenanted with the Devil?

Now in the heat of passion, Barnard in ringing tones thundered home the central message to which he had been building. The following are the words of Nathaniel Hawthorne. Barnard's words, now lost to history, must have been equally powerful. "Ye have found your nature and your destiny. There are all whom you have reverenced from youth. Ye deemed them holier than yourselves, and shrank from your own sin, contrasting it with their lives of righteousness, and prayerful aspirations heavenward. Yet, here are they all, in my worshipping assembly! This night it shall be granted that you to know their secret deeds; how hoary-bearded elders of the church have whispered wanton words to the young maids of their households; how many a woman, eager for widow's weeds, has given her husband a drink at bed-time, and let him sleep his last sleep in her bosom; how beardless youths have made haste to inherit their father's wealth; and how fair damsels—blush not, sweet ones—have dug little graves in the garden, and bidden me, the sole guest to an infant's funeral. By the sympathy of your human hearts for sin, ye shall scent out all the places—whether in church, bed-chamber, street, field or forest—where crime has been committed, and shall exult to behold the whole earth one stain of guilt, one mighty blood-spot. Far more than this! It shall be yours to penetrate, in every bosom, the deep mystery of sin, the foundation of all wicked arts. And now, my children, look upon each other." They did so, and the wretched man beheld his wife, and the wife her husband. The husband cried, "Look up to heaven and resist the Wicked One!"[207]

Five of the women present, Mary Osgood, Deliverance Dane, Sarah (Lord) Wilson, Mary (Lovett) Tyler, Abigail Barker, and

---

206 Ibid.
207 Hawthorne, *Young Goodman Brown*, 286-288.

one girl, Hannah Tyler, later made this statement about what followed. "After Mr. Barnard had been at prayer, we were blindfolded, and our hands were laid upon the afflicted persons, they being in their fits and falling into their fits at our coming into their presence, as they said. Some led us and laid our hands upon them, and then they said they were well, and that we were guilty of afflicting them; whereupon we were all seized, as prisoners, by a warrant from the justice of the peace [Dudley Bradstreet], and forthwith carried to Salem.

"And by reason of that sudden surprise, we knowing ourselves altogether innocent of that crime, we were all exceedingly astonished and amazed, and consternated and affrighted even out of our reason; and our nearest and dearest relations, seeing us in that dreadful condition, and knowing our great danger, apprehending that there was no other way to save our lives, as the case was then circumstantiated, but by our confessing ourselves to be such and such persons as the afflicted represented us to be, they, out of tender love and pity, persuaded us to confess what we did confess.

"And indeed that confession, that it is said we made, was no other than what was suggested to us by some gentlemen, they telling us that we were witches, and they knew it, and we knew it, and they knew that we knew it, which made us think it was so; and our understanding, our reason, our faculties almost gone, we were not capable of judging our condition; as also the hard measures they used with us rendered us incapable of making our defense, but said anything and everything which they desired, and most of what we said was but in effect a consenting to what they said. Some time after, when we were better composed, they telling us of what we had confessed, we did profess that we were innocent, and ignorant of such things; and we hearing that Samuel Wardwell had renounced his confession, and quickly after condemned and executed, some of us were told that we were going after Wardwell."[208]

---

208 Calef, *More Wonders*, 272-273. Wardwell renounced his confession on September 13, was condemned on September 17, and hanged on September 22.

On October 8, 1692, one month after the touch test, Thomas Brattle wrote, "Deacon Frye's wife, Captain Osgood's wife, and some others, remarkably pious and good people in repute, are apprehended and imprisoned [at the touch test]; and that that is more admirable, the forementioned women are become a kind of confessors, being first brought thereto by the urgings of their good husbands, who having taken up that corrupt and highly pernicious opinion, that whoever were accused by the afflicted, were guilty, did break charity with their dear wives, upon their being accused, and urged them to confess their guilt; which so far prevailed with them as to make them say, they were afraid they were in the snare of the Devil; and which, through the rude and barbarous methods that were afterwards used in Salem, issued in somewhat plainer degrees of confession, and was attended with prison. The good Deacon and Captain are now sensible of their error they were in; do now grieve and mourn bitterly, that they should break charity with their own wives, and urge them to confess themselves witches. They now see and acknowledge their rashness and uncharitableness."[209]

Torn from their homes without warning, stripped of their dignity and their rights, these women with terror in their hearts found themselves being carted off to Salem prison. A storm of slander was breaking over their heads; an inner storm raged too. When finally they emerged from the abyss of witchcraft madness, they recognized that they had penetrated the deepest and most painful layers of awareness and experience.

John Bridges, the blacksmith, was present during the touch test on September 7. A few weeks before he had doubted his own wife, Mary (Tyler) Post Bridges, who was now in prison, together with two of his own daughters and three of his stepdaughters. Now his sister-in-law, Mary (Lovett) Tyler, about 40, was accused at the touch test. That she might be innocent seemed preposterous to him.

On October 19, 1692 the Rev. Increase Mather went to Salem to visit the confessors in prison. He conferred with several of

---

209   Brattle, "Letter of October 8, 1692," in Burr, *Narratives*, 180-181.

them, and wrote the following account.[210]   "Goodwife [Mary (Lovett)] Tyler did say, that when she was first apprehended, she had no fears upon her, and did think that nothing could have made her confess against herself; but since, she has found to her great grief, that she has wronged the truth, and falsely accused herself.   She said, that when she was brought to Salem, her brother[-in-law John] Bridges rode with her; and that, all along the way from Andover to Salem, he kept telling her that she must needs be a witch, since the afflicted accused her, and at her touch were raised out of their fits, and urging her to confess herself a witch.   She as constantly told him that she was no witch, that she knew nothing of witchcraft, and begged him not to urge her to confess.   However, when she came to Salem, she was carried to a room, where her brother[-in-law John Bridges] on one side, and [the Rev.] Mr. John Emerson [of Gloucester], on the other side, did tell her that she was certainly a witch, and that she saw the Devil before her eyes at that time (and, accordingly, the said Emerson would attempt with his hand to beat him away from her eyes); and they so urged her to confess, that she wished herself in any dungeon, rather than be so treated.   Mr. Emerson told her, once and again, 'Well, I see you will not confess! Well, I will now leave you, and then you are undone, body and soul, for ever.'

"Her brother[-in-law John Bridges] urged her to confess, and told her that, in so doing, she could not lie. To which she answered, 'Good brother, do not say so; for I shall lie if I confess, and then who shall answer unto God for my lie?'   He still asserted it, and said that God would not suffer so many good men to be in such an error about it, and that she would be hanged if she did not confess; and continued so long and so violently to urge and press her to confess, that she thought, verily, that her life would have gone from her, and became so terrified in her mind that she owned, at length, almost anything that they propounded to her. That she had wronged her conscience in so doing; she was guilty of a great sin in belying of herself, and desire to mourn for it so long as she lived.   This she said, and a

---

210   The account written by Increase Mather is preserved in Upham, *Salem Witchcraft*, 2:404-405 and also in Burr, *Narratives*, 376.

great deal more of the like nature; and all with such affection, sorrow, relenting, grief, and mourning, as that it exceeds any pen to describe and express the same."

The following persons, called by the Rev. Barnard to take the touch-test on September 7, 1692, were arrested and imprisoned.

Mary (Clement) Osgood	about 55
Eunice (Potter) Frye	51
Abigail (Wheeler) Barker	36
Mary (Lovett) Tyler	40
Hannah Tyler	14
Joanna Tyler	11
Martha Tyler	11
Deliverance (Haseltine) Dane	about 37
Rebecca (Aslet) Johnson, widow	40
Rebecca Johnson, Jr.	17
Abigail Faulkner, Jr.	9
Dorothy Faulkner	12
Sarah (Lord) Wilson	44
Sarah Wilson, Jr.	14
John Sadie, Jr.	13
Henry Salter	about 65
Male slave of Nathaniel Dane	unknown
Joseph Draper	21

Why were these particular people singled out to come together at the meeting house in Andover to be put to the touch test? Carefully selected beforehand, all were members of the Andover elite. Mary Osgood was the second highest ranking woman in Andover, coming only after Dudley Bradstreet's wife, Ann. Eunice Frye was the deacon's wife. Abigail Barker was the daughter-in-law of proprietor Richard Barker. Deliverance (Haseltine) Dane was the Rev. Dane's daughter-in-law. Abigail Faulkner, Jr., and Dorothy Faulkner were the Rev. Dane's granddaughters. Throughout the Andover witch hunt, whenever the girls in the afflicted circle went into their fits, other children present would "be taken in fits, and have the same spectral sight."[211] The children present at the Andover touch test were no exception; they acted out the symptoms of demonic possession but, as the above table shows, eight of them were scooped up with the adults nonetheless and imprisoned as witches.

In the eight weeks from July 15, 1692, until the touch test on September 7, Dudley Bradstreet, acting in his capacity as justice of the peace, had granted out arrest warrants[212] against, and committed, some thirty Andover persons to prisons for supposed witchcrafts. Now, on September 7, Dudley Bradstreet dutifully wrote out the arrest warrants for the eighteen who were accused in the touch test. Finally, however, he understood that the leading citizens of Andover were being targeted. In the settlement of Andover, it had been first come, first serve; Johnny-come-lately was given the crumbs, small farms on marginal land. The controlling elite—those who gained their large land-holdings by the good fortune of being the town's first settlers—were now under attack. The Barkers, the third ranking family, and the Osgoods, the second ranking family, had been accused. The Bradstreets were the first ranking family; would they be next?

Dudley Bradstreet came to his senses. His warrants had put in jail nearly fifty Andover citizens. After the touch test, he refused to grant out any more warrants. Soon after his decision, Dudley Bradstreet and his wife, Ann, were cried out upon. The afflicted claimed he had killed nine persons by witchcraft. In response, Bradstreet and his wife found escape their safest course and in short order they fled from Massachusetts. "Captain [Dudley] Bradstreet and Mr. [Ephraim] Stevens are complained of by the afflicted, have left the town, and do abscond," wrote Thomas Brattle on October 8, 1692.[213]

---

211 Calef, *More Wonders*, 268. Despite their claimed spectral sight, these other children were never admitted to the privileged Andover afflicted circle made up entirely of children of the conspirators.

212 Provided the case had merit, an arrest warrant would be granted out by a justice or magistrate in response to a written, legal complaint filed by one or more accusers.

213 Brattle, "Letter of October 8, 1692," in Burr, *Narratives*, 180.

The touch test was cunningly executed. The elite of Andover were caught off guard. Captain Osgood, Deacon Frye, and others had urged their wives to confess. Apparently these men, pillars of the church, believed the message preached by Barnard that confession was the way to eternal life. They also may have hoped that confession would save the lives of their wives. It was a grotesque and horrifying scene. "Here it was that many accused themselves of riding upon poles through the air; many parents believing their children to be witches, and many husbands their wives, etc."[214]

Not until their wives and children were in prison, did the minds of these men begin to clear. They then realized that they had been deceived by the fanaticism of their younger minister, Thomas Barnard. These good men of Andover now began to comprehend the full implications of the storm raging in their midst. They turned to their older minister, the Rev. Francis Dane, and formed a resistance movement. Under his guidance they started to take the strong steps required to free the imprisoned members of their families.

214 Calef, *More Wonders*, 268.

15

FOURTH AND FIFTH TRIALS, SEPTEMBER 9 AND 17, 1692

M OST OF THE WOMEN ARRESTED at the Andover touch test were examined in Salem the next day, September 8, 1692. All confessed; many had been urged to admit they were agents of the Devil by their own husbands. Some husbands may have been convinced that confession would save the souls of their wives; others may have believed that confession would spare their wives' lives. All had fallen hopelessly under the spell of the black-hatted, black-frocked Andover minister, Thomas Barnard. They had been lured by his sermons "to barter the transitory pleasures of the world for the heavenly hope, that was to assume brighter substance as life grew dark."[215]

Contrast the behavior of the Andover group to that of the seventy-odd people imprisoned during the Salem Village phase of the witch hunt. Few, if any, of them had fallen under the spell of their ministers. Recall that only five—Abigail Hobbs, Deliverance Hobbs, Margaret Jacobs[216] and the slaves, Tituba and Candy—had confessed. Those remaining had refused to confess under any conditions; eleven of these non-confessors had been executed.

The fourth meeting of the Court of Oyer and Terminer was held on Friday, September 9, 1692, two days after the Andover touch test. Six women arrested during the Salem Village witch hunt were tried: Martha Corey of Salem Village, Mary Easty of Topsfield, Alice Parker of Salem, Ann Pudeator of Salem, Dorcas

---

215 Hawthorne, *The Scarlet Letter*, Chapter 20.
216 Margaret Jacobs retracted her confession on August 18, 1692.

Hoar of Beverly, and Mary Bradbury of Salisbury. These six adamantly refused to confess; they were condemned to death.

After the conviction of Martha Corey, the following entry was made in the church records of the Rev. Samuel Parris, "11 September, Lord's Day.—Sister Martha Corey was, after examination upon suspicion of witchcraft, committed to prison, and was condemned to the gallows for the same yesterday; and was this day in public voted to be excommunicated out of the church. Accordingly, this 14 September 1692, three brethren went with the pastor to her in Salem prison; whom we found very obdurate, justifying herself, and condemning all that had done anything to her just discovery or condemnation. Whereupon, after a little discourse, for her imperiousness would not suffer much, and after prayer—which she was willing to decline—the dreadful sentence of excommunication was pronounced against her."[217] Even as she awaited the hangman, Martha Corey would not yield an inch to the Rev. Samuel Parris.

On Saturday, September 17, 1692, the fifth and, as it turned out, the last meeting of the Court of Oyer and Terminer was held. John Hathorne was one of the justices sitting for this session. Eight women and one man were tried and sentenced to death. Two of the women had been arrested in the Salem Village witch hunt; they were Wilmot Redd of Marblehead and Abigail Hobbs of Topsfield. Six of the women and the man had been arrested in the Andover witch hunt; they were Margaret Scott of Rowley, Mary Parker of Andover, Abigail (Dane) Faulkner of Andover, Rebecca Eames of Boxford, Ann Foster of Andover, Mary (Foster) Lacey of Andover, and Samuel Wardwell of Andover. It is significant that the Andover residents, only recently imprisoned, were brought to trial abruptly whereas many others, long in prison, still were awaiting trial. The authorities apparently wanted to start confiscating property in Andover without further delay. However, by this time the families of the original proprietors were starting to join together in a resistance movement to oppose the witch hunt.

The September 17 court meeting was held primarily for people arrested during the Andover witch hunt; Wilmot Redd

217 Upham, *Salem Witchcraft*, 2:324-325.

and Abigail Hobbs apparently were afterthoughts. Margaret Scott, arrested during the Andover witch hunt, was not from Andover, Boxford or Haverhill, the three main towns involved, and so presents a special case. A seventy-year-old woman, a widow of twenty years, she was arrested about August 4. Little is known about the details of her arrest as there are no complaints, warrants or examinations extant. She would not confess.

Previous to the September 17 meeting of the court, no one who had confessed had been brought to trial. Because nearly everyone from Andover had confessed, the only way to have a trial for Andover people was to include confessors. Of the nine called for trial, Wilmot Redd, Margaret Scott, and Mary Parker never confessed; Samuel Wardwell confessed but afterwards recanted. The remaining five—Rebecca Eames, Abigail (Dane) Faulkner, Ann Foster, Mary (Foster) Lacey, and Abigail Hobbs—had confessed. Abigail Hobbs, aged 22, previously had been a darling of the court. She was the first (after Tituba) to confess in the Salem Village witch hunt, as noted earlier. While in prison she had willingly acted as an afflicted person in the courtroom. As a confessing witch she had accused many of witchcraft and worked to please the magistrates. But now that the court had many confessing witches from Andover, Abigail Hobbs was dispensable.

One explanation for the arrest of the children of Andover was to collect testimony against their parents and others.[218] For example, the authorities had not been able to get a satisfactory confession from Abigail (Dane) Faulkner. The best attempt was on August 30, when Abigail (Dane) Faulkner "at first denied witchcraft as she had done before, but afterwards she owned that she was angry at what folks said when her niece, Elizabeth Johnson, Jr., was taken up. She did look with an evil eye upon the afflicted persons & did consent that they should be afflicted, because they were the cause of bringing her kindred out. And she did wish them ill & her spirit being raised she did pinch her hands together but it was the Devil not she that afflicted them."

218 The authorities regarded a person eighteen years or under as a child when they allowed the release of imprisoned children on bail starting in October 1693.

This statement was the only concession that she made. Even to Puritan fanatics, it barely qualified as a confession. On September 7, two of her children, Abigail Faulkner, Jr., 9 and Dorothy Faulkner, 12, were arrested at the touch test. A memorandum was written that the two children "now in prison confessed before the honored magistrates upon their examination here in Salem, the 16 day of this instant September 1692, that [the specter of] their mother appeared before them and made them witches." The next day, September 17, at the trial of their mother, the two children were made to "affirm before the grand inquest that the above written evidences are truth."[219] The magistrates, as usual, twisted the terrified children's references to their mother into a witchcraft accusation.

Mercy Wardwell, 18, was among the children brought to the courtroom to read and affirm the confessions drawn up for them. On September 15 Mercy was shown her confession; it contained the statement, "Her companions were her father, mother, sister Sarah Hawkes, and William Barker."[220] Realizing that the magistrates intended to use this statement as evidence against her father at his trial, and against her mother if she came to trial, Mercy retracted her words. The scribe wrote, "Said she did not know that her father and mother were witches." On the next day, September 16, Mercy was again brought into the courtroom at the grand jury inquest for Mary Parker. Along with the other Andover children, Mercy had acted the role of an afflicted girl at the examination of Mary Parker on September 2. Mary Parker, aged 55 and a widow, had refused to confess.[221] When Mercy understood that the magistrates intended to use the part she played as an afflicted person as evidence against Mary Parker, Mercy once again refused to fall in line. The scribe wrote that Mercy said, "I did not certainly know that said Parker was a

219 Woodward, *Records of Salem Witchcraft*, 2:129-135.
220 Sarah Hawkes was not scheduled for trial and William Barker had escaped. William Barker and Samuel Wardwell, good friends, were free-thinkers of Andover.
221 On September 2, when John Hathorne asked, "How long have ye been in the snare of the Devil?" Mary Parker resolutely answered, "I know nothing of it." (Essex County Archives, *Witchcraft*, 2:30.)

witch."[222]   On both occasions Mercy might well have renounced more had she not been cut off by the hostile magistrates.

Giles Corey, the husband of the condemned Martha Corey, stood mute; that is, he refused to plead either guilty or not guilty. As a result, the law said that he could not be tried by jury. The enraged judges used an archaic law against this man. They would crush him by piling large stones upon him until he made a plea. Corey remained adamant and would not enter a plea. During the pressing, his tongue was pressed out of his mouth; Sheriff Corwin used his cane to force it in again as he lay dying. The day was September 19, 1692.

In the two court meetings in September, fourteen women and one man were condemned. The magistrates intended to hang them all. But the half-dozen or so ministers directing the clerical aspects of the witch hunt objected. To reject the charge that spectral evidence alone was used for conviction, these ministers had made valiant attempts to induce confessions. The Rev. Barnard, in sharp contrast to his Salem Village counterpart, Samuel Parris, had obtained a nearly perfect success ratio; everyone from his parish in Andover had confessed, except for two.[223] The execution of confessors at this juncture might bring further confessions to a screeching halt. The decision was made not to hang the five condemned who had confessed—Abigail (Dane) Faulkner,[224] Rebecca Eames, Mary (Foster) Lacey, Ann Foster, and Abigail Hobbs. Instead they would be held in prison until the time was ripe. But the ten condemned who were non-confessors would be hanged on schedule. One was Mary Bradbury, wife of Thomas Bradbury. Recall that he was the court clerk at

---

222   Essex Institute, *Witchcraft Collection*, "Examinations."

223   The two Andover non-confessors were Martha Carrier and Mary Parker. In addition, there were two Andover recanters, Samuel Wardwell, who completely renounced his confession, and his daughter Mercy Wardwell, who partially renounced hers.   Martha Carrier, arrested as part of the Salem Village witch hunt, was hanged on August 19, 1692. Mary Parker and Samuel Wardwell, both condemned on September 17, were hanged on September 22, 1692.

224   Abigail Faulkner had made a weak confession, if one at all. In any case Abigail Faulkner was temporarily safe from the hangman because she was pregnant.

Salisbury when the three Quaker women were flogged in 1662. Mary Bradbury was allowed to escape.

Now there were nine who would be hanged. Among them was Dorcas Hoar who belonged to the parish of the Rev. John Hale of Beverly. This was Hale's time to shine. He convinced Dorcas that confession would save her life, at least for a little while. John Hale, together with three other ministers, Nicholas Noyes, Daniel Epes, and John Emerson, drew up a petition in which they stated that Dorcas was ready to confess the witchcraft for which she was already condemned. They said that she had identified others guilty of the same crime. They requested that she be granted a month's additional time or more to prepare for death. They warned that, if she relapsed or again started afflicting others by witchcraft, there would be grounds to hasten her execution. The four ministers ended the petition by saying that her short reprieve might not only tend to save her soul, but also encourage others to confess and give glory to God. The four submitted the petition on Wednesday, September 21. Later that day magistrate Bartholomew Gedney heard her confession and consented that her execution be reprieved until further order. This petition, better than any other extant document, stated the explicit position of the clergy who were driving the witch hunt. They regarded confessions as essential; to encourage others to confess, they deemed that only non-confessing witches should be hanged until further developments.

With Dorcas Hoar plucked from the hangman, eight were left. These eight—seven women and one man—were hanged on Thursday, September 22, a chill and rainy day. They were Martha Corey, Mary Easty, Alice Parker, Ann Pudeator, Margaret Scott, Wilmot Redd, Mary Parker, and Samuel Wardwell. All had remained resolute in their refusals to confess. In the morning the eight were loaded onto a cart. When the cart reached the outskirts of the town, it turned off the main road and began to climb Gallows Hill. In going up the hill, the cart became stuck in a muddy rut. The afflicted girls following close behind chanted, "The Devil hinders the cart."[225]

---

225 Calef, *More Wonders*, 265.

The courage of these eight who had refused to fabricate confessions was truly astonishing. Martha Corey, wife to Giles Corey, protested her innocence upon the ladder and concluded her life with a prayer. Martha Corey had been imprisoned since March 21. Mary Easty, sister of Rebecca Nurse, took her last farewell of her husband, children and friends. Those present reported that it was distinct, devout, and affectionate, drawing tears from the eyes of many.

Ann Pudeator, widowed in 1682, held two valuable estates in Salem Town. After her condemnation she petitioned the Court, saying that "the evidence of John Best, Sr., and John Best, Jr., and Samuel Pickworth, which was given against me in Court, were all of them false and untrue, and, beside the above-said John Best has been formerly whipped and likewise is recorded for a liar. I would humbly beg of your honors to take it into your judicious and pious consideration, that my life not be taken away by such false evidences and witnesses as these be. Likewise, the evidence given in against me by Sarah Churchill and Mary Warren I am altogether ignorant of, and know nothing in the least measure about it, nor nothing else concerning the crime of witchcraft, for which I am condemned to die."[226] Not interested in the truth, the Court took no heed of her petition.

Mary Parker was the widow of Nathan Parker, an original proprietor of Andover. The Parker land was extensive and valuable, lying adjacent to the Wardwell farm. After Mary's execution, sheriff George Corwin, sent an officer to Andover to seize her estate, saying it was forfeited to the king. The officer seized the cattle, corn, and hay, and ordered her two sons to go to Salem and make a deal with Corwin, or else the land would be exposed to sale. Corwin settled with the sons, demanding £10 from them but taking £6. Apparently Corwin feared the mounting opposition of Andover's leading families, closing ranks to prevent land confiscation in Andover. The Parker land was saved.

When it was his turn, Wardwell spoke to the people claiming his innocence. The executioner stood beside him, smoking. Smoke blew into Wardwell's face and interrupted his

---

226 Upham, *Salem Witchcraft*, 2:329-330.

words.   The afflicted girls chanted, "The Devil hinders Wardwell with smoke."   After the execution the Rev. Nicholas Noyes, pointing to the bodies, declared, "What a sad thing it is to see eight firebrands of hell hanging there."[227]

That evening, Thursday September 22, justices William Stoughton, John Hathorne, and Samuel Sewall met with Cotton Mather to help him prepare his forthcoming book, *The Wonders of the Invisible World*.   These men were the hard core of the Puritan old-guard witch hunters.   It was raining so hard that William Stoughton stayed overnight and left early in the morning.   Cotton Mather recognized William Stoughton as "a real friend to New England."[228]

A commemorative stone for the executed victims has never been placed on Gallows Hill.   Today the place serves as a town park.   Except for a small corner set aside for a playing field, the hill still remains in its natural state.   There are few such fine views of Salem as from this tragic spot.   The city, embraced by two arms of the sea, extends from the foot of the hill to the harbor.   Beyond stretch the bay and the islands.   Mankind has desecrated the Earth, but time has not changed the ocean.   The sea looks as it did to those who died on Gallows Hill.   No one has identified the precise spot of the burials; the innocent rest in graves uncoffined and unknown.

> Fear no more the heat of the sun,
> Nor the furious winter's rages;
> Thou thy worldly task hast done,
> Home art gone, and ta'en thy wages.[229]

---

227 Calef, *More Wonders*, 262-265.
228 Thomas Hutchinson, *History of Massachusetts-Bay*, 1:365.
229 Shakespeare, *Cymbeline*, Act 4, Sc. 2.

16

THE ANDOVER CONFESSIONS

ONLY ABOUT A DOZEN MINISTERS were actively engaged in the witch hunt. Their acknowledged leader was Cotton Mather; he interacted directly with the civil authorities, giving advice and instructions when needed. It was essential that all confessions adhered to established church doctrine. Cotton Mather set the tone in his letter of May 31, 1692, giving instructions to John Richards, one of the justices of the Court of Oyer and Terminer. "Now first a credible confession of the guilty wretches is one of the most hopeful ways of coming at them, & I say a credible confession, because even confession itself sometimes is not credible. All the difficulty is how to obtain this confession. For this I am far from urging the un-English method of torture [physical torture]. What ever has a tendency to put the witches into confusion, is likely to bring them unto confession too. Here cross & swift questions have their use."[230] These words of Cotton Mather about a credible confession served as a guideline throughout the witch hunt.

Cotton Mather's father, Increase Mather, was also prominent at high levels in the witch hunt, but he was much less fanatic than his son. At the operational level of the witch hunt were the Rev. Samuel Parris, a member of the Salem Village conspiracy, and the Rev. Thomas Barnard, a member of the Andover conspiracy. Assisting from the sidelines were the Rev. Nicholas Noyes, assistant minister at Salem, the Rev. John Hale of Beverly, and the Rev. Deodat Lawson, a former minister at Salem Village who visited Salem Village during the initial phase of the Salem Village witch hunt. Other ministers,

---

230 Cotton Mather, "Letter of May 31, 1692 to John Richards."

including John Emerson, Daniel Epes, Zachariah Symmes, and Samuel Cheever, also played some role in the summer of 1692.[231]

Confessions were needed for various purposes. The civil authorities wanted to use accusations made by confessing witches to implicate others as witches. Some of the clergy were convinced that confessions helped to establish the reality of the invisible world of the Devil, a favorite theme in their sermons. Cotton Mather wrote, "There is witchcraft. First we have the testimony of Scripture for it: Exod. 22:18, *Thou shalt not suffer a witch to live.* Secondly we have the testimony of experience for it. Many witches have like those in Acts 19:18 confessed and showed their deeds. This confession is often made by them that are owners of as much reason as the people that laugh at all conceit of witchcraft. There can be no judgment left of any human affairs if such confessions must be ridiculed."[232]

The ministers visited the prisons to confer with the prisoners in an effort to elicit confessions. "The prison being full of persons committed on suspicion of witchcraft, I went and preached unto the persons in prison, (on Act. 24, 25) with a special help from the spirit of the Lord," wrote Cotton Mather of his activities during the summer of 1692.[233] The Rev. John Hale also wrote that he talked with the inmates of the prison. The Rev. John Emerson, on a visit to the prison, told Mary (Lovett) Tyler that she was certainly a witch and urged her to confess.

The following table lists all the known confessors in the Salem tragedy, their marital status and age, and the date of their first confession. The first five, Tituba, Abigail Hobbs, Deliverance Hobbs, Margaret Jacobs (who later recanted), and Candy were part of the Salem Village witch hunt; the rest, except Dorcas Hoar, were part of the Andover witch hunt. Eight of the confessors were brought to trial and condemned: Abigail

---

231 Because of the doings of a few ministers, the whole Puritan church has been disgraced in the eyes of history. In the fall of 1692, Increase Mather and other ministers representing the majority of the clergy played a significant role in bringing the tragedy to an end.

232 Cotton Mather, *A Discourse on Witchcraft.*

233 Cotton Mather, "Diary," Summer, 1692.

Hobbs, Ann Foster, Mary (Foster) Lacey, Rebecca Eames, and Abigail (Dane) Faulkner were condemned on September 17, 1692; the other three, Mary Post, Elizabeth Johnson, Jr., and Sarah Wardwell were condemned in January 1693. None of these eight were executed, although Ann Foster died in prison. Samuel Wardwell, who confessed and then recanted, was brought to trial and condemned on September 17 and was executed on September 22. Dorcas Hoar, who did not confess originally, was brought to trial and condemned on September 9, but confessed on September 21 and was spared execution.

Confessor	Status and age	Date of Confession
Tituba	Married slave	Mar. 2, 1692
Abigail Hobbs, condemned	Single, 22	Apr. 19
Deliverance Hobbs	Married, 45	Apr. 22
Margaret Jacobs	Single, 16	May 11; recanted August 18.
Candy	Slave	July 4
Ann (mnu) Foster, condemned	Widow, 72	July 15
Mary (Foster) Lacey, condemned	Married, 40	July 21
Mary Lacey, Jr.	Single, 18	July 21
Richard Carrier	Single, 18	July 22
Andrew Carrier	Single, 15	July 22
Martha (Toothaker) Emerson	Married, 24	July 23
Mary (Tyler) Post Bridges	Married, 50	c. July 30
Mary Toothaker	Widow, 47	July 30
Hannah Brumidge	Married, 59	July 30
Mary Post, condemned	Single, 28	Aug. 3
Thomas Carrier, Jr.	Single, 10	Aug. 10
Sarah Carrier	Single, 7	Aug. 10
Elizabeth Johnson, Jr., condemned	Single, 22	Aug. 11
Rebecca (Blake) Eames, condemned	Married, 51	Aug. 19
Sarah Bridges	Single, 17	Aug. 25
Mary Bridges, Jr.	Single, 13	Aug. 25
Hannah Post	Single, 26	Aug. 25
Susannah Post	Single, 31	Aug. 25
John Jackson, Jr.	Single, 22	Aug. 27
Mary (Osgood) Marston	Married, 27	Aug. 29
William Barker, Sr.	Married, 46	Aug. 29
Mary Barker	Single, 13	Aug. 29

Elizabeth (Dane) Johnson	Widow, 51	Aug. 30
Sarah Parker	Single, 22	Aug. 30
Abigail Johnson	Single, 10	Aug. 30
Abigail (Dane) Faulkner, condemned	Single, 40	Weak confession, Aug. 30
Stephen Johnson	Single, 13	Sept. 1
William Barker, Jr.	Single, 14	Sept. 1
Samuel Wardwell, condemned and executed	Married, 49	Sept. 1; recanted Sept. 13.
Sarah (Hooper) Hawkes Wardwell, condemned	Married, 42	Sept. 1
Sarah Hawkes	Single, 21	Sept. 1
Mercy Wardwell	Single, 18	Sept. 1; recanted in part Sept. 15.
Mary (Harrington) Taylor	Married, 34	Sept. 5
Henry Salter	64	Sept. 7
Rebecca (Aslet) Johnson	Widow, 40	Sept. 7
Rebecca Johnson, Jr.	Single, 17	Sept. 7
Mary (Clement) Osgood	Married, 55	Sept. 8
Deliverance (Haseltine) Dane	Married, 35	Sept. 8
Sarah (Lord) Wilson	Married, 44	Sept. 8
Mary (Lovett) Tyler	Married, 40	Sept. 8
Abigail (Wheeler) Barker	Married, 36	Sept. 8
Hannah Tyler	Single, 14	Sept. 8
Eunice (Potter) Frye	Married, 51	Sept. 8
Joseph Draper	Single, 21	Sept. 16
Dorothy Faulkner	Single, 10	Sept. 16
Abigail Faulkner, Jr.	Single, 8	Sept. 16
Martha Tyler	Single, 11	Sept. 16
Joanna Tyler	Single, 11	Sept. 16
Sarah Wilson, Jr.	Single, 14	Sept. 16
Dorcas (Galley) Hoar, condemned	Widow, 58	Sept. 21

Of the ministers taking part in the witch hunt, the Rev. Thomas Barnard was preeminent in eliciting confessions from his parishioners. Except for Tituba, Abigail Hobbs, Deliverance Hobbs, Margaret Jacobs (who later recanted), Candy, Martha Emerson, Mary Toothaker, Hannah Brumidge, John Jackson, Jr., Mary Taylor, and Dorcas Hoar, all the confessors belonged the Andover church. That is, out of a total of 55 known confessors, 44 belonged to Barnard's congregation. Barnard failed to obtain confessions from just two of his congregation, Martha Carrier and Mary Parker. In addition, two Andover confessors recanted: Samuel Wardwell completely and his daughter Mercy partially. After Wardwell's execution on September 22, a fear shot through the Andover confessors. Afraid of Wardwell's fate, none dared recant her confession. The following table lists the only three prisoners in the Salem witchcraft tragedy who recanted their confessions together with the only two Andover prisoners who refused to make any confession at all.

Margaret Jacobs	Single, 16	Recanted
Martha (Allen) Carrier, executed	Married, 38	Did not confess
Mary (Ayer) Parker, executed	Widow, 55	Did not confess
Samuel Wardwell, executed	Married, 49	Recanted
Mercy Wardwell	Single, 18	Recanted in part

The execution of the five women—Sarah Good, Rebecca Nurse, Susannah Martin, Elizabeth Howe, and Sarah Wildes— on July 19, 1692, was a bitter disappointment to the old-line clergy. The women went to their deaths refusing to make any last-minute confessions; all claimed they were innocent to the end. Their behavior at the time of their execution convinced a number of onlookers that in fact they were innocent.

At this point the Rev. Thomas Barnard of Andover entered the witch hunt in a serious way. He produced the miracle the clergy were praying for. On August 5, 1692, the day of the trial of the Rev. George Burroughs, Cotton Mather wrote, "Our good God is working of miracles. Five witches were lately executed [on July 19], impudently demanding of God a miraculous vindication of their innocence. Immediately upon this, our God miraculously sent in five Andover witches [Ann Foster, Mary (Foster) Lacey, Mary Lacey, Jr., Richard Carrier, Andrew Carrier], who made a most ample, surprising, amazing confession of all their villainies, and declared the five newly executed to have been of their company, discovering many more, but all agreeing in Burroughs being their ringleader, who, I suppose, this day receives his trial at Salem, whither a vast concourse of people is gone, my father [Increase Mather] this morning among the rest.

Since those, there have come in other confessors [Martha Emerson, Mary Bridges, Mary Toothaker, Hannah Brumidge, Mary Post]; yea, they come in daily. About this prodigious matter my soul has been refreshed with some little short of miraculous answers of prayer, which are not to be written; but they comfort me with a prospect of a hopeful issue."[234]"

The second mass execution, on August 19, 1692, was a triumph for the old-line clergy. Although none of the victims confessed, the Andover confessions implicated the two major figures, George Burroughs and Martha Carrier. The Rev. George Burroughs, the minister who did not strictly follow the Puritan code, but instead reached out to help all in need, was particularly repugnant to the hard-line ministers. Some of their group attended this signal event, including Cotton Mather; Zachariah Symmes, minister at Bradford; John Hale, minister at Beverly, 1657; Nicholas Noyes, assistant minister at Salem Town; and Samuel Cheever, minister at Marblehead.

Prior to Barnard's entry, the authorities had used intensive psychological torture against the prisoners taken in the Salem Village witch hunt—threats of the dungeon and gallows, forced wakefulness, and repeated examinations—but confessions were not forthcoming. Once the Rev. Thomas Barnard was called in, he fashioned new tactics. Barnard recognized that many of the New England colonists felt caught in a dangerous world; their fears were constantly nurtured by the teachings of the clergy. However, Barnard understood that his parishioners preferred guidance and direction to threats. He preached that witchcraft was a serious impediment to their happiness and spiritual life. In order to save their souls, he urged them to confess their sins. Rumors were circulated that many in Andover had been led by the Devil into the sin of witchcraft. "Now I am writing concerning Andover. I cannot omit the opportunity of sending you this information; that whereas there is a report spread about the country, how they were much addicted to sorcery in the said town, and that there were forty men in it that could raise the Devil as well as any astrologer, and the like," wrote Thomas

234 Cotton Mather, "Letter of August 5, 1692 to John Cotton."

Brattle on October 8, 1692.[235] Barnard preached that confession
purified the soul and confounded the Devil. By confession his
sinful parishioners could turn away from the Devil toward
redemption and salvation. His melodious and powerful sermons
made people hang on his every word. He not only preached of
the need for a credible confession, to use Cotton Mather's term, but
also explained how to make one. The congregation united behind
him.

The confessions of the Andover witches represented a major
turning point in the Salem witchcraft episode. Thomas Barnard,
acting in his spiritual role, imbued his parishioners with the
theologically correct concept of witchcraft. This doctrine they
obligingly regurgitated in their confessions. The confessors were
helped along by leading questions from magistrate John
Hathorne. If they stumbled on some fine point, he simply
reworded his question in such a way that a simple "yes" would
carry them over it. In this way the Andover witches were able to
produce extraordinarily similar, detailed confessions. In all the
confessions, the tracks of Cotton Mather, Thomas Barnard, and
other hard-line ministers are easy to identify. These confessions
are in effect the intellectual creations of these men, and in no way
the products of the accused witches. "Now, by these confessions
'tis agreed, that the Devil has made a dreadful knot of witches
in the country. Yea, that at prodigious witch meetings, the
wretches have proceeded so far, as to concert and consult the
methods of rooting out the Christian religion from this country,
and setting up instead of it, perhaps a more gross diabolism than
ever the world saw before," wrote Cotton Mather in his
fantasy.[236]

Cotton Mather attended many of the examinations of the
Andover accused. He wrote that he had "lately seen even poor
children of several ages, even from seven to twenty, more or less,

---

235 Brattle, "Letter of October 8, 1692," in Burr, *Narratives*, 181. But
      Brattle put the rumor to rest, writing, "After the best search I can make,
      it proves a mere slander, and a very unrighteous imputation."
236 Cotton Mather, *Wonders*, 16.

confessing their familiarity with Devils."[237]   A little torture or threat of torture, of course, made the prisoners divulge in their confessions the very information that Cotton Mather wanted to hear.   It was the account about the workings of the invisible world as originally put forth by Cotton Mather and echoed by his cohort Barnard.   Is it any wonder that virtually all the Andover confessions offered virtually the same account of the Devil's operation, the one espoused by Cotton Mather?

The Andover confessions represented to the clergy a manifestation of their most cherished objective. In their eyes the confessions gave proof of the existence of the invisible world of the Devil. This was an exciting achievement, as meaningful to them as our twentieth-century discovery of the invisible world of subatomic particles. The Andover confessions offered a complete verification of the clergy's forebodings about the attack of Satan on their church.   The revelations exposed by the confessions confirmed Puritan theology. The confessions gave as clear cut and directed a sequence of ideas as the Puritan catechism itself. "Goody Cloyce [an imprisoned witch], that excellent old Christian, stood in the early sunshine, at her own lattice catechizing a little girl, who had brought her a pint of morning's milk."[238]

The Rev. John Hale described the attributes of a credible confession, that is, a confession in line with the teachings of the church. Speaking of the confession of Tituba, he wrote, "Here were these things rendered her confession credible. (1.) That at this examination she answered every question as she did at first. A liar we say, had need of a good memory, but truth being always consistent with itself is the same today as it was yesterday. (2.) She seemed very penitent for her sin in covenanting with the Devil. (3.) She became a sufferer herself and, as she said, for her confession.   (4.) Her confession agreed exactly (which was afterwards verified in the other confessors) with the accusations of the afflicted. And the success of Tituba's confession encouraged

---

237 Cotton Mather, *Wonders*, 102-103.   The seven-year old was Sarah
      Carrier.
238 Hawthorne, *Young Goodman Brown.*

those in Authority to examine others that were suspected, and the event was that more confessed themselves guilty. And thus was this matter driven on."[239] This account written as early as 1698, but not published until 1702, blurred the fact that witchcraft confessions simply were not forthcoming until the onset of the Andover witch hunt on July 15, 1692, some four and one-half months after Tituba's confession at the beginning of March. In this way Hale minimized his own failure; he also, perhaps intentionally, slighted the outstanding success of his rival Thomas Barnard in obtaining confessions.

The Rev. Hale, continuing his account, described the flood of confessions obtained during the Andover witch hunt. "But that which chiefly carried on this matter to such a height, was the increasing of confessors till they amounted to nearly fifty, and four or six of them upon their trials owned their guilt of this crime, and were condemned for the same, but not executed.[240] And many of the confessors confirmed their confessions with very strong circumstances: As their exact agreement with the accusations of the afflicted; their punctual agreement with their fellow confessors; their relating the times when they convenanted with Satan, and the reasons that moved them thereunto; their witch meetings, and that they had their mock sacraments of baptism and the supper, in some of them; their signing the Devil's book: and some showed scars of the wounds which they said were made to fetch blood with, to sign the Devil's book; and some said they had imps to suck them, and showed sores raw where they said they were sucked by them."[241] This statement by the Rev. Hale listed the activities of witches as conceived by the clergy. The accused were expected to follow this scenario in their confession; otherwise the confession would not be credible.

239　Hale, *A Modest Enquiry*, in Burr, *Narratives*, 415.
240　The confessing witches Rebecca Eames, Abigail Faulkner, Ann Foster, Mary (Foster) Lacey, and Abigail Hobbs were condemned on September 17, 1692. If the weak confession of Abigail Faulkner is ruled out, Hale's number of four is obtained. Otherwise this group, together with Dorcas Hoar, who was condemned on September 9 but confessed the day before her scheduled execution, makes Hale's number of six.
241　Hale, *A Modest Enquiry*, in Burr, *Narratives*, 416-417.

An essential element of a credible confession was that the Devil be a deceiver. For example, in her confession Mary Bridges, Jr. said, "A yellow bird appeared to me out of doors, and bid me serve him. He promised me money and fine clothes, and I promised to serve him, but he gave me neither money nor fine clothes. I thought when he appeared, it was the Devil. I was to serve him two years, then was to be his body and soul. I admit I had been baptized by him." Another essential element was that the act of confessing gave immediate relief. "Then she was bid to go take the two afflicted persons by the hand and, when she did, they were not hurt."[242] The confession removed all pain from the afflicted.

The confession of Mary Bridges, Jr. contained essential references to the Devil's book, the witch meeting, the nighttime ride on a broomstick. "She said the next time she saw any such shape, it was a black bird. He would have her serve him and would have her touch a paper. When she did with her fingers, it made a red mark. Then she saw a black man. She owned that she was at the witch meeting at Chandler's at Andover, and thought there were nearly a hundred [witches] at it. She said her shape was there. She said she afflicted by sticking pins into things and clothes, while at the same time thinking of hurting them [the afflicted]. She said the dead taught her this way. She said they drank sack[243] at the witch meeting at Andover. It stood there in pots and they drew it out of a barrel. She also said that she rode to Salem Village meeting upon a pole and the black man carried the pole over the tops of the trees."[244]

This confession is typical. Puritan scruples did not permit the Salem witchcraft confessions to mention wild orgies, the kind that supposedly happened at European witch meetings. The most shocking event at a New England witches' sabbat was the taking of a mock sacrament or the drinking of wine or cider. The New England witches were required to be thoroughly proper in their behavior and follow accepted social convention. Indulgence

---

242 Suffolk County, *Court Records*, case 2729, page 73.
243 Sack, the drink of Shakespeare's day, beloved and praised by Falstaff, was passing out of favor by the year 1692.
244 Suffolk County, *Court Records*, case 2729, page 73.

in lascivious behavior, loud music, and dancing was not allowed. Their meetings were disappointingly sedate, almost like ordinary Sunday services. The Puritan ministers needed the existence of witchcraft to affirm their belief in God, but not to jar their sensibilities.

The confessions of the New England witches always contained statements that they never profited from their covenant with the evil spirit. The Devil never made good on his promises of fine clothes or money. Witchcraft, by necessity, was spectral in nature. The clergy and magistrates would have been hard-pressed indeed to find tangible evidence of witchcraft like a new dress or a pretty hat conferred by the Devil. Witchcraft was an abstraction embedded in the minds of the clergy; any worldly manifestation of its existence was completely unnecessary, mere clutter to a beautiful fantasy.

To the Puritan clergy the Devil made his presence known in the shape of a black man or an animal. Horns and cloven feet were unnecessary accouterments. Rebecca (Blake) Eames told them what they wanted to hear; "the Devil appeared to her in the likeness of a black man. She then gave herself soul and body to the Devil and promised to serve & obey him and keep his ways. She further declares that she did."[245] On another occasion Rebecca Eames said that "the Devil was in the shape of a horse when he carried her to afflict. The Devil appeared to her like a colt, very ugly."[246]

Ann Foster confessed that "the Devil appeared to her in the shape of a bird at several times, such a bird as she never saw the like before, & that she had had this gift (viz. of striking the afflicted down with her eye) ever since, & being asked why she thought that bird was the Devil she answered because he came white and vanished away black. The Devil told her that she should have this gift & that she must believe him & told her she should have prosperity. He had appeared to her three times & was always as a bird & the last time was about half a year since, & sat upon a table, had two legs & great eyes. The second time of his appearance he promised her prosperity." At another

245 Essex Institute, *Witchcraft Collection*, "Examinations."
246 Essex County Archives, *Witchcraft*, 2:25.

time, Ann Foster confessed that "the Devil in shape of a black man appeared to her with Goody Carrier about six years since when they made her a witch & that she promised to serve the Devil two years, upon which the Devil promised her prosperity & many things but never performed it."[247] The Devil never carried out his part of the bargain, thus reaffirming an important theological truth. The confession served as another vehicle of church teaching; the theological value of the confession lay in the message that it conveyed.

The Puritan church was preoccupied with the Devil to the point of obsession. Richard Carrier, after indoctrination in prison by Cotton Mather and torture authorized by John Hathorne, said at his examination that he saw "the shape of a man in the night. The man was black and had a high crowned hat. He asked me what I should be afraid of & proffered to go a little way with me. He bid me serve him & he would get me new clothes & give me a horse. He told me also that he was Christ, & I must believe him, & I think I did. I set my hand to his book. It was a little red book. I wrote with a stick & made a red color with it & I promised to serve him &, at parting, he bid me goodnight."[248] The black man, as far as outward appearances indicated, could well have been Cotton Mather in his black cloak and high-crowned hat. The book, of course, was the confession that Richard was forced to sign; the blood was his blood resulting from the torture that he had undergone.

Nathaniel Hawthorne picked up on this theme. "The next morning [after the witch meeting], young Goodman Brown came slowly into the street of Salem Village, staring around him like a bewildered man. The good old minister was taking a walk along the grave-yard, to get an appetite for breakfast and meditate his sermon, and bestow a blessing, as he passed, on Goodman Brown. He shrank from the venerable saint, as if to avoid an anathema. Had Goodman Brown fallen asleep in the forest, and only dreamed a wild dream of a witch-meeting? But, alas! it was a dream of evil omen. On the Sabbath day, he could not listen, because an anthem of sin rushed loudly upon his ear,

---

247 Woodward, *Records of Salem Witchcraft*, 2:136-139.
248 Woodward, *Records of Salem Witchcraft*, 2:198-199.

and drowned the blessed strain. When the minister spoke from the pulpit, with power and fervid eloquence, and, with his hand on the open Bible, of the sacred truths of our religion, and of future bliss or misery unutterable, then did Goodman Brown turn pale, dreading, lest the roof should thunder down upon the grey blasphemer [the minister] and his hearers."[249]

According to Puritan teaching, the Devil required the witches to undo their allegiance to the church by renouncing their Christian baptism. The Devil had them seal their covenants with him by writing their names or making their marks in his book. The Andover confessions described the Devil's methods of rebaptizing people and giving mock communion. There were only minor variations as to whether the book was red or made of birch bark, and whether he dipped heads to baptize or flung initiates bodily in the water.

Mary Toothaker imprisoned on May 31, 1692, refused to confess. For two months she held firm under repeated examinations. Another examination was held for her on July 30. "As she came to examination she promised herself twenty times by the way that, if she should die upon the Gallows, yet she would not say anything but that she was innocent & rejoiced in the thought of it, that she should go home innocent." Yet the magistrates, "after many questions and negative answers returned," were able to wring out a confession from her. Asked "if she did not sign the Devil's book," she answered that the Devil "brought something which she took to be a piece of birch bark, and she made a mark with her finger by rubbing off the white scurf. And he promised if she would serve him she should be safe from the Indians."[250]

Cotton Mather's crusade was directed against a diabolic conspiracy intent on overthrowing the church in New England. "I have indeed set myself to countermine the whole PLOT of the Devil, against New England," wrote Cotton Mather. For several years he had warned people of the dangers of witchcraft. Now in the summer of 1692, the Andover confessions provided spectacular confirmation of his worst fears. "The Devil,

---

249 Hawthorne, *Young Goodman Brown*.
250 Suffolk County, *Court Records*, case 2713, page 50.

exhibiting himself ordinarily as a small black man, has decoyed a fearful knot of proud, forward, ignorant, envious and malicious creatures, to lift themselves in his horrid service, by entering their names in a book by him tendered unto them. These witches, whereof above a score have now confessed, and show their deeds, have met in hellish rendezvouses, wherein the confessors do say, they have their diabolical sacraments, imitating the baptism and the supper of our Lord. In these hellish meetings, these monsters have associated themselves to do no less a thing than, to destroy the kingdom of our Lord Jesus Christ, in these parts of the world. They, each of them, have their specters, commissioned by them & representing of them, to be their engines of malice. By these wicked specters, they seize poor people about the country, with various & bloody torments. The people thus afflicted, are miserably scratched and bitten, so that the marks are most visible to all the world, but the causes utterly invisible, and the same invisible furies do most visibly stick pins into the bodies of the afflicted, and hideously distort, and disjoint all their members. Yea, they sometimes drag the poor people out of their chambers, and carry them over trees and hills, for diverse miles together."[251]

As Cotton Mather noted, the witches were not averse to flying over trees and hills. Nathaniel Hawthorne described a witch addressing the Devil for transportation. "'Ah, your worship,' cried the old lady, cackling aloud. 'So, as I was saying, being all ready for the meeting, and no horse to ride on, I made up my mind to foot it.' 'That can hardly be,' answered her friend [the Devil]. "Here is my staff, if you will.'"[252]

Many a witch testified to the riding on a pole, the Devil's staff, to the hellish rendezvouses at Salem Village. Ann Foster said that "she & Martha Carrier did both ride on a stick or pole when they went to the witch meeting at Salem Village & that the stick broke as they were carried in the air above the tops of the trees & they fell, but she did hang fast about the neck of Goody Carrier & they were presently at the village." Ann Foster's daughter, Mary (Foster) Lacey, confessed that "her

251 Cotton Mather, *Wonders*, 4, 80-81.
252 Hawthorne, *Young Goodman Brown*.

mother Foster, Goody Carrier & herself rode upon a pole to Salem Village meeting, and that the pole broke a little way off from the Village."[253]

Richard Carrier said, "I can not tell how long it is since I rode to Salem Village. I was there twice & rode with Mary Lacey, Jr. The Devil carried us, sometimes in the shape of a horse, sometimes in the shape of a man. The first time he was a horse; the second time, a man. When he was a horse our pole lay across the horse. When he was a man our pole was on his shoulder. When we went to Ballard's, he was a man. We were at Ballard's house and went in sometimes at the window & sometimes at the door. I got the cider out of the cellar & drew it in a pot belonging to the house & drank it in the orchard. I fetched the cider myself & went in my spirit for it." Mary Lacey, Jr. interjected the statement that Richard "went in his spirit & his body lay dead the while & out of doors." Richard said, "It was true."[254]

To confirm the worst forebodings of Cotton Mather, scores of witches were reported attending some meetings, plotting the ruin of New England's churches. Sarah Bridges said "she was to serve the Devil 4 years & he was to have body & soul. She admitted she had been to the witch meeting at Chandler's garrison at Andover & that she thought there were 200 witches there & that they ate bread & drank wine."[255] Susannah Post told magistrate Bartholomew Gedney that she was at a witch meeting at Andover attended by 200 witches, where she heard there were 500 witches in the county. Mary Bridges, Jr. said "she was at the witch meeting at Chandlers at Andover last week & she thought there were near a hundred at it. She said her shape was there."[256] Mary Toothaker testified that at a Salem Village witch meeting "they did talk of 305 witches in the county. Their discourse was about pulling down the kingdom of Christ and setting up the kingdom of Satan."[257] Elizabeth Johnson, Jr. said "she had been at the witches meeting. She said

253 Woodward, *Records of Salem Witchcraft*, 2:136-141.
254 Essex Institute, *Witchcraft Collection*, "Examinations."
255 Ibid.
256 Suffolk County, *Court Records*, case 2729, page 73.
257 Suffolk County, *Court Records*, case 2713, page 50.

there were about six score all the witch meeting all the Village that she saw. She said they had bread & wine at the witch sacrament at the Village & they filled the wine out into cups to drink. She said they agreed that time to afflict folk & to pull down the kingdom of Christ & to sell up the Devil's kingdom."[258]

To the magistrates and ministers, nothing was beyond belief. Cotton Mather wrote, "the sin of unbelief may be reckoned as perhaps the chief crime of our land. We are told, God swears in wrath against them that believe not. Never were the offers of the Gospel more freely tendered, or more basely despised, than in this New England. And thus by the just vengeance of heaven, the Devil becomes a master, a prince, a god, unto the miserable unbelievers."[259]

The confessions always included a description of how the witches afflicted their victims. Some said that they used puppets or other representations of people. Mary Bridges, Jr. said that "her afflicting was by sticking pins into things and clothes & think of hurting them. She said the dead taught her this way of afflicting."[260] Richard Carrier said that he "hurt the images of persons or the likeness of them by squeezing anything I had a mind to, between my hand. I hurt Swan in his spirit & struck him in the knee with a spindle. The Devil brought it & he was then in the shape of a black man & high crowned hat."[261]

Elizabeth Johnson, Jr. said, "she had afflicted Lawrence Lacey by sitting on his stomach. She said she afflicted Sarah Phelps by puppets. She brought out 3 puppets. Two of them were made of rags or strips of cloth; the other was made of a birch rind. One puppet had four pieces or strips of cloth wrapped one upon another, which she said was to afflict four persons with. There was thread in the middle under the rags. Lawrence Lacey & Ephraim Davis's child were told that she afflicted by pinching that puppet. A second puppet had two such pieces of rags rolled up together & 3 pins stuck into it, & she afflicted Ben

---

258 Massachusetts Archives, *Witchcraft*, 135:34.
259 Cotton Mather, *Wonders*, 98.
260 Suffolk County, *Court Records*, case 2729, page 73.
261 Essex Institute, *Witchcraft Collection*, "Examinations."

Abbot & James Frye's two children & Abraham Foster's children with that puppet & the other. She afflicted Ann Putnam with a spear & was asked whether the spear was iron or wood. She said either of them would do. She was asked where her familiar sucked her. She showed one of her knuckles of her finger & said there was one place. It looked red. She said she had two places more where they sucked her. Women were ordered to search them out & they found two little red specks that Johnson said were all that there were to be seen; they were plain to be seen when they were newly sucked. One of the places was behind her arm."[262]

Mary (Foster) Lacey said she would "take a rag, cloth or any such thing and roll it up together, and imagine it to represent such and such a person. Then whatsoever she does to that rag or cloth so rolled up, the person represented thereby will be in like manner afflicted."[263]

In his sermons about "a fresh drop of the burning brimstone," Cotton Mather condemned "the unpardonable sin committed by professors of the Christian religion, falling into witchcraft."[264] In contrast, the Rev. Barnard cleverly offered the hope of forgiveness of sin through confession. The final part of a confession often described the reconciliation made possible by the act of confession. Despite this reconciliation and all the talk about forgiveness, the magistrates were unrelenting. They unfailingly committed the confessors to prison; apparently, in their view, forgiveness was a matter for the next world.

Sarah Bridges "being bid to go and ask forgiveness of the afflicted she did & owned she had afflicted them but would do it no more, but would renounce the Devil & his works & the afflicted persons forgave her & she could talk with them & not hurt them."[265] Mary Bridges, Jr. "was bid to go take the two afflicted persons by the hand & she did & they were not hurt."[266]

---

262 Massachusetts Archives, *Witchcraft*, 135:34.
263 Woodward, *Records of Salem Witchcraft*, 2:136-141.
264 Cotton Mather, *Wonders*, 46, 120.
265 Essex Institute, *Witchcraft Collection*, "Examinations."
266 Suffolk County, *Court Records*, case 2729, page 73.

Magnalia Christi Americana:

OR, THE

Ecclesiastical History

OF

NEW-ENGLAND,

FROM

Its First Planting in the Year 1620. unto the Year
of our LORD, 1698.

In Seven BOOKS.

I. Antiquities : In Seven Chapters. With an Appendix.
II. Containing the Lives of the Governours, and Names of the Magistrates
of New-England : In Thirteen Chapters. With an Appendix.
III. The Lives of Sixty Famous Divines, by whose Ministry the Churches of
New-England have been Planted and Continued.
IV. An Account of the University of *Cambridge* in *New-England*; in Two
Parts. The First contains the Laws, the Benefactors, and Vicissitudes of
Harvard College; with Remarks upon it. The Second Part contains the Lives
of some Eminent Persons Educated in it.
V. Acts and Monuments of the Faith and Order in the Churches of *New-Eng-
land*, passed in their Synods; with Historical Remarks upon those Venerable
Assemblies; and a great Variety of Church-Cases occurring, and resolved by
the Synods of those Churches : In Four Parts.
VI. A Faithful Record of many Illustrious, Wonderful Providences, both
of Mercies and Judgments, on divers Persons in *New-England* : In Eight
Chapters.
VII. *The Wars of the Lord*. Being an History of the Manifold Afflictions and
Disturbances of the Churches in *New-England*, from their Various Adversa-
ries, and the Wonderful Methods and Mercies of God in their Deliverance :
In Six Chapters : To which is subjoined, An Appendix of Remarkable
Occurrences which *New-England* had in the Wars with the *Indian* Salvages,
from the Year 1688, to the Year 1698.

By the Reverend and Learned *COTTON MATHER*, M. A.
And Pastor of the North Church in *Boston*, *New-England*.

LONDON:

Printed for *Thomas Parkhurst*, at the *Bible* and *Three
Crowns* in *Cheapside*. MDCCII.

Title page of *Magnalia* by Cotton Mather

To all unto whom thefe Prefents, fhall co[...] **Greeting.**

KNOW YE, That WE have affigned and confti-
tuted, and do by thefe Prefents, with Advice and Confent of the
Council, conftitute and appoint *Stephen Barker Efq. of Methuen*
to be one of the Juftices to keep the Peace in our County of *Effex for the*
term of feven years of during that time, he fhall behave well in that
same Office
And to keep, and caufe to be kept, the Laws and Ordinances made for the
Good of the Peace, and for the Confervation of the fame, and for the Quiet,
Rule and Government of our Citizens and Subjects in the faid County, in all
and every the Articles thereof, according to the Force, Form and Effect of
the fame, and to chaftife and punifh all Perfons offending againft the Form
of thofe Laws and Ordinances, or any of them, in the County aforefaid, as
according to the Form of thofe Laws and Ordinances fhall be fit to be done ;
and to caufe to come before him the faid ; *Stephen Barker Efq.*
all thofe that fhall break the Peace, or attempt any
Thing againft the fame, or that fhall threaten any of the Citizens or fubjects
in their Perfons, or in burning their Houfes, to find fufficient Security for the
Peace, and for the good Behaviour towards the Citizens and Subjects of this
Government ; and if they fhall refufe to find fuch Security, then to caufe them
to be kept fafe in Prifon until they fhall find the fame ; and to do and perform in
the County aforefaid, and all whatfoever, according to our Laws and Ordinances,
or any of them, a Juftice of the Peace may and ought to do and perform ;

And with there juftices of the Peace in the same County

(according to the Tenor of the Commiffion to them granted) to enquire by the
Oaths of good and lawful Men of the faid County, by whom the Truth may
be better known, of all and all Manner of Thefts, Trefpaffes, Riots, Routs
and unlawful Affemblies whatfoever, and all and fingular other Mifdeeds and
Offences of which by Law, Juftices of the Peace in their General Seffions may
and ought to enquire, by whomfoever or howfoever done or perpetrated, or
which fhall hereafter happen, howfoever to be done or attempted in the
County aforefaid, contrary to the Form of the Laws and Ordinances aforefaid,
made for the common Good of our Citizens and Subjects ; *And with*

there juftices of the Peace in the same county

(according to the Tenor of the Commiffion to them granted as aforefaid) to
hear and determine, all and fingular the faid Thefts, Trefpaffes, Riots, Routs,
unlawful Affemblies, and all and fingular other the Premifes, and to do therein as to Juftice appertaineth, according to the Laws, Statutes and Ordinances
aforefaid.

IN TESTIMONY WHEREOF, WE have caufed our public Seal to
be hereunto affixed : WITNESS, *his excellency John Hancock Efq*

Our Governour, and Commander in Chief.

DATED at BOSTON, the *fifth* Day of *March* ANNO
DOMINI, One Thoufand Seven Hundred and Ninety *two* and in the
fixteenth YEAR of the INDEPENDENCE of the UNITED STATES
of AMERICA.

By HIS EXCELLENCY's Command,
with the Advice and Confent of the COUNCIL.

John Avery jun Secty

In 1792, one hundred years after William Barker was arrested for
witchcraft, saying that "all persons should be equal," his great-
great-nephew Stephen Barker received this commission signed by
John Hancock, a signer of the Declaration of Independence which
stated that "all men are created equal."

Sarah Wardwell's confession, typical of so many others, may be found in Chapter 24. Worth noting here, however, are suspicious elements in the initial sentence leading into her confession. These words (not her own) are one variation of the phrasing used to introduce many confessions. "After many denials of what she was accused . . . she was *required* to declare the truth in the fear of God and then she confesses as follows." The examiners, everyone present in the room, and Sarah herself knew full well, indeed assumed, that she was "required," from the outset, "to declare the truth in the fear of God." What persuaded her to alter her testimony from consistent denials of false accusations to full acquiescence to what was wanted? Was it fear of God or was it fear of the veiled threats of the examiners? Recall that Margaret Jacobs, aged 16, declared in writing that she was threatened with the dungeon and hanging if she refused to confess. The examiners already had resorted to the physical torture of Martha Carrier's two teenage sons to induce testimonies against their mother. If the examiners were willing to threaten an adolescent girl and torture adolescent boys, why would they not have been willing to threaten and torture adult women? It is possible that the Rev. Barnard's remarkable success at extracting confessions from his Andover congregation hinged upon a good deal more than sermons and charisma.

Thomas Brattle, Fellow of the Royal Society, mathematician, merchant, and Harvard's treasurer from 1693-1713, is generally accepted as an impeccable source. One of the very few to visit the prisons, witness the conditions, and talk with the prisoners, he wrote of the "rude and barbarous methods" used on them. Of particular bearing is his note written in the margin of his original manuscript, dated October 8, 1692. "You may possibly think that my terms are too severe; but should I tell you what a kind of Blade was employed in bringing these women to their confession; what methods from damnation were taken; with what violence urged; how unseasonably they were kept up; what buzzings and chuckings of the hand were used, and the like, I am sure that you would call them, (as I do), rude and barbarous methods."[267]

---

267 Brattle, "Letter of October 8, 1692," in Burr, *Narratives*, 181.

William Barker, Sr. understood exactly what the authorities wanted. His trumped-up confession stands as a minor masterpiece. Packed with vivid detail, it even included the cloven foot. It confirmed Satan's plan to eradicate the churches; 307 witches on the loose nicely emphasized the emergency. The confession, dated August 29, 1692, is as follows.

"He confesses he has been in the snare of the Devil three years. That the Devil first appeared to him like a black man and perceived he had a cloven foot. That the Devil demanded of him to give up himself soul & body unto him, which he promised to do. He said he had a great family, the world went hard with him and was willing to pay every man his own. And the Devil told him he would pay all his debts and he should live comfortably. He confesses he has afflicted Sprague, Foster and Martin, his three accusers. That he did sign the Devil's book with blood brought to him in a thing like an inkhorn, that he dipped his fingers therein and made a blot in the book, which was a confirmation of the covenant with the Devil.

"He confesses he was at a meeting of witches at Salem Village where he judges there was about a hundred of them. That the meeting was upon a green piece of ground near the minister's house. He said they met there to destroy that place by reason of the peoples being divided & their differing with their ministers.

"Satan's design was to set up his own worship, abolish all the churches in the land, to fall next upon Salem and so go through the country. He says the Devil promised that *all his people should live bravely, that all persons should be equal; that there should be no day of resurrection or of judgement, and neither punishment nor shame for sin.* He says there was a sacrament at that meeting, there was also bread & wine. Mr. Burse was a ringleader in that meeting. It was proposed at the meeting to make as many witches as they could. And they were all by Mr. Burse and the black man exhorted to pull down the kingdom of Christ and set up the kingdom of the Devil. He said he knew Mr. Burroughs and Goody Howe to be such persons. And that he heard a trumpet sounded at the meeting and thinks it

was Burse that did it.   The sound is heard many miles off, and
then they all come one after another.

"In the spring of the year the witches came from Connecticut
to afflict at Salem Village, but now they have left it off.   And
that he has been informed by some of the grandees that there are
about 307 witches in the country.   He says the witches are much
disturbed with the afflicted persons because they are discovered
by them.   They curse the judges because their society is brought
under.   They would have the afflicted persons counted as witches
but he thinks the afflicted persons are innocent & that they do
God good service.   And that he has not known or heard of one
innocent person taken up & put in prison.   He says he is heartily
sorry for what he has done and for hurting the afflicted persons,
his accusers; prays their forgiveness; desires prayers for himself,
promises to renounce the Devil and all his works.   And then he
could take them [the afflicted persons] all by the hand without
any harm by his eye or any otherwise.   5 September 1692.   The
above said is the truth as witness my hand, William Barker."[268]

Soon after his confession, William Barker, Sr. made a
successful escape from prison.   The deputy sheriff came to his
farm in Andover to seize his cattle, but his brother Lieut. John
Barker was already there.   Lieut. Barker saved the cattle by
paying off the deputy and prevented the seizure of any more
goods.

---

268 Massachusetts Archives, *Witchcraft*, 135:39.

17

COLLAPSE OF THE WITCH HUNT

T HE MASS EXECUTION OF EIGHT PEOPLE on September 22, 1692, marked a turning point in the witchcraft affair. On one hand, the witch hunters were going full tilt, destroying their enemies and taking their lands and goods. On the other hand, a strong reaction led by several high ranking citizens had begun to set in. When Governor Phipps returned from command of the army in Maine on September 29, 1692, he found people seriously alarmed at the Court's proceedings.

By this point, nineteen persons had been hanged, one pressed to death, and eight more condemned. Of these twenty-eight, more than a third were church members. Most had unblemished reputations, yet not one had been cleared. Many in the community believed that at least some, if not all of this number were innocent. About 150 accused witches were in prisons awaiting trial; another 200 had been accused but were not yet imprisoned. The prison at Salem was overflowing; many of the accused were in other prisons, also full. The names of most of the 150 that were imprisoned are known from official records. Because complaints had not been filed for the additional 200, none can be identified today except for the few mentioned in contemporary accounts.

In order to obtain confessions, some ministers had held out the hope of leniency, false though it may have been. As a result more than fifty of the prisoners had confessed witchcraft. However, five of these confessors did not find leniency but were condemned in September trials.[269] To placate these ministers, chief justice

---

269 The five were Abigail Hobbs, Ann Foster, Mary (Foster) Lacey, Abigail Faulkner, and Rebecca Eames.

Stoughton did not sign death warrants for these five, so they were spared from the mass execution of September 22. Also the condemned Dorcas Hoar was spared from that execution because she made a last minute confession. But Stoughton had no intention of keeping this policy in place. At the trials of the Superior Court of Judicature held in January 1693, he did sign death warrants for eight condemned women, including those whom he had spared in September.[270]

Spectral evidence was now the subject of furious controversy among the New England clergy. The idea of continuing the trials as before alarmed many people. Phipps was particularly unhappy about the use of the spectral evidence provided by the afflicted girls. On inquiry he was informed by the justices of the court that although they began with this spectral evidence, they also relied on human testimony. Human testimony consisted of nothing more than base slander against the accused offered by various witnesses. This type of slander was also spectral in nature. Despite objections, the court and chief judge Stoughton, in particular, insisted on trying the accused by the use of spectral evidence. They scheduled the next trial for November 1, 1692, in Salem.

On October 3, 1692, Increase Mather presented his *Cases of Conscience Concerning Evil Spirits* before a conference of ministers. Pointing out the dangers of "over-hasty suspecting or too precipitant judging," he came out strongly against the use of spectral evidence. In the same month the Rev. Increase Mather visited the Salem prison and made a revealing investigation of the conditions under which the confessions had been obtained.[271] The tide had finally turned and was ebbing.

---

270 Of the five confessing witches condemned in September, Ann Foster had died in jail and Abigail Faulkner was still pregnant. The three left, namely Abigail Hobbs, Mary (Foster) Lacey, and Rebecca Eames, plus Dorcas Hoar (the last minute confessor), plus Elizabeth Proctor, a non-confessing witch reprieved for pregnancy in August, plus the three confessing witches (Mary Post, Elizabeth Johnson, Jr., and Sarah Wardwell) condemned in January 1693, made up the eight.

271 Upham, *Salem Witchcraft*, 2:204.

A dog was supposedly afflicted by witchcraft in Salem Village.[272]   The afflicted girls examined the dog with their spectral sight and then accused John Bradstreet of causing the dog's afflictions.[273]   John Bradstreet made his escape into New Hampshire and the dog was put to death.

In Andover another dog entered the scene. An old ballad affirmed that "Griff was a dog of Puritan breed." He belonged to a little Andover girl, Deborah; "brown were her eyes as the robin's wing, and chestnut brown her waving hair." Griff was her loyal friend and protector, "for Deborah was ever safe from harm. Twice he had dragged her out of the stream, whose swollen current was bearing her down." Yet "that was the time when over the land, wisdom was naught, and counsel vain." The afflicted girls cried out upon Griff, falling into their fits whenever the dog chanced their way. When the constable came and took Griff away, Deborah was "numb with a child's great grief and pain." The constable led the dog down the road to the deserted Wardwell farm where "the witch-dog made a Christian end."[274]

Perhaps giddy with success, the conspiracies now made several fatal missteps. They had clearly overreached their bounds by accusing of people of such rank as the sons of the former governor, Simon Bradstreet. The witch hunt, which the ruling elite had allowed Cotton Mather to promote, had come full circle and now turned back upon its makers. Grown into a Frankenstein monster, it was placing in danger the same high ranking officials who had allowed its creation. A "worthy gentleman of Boston"

---

272 It is not known whether the dog was rabid.

273 John Bradstreet, aged 40 and a resident of Topsfield, was the younger brother of Dudley Bradstreet, the Andover justice of the peace. John's wife, Sarah (Perkins) Bradstreet, was the niece of Mary (Perkins) Bradbury, 77, who was imprisoned on June 29, 1692. Robert Pike of Salisbury, a magistrate and an assistant to the governor, used every legal means to free Mary (Perkins) Bradbury but his efforts were to no avail. However, after her condemnation on September 9, 1692, Mary (Perkins) Bradbury made an escape. For an elderly woman of infirm health to accomplish such a thing would require inside help. Other high-placed persons who were imprisoned also escaped, and none was ever recaptured.

274 C. H. Abbott, *The Andover Townsman*, March 12, 1897.

was accused by the conspiracy in Andover. Not one to be intimidated, he promptly sent back a writ, delivered by some friends, to arrest his accusers in a "thousand pound action for defamation."[275]   Although the writ was never exercised, its arrival stopped the Andover conspiracy dead in their tracks. This legal measure stymied the conspirators and helped to expose their deceit.   The complaint against the worthy gentleman vanished into thin air, like so much spectral evidence. From that time, no further accusations from Andover were made. A few residual accusations from other sources continued into October and November 1692, with the town of Gloucester as the focal point.   Despite these sporadic attempts to keep the witch hunt going, essentially it had collapsed.

For the 150 accused in prison, however, the terror was by no means over.   Governor Phipps felt certain that at least some of these were innocent, perhaps all.   He knew that many persons with fine reputations had been cried out upon as witches and wizards.   He saw that many in jail might perish.   At least fifty in prison were suffering acutely from the extreme cold and poverty, since prisoners were required to pay the jail keepers for their food and other expenses.   Phipps initiated a policy that allowed prisoners to be released on bail on the posting of recognizance bonds.   He directed the judges to relieve others to prevent them from dying in prison.

On October 29, 1692, to his great credit, Phipps put an end to the Court of Oyer and Terminer.   On November 25, the General Court passed an act constituting a Superior Court of Judicature,[276] with the first meeting set for January 3, 1693.   Because some of the justices acknowledged that the former proceedings had been too violent, Phipps decreed that spectral testimony would not be admitted as evidence in the newly created Superior Court.   The Council elected William Stoughton as chief justice as before, and Thomas Danforth, John Richards, Wait Still Winthrop, and Samuel Sewall as associate justices.   Except for Thomas

---

275   Calef, *More Wonders*, 269.
276   Its full name was the "Superior Court of Judicature, the Court of Assizes and General Gaol Delivery;" its purpose was to exercise jurisdiction over the most serious crimes tried in Massachusetts.

Danforth, all had been members of the old Court of Oyer and Terminer. The three Salem magistrates—John Hathorne, Jonathan Corwin, and Bartholomew Gedney—were not on the new court; these were the three who had been most active in confiscating property. Peter Sergeant was also not on the new court.

At the height of the witchcraft mania, accusers and accused were counted by scores. Andover was the first town to recover its senses. By October a resistance movement led by the Rev. Francis Dane and other prominent townspeople began to act. They chose to work through normal political channels by filing petitions with the governor and the courts.

The resistance first turned its attention to the imprisoned children of Andover. Its efforts were successful; the authorities let the Andover families post recognizance bonds for the release of their children on bail. The first children were set free on October 6. By October 15 eighteen of the nineteen imprisoned Andover children (aged 18 and under) were out of prison on bail.[277] Only Rebecca Johnson, Jr., aged 17, remained in prison to take care of her sick mother. About December 8 she and her mother were released on bail.

The release of the Andover women proved more difficult. On October 12, 1692, nine leading men of Andover addressed a petition to the General Court on behalf of their wives and children. The nine men spoke of the prisoners' condition—"a company of poor distressed creatures as full of inward grief and trouble as they are able to bear up in life withal." They referred to the want of "food convenient" for them, and stated that "the coldness of the winter season that is coming may soon dispatch

---

277 Bailey, *Historical Sketches of Andover*, 230. The eighteen children released in October were William Barker, Jr., Mary Barker, Sarah Bridges, Mary Bridges, Jr., Richard Carrier, Andrew Carrier, Thomas Carrier, Jr., Sarah Carrier, Dorothy Faulkner, Abigail Faulkner, Jr., Stephen Johnson, Abigail Johnson, Mary Lacey, Jr., John Sadie, Hannah Tyler, Martha Tyler, Joanna Tyler, and Sarah Wilson, Jr. Mercy Wardwell was not included; she had turned nineteen on October 3, 1692, just three days before October 6, when the first of the children were released.

such out of the way that have not been used to such hardships."
They told of the calamitous effects of their absence from their
families who were at the same time required to maintain them in
jail. They prayed that the prisoners might be released on bail,
"to remain as prisoners under bond in their own houses, where
they may be more tenderly cared for."[278]

A few weeks earlier, some of these men, whipped into a
frenzy of religious fervor at the Andover touch test, had been
duped into encouraging their wives and daughters to confess.
Others who may have been skeptical of the charming words of
Barnard nonetheless joined rank, their purpose being to urge
confession in the hope of leniency. Now, following the recent
execution of the eight condemned witches, and with their wives
next in line for the hangman, these men awoke to their terrible
mistake. Their frightened children at home wanted to know
when their mothers and sisters would return. At once the men fell
solidly behind the Rev. Dane in his efforts to reverse the damage
they had done while under the powerful spell of the Rev.
Barnard.

The Rev. Thomas Barnard, in what appears as a total about-
face, gladly jumped in to join the Rev. Francis Dane's crusade to
free the prisoners. Here Barnard displayed his uncanny knack
for shifting ground at precisely the critical moment. It was a
shift, however, that would have been a simple matter for a man
devoid of principle. On October 18, 1692, the Rev. Barnard joined
with the Rev. Dane and twenty-four citizens of Andover to
address a petition to the Governor and General Court. "Several
of the women that are accused are members of this church in full
communion, and had obtained a good report of blameless
conversation, and their walking as becometh women professing

---

278 Bailey, *Historical Sketches of Andover*, 225-235. The nine men
signing the petition of October 12 were "John Osgood in behalf of his
wife; John Frye in behalf of his wife; John Marston in behalf of his
wife, Mary Marston; Christopher Osgood in behalf of his daughter,
Mary Marston; Joseph Wilson in behalf of his wife and daughter; John
Bridges in behalf of his wife and children; Hopestill Tyler in behalf of
his wife and daughter; Ebenezer Barker for his wife; Nathaniel Dane for
his wife." Hopestill's daughters, Joanna and Martha Tyler, had already
been released on bail, about October 6.

godliness." The petition admits that "most of our people that have been apprehended for witchcraft have upon examination confessed it." However, it stated that there was "reason to think that the extreme urgency that was used with some of them by their friends and others who privately examined them, and the fear they were then under, hath been an inducement to them to admit such things." This represented the first attempt at a public explanation of the witchcraft confessions. Upon just such confessions had Cotton Mather and others justified the entire witchcraft proceedings.

The petition continued with a direct attack against the afflicted children or, more precisely, against the influence of the Devil on those children. "Our troubles we foresee are likely to continue and increase, if other methods be not taken then as yet have been; and we know not who can think himself safe, if the accusations of children and others who are under a diabolical influence shall be received against persons of good fame."[279] It was safer to point the finger at the afflicted girls than at their fathers and stepfathers who made up the conspiracy of accusers. Puritan teaching dictated that the basic tenet of a witchcraft plot could not be disturbed. The blame for any mistakes incurred had to be laid upon the Devil; the men carrying out the crime went scot-free. The existence of the Devil was not only of theological interest, but of practical use as well.

On December 6, 1692, eight Andover men petitioned on behalf of their wives and friends in prison. During their imprisonment they "have been exposed to great sufferings, which daily increase by reason of the winter coming on and they are in extreme danger of perishing." The petitioners asked that the prisoners be permitted to come home on "such terms as your honors may judge meet."[280]

Still the women of Andover were in jail. However the efforts of the Andover resistance were starting to take effect. The authorities allowed a few of the imprisoned women to be

---

279 Ibid.
280 Ibid.   The eight men signing this petition were the same as those signing the petition of October 12, except that the name of John Marston is missing.

released on bail.[281]   Husbands and kinsmen had to post stiff recognizance bonds which would be forfeited if the released prisoners did not appear at the meeting of the Superior Court of Judicature scheduled for January 3, 1693. The rest of the Andover women had to remain in prison.

Attention turned to the upcoming trials. Because no further arrests were being made, Dudley Bradstreet ventured out of hiding and made his return to Andover. In late December 1692, Dudley Bradstreet, the Rev. Dane, the Rev. Barnard, thirty-eight other men, and twelve women drew up a petition that was presented to the Superior Court of Judicature at Salem at its opening session on January 3, 1693. The petition was on behalf of Mary (Clement) Osgood, Eunice (Potter) Frye, Deliverance (Haseltine) Dane, Sarah (Lord) Wilson, and Abigail (Wheeler) Barker.   These women, all church members and part of the Andover elite, had been arrested together at the Andover touch test. "When these women were accused by some afflicted persons of the neighborhood, their relations and others, through a misrepresentation of the truth of that evidence, took great pains to persuade them to own what they were, by the afflicted, charged with and indeed did unreasonably urge them to confess themselves guilty. By the unwearied solicitations of those that privately discoursed them both at home and at Salem, they were at length persuaded publicly to own what they were charged with. Now though we cannot but judge it a thing very sinful for innocent persons to own a crime that they are not guilty of, yet considering the well-ordered conversation of those women while they lived among us, and what they now seriously and constantly affirm in a more composed frame, we cannot but in charity judge them innocent of the great transgression that has been imputed to them." The petition went on to speak for the other Andover imprisoned. "As for the rest of our neighbors, who are under the like circumstances with these that have been named, we can

---

281 Ibid. Abigail (Dane) Faulkner, Deliverance (Haseltine) Dane, Rebecca (Aslet) Johnson, and her daughter Rebecca Johnson, Jr. (the child not released in October) were released on bail about December 8; Sarah Parker, about December 12; Sarah (Lord) Wilson, Mary (Clement) Osgood, and Eunice (Potter) Frye, on December 20, 1692.

truly say of them that while they lived among us, we have had no cause to judge them such persons as, of late, they have been represented and reported to be, nor do we know that any of their neighbors had any just grounds to suspect them of that evil that they are now charged with."[282]   The petition affirmed the innocence of all, a bold step, indicative of the courage of the Rev. Dane.

On January 2, 1693, the day before the scheduled date for the trials of the Superior Court of Judicature at Salem, the Rev. Francis Dane, in a letter to an unnamed clergyman, made a statement concerning his parishioners who had been accused and imprisoned.   In his letter Dane vindicated Andover from the scandalous reports. "Many innocent persons have been accused & imprisoned. The conceit of specter evidence as an infallible mark did too far prevail.   Hence we so easily parted with our neighbors of honest & good report. Hence we so easily parted with our children, and thus things were hurried on, hence such strange breaches in families. Several that came before me, that spake with so much sobriety, professing their innocence, they were too much urged to confess."[283]   In a postscript the Rev. Dane said of his granddaughter Elizabeth Johnson, Jr., "she is but simplish at the best."[284]

Charles Upham in 1867 lucidly described Francis Dane's predicament and courage.   "The wrath of the accusers was concentrated upon him to an unparalleled extent from their entrance into Andover.   They did not venture to attack him directly.   His venerable age and commanding position made it inexpedient; but they struck as near him, and at as many points, as they dared. They accused, imprisoned, and caused to be convicted and sentenced to death, one of his daughters, Abigail (Dane) Faulkner. They accused, imprisoned, and brought to trial another, Elizabeth (Dane) Johnson. They imprisoned, and brought to the sentence of death, his granddaughter, Elizabeth

---

282 Ibid.
283 Ibid.
284 This statement by Dane confirms Calef's statement that Elizabeth Johnson, Jr. and Mary Post "were, as appears by their behavior, the most senseless and ignorant creatures that could be found."

Johnson, Jr. They cried out against, and caused to be imprisoned, several others of his grandchildren. They accused and imprisoned Deliverance the wife, and also the man-servant, of his son Nathaniel. Elizabeth (Jackson) Howe was the wife of his nephew. Surely, no one was more signalized by their malice and resentment than Francis Dane; and he deserves to be recognized as standing pre-eminent, and, for a time, almost alone, in bold denunciation and courageous resistance of the execrable proceedings of that dark day."[285]

The first meeting of the new Superior Court of Judicature was held at Salem, January 3, 1693, ten months after the start of the witchcraft affair.   Spectral testimony was not admitted as evidence in this court; this essentially left human testimony and confession as the only evidence to be allowed against the accused.

Fifty-six prisoners were brought to court. Thirty were cleared by the grand jury; the remaining twenty-six were bound over for trial by jury. Except for three, all were found innocent. According to Calef, "Two [Elizabeth Johnson, Jr. and Mary Post] of which were, as appears by their behavior, the most senseless and ignorant creatures that could be found; besides which it does not appear what came in against those was more than among the rest that were acquitted. The third [Sarah Wardwell] was the wife of Wardwell, who was one of the twenty executed, and it seems they had both confessed themselves guilty; but he retracting his said confession, was tried and executed; it is supposed that this woman fearing her husband's fate, was not so stiff in her denials of her former confession, such as it was. These three received sentence of death."[286]

The witchcraft epidemic had almost played itself out. Yet Sarah Wardwell found herself among the three condemned by the new court. From Calef's description, it might appear that the other two were condemned in order to avoid the impression that Sarah Wardwell was being singled out.

The next meeting of the Superior Court of Judicature was held at Charlestown on January 31, 1693. In his letter of February 21,

---

285 Upham, *Salem Witchcraft*, 2:460.
286 Calef, *More Wonders*, 332-333.

1693, Governor Phipps wrote, "I was informed by the Attorney General that there was the same reason to clear the three condemned as the rest according to his judgment. The deputy governor [Chief Justice William Stoughton] signed a warrant for their speedy execution, and also of five others[287] who were condemned at the former Court of Oyer and Terminer. I sent a reprieve whereby the execution was stopped. The lieutenant governor [Stoughton] upon this occasion was enraged and filled with passionate anger and refused to sit upon the bench in a Superior Court then held at Charlestown, and indeed has from the beginning hurried on these matters with great precipitancy and by his warrant has cause the estates, goods and chattels of the executed to be seized and disposed of without my knowledge and consent."[288]

Stoughton raved, "We were in a way to have cleared the land of these witches, etc. Who it was that obstructed the execution of justice, or hindered these good proceedings we had made, I know not, but thereby the Kingdom of Satan is advanced, etc., and the Lord have mercy on this country."[289] He went off the bench for the rest of the session.

During the trial, many witnesses were brought in to give human testimony against Lydia Dustin, 70, and a widow for twenty-one years. They offered "testimony as of accidents, illness, etc., befalling them, or theirs, after some quarrel; what these testified was much of it of actions said to be done twenty years before that time. The specter evidence was not made use of

---

287 The five others were Elizabeth Proctor, Dorcas Hoar, Rebecca Eames, Mary (Foster) Lacey, and Abigail Hobbs. Elizabeth Proctor, condemned on August 5, 1692 but reprieved until after giving birth, had a baby girl on January 27, 1693. Abigail Faulkner, condemned on September 17, 1692 but reprieved until after giving birth, was still pregnant in January. Her son was not born until March 1693, at which time the witch hunt was essentially over. Mary Bradbury had been allowed to escape soon after her condemnation on September 9, 1692, and was never recaptured. Ann Foster, condemned on September 17, 1692 had died in prison in December 1692. She was the mother of Mary (Foster) Lacey.

288 Phipps, "Letter dated at Boston, February 21, 1693," in Burr, *Narratives*, 201.

289 *Further Account of the Trials*, 216.

in these trials, so the jury soon brought her in not guilty. Her daughter and granddaughter, and the rest that were then tried, were also acquitted." Enraged, Thomas Danforth, acting as chief justice, railed at Lydia, "Woman, Woman, repent, there are shrewd things come in against you!"[290]   Well knowing that Lydia, her daughter, and granddaughter could not pay the exorbitant prison fees demanded for their release, Danforth ordered them back to prison. Lydia died in her cell from hunger and cold six weeks later.   Danforth's act was equivalent to a death warrant, made against a woman who had just been found innocent in trial by jury.

The Superior Court of Judicature met again in Boston on April 25, 1693, and at Ipswich on May 9. Everyone was cleared during these two sessions. Soon after, the governor, Sir William Phipps, issued a general jail release for all the alleged witches still remaining in prison. The release included those who had been condemned. As always, prison fees had to be paid before release. Mary Watkins, a young white woman unable to pay her fees, asked her jail keeper on August 11, 1693, to provide a master to carry her "out of the country into Virginia." At length "she was sold to Virginia."[291]   Since the Rev. Samuel Parris was finished with her, Tituba was also sold to a slave trader to pay her prison fees. What happened to her husband, John Indian, is unknown.

Massachusetts would never again witness another execution for witchcraft. A total of nineteen people were hanged, fourteen women and five men. Giles Corey was pressed to death and eight people died in prison. But not everyone in Massachusetts had been caught up the mania. Examination of the records shows that nearly all the inflammatory writings were produced by Cotton Mather and his cohorts. The responses of the average citizens that have come down to us in the form of petitions and letters were rational and displayed balanced judgment.

Because of their conceit in their own superior understanding, the justices, except for Samuel Sewall, never acknowledged their errors. In 1697 Sewall, who held a reputation of great integrity, gave a note to the minister during a public fast. His note

---

290 Calef, *More Wonders*, 334.
291 Burr, *Narratives*, 384.

acknowledged his mistakes and stated his desire to humble himself in the sight of God and his people. Sewall stood alone while the note was read in clear tones to the congregation.

When Sarah Wardwell came home after her release in May 1693 with her baby Rebecca, she found her children scattered and her Andover farm devastated. Sheriff George Corwin had come from Salem with his deputy and assistants during the past September. Vulture-like, they had seized all moveable property from the farm, including five cows, a heifer, a yearling, a horse, nine hogs, and eight loads of hay, and even had harvested six acres of corn upon the ground. They had taken her husband's carpenter tools. Fortunately their efforts to confiscate Andover land had been thwarted by the town's leading citizens who belonged to the resistance movement. The Wardwell land in Andover[292] was safe, but Sarah's more valuable land in Lynn, the legacy of Adam Hawkes, was gone.

In 1694 Governor Sir William Phipps left Boston for England, where he died in 1695. "Before he went he pardoned such as had been condemned, for which they gave about 30 shillings each to the King's attorney."[293] The leadership of Massachusetts fell upon William Stoughton who became acting governor. His old guard resisted and repressed any motion, even the slightest, toward redress and restitution of the property of the witchcraft victims.

The condemned were still under their attainders. John Proctor, executed on August 19, 1692, had been a rich man, with extensive acreage in Ipswich and in Salem Farms. In 1696 his widow Elizabeth Proctor, who had been among the condemned, petitioned the General Court for the recovery of her husband's lands. "Before my husband was executed, it is evident that somebody contrived a will wherein his whole estate is disposed of. Although the sentence was executed on my dear husband, yet I

---

292 Some of the Wardwell property now forms the campus of Andover Academy. In 1778 Samuel Phillips purchased the estate of Solomon Wardwell, a carpenter, and the first Academy building was his carpenter shop. Solomon was the great-grandson of Samuel Wardwell.
293 Calef, *More Wonders*, 336.

am still alive. Since my husband's death, the said will is proved and approved by the judge of probate and, by that kind of disposal, the whole estate is disposed of. Although God has granted my life, yet those who claim my husband's estate, by that which they call a will, will not suffer me to have one penny of the estate which, as I humbly conceive, does belong or ought to belong to me by the law, for they say I am dead in the law."[294] Nothing came of her petition.

After Stoughton's death on July 7, 1701, new hope was raised that some restitution would be made to the witchcraft victims. On March 2, 1703, twenty-one residents of Andover, Salem Village, and Topsfield petitioned the General Court requesting the reversal of attainders. Sarah Wardwell was among them. This was her last known act before her death, her final effort to recover her property in Lynn. Not until October 17, 1711 did the General Court pass an act to reverse the attainders of George Burroughs and others for witchcraft.[295] The executed Samuel Wardwell was included but not his wife, Sarah Wardwell. Her son, Samuel Wardwell, Jr. made one last attempt. In a petition on February 19, 1712, he wrote, "My mother Sarah Wardwell was condemned by the court at Salem sometime in January 1693, but her name is not inserted in the late Act of the General Court, for

---

294 Massachusetts Archives, *Witchcraft*, 135:110.
295 The others named on the act were the condemned Mary Bradbury, Martha Carrier, Giles Corey and his wife, Rebecca Eames, Mary Easty, Abigail Faulkner, Ann Foster, Sarah Good, Dorcas Hoar, Abigail Hobbs, Elizabeth Howe, George Jacobs, Sr., Mary (Foster) Lacey, Rebecca Nurse, Mary Parker, Mary Post, John Proctor, Samuel Wardwell, Sarah Wilds, and John Willard.   Intentionally left off the list were the condemned women Bridget Bishop, Elizabeth Johnson, Jr., Susannah Martin, Alice Parker, Elizabeth Proctor, Ann Pudeator, Wilmot Redd, Margaret Scott, and Sarah Wardwell.   Bridget Bishop's valuable house and land in Salem Town across the street from the house of the Rev. Noyes, Susannah Martin's land in Amesbury, Ann Pudeator's two estates on the north line of the common in Salem Town, Elizabeth Proctor's extensive acreage in Salem and Ipswich, and Sarah Wardwell's acreage in Lynn had been confiscated, not to be returned.   In 1700 magistrate Bartholomew Gedney, an owner of many properties in Salem, had possession of one of the Pudeator estates, and John Best, one of her accusers, the other.

the taking off the attainder of those who were condemned. My mother, being since deceased, I thought it my duty to endeavor that her name may have the benefit of that Act."[296] His petition failed.

Families struggled for years to recover their lands, but to no avail. On August 28, 1957, almost two hundred and fifty years later, the General Court passed a resolve declaring that "Whereas, one Ann Pudeator and certain other persons were indicted, tried, found guilty, sentenced to death, and executed in the year 1692 for witchcraft; and said persons may have been illegally tried, convicted and sentenced by a possibly illegal Court of Oyer and Terminer, and whereas the General Court of Massachusetts is informed that certain descendants of said Ann Pudeator and said other persons are still distressed by the record of such proceedings; therefore be it resolved that no disgrace or cause for distress attaches to said descendants, and be it further resolved that the passage of this resolve shall not affect in any way whatever the title to, or rights in any real or personal property, nor shall it require or permit the remission of any penalty, fine or forfeiture hitherto imposed or incurred."

The resolve did not lift any of the remaining attainders, and it further confirmed the status quo as to property rights. The ghost of Stoughton, slightly agitated by all the commotion, fell back again into peaceful repose. The spoils of witchcraft fanaticism were secure.

---

296 Bailey, *Historical Sketches of Andover*, 220.

18

MATTHEW MAULE, WIZARD

I MAGINE TRAVELING BACK IN TIME to the Salem of 1692, a small coastal settlement on a narrow neck of land jutting out into the harbor. In the center of town stands the meetinghouse with its bell tower pointing skyward. Houses and small cottages line the dirt tracks stretching down to the waterfront and its wharves. Merchant ships and fishing boats crowd the inner harbor. Inland, a deep forest blankets the land, broken only by a few scattered farms and villages.

In our day, the reality of seventeenth century New England lives on through the genius of Nathaniel Hawthorne and his narratives. An artist of exceptional sensitivity and insight, Hawthorne suffered most of his life from the knowledge of his ancestors' role in the enforcement of the Puritan code. Major William Hathorne persecuted the Quakers; magistrate John Hathorne persecuted the accused witches.

In the *The House of the Seven Gables*, Nathaniel Hawthorne wrote, "Old Matthew Maule, in a word, was executed for the crime of witchcraft. He was one of the martyrs to that terrible delusion, which should teach us that the influential classes are fully liable to all the passionate error that has ever characterized the maddest mob. Clergymen, judges, statesmen—the wisest, calmest, holiest persons of their day—stood in the inner circle round about the gallows, loudest to applaud the work of blood. If any one part of their proceedings can be said to deserve less blame than another, it was the singular indiscrimination with which they persecuted not merely the poor and aged, as in former judicial massacres, but people of all ranks; their own equals, brethren, and wives."

"Amid the disorder of such various ruin, it is not strange that a man of inconsiderable note, like Maule, should have trodden the martyr's path to the hill of execution almost unremarked in the throng of his fellow sufferers. But, in after days, when the frenzy of that hideous epoch had subsided, it was remembered how loudly Colonel Pyncheon had joined in the general cry, to purge the land from witchcraft; nor did it fail to be whispered that there was an invidious acrimony in the zeal with which he had sought the condemnation of Matthew Maule. It was well known that the victim had recognized the bitterness of personal enmity in his prosecutor's conduct towards him, and that he declared himself hunted to death for his spoil."[297]

Given that the real-life magistrate John Hathorne is the fictional Colonel Pyncheon, the question arises, who is the real-life counterpart of the fictional wizard Matthew Maule?

In the Salem witchcraft affair, only six men were executed as wizards. George Jacobs, Sr., John Willard, John Proctor, and the Rev. George Burroughs were hanged on August 19, 1692. Giles Corey was pressed to death on September 19, 1692. Finally, Samuel Wardwell was hanged on September 22, 1692.

A former minister of Salem Village, George Burroughs had been hounded out by the acrimony, snooping, and refusal on the part of some parishioners to pay their share of the minister's salary. Although he had been upheld and the parish reprimanded by the General Court, he preferred to leave rather than struggle further with the congregation. It is clear that Burroughs had incurred the wrath of the Putnam family of Salem Village, and it was they who accused him of witchcraft in 1692.

Under ordinary circumstances a Puritan minister would be immune to witchcraft accusations. However the ruling old guard deemed otherwise, and they threw the Virginia-born Burroughs to the wolves, the witch hunters. In 1692 Burroughs was the

297   Hawthorne, *The House of the Seven Gables*, Chapter 1

pastor of the church in Wells, Maine. His principal crime seemed to be a disbelief in witchcraft itself. Apparently the condemnation of a tolerant and forgiving minister was an important symbol for the staunch Puritans. A Harvard graduate and clergyman, George Burroughs was an important figure and does not fit the description of Matthew Maule in the novel, a man "of inconsiderable note."

Nathaniel Hawthorne described George Jacobs, Sr. in *Main-Street* as upright, quiet, blameless, a good husband, and a good father. He does not fit Hawthorne's description of the wizard Matthew Maule.

John Willard had been designated by the authorities to arrest several of those accused. Because of the promptings of his conscience, Willard refused, and so was accused himself. In *Main-Street*, Nathaniel Hawthorne described Willard as honest, shrewd, practical, active in his business at his place of trade. John Willard does not fit the description of the fictional Maule.

In *Main-Street*, Hawthorne described John Proctor and his wife Elizabeth as an aged couple who appeared to have led a truly Christian life. John Proctor, a well-known and wealthy innkeeper, is not the Matthew Maule of Nathaniel Hawthorne's book.

Eighty-year-old Giles Corey, a brave man, was not hanged but pressed to death for standing mute. He is not the character Matthew Maule.

This leaves one man, Samuel Wardwell, the last person, as it turned out, to be hanged for witchcraft in Salem. Wardwell was convinced that he was singled out for execution no matter how he pleaded. At first he refused to confess, but after his wife, stepdaughter and daughter were arrested he made a confession, desperately hoping that it would protect them. Up to that time, any accused witch who had confessed was not brought to trial. Despite his confession, Wardwell soon realized that he would be tried and convicted. An old hand at predictions, he foresaw that he would be sent to his death for witchcraft. On September 13, 1692, Samuel Wardwell renounced his confession and was immediately brought to trial. He was condemned on September 17 and hanged on September 22.

The Wardwells, a family of strong convictions, continually found themselves on the wrong side of Puritan law. They were Antinomian heretics, Quakers, and finally accused witches. Samuel Wardwell's father, Thomas Wardwell, a follower of Anne Hutchinson, was banished from Boston for heresy in 1637. Samuel Wardwell's brother Eliakim, and Eliakim's wife Lydia, converted Quakers, were forced to make their escape to New Jersey in 1664. For Samuel Wardwell, the accused wizard, there was neither banishment nor escape.

Calef gave the following eyewitness account, "Wardwell having formerly confessed himself guilty, and after denied it, was soon brought upon his trial; his former confession and specter testimony was all that appeared against him. At execution while he was speaking to the people, protesting his innocence, the executioner being at the same time smoking tobacco, the smoke coming in his face, interrupted his discourse, those accusers said, 'The Devil hinders him with smoke.' "

John Hathorne sat on horseback watching the execution. Eight were executed on that rainy day, September 22, 1692, on Gallows Hill. Compare the above contemporary account by Calef with this fictional account given by Nathaniel Hawthorne. "At the moment of execution—with the halter about his neck, and while Colonel Pyncheon [the real-life John Hathorne] sat on horseback, grimly gazing at the scene—Maule had addressed him from the scaffold and uttered a prophecy."

Of all the men accused in 1692, Samuel Wardwell alone had a history of telling fortunes and making prophecies. He alone found amusement as an amateur magician. Adding to the horror of this lapse of Puritan morality was his curiosity, imagination, and inclination toward independent thinking, traits that were unwelcome to the old guard.

Samuel Wardwell was a simple man, a carpenter, a person of small importance, "a man of inconsiderable note." The son of Matthew Maule in the novel was a carpenter named Thomas. The son of Samuel Wardwell in real life was a carpenter named Thomas. The fictional Matthew Maule corresponds to the real-life carpenter Samuel Wardwell.

Samuel Wardwell died in the final execution of the Salem witchcraft mania, a tragedy that was destined to lead to the fall of the New England Puritan oligarchy. Its demise is symbolized in the *The House of the Seven Gables* with the death of the fictitious Colonel Pyncheon, corresponding to the real-life John Hathorne, "The ironhearted Puritan, the relentless persecutor, the grasping and strong-willed man, was dead! Dead, in his new house!"[298]

---

298 Ibid.

19

THE LIFTING OF THE CURSE

U NTIL THE PRESENT CENTURY Salem was unique. No other city in America could boast of so many antique, wooden, gable-roofed houses. Three hundred years ago the occupants of those houses professed a full belief in the supernatural; they were eyewitnesses to the days of witchcraft. During this century nearly every one of those ancient structures was destroyed or mutilated beyond recognition. One wonders if the real reason was that the town of Salem wanted to purge itself of its past and get rid of the ghosts that haunted those antique houses. Although Nathaniel Hawthorne believed that ghost stories should not be treated seriously, he was tempted to play with the notion in his fiction. Now, in this chapter, the ghosts that inhabit the pages of *The House of the Seven Gables* are at last identified.

In Salem today, halfway down a narrow street, tourists can find three weather-beaten wooden houses. These ancient buildings, in the midst of a beautiful garden, face the blue waters of the harbor. The most famous, with its huge chimneys and acutely-peaked gables, is the House of the Seven Gables. In 1668 John Turner had the original structure built at its present location, which was then near "a natural spring of soft and pleasant water—a rare treasure on the sea-girt peninsula." Tradition says that the carpenter "did his work so faithfully that the timbered framework fastened by his hands still holds together." In 1782, the grandson of John Turner sold the house to Captain Samuel Ingersoll, whose wife was a Hathorne. Their daughter, Miss Susie Ingersoll, inherited the house and lived a solitary life in it. Her cousin, Nathaniel Hawthorne, eighteen years her junior, was almost her sole visitor. To Nathaniel Hawthorne, the house was "an object of curiosity from my

Hawthorne's birthplace as it appeared one hundred years ago

The Hooper house as it appeared one hundred years ago

boyhood, both as a specimen of the best and stateliest
architecture of a long-past epoch, and as the scene of events more
full of interest than a gray feudal castle."[299]

The second house on the site is the birthplace of Nathaniel
Hawthorne. Purchased by Hawthorne's grandfather in 1772, the
author was born here on July 4, 1804. After his birth, the family
lived there for only a few years. By 1900 it was owned by a
sturdy Irish woman and her husband, who kept the shutters
drawn, and allowed no one to tour the house, having refused,
apparently, offers as high as $5.00. In 1958 it was moved from its
original location on Union Street to the grounds of the House of
the Seven Gables.

The third house on the site is the Hooper house. In 1682
Benjamin Hooper built this house for his family in the center of
Salem. The clapboards covering the outside were cut from the log
by hand; the space between the outer and inner walls was
cemented with brick and mortar, a common means of protection
against fire. The beams, exposed in the low studded rooms, were
hewn from rough logs with an axe, and their crude ornamentation
was accomplished with an auger box. Years later the house
became a bakery. This "old bakery," was moved in 1911 to its
new foundation next to the House of the Seven Gables.

Remember that Sarah Hooper was born in 1650, the oldest
daughter of the well-to-do Hooper family. In 1670 at the age of
19, Sarah became the wife of the wealthy Adam Hawkes of
Lynn, 65 years old. In 1672, after moving from Salem to Andover,
"Samuel Wardwell, carpenter, wickedly and feloniously with
the Evil Spirit, the Devil, a covenant did make."[300] Adam
Hawkes died soon thereafter, leaving his handsome young
widow Sarah a small fortune in money and extensive and
valuable acreage in Lynn. Several young men of well-placed
Puritan families vied for her attention but "her eyes fell upon the
carpenter, clad in a green woolen jacket, a pair of loose breeches,
open at the knees, and with a long pocket for his rule, the end of
which protruded. A glow of artistic approval brightened over
her face; she was struck with admiration—which she made no

299 Ibid.
300 Woodward, *Records of Salem Witchcraft*, 2:147.

attempt to conceal—of the remarkable comeliness, strength and energy of his figure." Not long widowed, Sarah, 22, married the carpenter, 29, a man beneath her class. Did the rejected suitors believe that the carpenter had exercised a subtle influence over her? "Might not this influence be the same that was called witchcraft?"[301]

Did the carpenter, who became wealthy from his marriage to Sarah, also hope to gain social standing? "But, after all, what worked most to the young carpenter's disadvantage was, first, the reserve and sternness of his natural disposition, and next, the fact of his not being a church communicant, and the suspicion of his holding heretical tenets in matters of religion and polity."[302] It was well-known that Samuel Wardwell, like his father and brother before him, never lovingly embraced the Puritan church.

Remember that the wedding was performed on January 9, 1673 in Andover by the Puritan magistrate, Major William Hathorne; it was the only time he ever set foot in Andover for such an occasion.[303] The major saw all of his sons except John meet with mysterious and untimely deaths and did not rule out witchcraft as the cause. After the major's death in 1680, John Hathorne became a magistrate, carrying on in his father's footsteps.

The major's brother, also named John Hathorne, lived in Lynn and had worked closely with Adam Hawkes in the early days when that town was laid out and land was plentiful.[304] Adam's land, now the property of Samuel's wife, Sarah Wardwell, was especially valuable. "In the growth of the town, the site had become exceedingly desirable in the eyes of a prominent and powerful personage, who asserted plausible claims to the proprietorship of this, and a large adjacent tract of land. Colonel Pyncheon [magistrate John Hathorne], the claimant, as we

301 Hawthorne, *The House of the Seven Gables*, Chapter 13.
302 Ibid.
303 At the time of Sarah's marriage to Samuel Wardwell, the major had two unmarried sons, John, 31, and William, Jr., 26. The major's eldest son, Eleazer, 36, was married to Abigail Corwin.
304 At the time of Sarah's marriage to Samuel Wardwell, the Lynn John Hathorne had an unmarried son, John, Jr., aged 26, as well as two younger sons.

gather from whatever traits are preserved, was characterized by an iron energy of purpose. Matthew Maule [Samuel Wardwell], on the other hand, though an obscure man, was stubborn in the defense of what he considered his right. No written record of this dispute is known to be in existence. Our acquaintance with the whole subject is derived chiefly by tradition. This controversy between two ill-matched antagonists—at a period, moreover, when personal influence had far more weight than now—remained for years undecided, and came to a close only with the death of the party [Samuel Wardwell] occupying the disputed soil. The mode of his death, too, affects the mind differently, in our day, from what it did a century and a half ago. It was a death that blasted with strange horror the humble name of the dweller [Samuel Wardwell], and made it seem almost a religious act to obliterate his place and memory among men."[305]

"After the reported wizard's death, his humble homestead had fallen an easy spoil into Colonel Pyncheon's [magistrate John Hathorne's] grasp."[306] Julian Hawthorne, the son of Nathaniel, wrote that magistrate John Hathorne, "a punctiliously righteous person according to the Puritan code of morality, ended a poorer man than he began—the witch's curse having taken effect on the worldly prosperity of the family. The site of the present town of Raymond, in Maine, once belonged to the Hathornes [the eastern land]; but the title deeds were in some unaccountable way lost, and were not recovered until the lapse of time had rendered the claim obsolete."[307]

In 1792, one hundred years after the death of their great-grandfather Samuel Wardwell on Gallows Hill, the brothers Peter and Samuel Wardwell settled near Raymond, Maine, on the so-called Hathorne lands.[308] "In the course of time, the territory was partially cleared and occupied by actual settlers."[309] By Nathaniel Hathorne's day the Wardwells had spread over a significant area on "lands which they or their

---

305 Hawthorne, *The House of the Seven Gables*, Chapter 1.
306 Ibid.
307 Julian Hawthorne, *Nathaniel Hawthorne and his Wife*, 1:26.
308 W. S. Spur, *A History of Otisfield, Maine to 1944*.
309 Hawthorne, *The House of the Seven Gables*, Chapter 1.

fathers had wrested from the wild hand of nature by their own sturdy toil." Nathaniel Hawthorne wrote, "It was an ordinary saying that the old wizard, hanged though he was, had obtained the best end of the bargain in his contest with Colonel Pyncheon [magistrate John Hathorne]; inasmuch as he got possession of the the great Eastern claim [the eastern land in Maine]. A very old aged woman, recently dead, had often used the metaphorical expression, in fireside talk, that miles and miles of Pyncheon [Hathorne] land had been shoveled into Maule's [Wardwell's] grave; which, by the by, was but a very shallow nook, between two rocks, near the summit of Gallows Hill. Again, when the lawyers were making inquiry for the missing document, it was a byword that it would never be found, unless in the wizard's skeleton hand."[310]

"It is not the less certain, however, that awe and terror brooded over the memories of those who died for this horrible crime of witchcraft. Their graves, in the crevices of the rocks, were supposed to be incapable of retaining the occupants who had been so hastily thrust into them. Old Matthew Maule [Samuel Wardwell], especially, was known to have as little hesitation of difficulty in rising out of his grave as an ordinary man in getting out of bed, and was as often seen at midnight as living people at noonday. This pestilent wizard (in whom his just punishment seemed to have wrought no manner of amendment) had an inveterate habit of haunting a certain mansion, styled the House of the Seven Gables."[311]

"What sense, meaning, or moral such as ghost stories should be susceptible of, can be traced to the ridiculous legend that, at midnight, all the dead Pyncheons [Hathornes] assemble in the parlor. First comes the ancestor himself [magistrate John Hathorne], in his black cloak, steeple hat, and trunk breeches. The stout Colonel [magistrate John Hathorne] is dissatisfied! So decided is the look of discontent as to impart additional distinctness to his features; through which the moonlight passes, and flickers on the wall beyond. Something has strongly vexed the ancestor! With a grim shake of his head, he turns away.

---

310 Hawthorne, *The House of the Seven Gables*, Chapter 13.
311 Ibid.

Here come other Pyncheons, the whole tribe. A mother lifts her child.[312] In a corner, meanwhile, stands the figure of an elderly man [Samuel Wardwell], in a leather jerkin and breeches, with a carpenter's rule sticking out of his side pocket; he points his finger at the bearded Colonel and his descendants, nodding, jeering, mocking, and finally bursting into obstreperous, though inaudible laughter."[313]

Hathorne family tradition held that the condemned wizard had cursed the magistrate and his descendants. The novel's theme of an ancestral curse springs from Hawthorne's fancy that the wrongdoing of John Hathorne, the relentless witch-hunter, lived into successive generations, even to his own. And, in one very real sense, it did. For Hawthorne, the curse he inherited took a wrenching twist: Instead of dark portents and nebulous forebodings, Nathaniel Hawthorne wrestled with the more immediate, sinister forces of guilt, the guilt he so keenly felt on discovering the long, chilling catalog of his ancestors' misdeeds. Anthony Trollope perceptively commented that Hawthorne created *The House of the Seven Gables* because he had to write it. The book was Hawthorne's attempt to lift the curse of guilt and release himself from the heavy burden that it imposed upon him.

The characters of Phoebe and Holgrave in the novel are the key to the removal of the curse. Much of Phoebe's character is drawn from Nathaniel's wife Sophia (Peabody) Hawthorne, although in the novel Nathaniel makes Phoebe a Pyncheon. Holgrave, the artist and writer in the novel, is a thinly disguised image of Nathaniel himself. Significantly, Nathaniel makes Holgrave a descendant of the wizard. Holgrave does not disclose his relationship until, at the end of the book, he is confident that he has won Phoebe's love. On the death of Judge Pyncheon, Holgrave reveals the dusty secret

---

312 It is tempting to imagine that the mother and child are Sarah (Hooper) Hawkes Wardwell and her daughter Sarah Hawkes. By happy chance, the Hooper house was saved and moved to its present site next to the House of the Seven Gables.

313 Hawthorne, *The House of the Seven Gables*, Chapter 18.

hiding place of the now worthless Indian deed conveying the eastern land in Maine to the Pyncheons [Hathornes].

"But," said Phoebe, "how come you to know the secret?"

"My dearest Phoebe," said Holgrave, "how will it please you to assume the name of Maule? As for the secret it is the only inheritance that has come down to me from my ancestors. In this long drama of wrong and retribution, I represent the old wizard, and am probably as much a wizard as ever he was."[314]

Through the character of Holgrave, Hawthorne makes clear that he places himself not on the side of the oppressors, but squarely on the side of the oppressed. And he leaves no doubt that the weight of his ancestor's crimes was genuinely oppressive to him. But the love of Phoebe and Holgrave marks the lifting of the curse in the novel, much as the love of Sophia and Nathaniel does in real life.

In *The House of the Seven Gables*, Nathaniel Hawthorne has confronted the sins of his ancestors head on. For him, this required that his novel bring back to life not only his ancestors, but also their innocent victims. The tale he chooses to tell is not one of hatred or revenge, but ultimately of virtue, love, and forgiveness. His characters weave a charm of their own. They ring so true that they transcend time and place to win universal appeal to all people in all ages. The conflict Hawthorne struggled with for so long must have subsided as he approached the end of his story. The insight he gained is his gift to his readers. As one of America's finest writers, and as a man whose heritage was intimately linked with the Salem witchcraft affair, his is the final word.

---

314 Not coincidentally, Nathaniel Hawthorne addressed his own wife, Sophia, by his nickname for her, Phoebe.

20

THE ANDOVER CONSPIRACY

O F THE SALEM WITCHCRAFT AFFAIR, Nathaniel Hawthorne wrote, "If any one part of their proceedings can be said to deserve less blame than another, it was the singular indiscrimination with which they persecuted not merely the poor and aged, as in former judicial massacres, but people of all ranks; their own equals, brethren, and wives."[315] About fifty Andover residents were imprisoned for witchcraft in 1692, a number greater than Salem and Salem Village combined. Nowhere but in Andover do Hawthorne's words, "persecuted their own equals, brethren, and wives," take on such terrible meaning.

Contention, bickering, and altercations were present in abundance among the Puritans. In this atmosphere, accusations by one person against another were commonplace. Powerless to explain the reason for a sickness or catastrophe, the Puritan clergy turned to the Bible, and discovered witchcraft as the cause. "Witches are the doers of strange things. They do really torment, they do really afflict those that their spite shall extend unto," wrote Cotton Mather.[316] The policy of the church to blame witches as the cause of unexplained evils inevitably led to witchcraft accusations.

---

315 Hawthorne, *The House of the Seven Gables*, Chapter 1.
316 Cotton Mather, "A Discourse on Witchcraft."

A witchcraft accusation by itself would come to nothing. In order to turn an accusation into a prosecution, the accused person had to be charged. An accuser became a *plaintiff* or *complainant* when he filed an official written document, called a *complaint*, with the magistrates. If the magistrates felt that the complaint had merit, they made out an arrest warrant against the accused. A constable or marshal would carry out the arrest. After the arrest, the accused person, now a *defendant*, was taken before the magistrates for a preliminary *examination*.

Present at the preliminary examination were the afflicted persons. They threw fits and suffered the pains of torment, claiming that the specter of the accused person was hurting them at that very time. Of course, no one could see the specter except the afflicted, but the afflictions were considered hard evidence of the witchcraft of the accused. Witnesses for the prosecution might be called to give testimony about how the accused person had practiced witchcraft in the past. Previously imprisoned persons who had confessed witchcraft might also be present to claim that the accused person was one of their number. On the basis of the examination, the magistrates would decide whether to release the accused person or to commit her or him to prison to await trial. With the single exception of Nehemiah Abbot, Jr., every accused witch in 1692 was committed to prison after the preliminary examination.

The next legal step was the grand jury inquest. The grand jury could either clear or indict the accused. If indicted, the accused person would be given a trial by jury. In the case of a guilty verdict, the death sentence would be passed. In all phases of the prosecution, the accused person was never allowed representation by a lawyer or other counsel.

Throughout the entire process, accusations of witchcraft against the accused were rife. They came from all corners: from the afflicted girls, from the girls' parents, from witnesses for the prosecution, and from confessing witches. In this overall confusion the whole witchcraft affair appears as nothing more than an entangled morass of allegations brought on by mass hysteria. However, a careful analysis shows just the opposite.

The written complaint filed with the magistrates consisted of three parts: the accused witches, the afflicted children, and the adults making the complaint. The names of the accused witches and the afflicted children also appeared on the resulting arrest warrant.

Although many of the official documents in the case of the Andover witch hunt have been lost or destroyed, enough survive so that a reasonably detailed story can be reconstructed, despite some gaps. The first column gives the date of the complaint or arrest; the second column gives the name of the accused witch; the third column gives the plaintiffs; and the fourth column gives the afflicted girls. The names on the complaint or arrest warrant are used if either exists. Otherwise the names of the afflicted girls are taken from the examination document if it exists. Finally if all the preceding methods fail, the names are taken either from the indictments or from other evidence. In the last two columns, the earliest extant source is indicated, whether it be the complaint, the arrest warrant, the examination, the indictment, or an inference from ancillary information.

Date 1692	Accused Andover Witch	Plaintiffs	Afflicted
May 28	Martha (Allen) Carrier; about 38, condemned, hanged	*complaint:* Jonathan Walcott Joseph Houlton	*complaint:* Mary Walcott Ann Putnam, Jr. Abigail Williams Mercy Lewis
July 15	Ann Foster, about 72, condemned and died in prison	*inference:* Joseph Ballard	*inference:* Elizabeth (Phelps) Ballard
July 19	Mary (Foster) Lacey, 40, condemned, survived	*complaint:* Joseph Ballard	*complaint:* Elizabeth (Phelps) Ballard
July 19	Mary Lacey, Jr., 18	*complaint:* Joseph Ballard	*complaint:* Elizabeth (Phelps) Ballard
July 21	Richard Carrier, 18		*warrant:* Mary Warren
July 21	Andrew Carrier, 15		*warrant:* Mary Warren
July 22	Martha (Toothaker) Emerson, 24, of Haverhill		*warrant:* Mary Warren Mary Lacey, Jr.

July 28	Mary (Tyler) Post Bridges, about 50		*warrant:* Timothy Swan
About Aug. 1	Rebecca (Blake) Eames, 51, of Boxford (attended Andover Church)		*examination* Timothy Swan
Aug. 2	Mary Post, 28, condemned, survived	*complaint &* *warrant* Timothy Swan Mary Walcott Ann Putnam, Jr.	*complaint &* *warrant:* Timothy Swan Mary Walcott Ann Putnam, Jr.
Aug. 3	Mary (Johnson) Davis Clarke, about 52, of Haverhill (first accused of the Johnson Family)	*complaint:* Robert Swan John Swan	*complaint:* Timothy Swan Mary Walcott Ann Putnam, Jr.
by Aug. 10	Daniel Eames, 29, of Boxford (attended Andover Church)		
Aug. 10	Elizabeth Johnson, Jr., 22, condemned, survived		*examination:* Sarah Phelps Mary Walcott Ann Putnam, Jr. Timothy Swan
Aug. 10	Thomas Carrier, Jr., 10		*examination:* Sarah Phelps Ann Putnam. Jr. Mary Walcott
Aug. 10	Sarah Carrier, 7		*examination:* Sarah Phelps Ann Putnam, Jr.
Aug. 11	Abigail (Dane) Faulkner, 40, condemned, survived		*examination:* Sarah Phelps
Aug. 15	Edward Farrington, 30		*indictment:* Mary Warren
Aug. 15	Sarah Parker, 22		
Aug. 15	Samuel Wardwell, 49, condemned, hanged		*indictment:* Martha Sprague
Aug. 25	Mary Bridges, Jr., 13		*examination:* Martha Sprague Rose Foster

Aug. 25	Sarah Bridges, about 17		*examination:* Martha Sprague Rose Foster
Aug. 25	Hannah Post, 26		*examination:* Martha Sprague Rose Foster
Aug. 25	Susannah Post, about 31		*examination:* Martha Sprague Rose Foster
Aug. 25	William Barker, Sr., about 46	*warrant:* Samuel Martin Moses Tyler	*warrant:* Abigail Martin Martha Sprague Rose Foster
Aug. 25	Mary Barker, 13	*warrant:* Samuel Martin Moses Tyler	*warrant:* Abigail Martin Martha Sprague Rose Foster
Aug. 25	Mary (Osgood) Marston, 27	*warrant:* Samuel Martin Moses Tyler	*warrant:* Abigail Martin Martha Sprague Rose Foster
Aug. 25	John Jackson, Sr., about 49, of Rowley	*complaint:* Ephraim Foster Joseph Tyler	*complaint:* Rose Foster Martha Sprague
Aug. 25	John Jackson, Jr., 22, of Rowley	*complaint:* Ephraim Foster Joseph Tyler	*complaint:* Rose Foster Martha Sprague
Aug. 25	John Howard, about 47, of Rowley	*complaint:* Ephraim Foster Joseph Tyler	*complaint:* Rose Foster Martha Sprague
Aug. 29	Elizabeth (Dane) Johnson, about 51	*warrant:* Samuel Martin Moses Tyler	*warrant:* Abigail Martin Martha Sprague
Aug. 29	Abigail Johnson, 10	*warrant:* Samuel Martin Moses Tyler	*warrant:* Abigail Martin Martha Sprague
Aug. 29	Stephen Johnson, 13		*examination:* Martha Sprague Rose Foster Mary Lacey, Jr.
Sept. 1	William Barker, Jr., 14		*examination:* Martha Sprague Rose Foster Abigail Martin

Sept. 1	Sarah (Hooper) Hawkes Wardwell, 42, condemned, survived		*examination:* Martha Sprague Abigail Martin Rose Foster
Sept. 1	Sarah Hawkes, 21		*examination:* Martha Sprague Rose Foster
Sept. 1	Mercy Wardwell, 19		*examination:* Martha Sprague Rose Foster Timothy Swan
Sept. 1	Mary (Ayer) Parker, about 55, condemned, hanged		*examination:* Martha Sprague Sarah Phelps
Sept. 7	Mary (Clement) Osgood, about 55		*touch test*
Sept. 7	Eunice (Potter) Frye, 51		*touch test*
Sept. 7	Abigail (Wheeler) Barker, 36		*touch test*
Sept. 7	Mary (Lovett) Tyler, about 40		*touch test*
Sept. 7	Hannah Tyler, 14		*touch test*
Sept. 7	Joanna Tyler, 11		*touch test*
Sept. 7	Martha Tyler, 11		*touch test*
Sept. 7	Deliverance (Haseltine) Dane, about 37		*touch test*
Sept. 7	Rebecca (Aslet) Johnson, 40		*touch test*
Sept. 7	Rebecca Johnson Jr., 17		*touch test*
Sept. 7	Abigail Faulkner, Jr., 9		*touch test*
Sept. 7	Dorothy Faulkner, 12		*touch test*
Sept. 7	Sarah (Lord) Wilson, about 44		*touch test*
Sept. 7	Sarah Wilson, Jr., 14		*touch test*
Sept. 7	John Sadie, Jr., about 13		*touch test*
Sept. 7	Henry Salter, about 65		*touch test*
Sept. 7	Joseph Draper, 21		*touch test*
Sept. 7	Male Slave of the Rev. Dane		*touch test*

The first step in identifying the conspiracy is to eliminate the Salem Village girls Abigail Williams, Ann Putnam, Jr., Mercy Lewis, Mary Walcott, and Mary Warren, as they were instruments of the Salem Village conspiracy. Next eliminate Mary Lacey, Jr., an imprisoned witch, brought into the courtroom to act as an afflicted person. Associate each Andover afflicted girl with her father, or in the case of Martha Sprague with her stepfather and stepbrother. Three married women also were afflicted; associate them with their husbands. Timothy Swan acted both as an afflicted and an accuser; his two brothers were also accusers. The men so determined were the legal accusers, the plaintiffs. The following table is the result.

Legal accuser or plaintiff	Afflicted circle
Joseph Ballard, 50	Elizabeth (Phelps) Ballard, 46
Samuel Phelps, 41	Sarah Phelps, Jr., 10
Daniel Bigsby, 41	Hannah (Chandler) Bigsby, 35
Robert Swan, Jr., 35 Timothy Swan, 29 John Swan, 24	Timothy Swan, 29
Moses Tyler, about 50 Joseph Tyler, 21	Martha Sprague, 16
Ephraim Foster, 35	Hannah (Eames) Foster, 31 Rose Foster, 14
Samuel Martin, 47	Abigail Martin, Jr., 16

The table shows the names of ten legal accusers, a small group. To these add the names of the Rev. Thomas Barnard, who masterminded the Andover touch test where eighteen were arrested, and Thomas Chandler, father-in-law of accusers Daniel Bigsby and Samuel Phelps. Because this small and interwoven group of twelve filed all the complaints in the Andover witch hunt, it can be concluded that they formed a conspiracy. Thus the table plays the role of a "smoking gun" in exposing the conspiracy. Like the Salem Village witch hunt, the Andover witch hunt was not driven by uncontrolled mass hysteria, but by the planned and deliberate actions of a conspiracy.

Now follow short biographies of the twelve Andover conspirators and the eight in the afflicted circle. The first biography is that of Thomas Chandler.

Thomas Chandler   **Andover**
Married man, 65   *Conspirator*

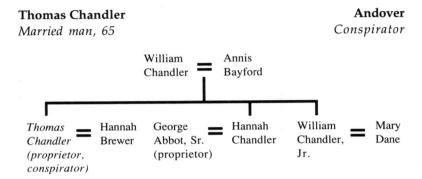

An important inter-family relationship in Andover was that of the Rev. Francis Dane. At the outset, it is helpful to give the structure of the Dane extended family and its relationship to the Chandler family. At the beginning of the seventeenth century, John Dane, a man of some pretensions, and William Chandler, a tanner, were friends in Hertfordshire, England. William Chandler and his wife, Annis (Bayford) Chandler, had Thomas Chandler, born about 1626, Hannah Chandler, born in 1629, and William Chandler, Jr., born in 1633. The Chandler family emigrated to New England and settled in Roxbury, then a town just southwest of Boston, and now a part of Boston.

Three children of John Dane and his wife, Frances (Boyer) Dane, enter the story. All born in England, the three are John Dane, Jr., born about 1610, Elizabeth Dane, born about 1612, and Francis Dane, born about 1615. John Dane, Jr., emigrated to New England, lived for a time with the Chandlers in Roxbury, and then left for Ipswich about 1638, where he became a chirurgeon.[317] His parents, John and Frances (Boyer) Dane, left

---

317 John Dane, Jr. left a dairy, a volume of manuscript, 132 leaves, 3.5 inches wide and 6 inches high, bound in parchment, with title page, "By John Dane of Ipswich, Chirurgeon, 1682." He also left some poems on the manner of preparation for death, two narrative poems, one in rhyme

England to join him in Ipswich, but soon moved to Roxbury to be near the Chandlers.

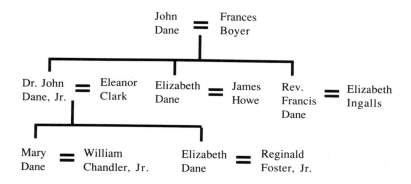

It seemed that John Dane and Annis (Bayford) Chandler were close, perhaps too close for the Puritan moral code. Except in unusual cases, divorces were forbidden. In any case William Chandler suddenly died in 1641 in Roxbury. "How many a woman, eager for widow's weeds, has given her husband a drink at bed-time, and let him sleep his last sleep in her bosom."[318] The next year, 1642, the healthy Frances (Boyer) Dane died suddenly in Roxbury. The following year, 1643, the widower John Dane married the widow Annis (Bayford) Chandler in Roxbury. Short accounts follow as to the fate of the children of the two families, now stepsiblings.

Hannah Chandler married George Abbot, Sr. in Roxbury in 1646. George Abbot, Sr. and Thomas Chandler, both ambitious, became original proprietors of the new settlement of Andover and moved to Andover to take up their positions. Thomas became a blacksmith and about 1651 married Hannah Brewer, the daughter of Daniel Brewer of Roxbury. William Chandler, Jr. also moved to Andover and in 1658 married Mary Dane, the daughter of his stepbrother John Dane, Jr. The three Chandler siblings became well established in Andover.

---

and the other not, and the minutes of sermons by the Rev. Dennison, the Rev. Hubbard, and the Rev. Grant.

318 Hawthorne, *Young Goodman Brown.*

In 1636 Francis Dane left London for Boston, being about six months on the journey, coming by way of the West Indies. He had no formal education, but received his theological training at the home of a clergyman, probably in Lynn.

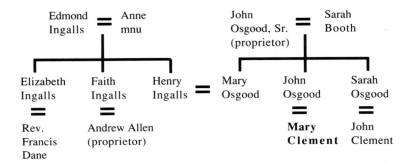

About 1644 Francis Dane married Elizabeth Ingalls, daughter of Edmond Ingalls of Lynn. Edmond Ingalls had two other children, Faith Ingalls and Henry Ingalls.[319] Faith Ingalls married Andrew Allen, a Scot, born about 1616. After coming to New England, he first lived in Lynn, where he is on record in 1642. About 1645 Andrew Allen became an original proprietor of Andover.

Elizabeth Dane married James Howe of Roxbury. They moved to Ipswich by 1648. In 1650 James Howe was granted 100 acres in the section known as Ipswich Farms, close to the Topsfield border. Both he and his wife became members of the Topsfield church. James Howe was a weaver by trade, but like other pioneers he was said to be able to build a house or butcher a swine. He could make a coffin or dig a grave. He could shoe a horse or make his own shoes. He could also write a deed or will, and practice in probate court. His wife, Elizabeth, died in 1694, and he died in 1702, at the age of 104, a man of three centuries.

---

319 Henry Ingalls, born in 1627, moved to Andover. He married, in 1653, Mary Osgood, daughter of John Osgood, Sr., who was an original proprietor of Andover. Mary's brother, John Osgood, married Mary Clement, who was imprisoned for witchcraft in 1692.

As stated above, Thomas Chandler and his brother-in-law, George Abbot, Sr., were original proprietors of Andover. Andrew Allen, the husband of the sister of Francis Dane's wife, was also an original proprietor. Because of the influence of these three proprietors, Francis Dane, aspiring for a pastorship, was made the minister in Andover in 1648. Francis Dane's brother-in-law Henry Ingalls also moved to Andover at that time.

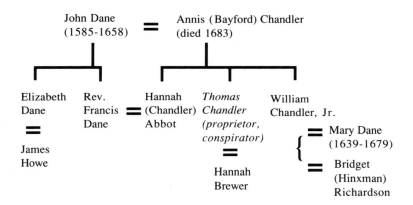

The Rev. Francis Dane was pastor at Andover for the 49 years from 1648 to his death in 1697. His wife, Elizabeth (Ingalls) Dane, died in 1676. The next year he married Mary Thomas, who died in 1689. In 1690, he married his stepsister, Hannah (Chandler) Abbot, widow of George Abbot, Sr. Abbot had died in 1682 at age 66. To Thomas Chandler, the marriage of his sister, Hannah, to her stepbrother, the Rev. Dane, paralleled the previous marriage of their mother, Annis, to John Dane, the father of the Rev. Dane. Bitter memories of this unhappy episode of the past stirred in the mind of Thomas Chandler.

Thomas Chandler, a blacksmith and ultimately a rich man, carried on a considerable iron works on the Shawsheen River. Thomas Chandler did not play an overt role in the conspiracy but participated in its action through his two sons-in-law, Samuel Phelps and Daniel Bigsby. As the original blacksmith of Andover, Thomas Chandler held a grudge against the two rival blacksmiths, John Bridges and Hopestill Tyler, and was instrumental in accusing their wives in 1692. The story of Hopestill's apprenticeship under Chandler is now outlined.

In 1658 Job Tyler apprenticed his young son Hopestill to Thomas Chandler, the blacksmith. Nathan Parker wrote the instrument of indenture and hid it in his house in a safe place. Soon afterwards, Job Tyler wanted to break the contract; Job entered Parker's house and stole the paper. Thomas Chandler always believed that Nathan Parker's wife, Mary (Ayer) Parker, had tipped off Job Tyler as to the hiding place. [On August 20, 1692, Thomas Chandler's son-in-law, Samuel Phelps, filed a complaint against the widowed Mary (Ayer) Parker, resulting in her execution on September 22, 1692.]

Hopestill Tyler's apprenticeship was the cause of a long controversy and several trials—Chandler vs. Tyler and Tyler vs. Chandler—extending over ten years and carried from court to court. Job Tyler used hostile words against Thomas Chandler. Chandler, wealthy and one of the principal citizens of Andover, made Tyler pay dearly. In 1665 in an action of defamation, the court decreed that "Job Tyler, being poor, he should not be fined above £6. We do order that Job Tyler shall nail up upon the post of Andover & Roxbury meetinghouses the acknowledgment, 'I, Job Tyler, have shamefully reproached Thomas Chandler by saying he is a base lying, cozening, cheating knave & that he has got his estate by cozening in a base reviling manner & that he was recorded for a liar & that he was a cheating, lying, whoring knave fit for all manner of bawdery, wishing the Devil had him. Therefore I, Job Tyler, do acknowledge that I have in these expressions most wickedly slandered Thomas Chandler & that without any just ground & therefore can do no less but express myself to be sorry for them.'"[320] Not one to give up easily for what he believed to be an unfair judgment, Job Tyler again brought suit against Chandler and was allowed to sue in *forma pauperis*, for he had no means of paying charges. The suit came to no avail; Job Tyler was ruined.

---

320 Bailey, *Historical Sketches of Andover*, 47-48.

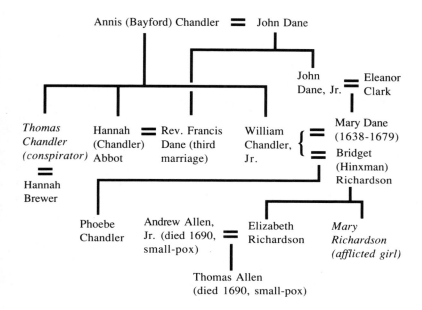

William Chandler, Jr., brother of Thomas Chandler, married, in 1658, Mary Dane, daughter of John Dane, Jr. William Chandler, Jr. was a brick-maker and later an innholder. Mary died in 1679, and five months later William Chandler, Jr. married Bridget (Hinxman) Richardson, the widow of James Richardson. The eldest child of Bridget and William was Phoebe Chandler, born in 1680. In 1692 Phoebe Chandler, 11, and her mother, Bridget, both testified against Martha (Allen) Carrier of Andover. Apparently Bridget blamed Martha for the deaths of her son-in-law, Andrew Allen, Jr., and of her grandson, Thomas Allen, both of whom died of smallpox in 1690. Andrew Allen, Jr. was the brother of Martha (Allen) Carrier, who many people believed brought the smallpox epidemic to Andover in 1690. Bridget's daughter, Mary Richardson, acted with the afflicted group in early September 1692.

A public house was called an inn, tavern, or ordinary. An innholder or taverner was licensed to sell wines and strong liquors to be drunk on the premises. A person licensed to sell liquors "out of doors," that is, liquors not to be drunk on the premises, was called a retailer. Andover was allowed two public houses and one retailer. Deacon John Frye of Andover was the retailer of strong spirits. Captain John Osgood was the innholder in the north part of Andover, and William Chandler, Jr. in the south part. Chandler's inn was on the road to Billerica. It was a custom then to denote shops and public houses by hanging out a "sign" or picture. The sign of Chandler's inn was a horseshoe. This quaint custom is still used in hamlets in England today.

In the years before 1692, Captain John Osgood made several complaints about the way that William Chandler, Jr. was conducting business. In 1690 Christopher Osgood, Deacon John Frye and others entered in court a petition about "a grievance which is grown so much an epidemical evil that overspreads and is like to corrupt the greater part of our town, if not speedily prevented by your help: viz. to put a stop to William Chandler's license of selling of drink. Servants and children are allowed by him in his house at all times unseasonably by night and day, sometimes till midnight and past & till break of day, till they know not their way to their habitations, and gaming is freely allowed in his house."[321] Nothing came of these petitions to the court. [In 1692, Captain John Osgood's wife, Mary (Clement) Osgood; Christopher Osgood's daughter, Mary (Osgood) Marston; and Deacon John Frye's wife, Eunice (Potter) Frye, were imprisoned for witchcraft.]

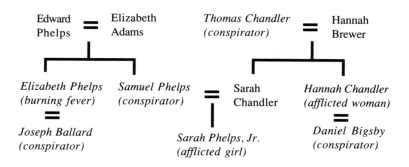

---

321 Bailey, *Historical Sketches of Andover*, 68-69.

Joseph Ballard   **Andover**
Married man, 50   *Conspirator*

Elizabeth (Phelps) Ballard   **Andover**
Married woman, 46   *Afflicted*

Joseph Ballard was born about 1642, the oldest child of Grace (mnu) and William Ballard, an original proprietor of Andover. In 1665 Joseph married Elizabeth Phelps, born about 1646, daughter of Elizabeth (Adams) and Edward Phelps. As the son of a first proprietor, Joseph Ballard had been elected a selectman three times (1687, 1688, 1690). When his father died in 1689, the family lands were divided between Joseph and his two brothers, John and William. These two brothers were married to Hooper sisters: John Ballard, the constable of the south part of Andover in 1692, to Rebecca Hooper; and William Ballard to Hannah Hooper. Also in 1689, Joseph and John were granted 20 acres on the Shawsheen River near Roger's Brook to establish saw, grist, and fulling mills. Another property holder near Roger's Brook was Ann Foster, widow of Andrew Foster, an original proprietor of Andover.

In 1692 Joseph Ballard, about 50, his wife, four sons, and two daughters were living in the south part of Andover. Their house was on the site of Seminary Hill (where the present Andover Library is situated) on the Boston Road, now Elm Street. The carpenter Samuel Wardwell, married to a third Hooper sister, Sarah, lived about one-half mile east on the same road.

In July 1692 Elizabeth (Phelps) Ballard, about 46, was dying. Her husband, Joseph Ballard, brought two of the afflicted girls of Salem Village, Ann Putnam, Jr. and Mary Walcott, to Andover to determine who was bewitching his wife. On July 15 the charge of witchcraft was brought against Ann Foster, about 72. On July 19 Joseph Ballard filed a complaint against Mary (Foster) Lacey, 40, and Mary Lacey, Jr., 18, for afflicting his wife, Elizabeth. On July 26 Ann Putnam, Jr. and Mary Walcott returned to Andover, and on July 27 Elizabeth died. On September 14 Joseph Ballard testified against Samuel Wardwell of Andover. On November 15, 1692, Joseph Ballard married Rebecca (Rea) Stevens Orne, who had been widowed twice.

Samuel Phelps   **Andover**
Married man, 41   *Conspirator*

Sarah Phelps, Jr.   **Andover**
Girl, 9   *Afflicted*

Samuel Phelps was born about 1651, son of Elizabeth (Adams) and Edward Phelps. Edward Phelps lived in Salem and Newbury before moving to Andover in 1661. He bought the Andover farm of John Godfrey, an estate of 40 acres with rights to other land. It was in the north part near Hagget's Pond and close to the farm of Job Tyler.

The parents of Edward Phelps's wife, Elizabeth, became Quakers. Both Edward's brothers, Henry Phelps, Jr. and Nicholas Phelps, were Quakers, and in 1661 Nicholas was imprisoned in Salem and then banished.

By 1679 Edward Phelps had sold his property in the north part and moved his family to the south part of Andover. In 1682 in Andover, Samuel Phelps married Sarah Chandler. Born in 1661, Sarah Chandler was the younger daughter of Hannah (Brewer) and Thomas Chandler, an original proprietor of Andover. The children of Sarah (Chandler) and Samuel Phelps included Sarah Phelps, Jr., born in 1682. Samuel's father, Edward Phelps, died in 1689. Samuel's sister Eleanor Phelps was married to Sarah's brother William Chandler, 3rd.

In 1692 Samuel Phelps was 41 and a weaver. He, his wife Sarah, and their five children were living in the south part of Andover. On July 27, 1692, Samuel's sister Elizabeth (Phelps) Ballard died reputedly by witchcraft. Samuel Phelps joined the Andover conspiracy. Two weeks after the death of his sister, Samuel Phelps filed a complaint against Elizabeth Johnson, Jr., 22, Sarah Carrier, 7, and Thomas Carrier, Jr., 10, for afflicting his daughter, Sarah Phelps, Jr. Next he accused Abigail (Dane) Faulkner and Mary (Ayer) Parker. On September 7 Sarah Phelps, Jr. was part of the afflicted circle at the Andover touch test, and on September 17 she testified against Abigail (Dane) Faulkner. The name of Sarah Phelps, Jr. appeared as the afflicted person on the indictments of Abigail (Dane) Faulkner, Elizabeth (Dane) Johnson, and Mary (Ayer) Parker.

In 1746 Samuel Phelps died, about 95 years of age. In 1757 his widow, Sarah (Chandler) Phelps, died, aged 95. Sarah Phelps, Jr. helped her mother raise the other nine Phelps children and did not marry until she was 38 years old. In 1771 Sarah (Phelps) Field died, aged 78.

Daniel Bigsby   **Andover**
Married man, 41   *Conspirator*

Hannah (Chandler) Bigsby   **Andover**
Married woman, 35   *Afflicted*

Daniel Bigsby was born about 1651 in Ipswich, son of Sarah (Wyatt) Heard and Joseph Bigsby. The family lived in Ipswich and then in Rowley Village.[322] In 1674 in Andover, Daniel Bigsby married Hannah Chandler, born about 1657, the older daughter of Hannah (Brewer) and Thomas Chandler, an original proprietor of Andover. In 1682 Hannah's sister, Sarah Chandler, married Samuel Phelps. In 1687 Hannah's brother, William Chandler, 3rd, married Eleanor Phelps.

In 1692 Daniel Bigsby, a carpenter about 41; his wife, Hannah, about 35; and six children were living in the south part of Andover. Hannah (Chandler) Bigsby, together with her niece, Sarah Phelps, Jr., were part of the afflicted circle at the examination of the widow Mary (Ayer) Parker on September 1. Mary Parker was hanged on September 22, 1692. Hannah was one of the afflicted at the Andover touch test on September 7. At the examination of Henry Salter on September 7, it was attested that he afflicted Hannah Bigsby among others.

---

322 In 1685 Rowley Village was incorporated as a separate town and its name was changed to Boxford. At that time the settlement consisted of about forty families. The town then embraced parts of the present towns of Groveland and Middleton.

Robert Swan, Jr.   **Andover**
Married man, 35   *Conspirator*

Timothy Swan   **Andover**
Single man, 29   *Afflicted and conspirator*

John Swan   **Andover**
Single man, 24   *Conspirator*

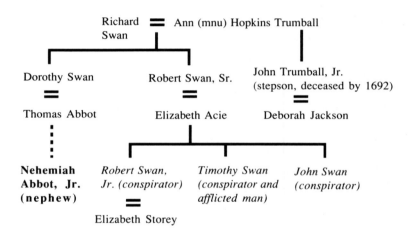

Robert Swan, Jr. was born in 1657; Timothy Swan, in 1663; and
John Swan in 1668. They were sons of Elizabeth (Acie) and Robert
Swan, Sr. of Haverhill. Robert Swan, Sr. was one of the most
prominent men of Haverhill, having served often as selectman
and representative to the General Court. In 1685, Robert Swan, Jr.
married Elizabeth Storey.

In 1692 the three Swan brothers were living in the north part
of Andover. Timothy, 29, a bachelor, was both an afflicted
person and a conspirator. There are no extant records of his
testimony despite the fact that he was involved in the
imprisonment of at least 18 persons. The Swan brothers played a
part in the cases of five of the six women accused in Haverhill;
the exception was Martha (Toothaker) Emerson. In the chart, as
in all the charts, the people charged with witchcraft are in

boldface. All of the people charged in 1692 were imprisoned, with the sole exception of Nehemiah Abbot, Jr.

Timothy Swan suffered from an unknown ailment that was to prove fatal. He first came to the attention of the Salem Village conspiracy of accusers because of a quarrel that he had had with Mary (Perkins) Bradbury of Salisbury, imprisoned on June 26, 1692. On July 15 Timothy Swan was brought to the courtroom as an afflicted person for the examination of Ann (mnu) Foster of Andover. On July 22, in answer to magistrate John Hathorne's leading question, Mary Lacey, Jr. said that Richard Carrier "burned Timothy Swan with his tobacco pipe in Swan's chamber in spirit. His spirit went in and did it. Sometimes we were in shapes and sometimes in body, but they did not see us. We rode upon hand poles & the Devil was also there in the shape of a black man & high crowned hat & bid us to kill Swan by stabbing him to death & we also stuck pins into his likeness." Hathorne then asked, "And what else had you—any hot irons or knitting needles?" She answered, "Yes, we had an iron spindle and Richard Carrier ran it through Swan's knee." Hathorne asked, "Had you any quarrel with him?" She said, "We all came in upon Mrs. Bradbury's quarrel with him."[323]

Hathorne next turned to Mary (Foster) Lacey, the mother of Mary Lacey, Jr., and asked, "Goody Lacey, did not you hurt Swan?" She responded, "No!" Her daughter interrupted, saying, "Yes, mother! Do not deny it!" The mother gave in and said, "The Devil made his imps do it. There were hot irons & the Devil held them." Hathorne immediately detected this major discrepancy in testimony, and cried, "Your daughter said it was an iron spindle." The mother, correcting herself, said, "Yes, yes. It was a spindle." (Hathorne was a man of excruciating detail in his quest to chronicle the wonders of the invisible world.) Mary Lacey, Jr. then "related something of the quarrel between Bradbury and Swan about thatching of a house."[324]

Magistrate Hathorne asked, "Richard Carrier, what say you to these two evidences that saw you with Timothy Swan?" Hathorne was, of course, referring to the type of evidence known

---

323 Essex Institute, *Witchcraft Collection*, "Examinations."
324 Ibid.

as spectral evidence. The "two evidences" provided by the confessing witch, Mary Lacey, Jr., were that she saw Richard's specter burn Timothy Swan with a tobacco pipe and run an iron spindle through Swan's knee. But Richard denied all. Infuriated with his impudence, Hathorne ordered him to be tortured. His mind and body broken, Richard was returned to the courtroom and testified that Mrs. Bradbury had him afflict Timothy Swan "because her husband & Timothy Swan fell out about a scythe, I think." Again Hathorne detected a major discrepancy in the testimony and retorted, "Did they not fall out about thatching of a barn?" Richard, not to be intimidated, defiantly answered, "No, not as I know of."[325] To this day it is not known whether the quarrel was over the thatching of a house or barn, or over a scythe.

On July 26, 1692 Ann Putnam, Jr. and Mary Walcott of the afflicted circle of Salem Village again visited Andover, and claimed that with their spectral sight they saw Mrs. Bradbury or her appearance tormenting Timothy Swan and nearly ready to kill him. Spurred on by this spectral evidence, Timothy Swan and his brothers were ready to act on his behalf. On July 28 they filed a complaint against Mary (Tyler) Post Bridges of Andover for committing witchcraft on the body of Timothy Swan. About July 29, they filed a complaint against Hannah (Varnum) Tyler Brumidge and Mary (Green) Green, both of Haverhill. On August 2 they filed a complaint against Mary Post. On August 3 they filed a complaint against Mary (Johnson) Davis Clarke of Haverhill. On August 19 they filed a complaint against Frances Hutchins and Ruth Wilford, both of Haverhill. On September 6 Timothy Swan testified in Salem against Mary (Perkins) Bradbury. On September 7 Timothy Swan was back in Andover as an afflicted at the touch test. Timothy Swan was named as the afflicted person on the indictments of Mary (Perkins) Bradbury, Mary Lacey, Jr., Richard Carrier, Mary (Tyler) Post Bridges, Mary Post, Rebecca (Blake) Eames, and Mercy Wardwell. Timothy Swan's gravestone in Andover reads, "Timothy Swan Died February ye 2, 1693 & in ye 30 year of His Age."[326]

325 Essex County Archives, *Witchcraft*, 2:53.
326 Bailey, *Historical Sketches of Andover*, 237.

Moses Tyler   **Boxford**
Married man, 51   *Conspirator*

Joseph Tyler   **Boxford**
Single man, 21   *Conspirator*

Martha Sprague   **Boxford**
Girl, 16   *Afflicted*

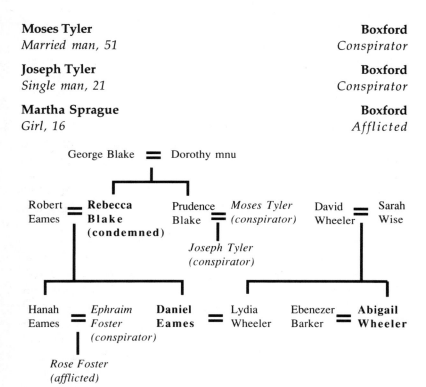

Moses Tyler was born about 1641 in Indian territory in the area that was to become Andover. He was the son of Mary (mnu) and Job Tyler. In 1666 he married Prudence Blake. Their children included Joseph Tyler, born 1671. Moses' wife, Prudence, was born in Gloucester in 1647, daughter of Dorothy (mnu) and George Blake, who later moved to Rowley Village (named Boxford in 1685). Prudence died in 1689 in Boxford.

In 1690 Moses Tyler married Sarah (Hasey) Sprague, born about 1647. Sarah was the daughter of Sarah (mnu) and Lieut. William Hasey of Boston, and was the widow of Phineas Sprague. Sarah (Hasey) and Phineas Sprague had eight children including Martha Sprague, born in 1676. In 1692 Martha Sprague, now the stepdaughter of Moses Tyler, was the leading girl in the Andover afflicted circle.

In 1692 Moses Tyler, about 51, and his family lived in Boxford so close to the Andover line that they attended the Andover church. At the beginning of the Andover witch hunt, Moses Tyler stood by as the conspiracy did its work. Silently Moses watched as his sister, Mary (Tyler) Post Bridges, was accused by Timothy Swan on July 28. About August 1 the conspiracy accused his sister-in-law, Rebecca (Blake) Eames; Moses Tyler said nothing. On August 2, 1692 the Swan brothers accused his niece Mary Post; Moses looked the other way, and he kept looking the other way when Mary Post was sentenced to death a half year later. By August 10, 1692 the conspiracy accused his nephew Daniel Eames; Moses did not protest. About August 15 the conspiracy accused his brother's sister-in-law Sarah Parker; Moses watched her go to prison.

Moses was biding his time. On August 15 he struck like a coiled serpent. He filed a complaint against Samuel Wardwell for afflicting his stepdaughter, Martha Sprague. Next Moses filed a complaint against his nieces Mary Bridges, Jr. and Hannah Post and his stepnieces Sarah Bridges and Susannah Post. On August 25 he filed a complaint against William Barker, Sr., Mary Barker, and Mary (Osgood) Marston. Moses' son Joseph Tyler filed a complaint against John Jackson, Sr., John Jackson, Jr., and John Howard. On August 29 Moses filed a complaint against Elizabeth (Dane) Johnson and Abigail Johnson. About August 31 he filed a complaint against Stephen Johnson, William Barker, Jr., Sarah Wardwell, Sarah Hawkes, Mercy Wardwell, and Mary (Ayer) Parker. Mary was his brother's mother-in-law; as a result of Moses' accusation, Mary was hanged three weeks later. On September 7 at the Andover touch test, Moses' stepdaughter Martha Sprague, a leader of the afflicted circle, was instrumental in the arrest of his sister-in-law, Mary (Lovett) Tyler, and his nieces Hannah Tyler, Martha Tyler, and Joanna Tyler. On September 14 Martha Sprague testified against Samuel Wardwell, and on September 16 against Abigail (Dane) Faulkner. Martha Sprague was in the courtroom much of the time from August 15 through September as an afflicted. Extant records show that she claimed to be afflicted by at least 20 persons.

In 1718 Sarah (Hasey) Sprague Tyler died at Boxford, and Moses married Martha Fiske of Wenham. On October 2, 1727, Moses Tyler died at Boxford in the 86th year of his age.

Ephraim Foster	**Andover**
Married man, 35	*Conspirator*
Hannah (Eames) Foster	**Andover**
Married woman, 31	*Afflicted*
Rose Foster	**Andover**
Girl, 14	*Afflicted*

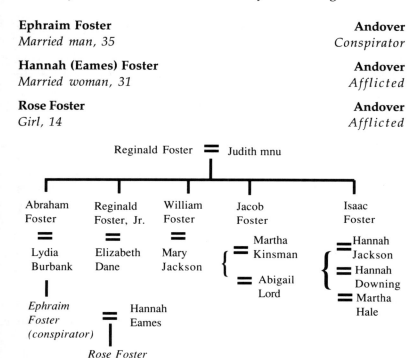

Ephraim Foster was born in Ipswich in 1657, the oldest child of Lydia (Burbank) and Abraham Foster of Ipswich.

Abraham's father, Reginald Foster, a wealthy and prominent citizen of Ipswich, had two daughters and four other sons. Son Reginald Foster, Jr. married Elizabeth Dane, daughter of Eleanor (Clark) and Dr. John Dane, Jr. of Ipswich. Son William Foster married Mary Jackson, daughter of Joanna and William Jackson of Rowley.   Jacob Foster married Martha Kinsman, and after her death married Abigail Lord,[327] daughter

---

327 One sister of Abigail (Lord) Foster was Sarah (Lord) Wilson, the wife of Joseph Wilson of Andover. Both Sarah (Lord) Wilson and her daughter

of Mary (Waite) and Robert Lord, Sr. of Ipswich. Isaac Foster married Hannah Jackson, and after her death in 1677 married Hannah Downing, daughter of Theophilus Downing of Salem. After Hannah's death, Isaac Foster married Martha Hale.

In 1677, Ephraim Foster, 20, married Hannah Eames, 16. She was born in 1661 in Rowley Village (named Boxford in 1685), eldest daughter of Rebecca (Blake) and Robert Eames. The Foster children included oldest child Rose, born in 1678 in Andover. In 1692 Ephraim Foster, 35, constable for the north part of Andover, his wife, Hannah (Eames) Foster, 31, and children were living in Andover close to the Boxford line. On May 13, 1692, their eighth child, Gideon, was born. On May 31, 1692, Elizabeth (Jackson) Howe of Ipswich Farms was imprisoned. About August 1 Hannah's mother, Rebecca (Blake) Eames, was imprisoned, and by August 9 Hannah's brother, Daniel Eames. About August 24 Ephraim Foster and Moses Tyler filed a complaint against Mary Bridges, Jr., Sarah Bridges, Hannah Post, and Susannah Post. On August 25, Ephraim Foster, Samuel Martin and Moses Tyler filed a complaint against William Barker, Sr., Mary Barker, and Mary (Osgood) Marston.

John Jackson, Sr. was the only son of William Jackson. William Jackson had three daughters, Elizabeth, Mary, and Deborah. On his death in 1688 William Jackson had left his large estate to his grandson John Jackson, Jr., with young John's father, John Jackson, Sr., acting as trustee. In the event of the death of John Jackson, Jr., the estate was to be divided between William Jackson's three daughters.

Sarah Wilson, Jr. were imprisoned in 1692. Another sister was Susannah (Lord) Osgood, the wife of Thomas Osgood of Andover. Thomas was the brother of Christopher Osgood, whose daughter Mary (Osgood) Marston was imprisoned in 1692.

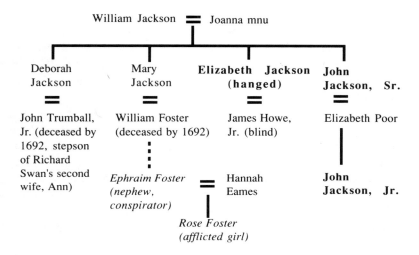

One of the daughters was already dead; she was Elizabeth (Jackson) Howe, hanged August 19, 1692. One of the remaining daughters was Mary (Jackson) Foster, a widow in Boxford. Her deceased husband was William Foster, the uncle of Ephraim Foster. The other remaining daughter was Deborah (Jackson) Trumball, also a widow. Her deceased husband was John Trumball, Jr., stepuncle of the Swan brothers of Andover. The elimination of John Jackson, Sr. and his son John Jackson, Jr. would leave the estate to the two widows, and in effect place it under the control of Ephraim Foster and the Swan brothers.

On August 25, 1692 Ephraim Foster and Joseph Tyler filed a complaint against John Jackson, Sr., John Jackson, Jr., and John Howard for afflicting Rose Foster and Martha Sprague. On August 31 Ephraim Foster, Moses Tyler, and Samuel Martin filed a complaint against Sarah Wardwell, Sarah Hawkes, Mercy Wardwell, William Barker, Jr., and Mary (Ayer) Parker. On September 7, Hannah (Eames) Foster and daughter Rose Foster were part the afflicted group at the Andover touch test. Among the accused was Sarah (Lord) Wilson, sister of Ephraim Foster's aunt, Abigail (Lord) Foster. On September 14 Ephraim Foster testified against Samuel Wardwell, who was hanged on September 22, 1692.

On January 7, 1693, Mary (Lovett) Tyler was tried on the indictment that she afflicted Hannah Foster, wife of Ephraim Foster, on September 7. The verdict was not guilty. On February 25, 1693, Rose Foster, aged 14 years and 10 months, died at Andover. In 1731, Hannah (Eames) Foster died at Andover, about 70. In 1746 Ephraim Foster died at Andover aged 88.

Rose Foster was afflicted by 15 persons. On September 17 she testified against Abigail (Dane) Faulkner who was sentenced to death on that day. Rose was a witness to the indictments of William Barker, Sr., John Jackson, Sr., John Jackson, Jr., Mary Bridges, Jr., Sarah Bridges, Henry Salter, and Rebecca (Aslet) Johnson. She was the afflicted person in the indictments of Abigail (Wheeler) Barker, Susannah Post, Mary Barker, Henry Salter, Mary Bridges, Jr., Hannah Tyler, and Stephen Johnson.

Samuel Martin   **Andover**
Married man, 47   *Conspirator*

Abigail Martin, Jr.   **Andover**
Girl, 16   *Afflicted*

Samuel Martin was born in 1645 in Gloucester, the only son of Mary (Pindar) and Solomon Martin, a shipwright. In 1648 Samuel's sister Mary was born and his mother, Mary, died soon after. A few months later his father, Solomon Martin, married Alice Farnum, widow of Ralph Farnum, 1st of Ipswich. Alice, 12 years older than Solomon, already had seven children ranging in age from about 4 to 20. In 1653, Alice and Solomon moved to Andover. Within a few years, Alice's two oldest sons, Thomas Farnum and Ralph Farnum, 2nd, also moved to Andover. Solomon continued his career and went out on voyages in his capacity as ship carpenter. In 1662 he was reported as absent from the country for seven years, presumed dead on a voyage across the seas.

Alice could barely manage the farm and meet expenses. At 17, her stepson Samuel Martin became rebellious, and the court placed him under the guardianship of Nathan Parker, an original proprietor of Andover and a learned man.[328] Parker was

---

328 C. H. Abbott, *The Andover Townsman*, September 17, 1897.

also to oversee the restoration of the Martin lands, which he managed to his own profit. Nathan Parker, a strict man, angered Samuel. The resentment reappeared in 1692 when Samuel Martin was one of the conspirators who accused Nathan Parker's widow, Mary (Ayer) Parker.

In 1676 Samuel Martin married Abigail Norton in Andover. Born in 1651, Abigail was the daughter of Mary and George Norton. After George's death, Mary married widower Philip Fowler of Ipswich, the maternal grandfather of Christopher Osgood of Andover. The children of Abigail and Samuel Martin included Abigail Martin, Jr., born in 1676 in Andover.

In 1692 Samuel Martin, 47, husbandman; his wife, Abigail; and children were living in the north part of Andover. Abigail was pregnant with their seventh child.

On January 8, 1692, Ralph Farnum, 2nd, who was Samuel Martin's stepbrother, died at Andover. John Farnum and Ralph Farnum, 3rd, both sons of Ralph Farnum, 2nd, testified against Martha (Allen) Carrier on June 28 and again on July 30. On August 25 Samuel Martin and Moses Tyler filed a complaint against William Barker, Sr., Mary Barker, and Mary (Osgood) Marston for afflicting Abigail Martin, Jr., Rose Foster, and Martha Sprague. Mary (Osgood) Marston was the daughter of Christopher Osgood. On August 25 at their examinations Mary Bridges, Jr., Sarah Bridges, Hannah Post, and Susannah Post were charged with afflicting Abigail Martin, Jr., Rose Foster, and Martha Sprague. On August 29 Samuel Martin and Moses Tyler filed a complaint against Elizabeth (Dane) Johnson and her daughter Abigail Johnson for afflicting Abigail Martin, Jr. and Martha Sprague. On August 30, Elizabeth (Dane) Johnson confessed that she afflicted Sarah Phelps and three of Samuel Martin's children and that her sister Abigail (Dane) Faulkner and Sarah Parker joined with her in afflicting them. About August 31 Sarah Wardwell, Sarah Hawkes, Mercy Wardwell, William Barker, Jr., and Mary (Ayer) Parker were complained of for afflicting Abigail Martin, Jr., Rose Foster, and Martha Sprague.

On September 7, 1692, Abigail Martin, Jr. and Ralph Farnum, 3rd were members of the afflicted circle at the Andover touch test. Abigail (Wheeler) Barker and Mary (Lovett) Tyler were indicted for practicing and exercising witchcraft against Ralph Farnum, 3rd on September 7.

On September 22, 1692, Mary (Ayer) Parker, widow of Nathan Parker, was hanged at Salem. Her daughter Sarah had been imprisoned by August 19. Another daughter, Hannah Parker, had married, in 1682, John Tyler, brother of Moses Tyler. A third daughter, Elizabeth Parker, had married in 1684 John Farnum, who was the brother of the afflicted Ralph Farnum, 3rd.

Abigail Martin, Jr. was afflicted by 13 persons. At the grand jury she testified against Samuel Wardwell. She signed three indictments, those of William Barker, Sr., Mary Barker, and Mary (Osgood) Marston.

In 1696 Ensign Samuel Martin died at Andover, aged 51.

The Rev. Thomas Barnard   Andover
Married man, 34   *Conspirator*

Thomas Barnard was born about 1658, in Hartford, Connecticut, son of Hannah (Marvin) and Francis Barnard, later of Hadley. In 1682 he became the assistant minister in Andover. In 1686 the Rev. Thomas Barnard married Elizabeth Price, the stepdaughter of Dudley Bradstreet of Andover. Barnard used his position of leadership to help engineer the witchcraft accusations in Andover, culminating in the infamous Andover touch test on September 7, 1692. In the fall of 1692, Barnard apparently had a change of heart and reluctantly became part of the Andover resistance.

21

THE ACCUSED: PROPRIETOR FAMILIES

A FEATURE OF THE SALEM WITCHCRAFT AFFAIR is that accusations were made against people of all ranks. In Andover a large number of accusations were directed against the ruling elite, the families of the first proprietors of Andover. "At first, it is true, only the friendless and the strange eccentric persons in the community or the high-tempered, or those who for any bold stand had incurred spite and made enemies, were selected. But, an epidemic of audacity seemed at length to seize the afflicted. The sort of vulgar satisfaction which rejoices in the degradation and humiliation of those above its own level, now revelled in reducing the pride of the lofty. Into the most honored households the tongue of accusation thrust itself, and fastened its venomous touch upon the purest and gentlest there. The ladies who had walked hitherto as examples of the community, the admired, but the envied of many, were brought low. Mistress Mary Osgood, and the wife of the deacon of the church, Mrs. Eunice Frye, a woman of all Christian virtues, and the Rev. Mr. Dane's daughter, Mrs. Abigail Faulkner, and her innocent children, Dorothy and Abigail Faulkner, and another of Mr. Dane's daughters, Elizabeth Johnson, and her daughter, Elizabeth Johnson, Jr., and Mr. Dane's daughter-in-law, Mrs. Deliverance (Haseltine) Dane, were accused; and finally Mr. Dane himself was hinted at, Mrs. Dudley Bradstreet named, and Mr. Dudley Bradstreet compelled to seek safety in flight. Such was the frenzy which seized the community and loosed its basest passions," wrote Sarah Loring Bailey in 1880.[329] Many nineteenth-century writers as well as later scholars viewed the

329 Bailey, *Historical Sketches of Andover*, 199.

witchcraft trials as an example of seventeenth-century religious hysteria. However, as James R. Mellow points out, Nathaniel Hawthorne, with a modern's foresight, suggested an economic motive behind the persecutions.[330] The economic motive, of course, was well spelled out at the time by Calef, who was a merchant.[331] It was also recorded by Governor Sir William Phipps, who in his letter of February 23, 1693, stated that William Stoughton, the lieutenant governor and the chief witchcraft justice, "has from the beginning hurried on these matters with great precipitancy and by his warrant has caused the estates, goods and chattels of the executed to be seized and disposed of without my knowledge or consent."[332] The three Salem magistrates, Jonathan Corwin, Bartholomew Gedney, and Hawthorne's great-great-grandfather, John Hathorne, were the most avid in the prosecutions and subsequent confiscations. These magistrates did not in any way discourage the Andover conspirators when they accused the families of proprietors, the owners of the large estates in Andover. However, after the executions on September 22, 1692, the Rev. Dane was able to form an effective Andover resistance group made up of the leading citizens of Andover; by petitions and other legal measures this group was instrumental in ending the witch hunt and preventing extensive confiscations of Andover property.

FOSTER FAMILY

Ann Foster	**Andover**
Widow, 72	*Charged about July 15, 1692*
Mary (Foster) Lacey	**Andover**
Married woman, 40	*Charged on July 19, 1692*
Mary Lacey, Jr.	**Andover**
Girl, 18	*Charged on July 19, 1692*

---

330 Mellow, *Nathaniel Hawthorne and his Times*, 352.
331 Calef, *More Wonders*, 265-267.
332 Phipps, "Letter of February 21, 1693," in Burr, *Narratives*, 210.

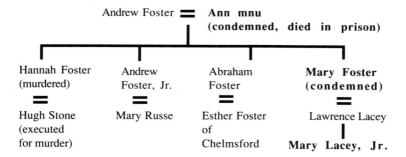

Andrew Foster,[333] an original proprietor of Andover, died in 1685, leaving his "dear and loving wife, Ann, use & sole liberty of living in that end of my house I now live in for her natural life; also 3 cows, 12 sheep." The house was in the south part of Andover.

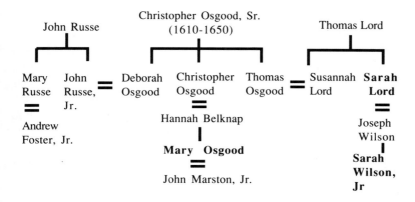

Elder son, Andrew Foster, Jr., and his wife, Mary (Russe) Foster, lived in the other end of the house.[334] The will continued, "Daughter Hannah [Stone] has hers already. To daughter Mary

---

333 The Andrew Foster family was not related to the family of Ephraim Foster of Andover, a conspirator.

334 Mary (Russe) Foster was the sister of John Russe, Jr. In 1663 John Russe, Jr. married Deborah Osgood, daughter of Christopher Osgood, Sr. Deborah's brother was Christopher Osgood, whose daughter Mary (Osgood) Marston was imprisoned in 1692.

[Lacey] 20 acres of land in Shawsheen fields near Cooper's land."[335] His sons Andrew and Abraham received the bulk of his land, much valuable acreage in the south part of Andover. Andrew was to pasture his mother's sheep and cows, and give her one-half of the corn, English and Indian, grown on the house lot, threshed and winnowed by the bushel. The younger son, Abraham, lived in the north part of Andover. Mary, the youngest daughter, born in 1652, married Lawrence Lacey of Andover in 1673. Their daughter Mary Lacey, Jr. was born in 1674. The Laceys lived in the north part of Andover.

In 1692, widow Ann Foster was about 72, her daughter Mary (Foster) Lacey was 40, and her granddaughter Mary Lacey, Jr. was 18. About July 14, 1692, Ann Foster was charged with afflicting Joseph Ballard's sick wife, Elizabeth (Phelps) Ballard. Ann's arrest on July 15 marks the beginning of the Andover witch hunt. The examination and confession of Ann Foster at Salem Village, July, 15 1692, stated, "After a while Ann Foster confessed that the Devil appeared to her in the shape of a bird several times, such a bird as she had never seen the like before. The Devil told her that she must believe him. He was always as a bird & sat upon the table and had two legs and great eyes & that he promised her prosperity & that it was Carrier's wife about three weeks ago that came and persuaded her to hurt these people [the afflicted girls]."[336] Since Martha Carrier had been safely behind bars for more than six weeks, it was clear that it must have been Martha's specter that appeared to Ann, proof positive that Martha was a witch. Ann Foster was imprisoned at Salem. One of Ann's crimes was that she supposedly had bewitched a hog of John Lovejoy's to death.

Examined again on July 16, Ann Foster said, "Goody Carrier came & told her of the meeting and would have her go, so they got upon sticks & went said journey & being there did see Mr. Burroughs, the minister, who spake to them all & this was about two months ago."[337] Since Burroughs had been tucked away in Salem prison for the past two and one-half months, her

---

335 Essex County, Massachusetts, *Court Records, Probate*, June 30, 1685.
336 Essex County Archives, *Witchcraft*, 2:22.
337 Ibid.

testimony provided hard evidence that Burroughs' specter attended that infamous witch meeting in Salem Village.

On July 18, the day before the execution of Rebecca Nurse and four other women, Ann Foster was examined again. "Ann Foster confessed that the Devil in the shape of a black man appeared to her. She further says that she heard some of the witches say that there was three hundred & five in the whole country, & that they would ruin that place, the Village; also says there was present at that meeting two men besides Mr. Burroughs, the minister, & one of them had gray hair."[338]

On July 19, the day of the execution, Joseph Ballard filed a complaint against Ann's daughter, Mary (Foster) Lacey, and Ann's granddaughter, Mary Lacey, Jr., for afflicting his ailing wife, Elizabeth. On the arrest warrant for Mary Lacey, Jr., dated July 20, the constable was directed to search diligently about the house for puppets. Constable Ephraim Foster, one of the conspirators, made the arrests on July 21. In his search he found a parcel of rags and a parcel of quills which none in the family could explain.

On July 21 and again on July 22 Ann Foster, daughter Mary (Foster) Lacey, and granddaughter Mary Lacey, Jr. were examined. The three women confessed; the older the woman, the weaker her confession. On one point Ann Foster was firm; she would not implicate her daughter. Hathorne lost patience with her and said, "You have already been three times examined, and yet you do not confess," meaning that she did not confess to making her daughter a witch.[339] On July 27, Elizabeth (Phelps) Ballard died of supposed witchcraft.

While in prison Mary Lacey, Jr. took on the role of an afflicted girl and was often taken to the courtroom to act with the afflicted circle. Mary Lacey, Jr. and Mary Warren (of the Salem Village circle) were the afflicted girls named on the warrant, dated July 23, for the arrest of Martha (Toothaker) Emerson of Haverhill. Mary Lacey, Jr. was one of the afflicted in the examinations of Martha (Toothaker) Emerson, July 23; Hannah (Varnum) Tyler Brumidge of Haverhill, July 30; John

---

338 Ibid.
339 Bailey, *Historical Sketches of Andover*, 214-215.

Jackson, Sr., John Jackson, Jr., and John Howard, August 27; William Barker, Sr., Mary Barker, and Mary (Osgood) Marston, August 29; William Barker, Jr., Stephen Johnson, Sarah Hawkes, Mercy Wardwell, and Sarah Wardwell, September 1; Mary (Harrington) Taylor, Jane (mnu) Lilly, and Mary (Dustin) Colson, September 5; and those arrested in the Andover touch test on September 7.

On September 17, 1692, Ann Foster and her daughter, Mary (Foster) Lacey, were condemned by the Court of Oyer and Terminer. Because they had confessed, they were not hanged but continued in prison. On October 6 Francis Faulkner and Lieut. John Barker posted a recognizance bond of £500 for Mary Lacey, Jr. Imprisoned 10 weeks, Mary was released from prison on bail. "The condition of this obligation is that Francis Faulkner and John Barker shall well and truly keep the aforesaid Mary Lacey, Jr. until they receive order from George Corwin, sheriff of the County of Essex, to deliver the aforesaid Mary Lacey, Jr. unto William Dounton, now keeper of their majesties' jail in Salem, & shall pay unto George Corwin, sheriff aforesaid, the forfeiture of said bond in case of default."[340] Faulkner and Barker were part of the Andover resistance group which by mid-October succeeded in freeing the imprisoned Andover children on bail. About December 9 widow Ann (mnu) Foster died in Salem prison. Her son, Abraham Foster, "was forced to pay the keeper before I could have the dead body of my mother to bury—£2. 10s. Money & provisions expended while she was in prison—£4."[341] The perpetuators of the witch hunt understood money.

On January 3, 1693, the grand jury at the Superior Court of Judicature at Salem entered the indictment, "Mary Lacey, Jr. of Andover, singlewoman, wickedly, maliciously, and feloniously, with the Devil a covenant did make, and renounced her former Christian baptism, and set her hand to the Devil's book, whereby the said Mary Lacey is become a wicked and detestable witch."[342] On many occasions during the witchcraft examinations

---

340 Massachusetts Archives, *Witchcraft*, 135:57.
341 Bailey, *Historical Sketches of Andover*, 216.
342 Suffolk County Archives, *Superior Court of Judicature Records*, "Case of Mary Lacey, Junior."

held in the hot summer, Mary had acted her part as an afflicted person alongside Timothy Swan and the others in the sanctioned circle. However her indictment in the cold winter showed she was not one of this privileged group. In fact, she was indicted for hurting her fellow sufferer, Timothy Swan, for she "on or about the 15th day of July last, in the year 1692, and divers other days and times, certain detestable acts, called witchcrafts and sorceries, wickedly, maliciously, and feloniously, has used, practiced, and exercised against one Timothy Swan," who "was and is tortured, afflicted, tormented, consumed, pined, & wasted, against the peace of our sovereign Lord and Lady, the King and Queen."[343] In a trial by jury on January 13 she was found "not guilty of the felony of witchcraft."[344] Timothy Swan died two and one-half weeks later.

In mid-January Chief Justice William Stoughton signed death warrants for Mary (Foster) Lacey and seven other condemned women; Governor Sir William Phipps reprieved her and the others. After more than seven months imprisonment, she was finally released in March 1693.

PARKER FAMILY

Mary (Ayer) Parker   **Andover**
Widow, 55   *Charged about September 1, 1692*

Sarah Parker   **Andover**
Single woman, 22   *Charged about August 15, 1692*

Mary Ayer was born about 1637 in England, daughter of Rebecca and John Ayer. The family emigrated to New England, settling in Hampton and then Haverhill. About 1652 Mary Ayer married widower Nathan Parker of Andover. Their children included Sarah Parker, born in 1670.

---

343 Ibid.
344 Ibid.

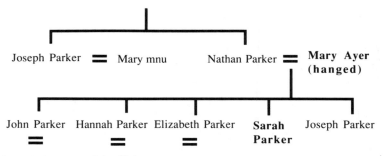

Nathan Parker and his brother, Joseph Parker, were original proprietors of Andover and "citizens of much consideration."[345] Joseph owned a tannery and had a corn mill, and Nathan was a scrivener and drew up most of the law papers of the settlement, including those for Hopestill Tyler's apprenticeship to Thomas Chandler. Nathan died a wealthy man in 1685, with a landed estate of more than 225 acres. "He evidently did not attend very carefully to the transfer of his own estate, but gives the whole undivided to the administration of his wife Mary and his [eldest] son John."[346]

In 1692 Mary (Ayer) Parker, about 55 and a widow for seven years, her sons, John Parker, 38, and Joseph Parker, 20, and daughter Sarah Parker, 22 were living on the Parker farm in the north part of Andover. Two other daughters were married. Hannah was the wife of John Tyler of Boxford, a brother of Moses Tyler, a conspirator; and Elizabeth was married to John Farnum of Andover.[347]

About August 15, 1692 Sarah Parker was imprisoned. On September 1 her mother, Mary (Ayer) Parker, was arrested. She was examined in Salem on September 2. Among the afflicted present were Martha Sprague of the afflicted circle, as well as the imprisoned Andover women and children, Hannah Post,

345 Bailey, *Historical Sketches of Andover*, 102-104; Abbott, *The Andover Townsman*, June 5, 1896.

346 Abbott, *The Andover Townsman*, June 19, 1896.

347 John Farnum, born 1664, and Ralph Farnum, 3rd, born 1666, were sons of Ralph Farnum, 2nd.

Sarah Bridges, Mary Lacey, Jr., Mercy Wardwell, and William Barker, Jr.[348] Mary (Ayer) Parker refused to confess. "I know nothing of it, there is another woman of the same name in Andover."[349] She was referring to her sister-in-law, Mary (mnu) Parker, the aged and senile widow of Joseph Parker.[350]

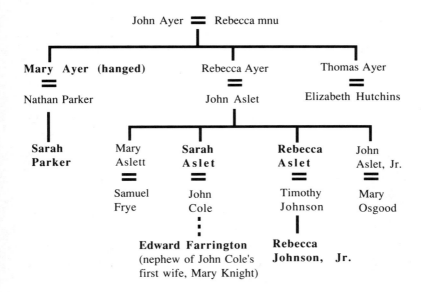

On September 7 Mary (Ayer) Parker's niece Rebecca (Aslet) Johnson and Rebecca's daughter Rebecca Johnson, Jr. were arrested at the Andover touch test. Also arrested at the touch test was Mary (Clement) Osgood, who was the mother of John Aslet, Jr.'s

348 Mercy Wardwell did her best to refute the rigged testimony against Mary Parker by stating, "But I did not certainly know that said Parker was a witch. This she owned to the Grand Inquest, September 16, 1692." This was three days after her father had refuted his own confession. (Essex County Archives, *Witchcraft*, 2:33.)

349 Woodward, *Records of Salem Witchcraft*, 2:153-154.

350 Although Bailey, *Historical Sketches of Andover*, 209, states that the widow Mary of Joseph Parker may have been the Mary Parker hanged for witchcraft, Abbott shows instead that the "widow Mary [of Nathan Parker] was the one who was hanged as a witch." Abbott, *The Andover Townsman*, June 19, 1896.

wife, Mary (Osgood) Aslet. (John Aslet, Jr. was the nephew of
Mary (Ayer) Parker.) Another arrested at the touch test was
Eunice (Potter) Frye, who was the wife of Samuel Frye's brother,
Deacon John Frye. (Samuel Frye's wife, Mary (Aslet) Frye, was
the niece of Mary (Ayer) Parker.)

On September 17 Mary (Ayer) Parker was condemned by the
Court of Oyer and Terminer, and on September 22 she was hanged.

On October 3 Mary (Ayer) Parker's niece, Sarah (Aslet) Cole
of Lynn, was accused and imprisoned. About December 12 Sarah
Parker's brothers, John Parker and Joseph Parker, posted a
recognizance bond for her release on bail. Sarah had suffered
imprisonment at Salem for 17 weeks.

On November 7, 1692 John Parker and Joseph Parker
petitioned, "That whereas our mother, Mary Parker of Andover,
was apprehended upon suspicion of witchcraft, and being brought
to a trial at Salem Court, was condemned: since her death the
sheriff of Essex sent an officer to seize on her estate. The said
officer required us in their majesties name to give him an account
of our mother's estate, pretending it was forfeited to the King; we
told him that our mother left no estate (which we are able to
make appear); notwithstanding which, he seized upon our cattle,
corn & hay, to a considerable value; and ordered us to go down to
Salem and make an agreement with the sheriff, otherwise the
estate would be exposed to sale.

"We not knowing what advantage the law might give him
against us, and fearing we should sustain greater damage by the
loss of our estate, went to the sheriff accordingly, who told us he
might take away all that was seized if he pleased, but was
willing to do us a kindness by giving us an opportunity to redeem
it. He at first demanded ten pounds of us, but at length was
willing to take six pounds, which he had obliged us by bill to pay
him within a month.

"Now if our mother had left an estate, we know not of any
law in force in this Province, by which it should be forfeited upon
her condemnation; much less can we understand that there is any
justice or reason, for the sheriff to seize upon our estate. And
though it is true our own act has obliged us to pay him a sum of
money, yet we declare that we were drawn to it partly by the
officers great pretenses of law for what he did, partly to prevent

the loss of our estate which we feared would be immediately sold."[351]   John and Joseph Parker retained their lands, which adjoined the estate of Samuel Wardwell to the south.

BARKER FAMILY

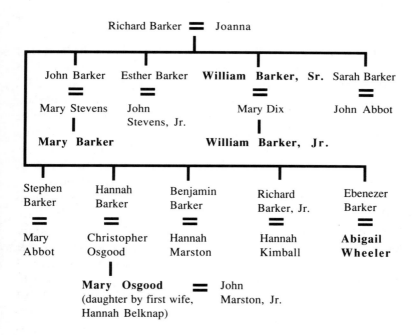

Richard Barker ▬ Joanna

John Barker	Esther Barker	**William Barker, Sr.**	Sarah Barker
▬	▬	▬	▬
Mary Stevens	John Stevens, Jr.	Mary Dix	John Abbot

Mary Barker   William Barker, Jr.

Stephen Barker	Hannah Barker	Benjamin Barker	Richard Barker, Jr.	Ebenezer Barker
▬	▬	▬	▬	▬
Mary Abbot	Christopher Osgood	Hannah Marston	Hannah Kimball	**Abigail Wheeler**

Mary Osgood ▬ John
(daughter by first wife,   Marston, Jr.
Hannah Belknap)

Mary Barker   **Andover**
Girl, 13   *Charged on August 25, 1692*

Richard Barker, an original proprietor of Andover, was one of the ten founders of the church in 1645.   Richard and his wife Joanna had nine children.[352]   His acreage in the north part of Andover was extensive, extending from the Merrimack River

---

351 Massachusetts Archives, *Witchcraft*, 135:65.
352 Stephen Barker and Mary Abbot were married in 1687, the first couple married by the new minister, the Rev. Thomas Barnard.   Stephen and Mary (Abbot) Barker as well as Richard, Jr. and Hannah (Kimball) Barker are six-times-great grandparents of the writer.

southward to Five Mile Pond. In 1692 Captain Dudley Bradstreet, Captain John Osgood, and Richard Barker were the leading men in town government. However, Richard Barker was aged and his duties were largely assumed by his eldest son, Lieut. John Barker. John Barker, born about 1644, married Mary Stevens in 1670. Their daughter Mary Barker was born in 1679. In 1692 Mary was 13.

On August 25, 1692 the Andover conspiracy struck the Barker family. "To the constables of Andover: Complaint being made to me this day, by Samuel Martin of Andover & Moses Tyler, Sr. of Boxford, against William Barker, Sr., Mary Marston, the wife of John Marston, Jr. & Mary Barker, the daughter of Lieut. John Barker, all of Andover, in that the above said William Barker, Sr., Mary Marston & Mary Barker, have woefully afflicted & abused, Abigail Martin, Jr. & Rose Foster of Andover, & Martha Sprague of Boxford by witchcraft, contrary to the peace of our sovereign Lord & Lady, William & Mary, King & Queen of England &c. & to their Majesties' laws in that case provided.

"These therefore require you in their Majesties' names upon sight hereof, to apprehend & seize the bodies of William Barker, Sr., Mary Marston, the wife of John Marston, Jr., & Mary Barker, the daughter of Lieut. John Barker, all of Andover, & them safely convey to Salem, before their Majesties' justices of the peace there, to be examined & proceeded with according to law, for which this shall be the warrant. Given under my hand & seal this 25th day of August, Anno Domini 1692, in the fourth year of their Majesties' reign. [Signed] Dudley Bradstreet, justice of peace. The said Martin & Tyler have given sufficient bond to prosecute said persons to effect, which bond remains with me."[353]

Mary Barker, her uncle William Barker, Sr., and Mary (Osgood) Marston were arrested on August 29, 1692 and conveyed the 15 difficult miles to Salem. Without anyone to speak in her defense, thirteen-year-old Mary was put up against the three Salem magistrates, all of them justices on the dreaded Court of Oyer and Terminer. After they questioned Mary, the following confession was drawn up and entered into the court records: "29 August 1692, Before Major Gedney, Mr. Hathorne and Mr. Corwin.

---

353   Boston Public Library, *Rare Books and Manuscripts*, "Warrants."

The examination and confession of Mary Barker of Andover. After several questions propounded and negative answers returned, she at last acknowledged that Goody Johnson[354] made her a witch. And sometime last summer she made a red mark in the Devil's book with the forefinger of her left hand. And the Devil would have her hurt Martha Sprague, Rose Foster and Abigail Martin, Jr. which she did upon Saturday and Sabbath Day last. She said she was not above a quarter of an hour in coming down from Andover to Salem to afflict. She says she afflicted the above three persons by squeezing her hands. She confesses she was at the witch meeting at Salem Village with her uncle. There was a great many there, and of her company there was only her uncle William Barker, Sr. and Mary Marston [the two arrested with her]. Martha Sprague said that Mary Barker's apparition told that she was baptized at Five Mile Pond.[355]

"Said Mary Barker said there was such a load & weight at her stomach that hindered her from speaking, and is afraid she has given up herself soul and body to the Devil. She says she promised to serve, worship and believe in him and he promised to pardon her sins, but finds he has deceived her, and that she was lost of God and all good people; that Goody Johnson and Goody Faulkner appeared at the same time and threatened to tear her in pieces if she did not do what she then did. She further says that she has seen no appearance since but a fly which did speak to her, and bid her afflict these poor creatures, which she did by pinching with, and clinching of her hands, for which she is sorry. And further the Devil told her it would be very brave and clever for her to come down here to Salem among these accused persons, and that she should never be brought out. She promises to confess what more she shall hereafter remember."[356]

The magistrates, not knowing any law, were obsessed with legalities. In order for Mary to be a witch, she must confess that

---

354 Elizabeth (Dane) Johnson. On the same day, August 29, 1692, the conspiracy filed a complaint against her.
355 Suffolk County, Court Records, case 2678, page 9.
356 Ibid.

she signed the Devil's book. Also her specter must have hurt someone. She did on Saturday and Sabbath Day last. She had to ride the broomstick. She did, taking only 15 minutes to go from Andover to the witch meeting at Salem Village. To be an authentic witch, Mary had to be baptized by the Devil. Because Mary could not remember, the afflicted Martha Sprague answered for her. The afflicted girls at Mary's examination were Rose Foster, 14, Abigail Martin, Jr., 16, and Martha Sprague, 16, of the Andover circle. They were teenagers not much older than the accused witch, Mary Barker, who hurt them with her specter. In the small closed community everyone knew one another.

One important thing to note in the above confession is the sentence: "She confesses she was at the witch meeting at Salem Village with her uncle." These words, put into her mouth by the leading questions of the magistrates, were legally interpreted that this child accused her uncle William Barker, Sr. of witchcraft. Thus, it has come down in history books that the accused children were depraved, because they bore witness against their own parents and relatives. But clearly such an interpretation is wrong; the evil lies not in the children, but in the magistrates who orchestrated these confessions, false then as now.

In Mary's confession is the statement, "Goody Faulkner appeared at the same time and threatened to tear her in pieces." This was interpreted as an accusation of Faulkner as a witch. Mary's confession was entered as evidence against Abigail (Dane) Faulkner at her trial at the Court of Oyer and Terminer on September 17. The magistrates required Mary to endorse the confession; the endorsement was indicated by the entry, "Mary Barker signed and owned the above said examination & confession. THE MARK of Mary Barker, 17 September 1692, before me, John Higginson, Jr., justice peace."[357]

The conspiracy struck at Mary but not at her father, Lieut. John Barker. His services were sorely needed in the Army. Throughout the examinations and trials in August and September

---

357 Ibid. John Higginson, Jr., justice of the peace in Salem, was the son of John Higginson, the elderly senior minister of Salem.

1692, the fighting in Maine against the French and Indians had heightened the frenzied atmosphere pervading the colony. Rumors of expected raids on Massachusetts spread fear and apprehension; the unsettled times were exploited by the old guard to carry out the trials in all haste. The case of Mary Barker is continued with the case of William Barker, Jr. which immediately follows.

William Barker, Sr.   **Andover**
Married man, 46   *Charged on August 25, 1692*

William Barker, Jr.   **Andover**
Boy, 14   *Charged on September 1, 1692*

William Barker, Sr. was born about 1646 in Andover, the second child of Joanna (mnu) and Richard Barker. William Barker, Sr. married, in 1677 in Andover, Mary Dix. They had two daughters and five sons; the eldest, William Barker, Jr., was born in 1678. In 1692 William Barker, Sr., about 46, his wife, and children were living on his father's land in the north part of Andover.

On August 25, 1692, the conspiracy filed a complaint against William Barker, Sr., his niece Mary Barker, and Mary (Osgood) Marston. On August 29 they were arrested and taken to Salem for examination. Three days later, on September 1, 1692, William's son, William Barker, Jr., 14, was arrested and imprisoned in Salem. After the boy's examination on September 1, the following confession was entered into the court records. "Before Major Gedney, Mr. Hathorne, Mr. Corwin, John Higginson, Jr., Esquire. The examination and confession of William Barker, Jr., aged 14 years or thereabouts. He is accused for exercising acts of witchcraft upon the bodies of Martha Sprague, Rose Foster and Abigail Martin, Jr. which he did not deny but could not remember it. He confesses now that he has not been in the snare of the Devil above six days, that as he was going into the woods one evening to look after cows he saw the shape of a black dog which looked very fiercely upon him and he was much disturbed in his mind about it and could not sleep well that night. And betimes next morning he met with a black man (he calls him a black man because he had black clothes and thinks he had a black skin) who bid him set his hand to his book and serve him as long as he, the said Barker, lived, which he promised. And thereupon he set his hand to this book by putting his finger thereon. He says the black man brought red stuff along with him in an inkhorn and he, the said Barker, dipped his finger into it and therewith made a red mark on the paper. He confesses he was to do any service the black man appointed him to do and was to have suit of clothes for it. He said further the black man would have him baptized but he never was. He says further that Goody Parker went with him last night to afflict Martha Sprague and that he afflicts by clinching his hands together. He says he now is sorry and hates the Devil, but yet struck down the afflicted with his eyes. And Martha Sprague, being recovered out of a fit, said that Barker's apparition and Goody Parker rode upon a pole and was baptized at Five Mile Pond. He now says there was such a load upon his stomach that he could not speak. A little after, he owned he was baptized by the black man at Five Mile Pond and did also renounce his former baptism. He knows Goody Parker to be a witch and says the Devil dipped his head into the water and spoke these words, that the said Barker was his forever and ever. He said he could not think of his baptism before and that the load that was upon his stomach is not so heavy as it was but just before. He still afflicted Martha Sprague & shut her mouth, but by laying his hand thereon opened it again. And afterwards confessed that there were of his company Goody Parker, Goody Johnson, Samuel Wardwell & his wife and two daughters. And then he could take the afflicted persons by the hand without doing them any harm. Wm. Barker, Jr. signed & owned the above said examination & confession before me, John Higginson, Jr., Justice Peace. The MARK of William Barker, Jr."[358]

This document once again displays the handiwork of the magistrates who drew up this so-called confession from notes taken by the scribe at the examination. Fourteen-year-old William Barker, Jr. was accused for "exercising acts of witchcraft ··· which he could not deny but could not remember it." This was a common trick. They told him that the mere fact that he could not remember had no bearing. He was guilty, and they would

---

help him fill in the details. Note that when he denied being baptized by the Devil, William Barker, Jr. "struck down the afflicted with his eyes, and [the afflicted] Martha Sprague being recovered out of a fit said that Barker's apparition rode upon a pole and was baptized at Five Mile Pond." But now comes the point of the confession, namely, that William Barker, Jr. "afterwards confessed that there were of his company, Goody Parker, Goody Johnson, Samuel Wardwell & his wife and two daughters. And then he could take the afflicted persons by the hand without doing them any harm." On the back of the document is the notation: "Confession of William Barker, Jr. Accused Goody Parker, Goody Johnson, Samuel Wardwell, his wife, & 2 daughters."[359] By this ruse the magistrates tried to give the impression that those making the accusations were not the plaintiffs but the defendants.

The first confession of William Barker, Sr., that of August 29, 1692, is given in Chapter 16. Of all the confessions, this one is outstanding. He expressed simply yet powerfully the hopes of the people for democracy and freedom of religion. Almost a century later the same ideas would be incorporated in the Declaration of Independence with similar words, "All men are created equal." The authorities by arresting respected men like William Barker, Sr. were either knowingly or unwittingly striking at the very foundations of their society, a society that was under military attack from the French and Indians. These men were needed to serve their country, yet they were being struck down in a tragic farce.

A few days after his first confession, William Barker, Sr., produced a second confession from prison. "God having called me to confess my sin and apostasy in that fall in giving the Devil advantage over me, appearing to me like a black man in the evening to set my hand to his book, as I have owned to my shame. He told me that I should not want, so doing. At Salem Village, there being a little off the meetinghouse, about a hundred five blades, some with rapiers by their side, which was called, and

---

359 Ibid.

might be more for ought I know, by Burse[360] and Burroughs, and the trumpet sounded, and bread and wine which they called the sacrament, but I had none, being carried all over on a stick, never being at any other meeting. I being at cart a Saturday last, all the day, of hay and English corn, the Devil brought my shape to Salem, and did afflict Martha Sprague and Rose Foster by clinching my hand; and a Sabbath day my shape afflicted Abigail Martin, Jr. and, at night, afflicted Martha Sprague and Abigail Martin, Jr. Elizabeth (Dane) Johnson and Abigail (Dane) Faulkner have been my enticers to this great abomination, as one[361] has owned and charged her to her sister with the same. And the design was to destroy Salem Village, and to begin at the ministers house, and to destroy the church of God, and to set up Satan's kingdom, and then all will be well. And now I hope God in some measure has made me something sensible of my sin and apostasy, begging pardon of God, and of the honorable magistrates and all God's people, hoping and promising by the help of God, to set to my heart and hand to do what in me lies to destroy such wicked worship, humbly begging the prayers of all God's people for me, I may walk humbly under this great affliction and that I may procure to myself the sure mercies of David, and the blessing of Abraham."[362]

Most of the imprisoned Andover people confessed that they joined the Devil's church. Their descriptions of this hellish church—its forms, ceremonies and sacraments—are the

---

360 The Rev. John Burse (or Buss), about 50, lived in Durham, New Hampshire, so was not subject to Massachusetts authority. His wife, Elizabeth, was the daughter of the imprisoned Mary (Perkins) Bradbury and her husband, Thomas. A physician and an unordained minister, John Burse at one time had been minister at Wells, Maine. His friend, the Rev. George Burroughs, became minister at Wells in 1690.

361 Elizabeth (Dane) Johnson in her confession taken on August 30 stated that she was carried to the witch meeting at the Village on a pole and her sister Faulkner was there and William Barker.

362 Hale, A Modest Enquiry, in Burr, Narratives, 419-420. This second confession is not one of the court documents; instead it first appeared in the book of the Rev. John Hale, published in 1702. Apparently Hale polished the language of the confession somewhat, as its style is different from Barker's first confession, as well as from other extant confessions.

imaginings of clerical minds. The thoughts of the ministers shine through in the words of the confessors. The confessions were extorted by persistent importunities; sometimes threats were used, and even torture. Certain fanatic clergymen were first and foremost in the efforts to extort confessions. These ministers molded the persecution into a religious shape and form. The ministers then quoted the works of their own minds (the confessions that they zealously elicited) as proof of the Devil's plot, which they themselves claimed to dread. Cotton Mather, chief of this class, was the most forward in molding the affair of 1692 into a shape acceptable to his own illusions. The fabricated confessions revealed the whole scope of his superstitions and fanaticism. Cotton Mather used the confessions, especially references to Satan's plan to abolish all the churches and to the existence of hundreds of witches in the country, as proof of his own fantasies.

On September 16 William Barker, Sr. admitted to his confession before the Court of Oyer and Terminer at Salem. Sometime afterwards he made his escape from prison. On the back of his indictment for practicing witchcraft against Abigail Martin, Jr., it is written, "fled, persons fled."[363] His cattle were immediately seized, but were redeemed by his brother, Lieut. John Barker, who paid £2. 10s. to the deputy sheriff.[364] About October 10 Lieut. John Barker and Francis Faulkner posted bonds for the release on bail of Mary Barker and William Barker, Jr. After six-weeks imprisonment the children were free, awaiting trial.

On January 3, 1693, the grand jury at the Superior Court of Judicature at Salem indicted both William Barker, Jr. and Mary Barker. However the two Barker children were not brought to trial at that time. A new bail bond had to be posted for the children to stay free. On January 13, 1673, Mary's father, Lieut. John Barker, together with Captain John Osgood posted "the sum of one hundred pounds to be levied on their or either of their lands & tenements, goods & chattels for the use of our said sovereign Lord & Lady, the King and Queen, on condition that

---

363 Massachusetts Archives, *Witchcraft*, 135:37.
364 Massachusetts Archives, *Witchcraft*, 135:138.

William Barker, Jr. and Mary Barker having stood committed for suspicion of witchcraft shall make their personal appearance at the next Court of Assizes and General Jail Delivery to be holden for the County of Essex."[365] At the May 10, 1693, meeting of the Superior Court of Judicature the two children made their appearance; each was tried by jury and found not guilty. Eleven years later, in 1704, Mary Barker and William Barker, Jr., first cousins, were married. Small wonder that these two, who had suffered hideous interrogation and imprisonment, should choose one another. They had eight children. He died in 1745, aged 66, and she died in 1752, aged 72. William Barker, Sr. died in 1718, aged 72; his wife, Mary, died in 1744, aged 88. The four graves may still be found in the old cemetery in North Andover.

Abigail (Wheeler) Barker   **Andover**
Married woman, 36   *Charged on September 7, 1692*

Abigail Wheeler was born 1656, daughter of Sarah (Wise) and David Wheeler of Rowley. In 1686 Abigail married Ebenezer Barker of Andover, fifth child of Joanna (mnu) and Richard Barker. In 1692 Abigail, 36, and her husband Ebenezer, a carpenter, were living in the south part of Andover. Abigail's sister, Lydia, and her husband, Daniel Eames, lived in Boxford but attended the Andover Church.

By the early part of August 1692 Daniel Eames and his mother, Rebecca (Blake) Eames, both found themselves in prison. On August 29, 1692 Ebenezer's niece, Mary Barker, and his brother, William Barker, Sr., were imprisoned and on September 1 William Barker, Jr. was imprisoned. On September 7 Abigail (Wheeler) Barker was arrested at the Andover touch test. Ebenezer Barker quickly joined the newly formed Andover resistance and was a signer of the petitions of October 12, October 18, and December 6. Abigail (Wheeler) Barker is specifically mentioned in the petition presented to the Superior Court of Judicature at Salem when it opened on January 3, 1693. The petition was signed by Dudley Bradstreet, the Rev. Dane, the

---

365 Massachusetts Archives, *Witchcraft*, 135:105.

Rev. Barnard, and fifty men and women of Andover.[366] Despite
the petition, the grand jury at the Superior Court of Judicature
indicted Abigail. However in a trial by jury on January 6 she was
found not guilty. She was released, having been imprisoned for
18 weeks in Salem. In 1743 Abigail (Wheeler) Barker died at
Andover, aged 87.

OSGOOD FAMILY

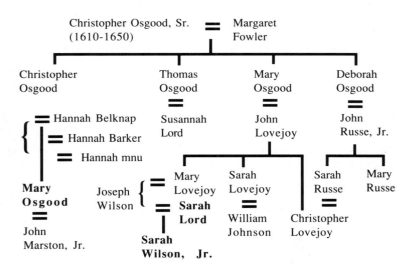

Mary (Osgood) Marston   **Andover**
Married woman, 27   *Charged on August 25, 1692*

Mary Osgood was born in 1665, eldest daughter of Hannah
(Belknap) and Christopher Osgood of the south part of
Andover.[367] In 1689 Mary Osgood married John Marston, Jr., born

---

366 Bailey, *Historical Sketches of Andover*, 225-235.
367 There were two branches of the Osgood family in Andover. In 1692 one
     was led by Captain John Osgood (1630-1693), son of Andover original
     proprietor John Osgood, Sr. (1595-1651). The other branch was led by
     Christopher Osgood (1643-1723), son of Christopher Osgood, Sr.

in 1653 in Hampton, son of Martha (mnu) and John Marston, Sr. The Marston family moved to Andover in 1664. John Marston, Sr., who served twice as a selectman, was the only outsider allowed into the ruling group of Andover's first-settler families. In 1692 Mary, 27, and her husband were living in the north part of Andover. On August 25 Samuel Martin and Moses Tyler filed a complaint against Mary (Osgood) Marston, and on August 29 she was arrested and examined before the three Salem magistrates. Mary confessed, saying that about three years previously, about the time her mother[368] died, she was overcome with melancholy. She was imprisoned.

John Marston, Jr. and Christopher Osgood, both in the Andover resistance, signed the various petitions. On January 3, 1693, the grand jury at the Superior Court of Judicature at Salem indicted Mary (Osgood) Marston. On January 6 in a trial by jury, she was found not guilty. Mary, who had suffered imprisonment for about 20 weeks, was released upon payment of fees.

Mary (Clement) Osgood   **Andover**
Married woman, 55   *Charged on September 7, 1692*

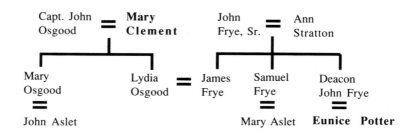

Mary Clement was born about 1637 in England, daughter of Robert Clement who settled in Haverhill, Massachusetts. In

---

(1610-1650) of Ipswich. The two branches were related, but the relationship is unknown. Both branches were part of the elite ruling class of Andover.

368 Mary was referring to her second stepmother, Hannah (mnu) Marston, who died in 1689. Her first stepmother had been Hannah Barker (died 1687), daughter of Joanna (mnu) and Richard Barker.

1653, she married John Osgood of Andover. He was born about 1630 in England, elder son of Sarah (Booth) and John Osgood, Sr., (1595-1651), an original proprietor of Andover. John Osgood, Sr. was one of the ten founders of the Andover Church in 1645, and was Andover's first representative to the General Court. He died in 1651. Between 1670 and 1690, his son John Osgood often served as a selectman in town government and as a representative in colonial government.

Mary (Clement) Osgood, about 55 in 1692, was one of the most highly respected women in Andover. Her husband Captain John Osgood was the commander of a company of Andover militia. Mary and John lived in the north part of Andover and were prominent members of the church. They had nine children, three at home and six married. Son Peter Osgood was a constable in Salem; he had to carry out the arrests of several accused witches in Salem.

On September 7, 1692 Mary (Clement) Osgood was arrested at the Andover touch test. At her examination in Salem on the next day, Mary made the following confession. "She confesses, that about 11 years ago, when she was in a melancholy state and condition, she used to walk abroad in her orchard; and upon a certain time, she saw the appearance of a cat, at the end of the house, which yet she thought was a real cat. However, at that time, it diverted her from praying to God, and instead thereof she prayed to the Devil; about which time she made a covenant with the Devil, who, as a black man, came to her and presented her a book, upon which she laid her finger and that left a red spot. And that upon her signing, the Devil told her he was her god, and that she should serve and worship him, and, she believes, she consented to it. She says further, that about two years ago, she was carried through the air, in company with Deacon Frye's wife, Ebenezer Barker's wife, and Goody Tyler, to Five Mile Pond, where she was baptized by the Devil, who dipped her face in the water and made her renounce her former baptism, and told her she must be his, soul and body, forever, and that she must serve him, which she promised to do. She says, the renouncing her first baptism was after her dipping, and that she was transported back again through the air, in company with the fore-named persons, in the same manner as she went, and believes they were carried upon a pole. Q. How many persons were upon the pole? A. As I said before, viz. four persons and no more but whom she had named above. She confesses she has afflicted three persons, John Sadie, Jr., Martha Sprague, and Rose Foster, and that she did it by pinching her bed clothes, and giving consent the Devil should do it in her shape, and that the Devil could not do it without her consent. She confesses afflicting persons in the court, by the glance of her eye.

"Her husband being present was asked if he judged his wife to be any way discomposed. He answered, that having lived with her so long, he doth not judge her to be any ways discomposed, but has cause to believe what she had said is true."[369]

Present in the courtroom at the examination were the Andover afflicted girls Martha Sprague and Rose Foster, as well as Mary Richardson, the stepdaughter of Thomas Chandler's brother, William Chandler, Jr. Also present were the imprisoned Mary Lacey, Jr., Elizabeth Johnson, Jr., and Hannah Post playing their parts as afflicted persons.

In October 1692, the Rev. Increase Mather interviewed Mary (Clement) Osgood in prison. "Being asked why she prefixed a time, and spake of her being baptized, &c., about twelve years since, she replied and said, that, when she had owned the thing, they asked the time, to which she answered that she knew not the time. But, being told that she did know the time, and must tell the time, and the like, she considered that about twelve years before (when she had her last child) she had a fit of sickness, and was melancholy; and so thought that that time might be as proper a time to mention as any, and accordingly did prefix the said time. Being asked about the cat, in the shape of which she had confessed that the Devil had appeared to her, and must needs appear to her, &c., (she being a witch), she at length did own that the Devil had appeared to her; and, being pressed to say in what creature's shape he appeared, she at length did say that it was in the shape of a cat. Remembering that, some time before her being apprehended, as she went out her door, she saw a cat, &c.; not as though she any whit

---

369 Hutchinson, "The Witchcraft Delusion of 1692," 398.

suspected the said cat to be the Devil, in the day of it, but because some creature she must mention, and this came to her mind at that time."[370]

Captain John Osgood was a tireless member of the Andover resistance and posted several bonds for the release of the imprisoned Andover children on bail. The children were released by mid-October. On October 12 John Osgood and eight other Andover men of Andover petitioned for the release of their families on bail. On October 18 twenty-six men of Andover, including John Osgood, his sons Timothy and Samuel Osgood, nephew Hooker Osgood, and kinsman Christopher Osgood, petitioned for the release of prisoners on bail. On December 6 John Osgood, Christopher Osgood, and six other men of Andover again petitioned for release of their wives and neighbors on bail. On December 20 Captain John Osgood and Deacon John Frye were allowed to post bonds for the release of their wives, Mary (Clement) Osgood and Eunice (Potter) Frye, on bail. Both women had been in prison for 15 weeks. On January 5, 1693, the grand jury at the Superior Court of Judicature at Salem indicted Mary. On January 12 in a trial by jury, Mary was found not guilty and released. About three months later, on April 21, 1693, her husband Captain John Osgood died in Andover, aged 62.

FRYE FAMILY

Eunice (Potter) Frye   **Andover**
Married woman, 51   *Charged on September 7, 1692*

Eunice Potter was born in 1641, daughter of Mary and Luke Potter of Concord. In 1660 Eunice married John Frye of Andover. He was born about 1633 in England, son of Anne (Stratton) and John Frye, Sr. John Frye, Sr. was an original proprietor of Andover. His son John Frye became the Deacon of the Andover Church. James Frye, the brother of Deacon John Frye, was married to Lydia Osgood, daughter of Mary (Clement) Osgood and John Osgood. In 1692 Eunice, 51, and her husband, Deacon

---

370 Upham, *Salem Witchcraft*, 2:406-407.

John Frye, were living in the south part of Andover. In that year the deacon was also serving as a selectman.

On September 7, 1692, Eunice (Potter) Frye was arrested at the Andover touch test and imprisoned in Salem. Deacon John Frye soon became an active member of the Andover resistance and signed the petitions of October 12 and December 6 for the release of his wife and others on bail. On December 20 Deacon John Frye and Captain John Osgood were allowed to post recognizance bonds for the release on bail of their wives, Eunice (Potter) Frye and Mary (Clement) Osgood. The two women had been in prison for 15 weeks.

On January 3, 1693, the grand jury at the Superior Court of Judicature at Salem indicted Eunice Frye but she was not brought to trial at that time. On January 12 John Osgood and James Frye posted a recognizance bond for her continued freedom on bail. On May 10, 1693 in a trial by jury at the Superior Court of Judicature at Ipswich, Eunice Frye was found not guilty.

Samuel Frye, the son of Ann (Stratton) and John Frye, Sr., was born in 1649 and married Mary Aslet in 1671. At the end of September 1692 Mary and Samuel Frye took William Wardwell, twelve-year-old son of the executed Samuel Wardwell and the imprisoned Sarah Wardwell, to live in their family until he was twenty-one and to teach him the trade of weaver.[371]

BRADSTREET FAMILY

Dudley Bradstreet   **Andover**
Married man, 44   *Cried out upon after September 7, 1692*

Captain Dudley Bradstreet, 44, was the son of Anne (Dudley) and Simon Bradstreet.[372] Dudley Bradstreet and his wife, Ann (Wood) Price Bradstreet, were the foremost residents of Andover, both 44 years old in 1692. Dudley had served in every important

---

371 William and Dorothy (Wright) Wardwell are five-times-great grandparents of the writer.

372 On May 14, 1692 Simon Bradstreet, the elected governor of Massachusetts, was replaced by the royal governor, Sir William Phipps, appointed by the crown.

town position and was a selectman many times. In 1692 he was serving as Andover's representative to the General Court and was Andover's justice of the peace.[373] In that judicial capacity he signed arrest warrants and examined some of the accused. "He seems to deprecate the necessity laid upon him, and to disclaim any judgment in the matter. He evidently, though humane and not so credulous as many in regard to the wild stories current, had not the determination and strength that characterize the minister, Mr. Dane."[374]

After the Andover touch test on September 7, 1692, Dudley Bradstreet refused to sign any more arrest warrants. The afflicted girls then started to cry out upon him and his wife. They quickly escaped from town. For that reason his name appears neither on the Andover petitions nor the selectmen decisions that fall. However by the end of December, Dudley Bradstreet had returned to Andover. His name is the first name on the Andover petition presented to the Superior Court of Judicature on January 3, 1693.

John Bradstreet   **Topsfield**
Married man, 40   *Cried out upon after September 7, 1692*

In 1692 the younger brother of Dudley, John Bradstreet, 40, lived in Topsfield. His wife, Sarah (Perkins) Bradstreet, 35, was a niece of Mary (Perkins) Bradbury who was condemned on September 9 but then escaped from prison. Her escape was possible because of the intercessions of some high officials, who most likely included the Bradstreets. A Salem Village dog became afflicted. The girls with their spectral sight were sent for and behold, they saw the specter of John Bradstreet riding on the back of the dog. They cried out upon John saying that he was the cause of the dog's afflictions. John wisely fled to New

---

373 A representative was a member of the lower legislative body (the House of Representatives); on the other hand, an assistant to the governor (like John Hathorne) was a member of the upper legislative body (the Board of Assistants, later called the Council). Justice of the peace was a judicial office below that of a magistrate.

374 Bailey, *Historical Sketches of Andover*, 224.

Hampshire. The dog was put to death; this act was inconsistent because the dog did not afflict anyone but was afflicted.

STEVENS FAMILY

Ephraim Stevens   **Andover**
Married man, 43   *Cried out upon after September 7, 1692*

John Stevens, born in 1605, landed in Newbury in 1648 on the ship *Confidence* from Southampton, England. He was an original proprietor of Andover. His stone in the old cemetery reads, "Here Lyes Buried the Body of Mr. John Stevens, who Deceased ye 11 Day of April 1662 in ye 57 Year of His Age." His children included John Stevens, Jr., born 1639, Ephraim Stevens, born 1648, and Mary Stevens, born 1649. Mary married John Barker in 1670, and their daughter, Mary Barker, born in 1679, was imprisoned for witchcraft on August 29, 1692.

Ephraim Stevens married, in 1680, Sarah Abbot, daughter of Hannah (Chandler) and George Abbot, Sr. After the death of her husband, Hannah (Chandler) Abbot became the third wife of the Rev. Francis Dane.

In 1692 Ephraim Stevens was 43. After the Andover touch test on September 7, 1692, the afflicted girls cried out upon him, and he left town.

John Stevens, 3rd, the son of John Stevens, Jr., was born in 1663 and married Ruth Poor in 1689. At the end of September 1692 John and Ruth took baby Elizabeth Wardwell, daughter of the executed Samuel Wardwell and the imprisoned Sarah Wardwell, to live in their family until she was eighteen years of age.

22

THE ACCUSED: THE DANE FAMILY

A NDOVER'S FIRST MINISTER, the Rev. John Woodbridge,
served only until 1647, when he left Andover and returned
to England with his brother, Benjamin Woodbridge. The Rev.
Woodbridge was succeeded by the Rev. Francis Dane, born about
1615 in England, the son of John Dane, pioneer of Ipswich and
Roxbury, Massachusetts. Francis Dane, about 33 years of age,
settled in Andover in 1648 and was ordained as minister. He had
no formal education for the ministry. He served as Andover's
only minister until 1682. In that year the Rev. Thomas Barnard
of Hadley was appointed assistant minister. The Rev. Dane
continued to serve, now as senior minister, until his death in 1697
at age 82.

No single family had more members accused in 1692 than did
the family of the Rev. Dane. In addition, many members of his
extended family were also accused. The following chart shows
the three main branches of the extended family of the Rev.
Francis Dane.

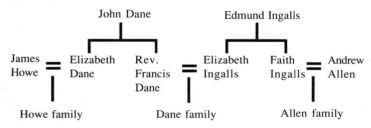

The following table lists the members of the extended Dane
family who were accused of witchcraft in 1692. All of the

accused were from Andover unless otherwise noted. All were imprisoned except Nehemiah Abbot, Jr.

Charged	Accused person, age, town	Family branch
Apr. 21	Nehemiah Abbot, Jr., 29, of Topsfield	Howe family
May 18	Dr. Roger Toothaker, 58, of Billerica—**Died in prison**	Allen family
May 28	Martha (Allen) Carrier, 38—**Hanged**	Allen family
May 28	Elizabeth (Jackson) Howe, 53, of Topsfield—**Hanged**	Howe family
May 28	Margaret Toothaker, 9, of Billerica	Allen family
May 28	Mary (Allen) Toothaker, 47, of Billerica	Allen family
July 21	Andrew Carrier, 15	Allen family
July 21	Richard Carrier, 18	Allen family
July 22	Martha (Toothaker) Emerson, 24, of Haverhill	Allen family
Aug. 3	Mary (Johnson) Davis Clarke, 52, of Haverhill	Sister-in-law of the Rev. Dane's daughter
Aug. 10	Elizabeth Johnson, Jr., 22—**Condemned**	Dane family
Aug. 10	Sarah Carrier, 7	Allen family
Aug. 10	Thomas Carrier, Jr., 10	Allen family
Aug. 11	Abigail (Dane) Faulkner, 40—**Condemned**	Dane family
Aug. 24	Sarah Bridges, 17r	Howe family
Aug. 25	John Jackson, Sr., 50, of Rowley	Howe family
Aug. 25	John Jackson, Jr., 22, of Rowley	Howe family
Aug. 29	Abigail Johnson, 10	Dane family
Aug. 29	Elizabeth (Dane) Johnson, 51	Dane family
Aug. 30	Stephen Johnson, 13	Dane family
Sep. 7	Deliverance (Haseltine) Dane, 37	Dane family
Sep. 7	Rebecca (Aslet) Johnson, 40,	Dane family
Sep. 7	Rebecca Johnson, Jr., 17	Dane family
Sep. 7	Male slave of Nathaniel Dane	Dane family
Sep. 7	Abigail Faulkner, Jr., 9	Dane family
Sep. 7	Dorothy Faulkner, 12	Dane family
Sep. 7	John Sadie, Jr., 13	Stepnephew of the Rev. Dane's daughter

Not included in the table is Sarah Bridges' aunt, Sarah (Towne) Bridges Cloyce, who was imprisoned. Sarah Cloyce's two sisters, Mary (Towne) Easty and Rebecca (Towne) Nurse, were hanged. Also not listed in the table are three other relatives who were imprisoned, namely Rebecca (Aslet) Johnson's sister, Sarah (Aslet) Cole of Lynn; Rebecca (Aslet) Johnson's stepnephew, Edward Farrington of Andover; and Cole's sister-in-law, Sarah (Davis) Cole of Salem. In addition, the Aslet sisters' aunt, Mary (Ayer) Parker, was hanged and her daughter, Sarah Parker, was imprisoned.

ALLEN FAMILY

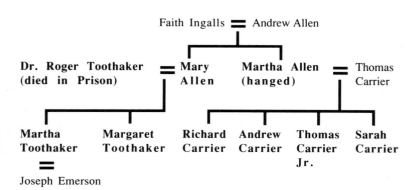

The chart shows two branches of the Allen family, namely the Toothakers and the Carriers. The patriarch Andrew Allen, born in England in 1616, was an original proprietor of Andover. In 1643, at age 27, he moved from Lynn, Massachusetts, to Andover. His farm was in the south part of Andover near Sunset Rock and close to the farm of Andrew Foster. His wife, Faith (Ingalls) Allen, was the sister of the Rev. Francis Dane's first wife, Elizabeth (Ingalls) Dane, who died in 1676. Sons Andrew Allen, Jr. and John Allen died of smallpox in 1690.

Dr. Roger Toothaker   **Billerica**
Married man, 58   *Charged on May 18, 1692*

Mary (Allen) Toothaker   **Billerica**
Married woman, 47   *Charged on May 28, 1692*

Margaret Toothaker   **Billerica**
Girl, 9   *Charged on May 28, 1692*

Roger Toothaker was born about 1634 in England, son of Margaret and Roger Toothaker. The son Roger became a physician and settled in Billerica, Massachusetts. In 1665 he married Mary Allen. She was born about 1645 in Andover, daughter of Faith (Ingalls) and Andrew Allen.

In 1692 Roger, about 58; his wife Mary, about 47; two sons, Roger, Jr., 19, and Andrew, 12; and daughter Margaret, 9, were living in Billerica. The other living daughter, Martha, 24 years old on July 23, 1692, was married to Joseph Emerson in Haverhill. Son Allen Toothaker, 21, lived in Andover. A son, Nathaniel, and three daughters, each named Mary, all had died young.

On May 18, 1692, the conspiracy of accusers in Salem Village filed a complaint against Dr. Roger Toothaker. They charged him with afflicting, among others, Elizabeth Hubbard, servant of his rival, Dr. William Griggs of Salem Village. Dr. Toothaker was arrested and sent to Boston prison. On May 28 the Salem Village conspiracy filed a complaint against his wife, Mary (Allen) Toothaker, his young daughter, Margaret Toothaker, and his sister-in-law, Martha (Allen) Carrier of Andover. On May 31 they were arrested and imprisoned in Salem.

Thomas Gage, 36, and Elias Pickworth, 34, gave depositions about the illnesses of two children that spring. The two men claimed that Dr. Toothaker had said, "I have already seen both the children, and my opinion is they are under an evil hand. My daughter [Martha Emerson] had killed a witch. She had learned something from me. She got some of the afflicted person's urine and put it into an earthen pot. She stopped the pot very close, and put the pot into a hot oven and stopped up the oven. The next morning the witch was dead."[375]

On June 16, 1692, Dr. Roger Toothaker died in the Boston prison. Twenty-four men were named to a coroner's jury. They reported that they viewed the body and obtained the best information they could from persons near and present at his death. They concluded that he died from natural causes. However, the very fact that a coroner's jury was impaneled indicates that Dr. Toothaker died under suspicious circumstances.

On July 23, 1692, Mary's daughter Martha (Toothaker) Emerson was accused and arrested. On July 30 the imprisoned Mary Toothaker, now a widow, made a confession before the magistrates at Salem. When asked if her husband instructed his daughter to kill Button, a reputed witch, Mary answered in the affirmative. Mary then added that she and her husband used to read many histories, especially one that treated the twelve signs of the zodiac, from which they could tell a great deal. She related her terror of the Indians, a well-grounded fear as Billerica was still subject to Indian raids. Mary confessed to having made a covenant with the Devil in the past May for protection from the Indians.

About a week later, on August 1, 1692, the Indians attacked Billerica and at least six persons were slain. The Indians returned a few days later and burned down the deserted Toothaker farm. On August 5, 1692, Mary's sister Martha (Allen) Carrier was condemned by the Court of Oyer and Terminer, and on August 10 she was hanged at Salem.

On February 1, 1693, at the Superior Court of Judicature at Charlestown for Middlesex County, Mary Toothaker was found not guilty in a trial by jury. Her daughter Margaret was also released. In 1695 the Indians raided Billerica. They killed widow Mary (Allen) Toothaker and carried off Margaret, now 12, who was never heard of again.

Martha (Toothaker) Emerson   **Haverhill**
Married woman, 24   *Charged on July 22, 1692*

---

375 Essex County Archives, *Witchcraft*, 1:117.

Martha Toothaker, born in 1668, was the daughter of Mary (Allen) and Dr. Roger Toothaker of Billerica. Martha Toothaker married, in 1690, Joseph Emerson of Haverhill, born in 1669, son of Ann (Grant) and Robert Emerson. In the spring of 1692 Martha, 23, and Joseph Emerson, a millwright and carpenter, were living in Haverhill with their infant. Martha was a member of the Haverhill Church. On May 18, 1692, her father, Dr. Roger Toothaker, was imprisoned. On May 31 her mother, Mary (Allen) Toothaker; her sister, Margaret Toothaker, 9; and her aunt, Martha (Allen) Carrier were imprisoned. On June 16 her father died in Boston prison. On July 22, 1692, Richard Carrier, 18, and Andrew Carrier, 15, of Andover, were imprisoned. The two boys were Martha's first cousins.

On July 22, 1692, the three Salem magistrates, Bartholomew Gedney, John Hathorne, and Jonathan Corwin, together with the Salem justice of the peace, John Higginson, Jr., issued an arrest warrant for Martha (Toothaker) Emerson. They accused her of afflicting Mary Warren, 20, a long-standing member of the Salem Village afflicted circle, and Mary Lacey, Jr., 18, of Andover.[376] The warrant required the arresting officer to make a diligent search for any images or puppets in the Emerson house or about it. Martha Emerson was arrested the same day by William Starling, constable of Haverhill, and imprisoned in Salem.

The next day, her twenty-fourth birthday, July 23, 1692, Martha (Toothaker) Emerson was examined. Mary Warren accused Martha Emerson of practicing witchcraft right in the courtroom, a *pro-forma* accusation in 1692. Martha at first refused to confess. "Emerson was told that her father had said he had taught his daughter Martha so that she had killed a witch, and that was to take the afflicted person's water & put it in a glass or bottle, and set it into an oven. Emerson owned she had kept a woman's urine in a glass."[377] This revelation was

---

376 Mary Lacey, Jr., after her arrest, had made a long confession at her examination on July 21 and played the role of an afflicted girl. From then on, the three Salem magistrates often brought her from jail to the courtroom to serve as an afflicted girl.
377 Suffolk County, Court Records, case 2708, page 32.

taken as proof of witchcraft, even though such things were part of the common medical practice of the day.

On August 5, 1692, Martha Emerson's aunt, Martha (Allen) Carrier, was condemned by the Court of Oyer and Terminer. On August 10 Martha Emerson's first cousins, Thomas Carrier, Jr., 10, and Sarah Carrier, 7, were imprisoned. On August 19 Martha (Allen) Carrier was hanged at Salem.

On January 10, 1693, the grand jury at the Superior Court of Judicature at Salem cleared Martha Emerson and she was released. Martha (Toothaker) Emerson died at Haverhill, aged 57, in 1726.

Martha (Allen) Carrier	*Andover*
Married woman, 38	*Charged on May 28, 1692*
Richard Carrier	*Andover*
Boy, 18	*Charged on July 21, 1692*
Andrew Carrier	*Andover*
Boy, 15	*Charged on July 21, 1692*
Thomas Carrier, Jr.	*Andover*
Boy, 10	*Charged on August 10, 1692*
Sarah Carrier	*Andover*
Girl, 7	*Charged on August 10, 1692*

Martha Allen was born about 1654 in Andover, daughter of Faith (Ingalls) and Andrew Allen, an original proprietor of Andover. In 1674 Martha Allen married Thomas Carrier, Sr. of Billerica, who was at least twenty years her senior. Their children included Richard Carrier, born 1674, Andrew Carrier, born 1677, Thomas Carrier, Jr., born 1682, and Sarah Carrier, born 1684. When first married, the Carriers had lived in Billerica, where Martha's sister, Mary (Allen) Toothaker, and her family lived. Around 1686, the Carrier family moved to Andover. In the fall of 1690, the smallpox epidemic, which had begun in Boston in late 1689, reached Andover, killing over a dozen people there. Included in this number were seven members of the Allen family. The Carriers were accused of bringing smallpox to Andover and were banned from entering public places.

In 1692 Martha (Allen) Carrier, about 38, her husband, Thomas, and their five children (the above four plus a younger sister) were living in the south part of Andover. On May 18, 1692, Dr. Roger Toothaker of Billerica was accused, examined, and imprisoned at Boston. On May 28 the Salem Village conspiracy filed a complaint against Martha Carrier. She was the first person from Andover to be accused in 1692. On May 31 she was arrested and taken to Salem Village for examination. Martha refused to confess. Magistrate John Hathorne asked the girls of the Salem Village afflicted circle, "Who hurts you?" Susannah Sheldon answered, "Goody Carrier. She bites me, pinches me, & tells me she would cut my throat, if I did not sign her book." Ann Putnam, Jr. complained of a pin stuck in her. Mary Warren cried out that she was pricked. Hathorne told Martha Carrier, "You see. You look upon them & they fall down." Martha answered, "It is false. The Devil is a liar. I looked upon none since I came into the room, but you."[378] The record of the examination ends with the passage, "The tortures of the afflicted were so great that there was no enduring of it, so that she was ordered away & to be bound hand & foot with all expedition; the afflicted in the meanwhile almost killed, to the great trouble of all the spectators, magistrates, & others. Note, as soon as she was well bound, they all had strange & sudden ease. Mary Walcott told the magistrates that this woman told her that she had been a witch these 40 years."[379] Martha Carrier was committed to the chains of Salem prison.

On June 28, 1692, a summons for witnesses against Martha (Allen) Carrier included Samuel Preston, Jr.,[380] Phoebe Chandler,[381] and John Rogers.[382] Samuel Preston, Jr., aged 41, testified that two years previously he had some difference with

---

378 Woodward, *Records of Salem Witchcraft*, 2:56-57.
379 Ibid.
380 His brother, Thomas Preston of Salem Village, was married to Rebecca Nurse, daughter of Rebecca (Towne) and Francis Nurse.
381 Born in 1680 Phoebe was the daughter of William Chandler, Jr. by his second wife, Bridget (Hinxman) Richardson Chandler. William Chandler, Jr. was the brother of conspirator Thomas Chandler.
382 Three years later, on August 5, 1695, John Rogers was slain by the Indians in Billerica.

Martha Carrier, and soon after he "lost a cow in a strange manner, being cast upon her back with her heels up in firm ground when she was very lusty, it being in June." Phoebe Chandler, aged 11, testified, "The last Sabbath day I went to meeting, & Richard Carrier, son of Martha Carrier, looked very earnestly upon me, & immediately my hand began to pain me greatly, & I had a strange burning at my stomach, & then was struck deaf that I could not hear any of the prayer, nor the singing, till the two or three last words of the singing." John Rogers, aged 50, testified that seven years ago, in a dispute with Martha, "she gave forth several threatening words as she often used to do and in a short time this deponent had two large lusty sows that were lost." Thomas Putnam and John Putnam, Jr., members of the Salem Village conspiracy, also testified against her.[383]

On July 21, 1692, Mary Lacey, Jr., 18, just arrested, was examined. She confessed and then assumed the role of an afflicted girl herself with spectral sight. As one who could see spirits and apparitions, Mary said, "Goody Carrier came to us in her spirit, sometimes in the likeness of a cat, sometimes in the likeness of a bird." Nathaniel Hawthorne's ancestor wanted to know what color the cats were. Finding out the cats were black, he then wanted to know where or in what places do those cats suck. Mary gravely answered, "I cannot tell but believe they do suck her body." The Puritan ancestor then asked, "Did you hear the 77 witches names called over?" Mary answered affirmatively and then went on to confirm the worst fears of Cotton Mather. She said, "Goody Carrier told me the Devil said to her she should be a Queen in Hell." Hathorne, delighted, asked, "Who was to be King?" Mary answered. "The minister, Mr. Burroughs, a pretty little man, and he has come to us sometimes in his spirit in the shape of a cat & I think sometimes in his proper shape." As the July 21 examination continued, Mary Warren, a Salem Village afflicted girl, "had a fit and cried out upon Richard Carrier, and Mary Lacey, Jr. prayed that he might be sent for."[384]

---

383 Woodward, *Records of Salem Witchcraft*, 2:61-66.
384 Essex Institute, *Witchcraft Collection*, "Examinations."

Obligingly, the Salem magistrates, Bartholomew Gedney, John Hathorne, and Jonathan Corwin, who were carrying out the examination, issued an arrest warrant for Martha Carrier's two oldest sons, Richard Carrier, 18, and Andrew Carrier, 15. The three magistrates charged the two boys with afflicting Mary Warren of Salem Village; they had just witnessed her fit with their own eyes, so there was no doubt in their minds of the boys' guilt. The warrant advised the arresting officer to ask about and search for any paper or puppets that might relate to witchcraft.

On the next day, July 22, the two boys were duly arrested and taken to Salem. Richard Carrier and his brother were brought into the courtroom. The three Salem magistrates asked many questions, but the Carrier boys returned negative answers to all of them and refused to confess anything. Playing their parts well, the afflicted girls cried out that they saw the black man and the specter of Martha Carrier stand on the table before the boys to hinder their confession. In answer to one of Hathorne's many leading questions, Mary Lacey, Jr. said, "It was about a fortnight since we went upon poles in the night, and we got into the house & this Richard afflicted [Elizabeth (Phelps)] Ballard by pinching & choking of her."[385]

The two Carrier boys would neither confess nor accuse their mother of witchcraft. The afflicted girl Mary Warren fell into "a bad fit & blood running out of her mouth. The afflicted persons were [so] grievously tormented that Richard and Andrew were carried out to another chamber, and their feet and hands bound a little while." Each was tied neck and heels until blood was ready to come out of their noses. "After, Richard was brought in again. Q. Richard, though you have been very obstinate, yet tell us how long ago it is since you were taken in this snare? A. A year last May and no more. Unto many questions propounded, he answered affirmatively as follows." The result was a confession induced by Hathorne's leading questions. "I hurt Swan in spirit & struck him in the knee with a spindle. The Devil brought it & was then in the shape of a black man with a high crowned hat. My mother was with me sometimes, but not often—mother was bodily with me—I have seen her once in spirit since her

385 Ibid.

imprisonment & in the shape of a cat. I was present when brother signed the book & I think mother was there also & the Devil—I rode the first time on a horse & the second time on a man to Salem Village & think there might be seventy there at each meeting."[386]

"Andrew Carrier brought in and his brother told him that he had acknowledged all. Unto many questions asked, he returned the following answers. The Devil is a black man. He was to serve the Devil five years and the Devil was to give him house and land in Andover. Memorandum. This Andrew in his examination stammered and stuttered exceedingly in speaking which some of his neighbors present said he was not wont to do."[387]

Mary Lacey, Jr. and the Carrier boys were committed to prison. In the following days Hathorne often called Mary Lacey, Jr. back to the courtroom to act as an afflicted person when other alleged witches were examined. Richard Carrier also was sometimes brought back to the courtroom to act an afflicted person. In prison the terrified children were under Hathorne's command.

On August 5, 1692, Martha (Allen) Carrier was condemned by the Court of Oyer and Terminer. About August 10, 1692, a complaint was filed against Thomas Carrier, Jr., Sarah Carrier, and their cousin Elizabeth Johnson, Jr. (granddaughter of the Rev. Francis Dane) for afflicting Sarah Phelps of Andover and Ann Putnam, Jr. and Mary Walcott of Salem Village. On August 11 Thomas Carrier, Jr., 10, and Sarah Carrier, 7, were tricked by magistrate Hathorne into naming their mother as a witch. The abuse of Martha Carrier's four children was a tactic used by the court to induce her to confess; she never did. On August 19, 1692, Martha Carrier was hanged at Salem.

The Rev. Cotton Mather would later write of Martha Carrier, "This rampant hag was the person of whom the confessions of the witches, and of her own children among the rest, agreed that the Devil had promised her that she should be

---

386 Ibid.
387 Ibid.

Queen of Hell."[388]   The confessions were those of Mary (Foster) Lacey and her daughter Mary Lacey, Jr., who, terrified, affirmed every leading question put to them; of Martha's sons Richard and Andrew Carrier, who had been tortured; and of Martha's two small children Thomas, Jr. and Sarah Carrier, who were too young to fend off Hathorne's abusive questions.

On October 6, 1692, Thomas Carrier, Sr., Walter Wright, and Francis Johnson posted a recognizance bond of £500 for the release of Sarah Carrier, Abigail Johnson, and Stephen Johnson on bail. The three Carrier boys were also released on recognizance bonds posted by men of the Andover resistance. All the children were to appear at the next court. At the meeting of the Superior Court of Judicature at Salem in January 1693, the only extant document pertaining to the Carrier children is an indictment of Richard Carrier for afflicting Timothy Swan in the month of June 1692.

HOWE FAMILY

The first member of the Howe family accused of witchcraft was Nehemiah Abbot, Jr., son of Mary (Howe) and Nehemiah Abbot, Sr. Nehemiah Abbot, Sr. was a son of George Abbot (1600-1647) of Rowley. Another son was George Abbot, who after completing his apprenticeship as a tailor, left Rowley and settled in Andover. Already in Andover was George Abbot, Sr., an original proprietor. To differentiate the two men with the same name, the original proprietor was always designated as George Abbot, Sr., and the new resident was called George Abbot, "the tailor" on the town records.[389]

About 29 years old in 1692, Nehemiah Abbot, Jr., a great-nephew of the Rev. Francis Dane, lived in Topsfield. He was accused of witchcraft by the Salem Village conspirators on April 21, 1692. Because the afflicted girls had not received adequate instructions from the conspirators, they simply could not properly identify him. After two examinations on April 22, he was

---

388 Cotton Mather, *Wonders*, 159.
389 Sarah (Farnum) and George Abbot, the tailor, are seven-times-great grandparents of the writer.

released. His was the only case in which an accused person was released after examination. The second member of the Howe family accused was Elizabeth (Jackson) Howe, daughter-in-law of the Rev. Dane' sister. Elizabeth (Jackson) Howe was imprisoned on May 31 and hanged on July 19, 1692. Sarah Bridges, a great-niece of the Rev. Dane, was the third member of the Howe family branch to be accused. Sarah Bridges is treated in Chapter 23.

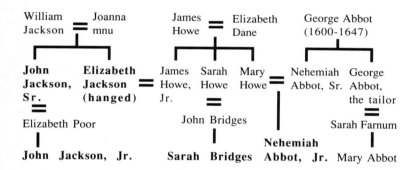

Elizabeth (Jackson) Howe   **Ipswich Farms**
Married woman, 53   *Charged on May 28, 1692*

Elizabeth Jackson was born about 1637 in England, the daughter of Joanna and William Jackson. The family emigrated to New England and were original settlers of Rowley. In 1658 Elizabeth Jackson married James Howe, Jr., born about 1633. He was the son of Elizabeth (Dane) and James Howe, who lived in the section of Ipswich known as Ipswich Farms. Elizabeth (Dane) Howe was the sister of the Rev. Francis Dane of Andover.

Elizabeth Jackson was one of four children. Upon William Jackson's death in 1688, his large estate had gone to his grandson, John Jackson, Jr., to be held in trust for him by his father, John Jackson, Sr. In case the John Jackson, Jr. died, the estate would be divided between the three Jackson sisters. Both of Elizabeth's sisters were widowed by the year 1691.

In 1682 Elizabeth Howe and her husband had a quarrel with Samuel Perley of Topsfield. Elizabeth applied for membership in the Ipswich church, but this was denied, blocked by Samuel

Perley and Isaac Foster of Ipswich. Isaac Foster was the brother-in-law of Mary (Jackson) Foster (Elizabeth's sister) and Elizabeth (Dane) Foster (James Howe, Jr.'s first cousin). Isaac Foster was also the uncle of Ephraim Foster of Andover, who brought charges of witchcraft against John Jackson, Sr. and John Jackson, Jr.

In 1692 Elizabeth (Jackson) Howe, about 53, her blind husband, James Howe, Jr., and their children were living on the Howe estate in Ipswich Farms. James Howe, Jr. had been without sight for about seven years, and Elizabeth had assumed the full burden of caring for him and managing the farm. The Howe farm was close to the Topsfield boundary, and Elizabeth's husband was included with the Topsfield men targeted by the Salem Village conspiracy. Also in the background there was a great deal of envy stirred up by the legacy left by William Jackson.

On May 28, 1692, the Salem Village conspiracy filed a complaint against Elizabeth Howe for afflicting Mary Walcott, Abigail Williams, Mercy Lewis, and Ann Putnam, Jr. On May 31, 1692, Elizabeth Howe was arrested. At her examination she refused to confess, saying, "If it was the last moment I was to live, God knows I am innocent of anything in this nature." On June 30, 1692, Elizabeth Howe was tried at the second sitting of the Court of Oyer and Terminer at Salem. Depositions supporting Elizabeth's character and Christian behavior were given by many of her neighbors. Her husband's father, James Howe, about ninety-four, stated that Elizabeth was "very dutiful, careful, loving, obedient and kind, tenderly leading her husband about by the hand in his want of eyesight."[390] On July 2, 1692, Elizabeth was condemned by the Court of Oyer and Terminer, and on July 19, 1692, Elizabeth (Jackson) Howe was hanged at Salem.

In 1704, James Howe, Jr. died at Topsfield. In 1710 his surviving daughters, Mary and Abigail Howe, gave the account, "Our honored father went twice a week the whole time of our mother's imprisonment to carry her maintenance which was provided with much difficulty, and one of us went with him because he could not go alone for want of sight."[391]

---

390 M. V. B. Perley, *Salem Village Witchcraft Trials*, 33-59.
391 Ibid.

John Howard   **Rowley**
Man, 47   *Charged on August 25, 1692*

John Jackson, Sr.   **Rowley**
Widower, 50   *Charged on August 25, 1692*

John Jackson, Jr.   **Rowley**
Single man. 22   *Charged on August 25, 1692*

John Jackson, Sr. was born about 1643, the only son of Joanna and William Jackson, an original settler of Rowley. John Jackson, Sr. married, in 1669 in Rowley, Elizabeth Poor, daughter of John Poor of Newbury. Their only child was John Jackson, Jr., born in 1670. In the spring of 1671 John's wife, Elizabeth, was drowned in the swift current of a tidal creek on the ebb tide after she had lost her way on the Rowley marshes. John's father, William Jackson, died in 1688. "William Jackson of Rowley in 1688, in his parting advise to his only son John [John Jackson, Sr.], alludes to the promise, 'when he [William Jackson] matched with brother Poor, his daughter,' of one-half of the estate, 'notwithstanding he [John Jackson, Sr.] has not been a good husband to himself, nor so helpful to his parents, since it has pleased God to take his wife away,' still the loving father [William Jackson] gives the estate, on account of the only grandson John [John Jackson, Jr.], only son of Elizabeth Poor. The sisters of John Jackson, Sr. get the estate in case young Jackson [John Jackson, Jr.] comes to grief."[392]

In 1692 John Howard, about 47, John Jackson, Sr., about 50, and his son John Jackson, Jr., 22, all living in Rowley, worked together. John Jackson, Sr. had three living sisters, Mary, Deborah, and Elizabeth. At that time two of the sisters were widows. One was widow Mary (Jackson) Foster of Boxford, who was the aunt of Ephraim Foster. The other was widow Deborah (Jackson) Trumball, who was the stepsister-in-law of Robert Swan, Sr. of Haverhill. Ephraim Foster and three sons of Robert Swan, Sr. were members of the Andover conspiracy. The third sister was Elizabeth (Jackson) Howe of Topsfield. She was

---

392 C. H. Abbott, *The Andover Townsman*, October 7, 1898.

arrested and imprisoned on May 31, condemned on July 2, and hanged at Salem on July 19, 1692.

On August 25, 1692, Ephraim Foster, constable of Andover, and Joseph Tyler of Boxford, filed a complaint against John Jackson, Sr., John Jackson, Jr., and John Howard for afflicting Rose Foster of Andover and Martha Sprague of Boxford. The three accused men were called "laborers" in the bond posted for the complaint. However the term laborer must have been used in a generic sense, as the Jacksons were quite wealthy, and Susannah Post, 31, referred to Howard with the honorific title "Mr." during her preliminary examination of August 25. The three accused men were arrested on August 26.

On August 27, 1692, at his examination at Salem, John Jackson, Sr. refused to confess. "The afflicted persons fell into a bad fit before Jackson came into the room and said he is coming. Question, John Jackson, why do you afflict these persons? Answer. I desire to cry to God to keep both me and mine from this sin. I never did since the day I was born. Question. John Jackson, you are here accused for hurting Martha Sprague and Rose Foster by witchcraft. Answer. I am innocent."[393]

At his examination John Jackson, Jr. confessed that the Devil appeared to him in the shape of a black man and would not let him sleep at night. The son said his father stood by him and ordered him not to confess. When asked if his father had bewitched him he did not answer. Jackson, his son, and John Howard were placed in irons in Ipswich prison. On January 7, 1693, the grand jury for the Superior Court of Judicature at Salem cleared the Jacksons, father and son. In 1718 John Jackson, Sr. died at Rowley.

IMMEDIATE FAMILY OF REV. DANE

The following chart shows some of the members of the immediate family of the Rev. Francis Dane, with the imprisoned in boldface.

---

393 Suffolk County, Court Records, case 2704, page 26.

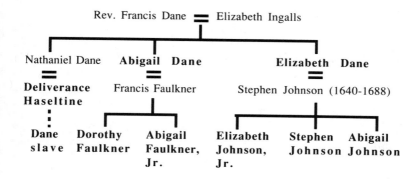

| **Abigail (Dane) Faulkner** | **Andover** |
| *Married woman, 40* | *Charged on August 11, 1692* |

| **Abigail Faulkner, Jr.** | **Andover** |
| *Girl, 9* | *Charged on September 7, 1692* |

| **Dorothy Faulkner** | **Andover** |
| *Girl, 12* | *Charged on September 7, 1692* |

Abigail Dane was born in 1652, Andover, daughter of Elizabeth (Ingalls) and the Rev. Francis Dane. In 1675 Abigail Dane married Francis Faulkner, eldest son of Dorothy (mnu) Robinson and Edmond Faulkner, an original proprietor of Andover. Their children included Dorothy Faulkner, born 1680, and Abigail Faulkner, Jr., born 1683. In 1687 Francis had been "taken with fits which did very much impair his memory and understanding, but with the blessing of the Lord upon his wife's endeavors did recover."

In 1692 the Faulkners were a family of high position in the community. Abigail, 40, her husband, Francis, and their six children, including Dorothy, 12, and Abigail, 9, were living on their farm in the north part of Andover. On August 10, 1692, Elizabeth Johnson, Jr., 22, granddaughter of the Rev. Dane, was arrested. She was the first member of the immediate Dane family to be accused. On the next day, August 11, Abigail (Dane) Faulkner was arrested for afflicting Sarah Phelps of the Andover afflicted circle. Abigail was two months pregnant with her seventh child. The examination of Abigail (Dane) Faulkner in Salem on August 11 states, "Mary Walcott said she had seen her two months ago but was not hurt by her [Abigail] till last night; Ann Putnam, Jr. said she had seen Faulkner but was not hurt by her till last night & then she pulled me off my horse. Mary Warren and others of the afflicted were struck down into fits & helped out of their fits by a touch of Abigail Faulkner's hand. She was urged to confess the truth for the credit of her town. Her niece, Elizabeth Johnson, Jr. urged her, but she [Abigail] refused to do it, saying God would not require her to confess that; that she was not guilty. She denied that she had anything to do with witchcraft. She [Abigail] said she had looked on some of these afflicted when they came to Andover & hurt them not; but she was told it was before she began to afflict them. She was told that it was reported that she used to conjure with a sieve, but she said it was not so."[394]

Of Abigail Faulkner's examination, Sarah Loring Bailey wrote, "Her conduct in the courts was worthy of her position, free alike from credulous weakness on the one hand and scornful defiance on the other. Either from her own good sense, or upheld by the wise counsels of her father (who never yielded to the delusion), she showed the greatest discretion, paying due deference to the court, yet never losing her firmness and dignity. That she was not to be intimidated by superstitious terrors, the examiners knew, it is evident, for they forbore to argue with her about 'peace and judgment to come,' but they urged her to confess 'for the credit of her town!' This seems almost to have a spice of malice and meanness in it, for to hint even that the fair name of the town was to suffer from the family of the minister was not to help him who had recently been involved in difficulties with his parishioners."[395] This last sentence refers to the war that the Rev. Barnard and his followers had been waging against the Rev. Dane.

Elizabeth (Dane) Johnson and her daughter, Abigail Johnson, 10, were imprisoned on August 30, 1692. On the same day Abigail (Dane) Faulkner was examined again. "At first she denied witchcraft as she had done before. But afterward she admitted that she was angry at what folk said when her cousin [niece]

---

394 Woodward, *Records of Salem Witchcraft*, 2:129-130.
395 Bailey, *Historical Sketches of Andover*, 216.

Elizabeth Johnson, Jr. was taken up [arrested] & folk laughed & said her sister Johnson [Elizabeth (Dane) Johnson] would come out next. She [Abigail] did look with an evil eye on the afflicted persons & did consent that they should be afflicted because they were the cause of bringing her kindred out; and she did wish them ill. Her spirit being raised she did pinch her hands together and she knew not but that the Devil might take that advantage, but it was the Devil not she that afflicted them."[396] In other words, Abigail Faulkner admitted that she had become angry at the ones who caused her niece to be imprisoned. The authorities were pleased to interpret her anger as the practice of witchcraft. In Andover the most religious of the people were the easiest targets, because they were honest enough to admit their anger to the authorities. The Puritan concept of perfection had been distorted to the point that a person could be hanged for harboring anger, not necessarily expressed but merely felt, against ruthless accusers intent on destroying the person's family. On the other hand, the accusers, sanctioned by the old guard, operated with immunity; any outrage of theirs was condoned, even applauded.

In 1880 Sarah Loring Bailey gave this analysis of the Andover phase of the witch hunt. "It will be noticed in considering these confessions that it was not the least conscientious, the least scrupulous in morals, who uttered the seeming falsehoods and perjuries. It was the religiously brought up, the shrinking woman and children, accustomed to rely implicitly on the judgment and advice of their superiors in worldly wisdom, or in theological learning.[397] Martha Carrier, having no importunate advisers begging her not to ruin herself and them, and being used to depend upon her own judgment, stood

---

396 Woodward, *Records of Salem Witchcraft*, 2:131.

397 In looking at the entire Salem witchcraft affair, it should be noted that Rebecca Nurse of Salem Village and others as "religiously brought up" as any from Andover went to their deaths in preference to uttering "seeming falsehoods and perjuries." The fact is that, with few exceptions, only the parishioners of the Rev. Thomas Barnard of Andover "were accustomed to rely implicitly on the advice of their superiors."

firm, the sole one[398] of forty or more who did not make an admission of complicity of the Devil's works, and who did not indeed even admit (what the wisest believed) that there was Satanic agency in the matter. Abigail Faulkner, who made only partial admissions, acted no doubt under the instructions of her father, who saw that only concession of some points would save her, and could advise it conscientiously, since neither he nor any one else could know for a certainty that the Devil was not concerned in these extraordinary manifestations."[399]

On August 30, 1692, Abigail Faulkner's nephew Stephen Johnson, 13, was imprisoned. On September 7 her daughters, Dorothy Faulkner, 12, and Abigail Faulkner, Jr., 9, and her sister-in-law, Deliverance (Haseltine) Dane, were imprisoned, victims of the Andover touch test.

On September 16, 1692, Dorothy Faulkner and Abigail Faulkner, Jr. confessed to the grand jury that their mother had led them into witchcraft. On the next day, Dorothy Faulkner and Abigail Faulkner, Jr., Martha and Joanna Tyler, twins, 11, Sarah Wilson, Jr., 14, (all imprisoned children of Andover) and Joseph Draper, 21, confessed that "they were led into that dreadful sin of witchcraft by Abigail (Dane) Faulkner."[400] Rose Foster, Martha Sprague, and Sarah Phelps (all members of the Andover afflicted circle) as well as some of the afflicted girls of Salem Village testified against Abigail Faulkner.

On September 17, 1692, Abigail Faulkner of Andover was tried before the Court of Oyer an Terminer. The verdict was written in a clear hand on a document now in the State Archives: "The jury find Abigail Faulkner, wife of Francis Faulkner of

---

398 Mary Parker should be included with Martha Carrier as the only two from Andover who did not confess. Like Martha Carrier, Mary Parker was executed. Samuel Wardwell of Andover recanted his confession and was executed. His daughter Mercy Wardwell recanted the parts of her confession that were to be used against others. The real crime of Martha Carrier was not witchcraft, but that she was "used to depend upon her own judgment." As Bailey clearly indicates, the Salem witchcraft affair was not a "popular delusion" of the people but a manifestation of "what the wisest believed."

399 Bailey, *Historical Sketches of Andover*, 224.

400 Woodward, *Records of Salem Witchcraft*, 2:134-135.

Andover, guilty of the felony of witchcraft committed on the body of Martha Sprague, also on the body of Sarah Phelps. SENTENCE OF DEATH PASSED ON ABIGAIL FAULKNER. Copia vera."[401] Abigail, pregnant, was reprieved until after the birth of her child.

On October 6, John Osgood and Nathaniel Dane posted a recognizance bond of £500 to bail out Dorothy Faulkner and Abigail Faulkner, Jr.; the two children were released, having spent about a month in jail. On December 3, 1692, Abigail petitioned Governor Sir William Phipps from Salem prison. She said that the only evidence used against her was spectral evidence and the accusations of the confessors. She pointed out that, after she was condemned, the confessors admitted to her and others that they wronged her and what they had said against her was false. A few days later Abigail (Dane) Faulkner was released from prison.[402]

Abigail's two daughters, Dorothy Faulkner and Abigail Faulkner, Jr. were not tried in January. Because of a recognizance bond of £100 posted on January 13, 1693, by their father, Francis Faulkner, and their uncle, Joseph Marble, they remained free on bail. In March Abigail's son was born at Andover; she named him Amniruhamah, the name meaning "mercy for my people." On May 10, 1693, at the Superior Court of Judicature at Ipswich, the two girls were cleared by proclamation. On February 17, 1697, the Rev. Francis Dane died in Andover.

In 1703 Abigail (Dane) Faulkner wrote, "That whereas in the year 1692 when many were accused and imprisoned at Salem as witches and some executed, myself was accused by the afflicted who pretended to see me by their spectral sight (not with their bodily eyes) and that I afflicted them, upon whose accusations (and theirs only) I was examined, imprisoned, and brought to trial, these being all that gave in any evidence against me upon oath, yet the jury (upon only their testimony) brought me in guilty, & the sentence of death was passed upon me. But it pleased God to put into the heart of his excellency Sir William Phipps to grant me a reprieve and at length, a pardon. The

---

401 Bailey, *Historical Sketches of Andover*, 218.
402 Upham, *Salem Witchcraft*, 2:332.

pardon has so far had its effect, as that I am as yet suffered to live, but this only as a malefactor convict upon record of the most heinous crimes that mankind can supposed to be guilty of, which besides its utter ruining and defacing my reputation, will certainly expose myself to imminent danger by new accusations, which will thereby be the more readily believed, will remain as a perpetual brand of infamy upon my family."[403]

On July 20, 1703, the House of Representatives replied to the "Petitions of Abigail Faulkner and sundry of the inhabitants of Andover. Whereas it is conceived by many worthy and pious persons that the evidence given against many of the said condemned persons was weak and insufficient as to taking away the lives of sundry so condemned, it is hereby ordered that a bill be drawn up for preventing the like procedure for the future, and that no specter evidence may hereafter be accounted valid, or sufficient to take away the life, or good name, of any person or persons within this Province, and that the infamy, and reproach, cast on the names and posterity of the said accused and condemned persons may in some measure be rolled away."[404]

In 1708 Abigail Faulkner, Jr. married Thomas Lamson of Ipswich, and Dorothy Faulkner married Samuel Nurse of Salem Village, son of Rebecca Nurse, who was hanged. In 1730 Abigail (Dane) Faulkner died at Andover at the age of 78, and in 1732 her husband Francis Faulkner died at Andover at the age of 80.

Elizabeth (Dane) Johnson	**Andover**
Widow, 51	*Charged on August 29, 1692*
Elizabeth Johnson, Jr.	**Andover**
Single woman, 22	*Charged on August 10, 1692*
Stephen Johnson	**Andover**
Boy, 13	*Charged on August 30, 1692*
Abigail Johnson	**Andover**
Girl, 10	*Charged on August 29, 1692*

---

403 Massachusetts Archives, *Witchcraft*, 135:103.
404 Massachusetts Archives, *Witchcraft*, 135:109.

Elizabeth Dane was born about 1641, daughter of Elizabeth (Ingalls) and the Rev. Francis Dane of Andover. In 1661 she married Stephen Johnson, Sr., son of Susannah and John Johnson, who was an early settler of Andover. The children of Elizabeth (Dane) and Stephen Johnson, Sr. included eldest child Francis Johnson, born 1666, Elizabeth Johnson, Jr., born 1670, Stephen Johnson, born 1679, and Abigail Johnson, born 1682. The father, Stephen Johnson, Sr., died in 1688.

In 1692 Elizabeth, about 51 and a widow of 4 years, and her children were living in the north part of Andover. The children included Elizabeth, Jr., 22, Stephen, 13, and Abigail, 10. On August 3, 1692, Elizabeth (Dane) Johnson's sister-in-law, Mary (Johnson) Davis Clarke of Haverhill, was accused and imprisoned.

On August 10, 1692, Elizabeth Johnson, Jr., 22, was arrested and examined in Andover by Dudley Bradstreet in his office as justice of the peace. The accusation against her was the first direct attack on the immediate family of the Rev. Francis Dane. Elizabeth Johnson, Jr. readily confessed everything put to her. The next day she was sent to Salem, again examined, admitting everything required by the magistrates, and imprisoned. On the same day, August 11, her aunt, Abigail (Dane) Faulkner, was imprisoned.

On August 29, 1692, Samuel Martin of Andover and Moses Tyler of Boxford filed a complaint against Elizabeth (Dane) Johnson and her daughter, Abigail, for afflicting Abigail Martin and Martha Sprague. On the next day the Constable Ephraim Foster came to arrest them. Young Stephen Johnson came to the defense of his mother and sister and bravely resisted the constable. Stephen too was taken and the three were imprisoned in Salem. The mother's examination typifies a terrified prisoner trying to please the magistrates by answering their bullying and absurd leading questions in the affirmative. "The Devil had made her promise to renounce God and Christ & she did so, & being asked how long she had been a witch, she said that she knew not, but that she was 30 years old when she was married & now she was 51 & when she had 3 children the Devil came to her & the Devil appeared to her like a bird, a black bird, & then she did not sign but a year after she signed."[405] On September 1, 1692, Stephen Johnson confessed at his examination. On October 6 Walter Wright, Francis Johnson, and Thomas Carrier, Sr. posted a recognizance bond of £500 to bail out Stephen Johnson, Abigail Johnson, and Sarah Carrier.

About January 2, 1693, the Rev. Francis Dane made the statement, "Concerning my daughter Elizabeth Johnson, I never had ground to suspect her; neither have I heard any other to accuse, till by specter evidence she was brought forth; but this I must say, she was weak, and incapacious, fearful, and in that respect, I fear she hath falsely accused herself and others. Not long before she was sent for, she spake as to her own particular, that she was sure she was no witch, and for her daughter Elizabeth she is but simplish at the best."[406]

On January 3, 1693, at the Superior Court of Judicature at Salem, the grand jury indicted Elizabeth (Dane) Johnson, Elizabeth Johnson, Jr. and Stephen Johnson. On January 5, 1693, before the grand jury, the intimidated Elizabeth Johnson, Jr. signed and admitted her confession of August 11. On January 7, 1693, in a trial by jury, Elizabeth (Dane) Johnson was found not guilty and was released after imprisonment of five months. On January 12 in a trial by jury, Elizabeth Johnson, Jr. was found guilty. Chief Justice William Stoughton signed death warrants for Elizabeth Johnson, Jr. and seven other condemned women but they were reprieved by Governor Sir William Phipps. On February 1, 1693, Francis Johnson married Sarah Hawkes, daughter of Sarah Wardwell. Elizabeth Johnson, Jr. was released in February 1693 after about six months imprisonment. In 1708 Stephen Johnson married Sarah Whittaker of Haverhill. By 1717 Abigail Johnson married James Black of Boxford.

Rebecca (Aslet) Johnson	**Andover**
Widow, 40	*Charged on September 7, 1692*
Rebecca Johnson, Jr.	**Andover**
Girl, 17	*Charged on September 7, 1692*

---

405 Essex Institute, *Witchcraft Collection*, "Examinations."
406 Bailey, *Historical Sketches of Andover*, 233.

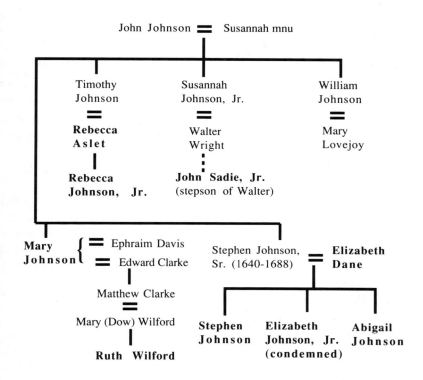

Rebecca Aslet was born in 1652 in Andover, daughter of Rebecca (Ayer) and John Aslet. He was an original proprietor of Andover. In 1674 Rebecca Aslet married Timothy Johnson, son of Susannah (mnu) and John Johnson of Andover. Rebecca Johnson, Jr., born in 1675, was the eldest child of Rebecca and Timothy. Timothy died in 1688. In 1690, Rebecca (Aslet) Johnson was appointed the sexton of the Andover Church, "for sweeping the meetinghouse & ringing the the bell."[407] She held the position for eight years, earning forty shillings annually. She was the only woman ever appointed by the town to this position.

In 1692 Rebecca (Aslet) Johnson, 40 and a widow for four years, her daughter Rebecca Johnson, Jr., 17, and her other children were living in the north part of Andover. In 1692, two of

407 Bailey, *Historical Sketches of Andover*, 412.

the five selectmen of Andover were her only brother, John Aslet, Jr., who was quite wealthy, and her brother-in-law, Samuel Frye. Her aunt was widow Mary (Ayer) Parker. Rebecca's sister was Sarah (Aslet) Cole of Lynn.

The following relatives of Rebecca (Aslet) Johnson were imprisoned: on August 3, 1692, her sister-in-law Mary (Johnson) Davis Clarke of Haverhill; on August 11 her niece Elizabeth Johnson, Jr.; about August 15 her cousin Sarah Parker; on August 30 her sister-in-law Elizabeth (Dane) Johnson, her niece Abigail Johnson, and her nephew Stephen Johnson; on September 2, her aunt Mary (Ayer) Parker (who was hanged on September 22); and on October 3 her sister, Sarah (Aslet) Cole of Lynn.

On September 7, 1692, Rebecca (Aslet) Johnson and her daughter, Rebecca Johnson, Jr., were arrested at the Andover touch test. At her examination, Rebecca, the mother, "denied what she was accused of, but she acknowledged the turning of the sieve in her house by her daughter, when she desired to know if her brother[-in-law] Moses Hagget was alive or dead. And that if the sieve turned he was dead, and so the sieve did turn. And my daughter said that Mr. Barnard's mind told her the way the words were, —By Saint Peter & Saint Paul, if Hagget be dead let this sieve turn round. And so it did."[408] This was indeed a weak confession. About December 8, 1692, Rebecca and her daughter, after thirteen weeks imprisonment at Salem, were released on bail posted by the Andover resistance. On January 7, 1693, at the Superior Court of Judicature at Salem, the grand jury cleared Rebecca (Aslet) Johnson. In 1698 Rebecca Johnson, Jr. married Joseph Ballard, Jr., the son of the man who made the first witchcraft accusation in Andover. In 1734, Rebecca (Johnson) Ballard died at Andover, aged 58.

Deliverance (Haseltine) Dane   Andover
Married woman, 37   *Charged on September 7, 1692*

Robert and Ann (mnu) of Rowley Village-by-the-Merrimack (later named Bradford) had children David Haseltine, born in 1643, Mercy Haseltine, born in 1646, and Deliverance Haseltine

---

408   Suffolk County, Court Records, case 2707, page 30.

born in 1655.[409] Deliverance married, in 1672, Nathaniel Dane, born about 1645, son of Elizabeth (Ingalls) and the Rev. Francis Dane of Andover. In 1692 Deliverance, about 37, her husband, and children were living in the north part of Andover. She and Nathaniel were respected members of the community.

On September 7, 1692, Deliverance Dane was arrested at the Andover touch test. She was more than three months pregnant at the time of her arrest. Her husband, Nathaniel, became an active member of the Andover resistance. On October 6, 1692, he and John Osgood posted a recognizance Bond of £500 for the release of Dorothy and Abigail Faulkner. Nathaniel signed the various petitions for the release of the prisoners on bail. About December 8, 1692, Nathaniel Dane posted a recognizance bond for the release of his wife on bail, after imprisonment of thirteen weeks. On February 20, 1693, their daughter was born at Andover and named Deliverance.

Male Slave of Nathaniel Dane   **Andover**
Man   *Charged on September 7, 1692*

A male slave of Nathaniel Dane, arrested about the time of the Andover touch test, was imprisoned about eight weeks.

John Sadie, Jr.   **Andover**
Boy, 13   *Charged on September 7, 1692*

John Sadie, Jr. was born about 1679 in Ipswich, son of Elizabeth (Peters) and John Sadie. After John's death, his widow married, in 1684, widower Walter Wright of Andover. His first wife had been Susannah Johnson, Jr., daughter of Susannah (mnu) and John Johnson, early settlers of Andover. In 1692, John Sadie, Jr. about 13, lived in the south part of Andover with his mother and stepfather. On September 7, 1692, John Sadie, Jr., along with several other children of Andover, was arrested at the Andover touch test. On October 6 he was bailed out by Walter Wright and Francis Faulkner. In 1702 John Sadie, Jr. died at Andover, a bachelor, aged about 24.

---

409 David and Mary (Jewett) Haseltine as well as Benjamin and Mercy (Haseltine) Kimball are seven-times-great grandparents of the writer.

Edward Farrington   **Andover**
Married man, 30   *Charged about August 15, 1692*

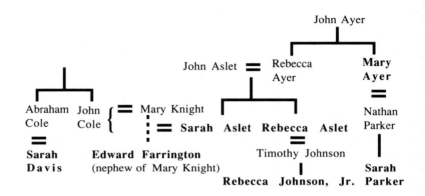

Edward Farrington was born in 1662 in Lynn, son of Elizabeth (Knight) and John Farrington. In 1667 Edward's widowed mother married widower Mark Graves, a weaver of Andover. In 1690 Edward Farrington married Martha Browne. Edward's maternal aunt, Mary Knight, had married John Cole of Lynn in 1661. She died in 1675 and John Cole then married Sarah Aslet of Andover. Sarah's sister, Rebecca Aslet, married in 1674 Timothy Johnson of Andover, thereby linking Edward Farrington to the Johnson family. In 1692 Edward Farrington, 30, and his wife were living in the north part of Andover on the farm later given to him by his stepfather, Mark Graves. About August 15, 1692, Edward Farrington was arrested for witchcraft. On September 7 Rebecca (Aslet) Johnson was imprisoned. John Cole's sister-in-law, Sarah (Davis) Cole of Salem, was accused on September 10 and imprisoned. On October 1 Sarah (Aslet) Cole of Lynn was accused and on October 3 imprisoned. On January 3, 1693, Edward Farrington was indicted. There are no further records extant.

23

THE ACCUSED: THE TYLER FAMILY

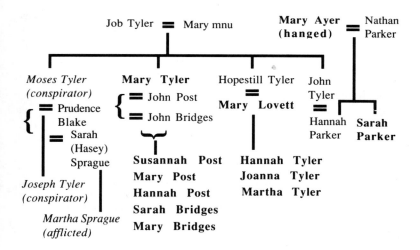

THE ABOVE CHART DEPICTS the Tyler family. (The accused are shown in bold). The Tyler siblings, Moses, Mary, Hopestill, and John, were children of Mary (mnu) and Job Tyler, originally of Andover, but subsequently of Mendon and Boxford. As seen on the chart, Moses Tyler and the rest of the conspiracy made witchcraft accusations against members of the families of his sister Mary (Tyler) Post Bridges, his brother Hopestill Tyler, and his brother John Tyler.

Sarah Parker, the sister of John Tyler's wife, was imprisoned and Mary (Ayer) Parker, the mother of John's wife, was hanged. The Parkers have already been treated in Chapter 21.

BRIDGES FAMILY

Mary (Tyler) Post Bridges	**Andover**
Married woman, 48	*Charged on July 28, 1692*
Mary Post	**Andover/Rowley**
Single woman, 28	*Charged on August 2, 1692*
Susannah Post	**Andover**
Single woman, 31	*Charged on August 24, 1692*
Hannah Post	**Andover/Boxford**
Single woman, 26	*Charged on August 24, 1692*
Sarah Bridges	**Andover**
Girl, 17	*Charged on August 24, 1692*
Mary Bridges, Jr.	**Andover**
Girl, 13	*Charged on August 24, 1692*

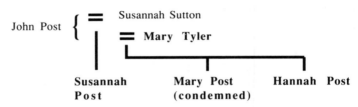

Moses' sister, Mary Tyler, was born in 1644 in Andover. In 1662, Mary Tyler married widower John Post. His daughter Susannah Post was born about 1661; their daughter Mary Post, in 1664; and their daughter Hannah Post, in 1666. John Post was killed by Indians in 1675 at Mendon. In 1678, the widow Mary (Tyler) Post married widower John Bridges, a blacksmith, son of Alice (mnu) and Edmond Bridges of Ipswich. Mary Bridges, Jr. was born 1679 in Andover, daughter of Mary (Tyler) Post and John Bridges.

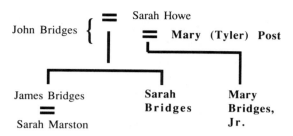

John Bridges had interesting family relationships. His first wife was Sarah Howe, daughter of Elizabeth (Dane) and James Howe of Topsfield.[410] Elizabeth (Dane) Howe was the sister of the Rev. Francis Dane of Andover. Sarah Bridges, born about 1675, the daughter of Sarah (Howe) and John Bridges, was thus a blood great-niece of the Rev. Francis Dane. Sarah Bridges was the third member of the Howe family branch to be accused. The two other previously accused members were Nehemiah Abbot, Jr. and Elizabeth (Jackson) Howe. Elizabeth (Jackson) Howe was hanged on July 19.

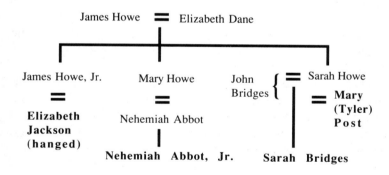

---

410 On May 24, 1692, James Bridges, born in 1673, the son of Sarah (Howe) and John Bridges, married Sarah Marston, born 1661, daughter of Martha (Lombard) and John Marston, Sr. Prior to the marriage, Samuel Wardwell had told the fortune of James Bridges, "that he loved a girl at fourteen years old, which said Bridges owned to be the truth." (Woodward, *Records of Salem Witchcraft*, 2:152-153.) The brother of Sarah (Marston) Bridges was John Marston, Jr. His wife, Mary (Osgood) Marston, was imprisoned at the Andover touch test on September 7, 1692.

Mary (Tyler) Post Bridges, 48, and her husband, John Bridges, were living in the north part of Andover in 1692. Living with them were Susannah Post, about 31, Sarah Bridges, about 17, and their four children; the oldest of the four was Mary Bridges, Jr., 13. Mary Post, 28, lived in Rowley. Hannah Post, 26, lived in Boxford with her brother, John Post, Jr.; although Boxford residents, they attended the Andover Church.

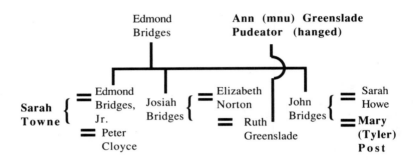

John Bridge's sister-in-law, Sarah (Towne) Bridges Cloyce of Salem Village, was imprisoned on April 11, 1692. Ann (mnu) Greenslade Pudeator of Salem was imprisoned on May 12 and hanged on September 22. Ann was the mother-in-law of John Bridge's half-brother, Josiah Bridges of Boxford.

On July 28, 1692, a complaint was filed against Mary (Tyler) Post Bridges for afflicting Timothy Swan of Andover, Ann Putnam, Jr., and Mary Walcott. Mary (Tyler) Post Bridges was arrested and imprisoned in Salem. Her husband, John Bridges, was one of the God-fearing men of Andover completely under the spell of the Rev. Thomas Barnard. In October 1692, when interviewed by the Rev. Increase Mather in prison, Mary said that "she had confessed against herself things which were all utterly false; and that she was brought to her confession by being told that she certainly was a witch, and so made to believe it—though she had no other grounds so to believe."[411]   On July 30 Mary was taken to the preliminary examination of Hannah

---

411 Upham, *Salem Witchcraft*, 2:406.

(mnu) Tyler Brumidge of Haverhill; Mary urged Hannah to make a confession, saying that it was the way to eternal life. On August 2 Mary Post was arrested and imprisoned for afflicting Timothy Swan, Ann Putnam, Jr., and Mary Walcott. Mary Post confessed.

On August 24, 1692, in his first overt action against his own family, Moses Tyler with Ephraim Foster filed a complaint against Hannah Post, Sarah Bridges, Mary Bridges, Jr., and Susannah Post for afflicting Martha Sprague and Rose Foster. The next day the four accused young women were arrested and taken to Salem for examination. Their sister, Mary Post, arrested on August 2, was in the courtroom during their examinations.

Hannah Post was the first examined. She confessed to making a covenant with the Devil. At her examination, Sarah Bridges was told that her stepsister Hannah Post had confessed. Sarah Bridges then confessed that she had made a covenant with the Devil last winter. Mary Bridges, Jr. confessed that she might have afflicted Mary Warren, but said she did not know that her mother was a witch. Susannah Post, the last of the four examined, confessed to a covenant with the Devil made three years ago and said that she had heard there were about 500 witches in the country.

Imprisoned at Salem with their mother, the sisters were returned to the courtroom on several occasions to act as afflicted. On August 27 Sarah Bridges and Susannah Post were present at the examinations of John Jackson, Sr., John Jackson, Jr., and John Howard. On September 1 and 2 Sarah Bridges was at the examinations of William Barker, Jr., Stephen Johnson, Sarah Wardwell, Sarah Hawkes, Mercy Wardwell and widow Mary (Ayer) Parker. On September 5 Susannah Post was at the preliminary examination of Mary (Harrington) Taylor of Reading.

On September 7 Mary (Lovett) Tyler, sister-in-law of John Bridges, was arrested at the Andover touch test. John Bridges kept telling her that she must be a witch because the afflicted girls accused her, and at her touch their fits subsided. He pressed her to make a confession, which she finally did. After the executions on September 22, John Bridges had a change of heart. On October 12 John Bridges was one of the nine Andover men who petitioned for the release of prisoners on bail. On October 15 John Osgood and John Bridges posted a bond of £500 for the release of Mary Bridges, Jr. It can be determined that Sarah Bridges was also released on bail by that date (although her bail bond is not extant). On October 18 John Bridges was one of the twenty-six men who petitioned for the release of prisoners on bail. The petition decried the accusations of afflicted children and others who were under a diabolical influence. This position represented a complete about face to John Bridges' previous statement to Mary Tyler saying that she must be a witch because the afflicted girls accused her. On December 6 John Bridges and his brother-in-law, Hopestill Tyler, were among the eight Andover men who petitioned for the release of prisoners.[412]

On January 12, 1693, Mary (Tyler) Post Bridges was found not guilty in a trial by jury at the Superior Court of Judicature at Salem. The trial of Mary Post followed next, and she was found guilty. The trials of Sarah Bridges and Hannah Post were also held and they were found not guilty. Mary Bridges, Jr. and Susannah Post, not brought to trial, remained free on a recognizance bond of £100 posted by John Bridges and John Osgood on January 12, 1693. About the middle of January, Chief Justice William Stoughton signed death warrants for Mary Post and seven other condemned women, but they were reprieved by Governor Sir William Phipps. Mary Post was released in April after imprisonment of more than eight months. On May 10, 1693, Mary Bridges, Jr. and Susannah Post in trials by jury at the Superior Court of Judicature at Ipswich were both found not guilty. In 1694 Sarah Bridges married Samuel Preston, Jr. of Andover.

TYLER FAMILY

Mary (Lovett) Tyler   **Andover**
Married woman, 40   *Charged on September 7, 1692*

---

412 Bailey, *Historical Sketches of Andover*, 225-230.

Hannah Tyler   **Andover**
Girl, 14   *Charged on September 7, 1692*

Martha Tyler   **Andover**
Girl, 11   *Charged on September 7, 1692*

Joanna Tyler   **Andover**
Girl, 11   *Charged on September 7, 1692*

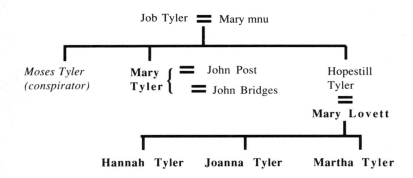

Mary Lovett was born about 1652, daughter of Joanna (Blott) and Richard Lovett of Mendon. In 1668 Mary Lovett married Hopestill Tyler, son of Mary (mnu) and Job Tyler. Their children included Hannah, born 1678, and twins Martha and Joanna, born 1681. As a youth, Hopestill had been apprenticed to Thomas Chandler, blacksmith of Andover, but Job Tyler soon sued to retract the contract. Other parents also brought suit against Thomas Chandler for his treatment of apprentices. However Hopestill completed the apprenticeship and became a blacksmith. In 1692 Hopestill's wife would be accused of witchcraft by the Andover conspiracy, which included not only Thomas Chandler but also Hopestill's brother, Moses Tyler.

In 1692 Mary, about 40, and her husband, Hopestill Tyler, were living in the south part of Andover with their five children, including Hannah, 14, and twins Martha and Joanna, 11. On July 28 Hopestill's sister, Mary (Tyler) Post Bridges, was imprisoned, and within a month five daughters or stepdaughters of Mary were also imprisoned.

On September 7 Mary (Lovett) Tyler and her daughters Hannah, Martha, and Joanna were arrested during the Andover touch test.   Their stepcousin Martha Sprague was in the courtroom in her role as an afflicted.   On September 16, Martha Tyler and Joanna Tyler confessed that they were led into the dreadful sin of witchcraft.

In October 1692, the Rev. Increase Mather interviewed Mary (Lovett) Tyler in Salem prison.   His account, colored by his own preconceptions, still managed to describe her terror and confusion. "Goodwife Tyler did say, that, when she was first apprehended, she had no fears upon her, and did think that nothing could have made her confess against herself.   But since, she had found, to her great grief, that she had wronged the truth, and falsely accused herself."[413]   According to Increase Mather's story, accused women who refused to confess were relentlessly pressed to do so by their next of kin.   Was it because their husbands, to quote Thomas Brattle, "did break charity with their dear wives,"[414] aghast to find themselves married to witches?   Or was it because their husbands wanted confessions, true or false, believing that in that way their wives would escape the gallows?

Hopestill Tyler became an active member of the Andover resistance and helped in the release, by mid-October, of the imprisoned children of Andover.   Hopestill signed the petitions of October 12, October 18, and December 6, 1692.   On January 5, 1693, Hannah Tyler was found not guilty in a trial by jury at the Superior Court of Judicature at Salem.   Two days later Mary (Lovett) Tyler was also found not guilty.   Because the Tyler twins, Martha and Joanna, were not tried at that time, John Bridges and Hopestill Tyler on January 13 posted a £100 bond to keep them free on bail.   On May 10, 1693, the twins appeared at the Superior Court of Judicature at Ipswich according to the terms of the recognizance bond and were cleared.   John Bridges and Hopestill Tyler, two men initially under the control of the Rev. Thomas Barnard, had finally redeemed themselves.

---

413   Upham, *Salem Witchcraft*, 2:404.
414   Brattle, "Letter of October 8, 1692," in Burr, *Narratives*, 180.

EAMES FAMILY

Rebecca (Blake) Eames	**Boxford**
Married woman, 51	*Charged about August 1, 1692*

Daniel Eames	**Boxford**
Married man, 29	*Charged by August 9, 1692*

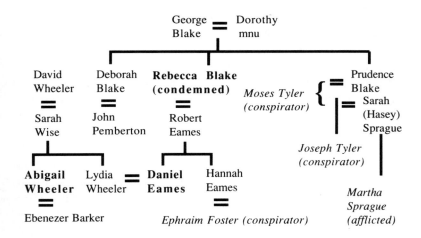

Dorothy (mnu) and George Blake, original settlers of Gloucester, had children Rebecca Blake, born in 1641, Deborah Blake, born in 1644, and Prudence Blake, born in 1647.[415] About 1661 Rebecca Blake married Robert Eames of Rowley Village (named Boxford in 1685). Their children included Hannah Eames, born in 1661, and Daniel Eames, second child and eldest son, born in 1663. Hannah Eames married Ephraim Foster about 1678. In 1666 Rebecca's sister, Prudence Blake, married Moses Tyler, a neighbor of Robert Eames in Rowley Village (named Boxford in 1685). In 1669 Dorothy (mnu) and George Blake sold their Gloucester property and moved to Rowley Village (named Boxford in 1685), close to their two daughters. Daughter Prudence (Blake) Tyler died in 1689; Moses Tyler took the widow

---

415 Deborah Blake married John Pemberton in 1668. They are seven-times-great grandparents of the writer.

Sarah (Hasey) Sprague as his second wife. The Blakes, Eameses, and Tylers all lived so close to the Andover line that they attended the Andover Church.

In 1683 Daniel Eames married Lydia Wheeler, born in 1662, daughter of Sarah (Wise) and David Wheeler of Rowley. Lydia's sister, Abigail (Wheeler) Barker, and Daniel's sister, Hannah (Eames) Foster, both lived in Andover. Abigail (Wheeler) Barker was imprisoned in 1692; Ephraim Foster, the husband of Hannah (Eames) Foster, was a conspirator in 1692.

In 1692 Rebecca (Blake) Eames, 51, and her husband, Robert Eames, were living on their farm in Boxford near the Andover line. In 1692 Robert Eames was a Boxford selectman. Their son Daniel Eames, 29, lived nearby with his wife and children. At the beginning of August a complaint was filed against Rebecca (Blake) Eames for afflicting Timothy Swan of Andover and Mary Warren. Rebecca Eames was imprisoned in Salem, and her son Daniel Eames was imprisoned a few days later.

On August 19, 1692, the day of the execution of five condemned witches, Rebecca was examined. "She owned that she had been in the snare a month or two, and had been persuaded to it three months. The Devil appeared to her like a colt, very ugly, the first time but she would not own that she had been baptized by him. She did not know but that the Devil did persuade her to renounce God and Christ, and follow his wicked ways, but she did take his council and afflict Timothy Swan. She did not know but that the Devil might ask her body and soul & she knows not but that she did give him soul and body. Afterward she said she did do it & that she would forsake God and his works, and the Devil promised her to give her power and to avenge herself on them that offended her. Afterward she said the Devil appeared to her seven years ago & he had tempted her to lie, and had made her afflict persons." Barraged by leading questions, she answered, "A ragged girl came together with the Devil, and they persuaded me to afflict. I afflicted Mary Warren and another fair face. It is about a quarter of a year ago. I did it by sticking of pins." When asked where she kept her spear, she answered, "I had nothing but an awl." Asked whether she came with her body or spirit to hurt these maids, she answered, "with my spirit." Now was the time for atonement.

When asked whether she would ask their forgiveness, she said, "I will fall down on my knees to ask forgiveness of them."[416]   On September 17, 1692 Rebecca (Blake) Eames was condemned. However, each condemned person who confessed was given a temporary reprieve from death, though kept in prison.

On December 5 Rebecca petitioned Governor Phipps for a pardon, saying she did not deserve to die for witchcraft or any other sin.   In the petition she said that the only evidence used against her was specter evidence and her own confession. She said that her confession was altogether false and untrue, as she was pressured out of her senses by the afflicted girls, Abigail Hobbs and Mary Lacey, Jr. She said that these two cried out against her and charged her with witchcraft, taunting her, spitting in her face, calling her an old witch, and saying that, if she would not confess, she would hang. She said that their actions led her to confess. She explained that she did not deny her confession at her trial because she was so confused that she did not understand what she was saying. Finally in the petition, Rebecca said that, when the Rev. Increase Mather and Mr. Thomas Brattle visited the Salem prison in October, Abigail Hobbs and Mary Lacey, Jr. repudiated what they previously had said against her, stating that it was nothing but the Devil's delusions and that they knew of no witchcraft by her. Despite her petition, Rebecca remained in jail. In the middle of January Chief Justice William Stoughton signed death warrants for Rebecca (Blake) Eames and seven other condemned women, but Governor Phipps issued reprieves. In March 1693, Rebecca was released after more than seven months imprisonment. On July 22, 1693, her husband, Robert Eames, died at Boxford, aged about 53. In 1721 widow Rebecca died at Boxford aged 81.

---

416 Woodward, *Records of Salem Witchcraft*, 2:143-146.

24

THE ACCUSED: OTHER FAMILIES

COTTON MATHER WROTE, "We have seen a horrible thing done in our land! O 'tis a most humbling thing, to think, that ever there should be such an abomination among us, as for a crew of human race, to renounce their Maker, and to unite with the Devil, for the troubling of mankind, and for the people to be, as is seen by some confessed, baptized by a fiend, using this form upon them, *Thou art mine, and I have full power over thee!* afterwards communicating in an hellish bread and wine, by that fiend administrated unto them. O 'tis a defiled land wherein we live."[417]

Yet how were the confessions obtained? Sarah Loring Bailey wrote, "The examiners proceeded on the assumption that the accused were guilty; they invited evidences against them, in their zeal almost put words into the mouths of reluctant confessors and faltering witnesses, and they placed implicit faith in every statement corroborative of their preconceived opinions."[418] The magistrates gravely maintained that the accused witches could fly on broomsticks in virtue of their compact with the Devil; their authority was that, in the Lord's temptation, Satan transported Christ through the air to the summit of a high mountain. Cotton Mather argued that the remarkable instances of the Devil's operations disclosed by the witchcraft trials represented a marvelous revelation of scripture. In his introduction to *The Wonders of the Invisible World*, Cotton Mather wrote, "For the dogmatical part of my discourse, I want no defense; for the historical part of it, I have a very great one;

---

417 Cotton Mather, *Wonders*, 87.
418 Bailey, *Historical Sketches of Andover*, 195.

the Lieutenant Governor of New England, having perused it, has done me the honor of giving me a shield." William Stoughton wrote to Cotton Mather, "Having now perused so fruitful and happy a composure, and considering the place I hold in the Court of Oyer and Terminer, still laboring and proceeding in the trial of persons accused and convicted of witchcraft, I express my obligation and thankfulness to you for so great pains. Such is your design, such your zeal for God, your enmity to Satan and his kingdom, your faithfulness and compassion to this poor people, your care of truth, your wisdom and dexterity, such your clear discerning of Divine providences, now running on apace towards their glorious issues in the world, and finally, such your good news of the shortness of the Devil's time, that all good men must needs desire the making of your discourse public to the world."[419]

Cotton Mather's book was hastily put together and published in the two weeks following the execution of Mary Parker and Samuel Wardwell of Andover and six other condemned women on September 22, 1692. Despite the praise lavished on the book by Lieutenant Governor Stoughton, Cotton Mather's arguments were soon to be dispelled by a rising tide of reasonable people determined to put a stop to the witchcraft proceedings. Not least among them were the Rev. Francis Dane and his resistance group of Andover citizens.

WARDWELL FAMILY

Samuel Wardwell   **Andover**
Married man, 49   *Charged on August 15, 1692*

Sarah (Hooper) Hawkes Wardwell   **Andover**
Married woman, 41   *Charged on September 1, 1692*

Sarah Hawkes   **Andover**
Single woman, 21   *Charged on September 1, 1692*

Mercy Wardwell   **Andover**
Girl, 18   *Charged on September 1, 1692*

---

419 Cotton Mather, *Wonders*, 5-7.

Samuel Wardwell was born in 1643 in Exeter, New Hampshire, son of Elizabeth (Woodruff) and Thomas Wardwell. Samuel became a carpenter. He married about 1668 and had a son, Thomas, born about 1670. After his wife's death, Samuel Wardwell and his son moved to Andover.

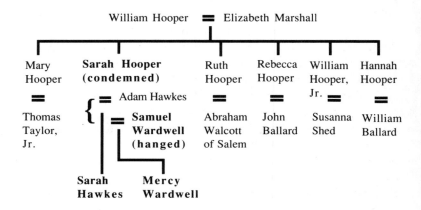

Sarah Hooper was born December 7, 1650, in Reading, daughter of Elizabeth (Marshall) and William Hooper. Their other children included daughters Rebecca, born in 1656, and Hannah, born in 1662.

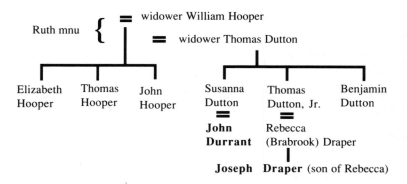

After his wife Elizabeth's death, William Hooper, married, about 1664, Ruth (mnu) and they had three children, Elizabeth Hooper, born in 1665, Thomas Hooper, born in 1668, and John

Hooper, born in 1670. After William's death, Ruth married, in 1685, widower Thomas Dutton, Sr. of Billerica who had several children by his first wife.

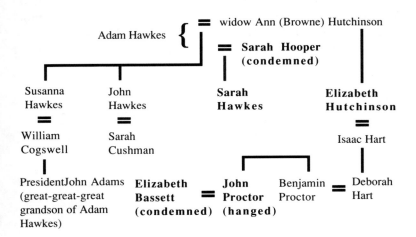

Adam Hawkes was born about 1605 and in 1630 became the first settler of the Saugus section of the original township of Lynn, Massachusetts. His first wife was Ann (Browne) Hutchinson, a widow with five children. Ann had two more children, twins John Hawkes and Susanna Hawkes, by Adam Hawkes. Ann died in 1669, at which time all her children were married.

In 1670 Sarah Hooper, aged 19, married widower Adam Hawkes, 65. With Sarah, Adam had only one child, Sarah Hawkes, born in 1671 in Lynn. Sarah Hawkes was eight months old when Adam Hawkes died in 1672. Adam Hawkes' death made his widow, Sarah (Hooper) Hawkes, wealthy at the age of 22. In 1673 Sarah (Hooper) Hawkes married Samuel Wardwell in Andover. Their marriage was performed by Major William Hathorne of Salem. Their eldest child, Mercy Wardwell, was born in 1673. They had six more children, but one daughter died in infancy. Sarah Wardwell's sister Rebecca Hooper married John Ballard in 1681; and her sister Hannah Hooper married his brother William Ballard in 1682. The

Ballards lived in Andover. Sarah's half-brothers, Thomas Hooper and John Hooper, also settled in Andover by 1690.

In 1692 Samuel Wardwell, 49, and his wife, Sarah, 41, were living in the south part of Andover with Sarah's daughter Sarah Hawkes, 21, and their children Mercy Wardwell, 18, Samuel Wardwell, Jr., 15, William Wardwell, 12, Eliakim Wardwell, 4, Elizabeth Wardwell, about 3, and Rebecca Wardwell, not yet one.

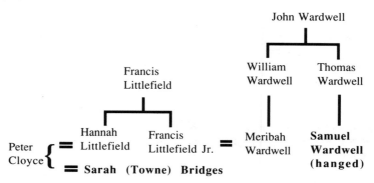

On April 4, 1692, Sarah (Towne) Bridges Cloyce of Salem Village was accused and subsequently imprisoned. She was the wife of widower Peter Cloyce. By his first marriage Peter was a brother-in-law of Samuel Wardwell's first cousin, Meribah (Wardwell) Littlefield of Wells, Maine.

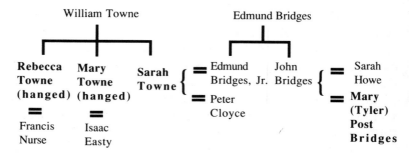

By her first marriage to Edmond Bridges, Jr., who died in 1680, Sarah Cloyce was the sister-in-law of Mary (Tyler) Post

Bridges, who is treated in Chapter 23. Sarah Cloyce's sisters, Rebecca Nurse and Mary Easty, were hanged in 1692.

On May 14, 1692, Elizabeth (Hutchinson) Hart of Lynn was accused and subsequently imprisoned She was the daughter of Adam Hawkes' first wife, Anne (Browne) Hutchinson. On August 3 Sarah (Hooper) Hawkes Wardwell's first cousin, Edward Marshall of Malden, 50, died. Five days later, Sarah's brother, William Hooper, Jr. of Reading, died. During the funeral his house caught fire and burned down.

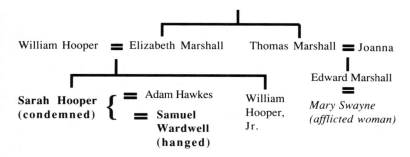

On August 15, 1692, Samuel Wardwell was arrested and imprisoned. About August 31 Sarah Wardwell, Sarah Hawkes, and Mercy Wardwell were arrested. They were accused of afflicting Rose Foster, Abigail Martin, and Martha Sprague. Sarah Wardwell carried her baby, Rebecca Wardwell, with her to prison.[420]

On September 1, the four family members, Samuel, his wife Sarah, his stepdaughter Sarah Hawkes, and his daughter Mercy made confessions. Samuel's confession is discussed in Chapters 5 and 13. Samuel's confession was taken before John Higginson, Jr., justice of the peace, whereas the confessions of the three women were before Major Gedney, Mr. Hathorne, Mr. Corwin, and John Higginson, Jr. It is not known why the names of the three Salem magistrates did not appear on Samuel's confession.

Sarah Wardwell confessed, "After many denials of what she was accused for & particularly of tormenting the afflicted persons by looking on them with her eyes before the justices

---

420 C. H. Abbott, *The Andover Townsman*, March 26, 1897.

which not withstanding was evident to the beholders, she was required to declare the truth in the fear of God, & then she confesses as follows. That she thinks she has been in the snare of the Devil 6 years at which time a man appeared to her & required her to worship him & do him service. He said he was God & should be worshiped & promised me such things as I wanted as clothing & the like. She says she signed a piece of paper by putting her finger to it which, as she think, made a black mark. Being asked why she did not weep & lament for it, she answered she could not weep. She said she was baptized in Shawsheen River & he dipped her face in the water & at her baptism she gave herself soul & body to him & he told her she was his servant. She says she both went & returned on foot & was alone. She was also once at Salem Village witch meeting where there were many people & that she was carried upon a pole in company with 3 more, viz., Goody Foster, Goody Carrier, & Goody Lawrence.[421] There was also a minister there & some men with pretty handsome apparel & that she saw a woman carry wine & amongst them she said she knew Goody Carrier to be a witch. She said she afflicted none but Martha Sprague last night—being asked how she did it, said that Martha Sprague was a means of taking up her husband[422] & because he was gone from home & she much vexed at it & thereupon suddenly caught up her child in her arms & wished Sprague might be afflicted a little after. Said she squeezed her child with an intention that the persons should be afflicted. She said she never knew her husband to be a witch till she was such an one herself & thinks her daughters have been so but a little while, not above a month."[423]

Sarah Hawkes' confession: "After the afflicted persons had accused her & the rest of her company with afflicting of them and particularly making them dance & sing several hours at Mr.

---

421 The scribe most likely wrote, by mistake, the name Goody Lawrence instead of Goody Lacey, the wife of Lawrence Lacey.

422 Two weeks previously the accusations of Martha Sprague led to the arrest of Sarah's husband, Samuel Wardwell.

423 Essex Institute, *Witchcraft Collection*, "Examinations."

Tyler's house,[424] and after her striking them down with the glance of her eyes in the court & recovering them again, she confesses as follows, viz. That this last spring, after she had turned the sieve & scissors, the Devil came to her and got a promise of her, but she never had anything of him. She says she went to Salem Village meeting of witches with Goody Carrier. She promised to serve the Devil 3 or 4 years & to give him her soul & body & that she signed a paper he offered to her by making a black scrawl or mark with a stick as a confirmation of the covenant & he promised she should have what she wanted, but never had anything of him. She says she never afflicted till last night, when she afflicted Martha Sprague & Rose Foster. She says she knows that when she pulled off her glove in court she afflicted them. Note that Sarah Hawkes in recovering Sprague out of her fit gripped her wrist so hard that presently it swelled & Sprague could not stir it. But upon Hawkes laying her hand gently upon it, it was presently well again. She says the paper she signed seemed to her to hang upon nothing. At the 1st & 2nd appearance of the Devil, he was like a man, but the 3rd appearance was like a shadow. She says the Devil does carry things out of her mind strangely, for when she came upstairs[425] she had a mind to confess but now cannot. She says further that William Barker was one of her company when they danced at Mr. Tyler's house & that they caused Ephraim Foster's wife to dance at home & Martha Sprague sung at Mr. Tyler's almost all day till she was almost killed. She confesses that Stephen Johnson, her father [Samuel Wardwell] & mother & her sister Mercy were of her company. She was baptized a little above a

---

424 Nathaniel Hawthorne, in Chapter 13 of *The House of the Seven Gables*, wrote, "Seated by his humble fireside, Maule had but to wave his hand; and, wherever the proud lady chanced to be, her spirit passed from beneath her own control, and bowed itself to Maule. 'Alice laugh!' the carpenter would say. And even if it were prayer time, Alice must break into wild laughter. 'Alice dance!' and dance she would, not in such courtlike measures as she has learned abroad, but some high-paced jig befitting the brisk lasses at a rustic merrymaking."

425 The examination was carried out in the large upstairs chamber of magistrate Jonathan Corwin's house in Salem, today known as the Witch House and open for visitors.

month ago in Five Mile Pond & renounced her former baptism. The Devil dipped her face in the water & he was then in the shape of a black man & has seen him several times since. As to the witch meeting at the Village, she saw there a dozen of strangers riding upon poles but knew them not. There was a man or 2, the rest were women. One of the men was tall; the other, short & fat. Note here that when she had confessed all as above, except the renouncing of her former baptism, she could not come near any of the afflicted persons without tormenting them with her eyes. But when she did remember & confessed that she had renounced her former baptism, then they were reconciled & could all take one another by the hand freely."[426]   The last sentence, a typical product of the clerical minds fashioning the content of the confessions, describes a reconciliation made possible by Sarah's complete acquiescence to their demands.

Mercy Wardwell's confession: "She confesses she hath been in the snare of the Devil a quarter of a year. The cause of her being enticed was her discontent & the occasion of her discontent was because that people told her that she should never have such a young man who loved her & he finding no encouragement threatened to drown himself, at which she was much troubled. Sometime after, to her apprehension, he that made love to her came & entreated her to be his & she did not then consent & so dismissed him with that answer. The next time he appeared in the shape of a dog & told her she must be his, for he was God & Christ & she should serve him and she did then believe him & promised to serve him. He told her she must always wish the Devil had this or that & that she must curse & lie. She confesses she covenanted to serve the Devil twenty years & he promised that she should be happy & she made a red mark upon a piece of paper, where she saw no other names. And thinks he keeps the paper, because he carried it away with him. She owned she afflicted Martha Sprague & Rose Foster but never any before. Her companions were her father, mother, sister Sarah Hawkes & William Barker. She said further, which is remarkable, that when she looked down upon the table she could confess nothing. She confesses she was baptized at home in a pail of water in

---

426 Essex Institute, *Witchcraft Collection*, "Examinations."

which he dipped her face, telling her she must serve him & that it is about a quarter of a year ago since she was baptized. She says also that she afflicted Timothy Swan by squeezing her hands & thinking upon him & the Devil made her do it, whom she has not seen but 4 times. Note here a thing remarkable that notwithstanding all this confession, yet the afflicted persons could not come near to her, but upon the Major [Gedney] asking of her if the Devil had not made her renounce her former baptism, and she answering yes, then they could all take one another by the hand without any hurt."[427]

Samuel renounced his confession on September 13. On September 15 Mercy Wardwell renounced her confession concerning her father and mother. Mercy "said she did not know her father and mother were witches."[428]

On September 16 in testimony before the grand jury, Mercy also renounced her confession concerning Mary (Ayer) Parker. Mercy said, "I did not certainly know that said Parker was a witch."[429] Samuel Wardwell and Mary Parker were condemned on September 17, and hanged on September 22.

The sheriff seized the moveables from Samuel Wardwell's farm: 5 cows, 1 heifer and a yearling, 1 horse, 9 hogs, 8 loads of hay, 1 set of carpenter tools, and 6 acres of corn upon the ground.[430] Five days after Samuel was executed, the selectmen of Andover asked the Ipswich court for permission to place the Wardwell minor children left on the farm with other Andover families. The petition began, "That whereas Samuel Wardwell and his wife of Andover were lately apprehended and committed to prison for witchcraft, and have left several small children who are incapable of providing for themselves and are now in a suffering condition, we have thought it necessary and convenient that they should be disposed of in some families where they may be due care taken of them." Permission was granted, and the following entry was made in the town records. "We the subscribers, selectmen of Andover, the above said year, having

---

427 Ibid.
428 Ibid.
429 Woodward, *Records of Salem Witchcraft*, 2:157.
430 Massachusetts Archives, *Witchcraft*, 135:140.

informed the Quarter Sessions at Ipswich the 27th of the above said September that there were several children of Samuel Wardwell's that were in a suffering condition, begging their advice, direction and order therein, which they were pleased to consider of & order as follows, that the selectmen for the time being should place out, or if need require bind out, said children in good and honest families. Pursuant to this order of the Court we have placed them as follows; viz., Samuel Wardwell, Jr. we placed with John Ballard, his uncle, for one year; William we placed with Corporal Samuel Frye till he become to be of the age one and twenty years; said Frye to learn him the trade of weaver; Eliakim we placed to Daniel Poor till he was twenty-one years of age; & Elizabeth we placed with John Stevens [3rd] till eighteen years of age; all of the aforesaid were to find them with suits of apparel at the end of said time."[431]

On January 3, 1693, the grand jury at the Superior Court of Judicature at Salem indicted Sarah Wardwell, Sarah Hawkes, and Mercy Wardwell. The three were tried by jury on January 10. Sarah Wardwell was found guilty. Sarah Hawkes and Mercy Wardwell were found not guilty and released, each having been imprisoned about five months. In the middle of January Chief Justice William Stoughton signed death warrants for Sarah Wardwell and seven other condemned women but they were reprieved by Governor Sir William Phipps.

On February 1, 1693, Sarah Hawkes married Francis Johnson of Andover. He was the son of Elizabeth (Dane) Johnson, who had been imprisoned. Francis' two sisters, Abigail and Elizabeth, Jr., and his brother, Stephen, had been imprisoned. In 1697, Mercy Wardwell married John Wright, son of Walter Wright of Andover and his first wife Susannah (Johnson) Wright. In 1706, William Wardwell married Dorothy Wright, daughter of Walter Wright and his second wife, Elizabeth (Peters) Sadie Wright. Sometime between 1703 and 1711, widow Sarah Wardwell died at Andover, the date unknown. In 1716 Sarah (Hawkes) Johnson died at Andover, aged 45. In 1754 Mercy (Wardwell) Wright died at Andover in her 81st year.

---

431 Bailey, *Historical Sketches of Andover*, 220-221.

Joseph Draper   **Andover**
Single man, 21   *Charged on September 7, 1692*

Joseph Draper was born in 1671, son of Rebecca (Brabrook) and
Adam Draper of Concord. Adam Draper died by 1678, and his
widow married Thomas Dutton, Jr. of Billerica. Joseph Draper's
maternal aunt, Rachel (Brabrook) Fuller of Hampton, had been
tried for witchcraft in 1680 and was acquitted.

In 1692 Joseph Draper, 21, was living in the south part of
Andover. His stepgrandmother was Ruth (mnu) Hooper Dutton.
She was the stepmother of the three Hooper sisters living in
Andover. The sisters were Rebecca (Hooper) Ballard, wife of
John Ballard; Hannah (Hooper) Ballard, wife of William
Ballard; and Sarah (Hooper) Hawkes Wardwell, wife of
Samuel Wardwell. Also living in Andover were Ruth's sons,
Thomas Hooper and John Hooper, who were half-brothers of the
three Hooper sisters. Joseph Draper worked for the Hooper
family members living in Andover.

Joseph Draper was arrested at the Andover touch test on
September 7. On September 16 Joseph Draper acknowledged that
he was led into the sin of witchcraft by Abigail (Dane) Faulkner.
On Oct. 27, Joseph Draper's stepuncle, John Durrant of Billerica,
died at Cambridge prison.

John Durrant   **Billerica**
Married man, 47   *Charged (date unknown)*

John Durrant was born about 1645 in the part of Lynn which
later became Reading. He married, in 1670 in Billerica,
Susannah Dutton, daughter of Thomas Dutton, Sr. of Billerica by
his first wife. After his first wife's death Thomas Dutton, Sr.
married in 1685, Ruth (mnu) Hooper, the widow of William
Hooper of Reading. In 1692 John Durrant was about 47. It is not
known when John Durrant was imprisoned, but on October 27, 1692
he died in Cambridge prison.

WILSON FAMILY

Sarah (Lord) Wilson   **Andover**
Married woman, 44   *Charged on September 7, 1692*

Sarah Wilson, Jr.   **Andover**
Girl, 14   *Charged on September 7, 1692*

Sarah Lord was born about 1648 in Ipswich, daughter of Mary (Waite) and Robert Lord, a prominent resident of Ipswich. Sarah's sister, Abigail Lord, married Jacob Foster of Ipswich, an uncle of Ephraim Foster of Andover, a conspirator. Sarah's sister, Susannah Lord, married Thomas Osgood of Andover, brother of Christopher Osgood. About 1669 Joseph Wilson moved to Andover, where he married Mary Lovejoy, niece of Christopher Osgood. In 1678 Sarah Lord married widower Joseph Wilson of Andover. Their children included daughter Sarah Wilson, Jr., born in 1678.

In 1692 Sarah, about 44, her husband, Joseph, their daughter Sarah Wilson, Jr., 14, and their other children were living in the south part of Andover. Joseph and his wife were both members of the Andover Church.

On September 7, 1692, Sarah (Lord) Wilson and her daughter Sarah Wilson, Jr. were arrested at the Andover touch test. On September 16 the Andover children Sarah Wilson, Jr., Dorothy Faulkner, 12, Abigail Faulkner, Jr., 9, Joanna Tyler, 11, and Martha Tyler, 11, as well as Joseph Draper, 21, were made to confess that they had been led into witchcraft by Abigail (Dane) Faulkner. The officials were desperate for evidence to use against Abigail (Dane) Faulkner in her forthcoming trial, as she had made only a partial confession.

In October 1692 the Rev. Increase Mather visited the Salem prison and interviewed Sarah (Lord) Wilson. "Goodwife Wilson said that she was in the dark as to some things in her confession. Yet she asserted that, knowingly, she never had familiarity with the Devil; that, knowingly, she never consented to the afflicting of any person, &c. However, she said that truly she was in the dark as to the matter of her being a witch. And being asked how she was in the dark, she replied, that the afflicted persons crying out of her as afflicting them made her fearful of herself; and that was all that made her say that she was in the dark."[432]

On October 12 Joseph Wilson, on behalf of his wife and daughter, petitioned, along with eight other men of Andover, for the release of their families on bail. On October 15 the officials allowed Sarah Wilson, Jr. to be released on bail after six weeks imprisonment. The other imprisoned Andover children were also allowed to be released on bail about the same time. On October 18 Joseph Wilson and twenty-five other men of Andover petitioned for the release of prisoners on bail. On December 6 Joseph Wilson and seven other men of Andover again petitioned for release of the prisoners on bail. On December 20, Sarah (Lord) Wilson was released on bail after 15 weeks imprisonment. She was ordered to appear at the meeting of the Superior Court of Judicature on January 3, 1693. However, neither Sarah (Lord) Wilson nor her daughter were tried in January 1693. On January 13, Joseph Wilson and John Osgood posted a recognizance bond of £100 for the continued freedom of Sarah (Lord) Wilson and Sarah Wilson, Jr. on bail. On May 10, 1693, mother and daughter appeared at the Superior Court of Judicature at Ipswich and were cleared.

SALTER FAMILY

Henry Salter   **Andover**
Widower, 64   *Charged on September 7, 1692*

Henry Salter was born about 1628 in England. About 1653, he married Hannah (mnu), born in 1633. They moved to Andover and in 1678 he was involved in a law suit with John Godfrey. His wife died in 1686.

In 1692 Henry, a widower aged 64, was living in the south part of Andover. He was arrested at the Andover touch test on September 7. At his examination, "he struck down with his eye Mary Warren, Mary Walcott, Rose Foster, and Mary Lacey, Jr., and recovered them with a touch of his hand. Mary Walcott

---

432 Upham, *Salem Witchcraft*, 2:406.

said he [more precisely, his specter] hurt her the last Thursday [September 1], and almost choked her to death upon the last Sabbath day [September 4]. Mary Warren [a Salem Village girl who knew nothing about him or his personal life] said he [his specter again] told her he used his witchcraft by the key & Bible, and sometimes by the sieve & scissors." To these typical lies by the afflicted girls, Henry said, "I never knew any such thing." Magistrate John Hathorne, angry at Henry's defiance, reversed the situation and painted Henry as the liar. "He owns he has told lies before and been in drink."[433]

On January 5, 1693, Henry Salter was cleared by the grand jury at the Superior Court of Judicature in Salem and released after spending four months in jail.

---

433 Suffolk County, Court Records, case 2702, page 24.

25

THE END OF THE AFFAIR

I N DECEMBER 1692, A GROUP OF PRISONERS at Ipswich prison, a dank and bone-chilling spot that amounted to little more than an unheated, vermin-ridden pit, submitted a petition to their honorable governor, Council (the upper house), and General Assembly (the lower house). Ten women signed the petition. They were widow Joanna Penny, 72; widow Rachel Vinson, 61; widow Margaret Prince, 62; Mary Green, 34; Mary Rowe, 34; Mehitabel Downing, 40; Phoebe Day, 39; Elizabeth Dicer; Hannah Brumidge; 59; and Rachel (Haffield) Clinton, 63. The petition stated that, though charged with witchcraft, the signers did not believe they were guilty. They requested their release on bail. They stated their willingness to abide trial before any judicature. They asked that their suffering from long-term imprisonment be considered; they were likely to perish in midwinter. Some were elderly; all were weak and sick, one in fetters for the past six months. In conclusion, they pleaded for their lives: that they not be left to die under the miserable conditions of prison.

In the seventeenth-century extended imprisonments were unusual. A prisoner who was neither executed nor released usually died in such an environment—an efficient, if inhumane, method to keep down the prison populations. The winter of 1692-1693, at the center of the so-called little ice-age, was one of the coldest in the history of civilization.

This chapter supplies a brief look at the 25 women and men accused of witchcraft who were imprisoned after July 15, 1692 but do not fall under the heading of the Andover witch hunt. This group, mostly from the towns of Haverhill, Reading, and Gloucester, represents the end of the Salem witchcraft affair.

HAVERHILL

Hannah (Varnum) Tyler Brumidge   Haverhill
Married woman, 59   *Charged about July 30, 1692*

Hannah Varnum was born about 1633, daughter of George Varnum of Ipswich, who died in 1649. In 1650 in Haverhill, Hannah married Abraham Tyler,[434] who died in 1673; in 1674, she married widower Edward Brumidge of Haverhill.

In 1692 Hannah, aged 59, was living in Haverhill with her husband. On July 30, 1692, she and Mary Green of Haverhill were arrested and put in irons at Ipswich prison. At Hannah's examination on July 30, many accusations were thrown at her. Mary (Tyler) Post Bridges who was present "said that Brumidge was in her society at Ballard's house, [Bridges] telling her to her face she was there in her spirit, & [Bridges] urged her to confess, that being the way to eternal life. Said Bridges told Brumidge that the Devil would not leave her until she did confess and therefore urged her to do so." When Ann Putnam, Jr. fell into a violent fit, Bridges claimed that she saw the specter of Hannah upon Putnam. Mary Walcott said she saw the specter of Hannah stab Putnam with a spear. Hannah's confession, if it was one, was indeed weak. "Said Brumidge said she had been under some deadness with respect to the ordnances for the matter of 6 weeks. And a sudden suggestion came to her head, saying I can help thee with strength, to which she answered, avoid Satan. She, being asked what shape the Devil appeared to her, answered she believed the Devil was in her heart. And being asked several other questions, she returned negative answers."[435]

In December Hannah was one of the signers of the petition from Ipswich Prison. On January 3, 1693 the Grand Jury at the Superior Court of Judicature at Salem cleared Hannah Brumidge.

Mary (Green) Green   Haverhill
Married woman, 34   *Charged about July 30, 1692*

---

434 The kinship, if any, between Abraham Tyler of Haverhill and Job Tyler of Boxford is unknown.
435 Suffolk County, *Court Records*, case 2674, page 5.

Mary Green, born about 1658, married, in 1678, widower Peter Green, a weaver of Haverhill. His first wife had been Elizabeth (Dustin) Kingsbury, widow of John Kingsbury of Haverhill. In 1692 Mary, about 34, and her husband were living in Haverhill. On July 30, 1692, Mary Green and Hannah Brumidge of Haverhill were arrested and imprisoned at Ipswich. An account of Robert Lord, blacksmith of Ipswich specified that he made iron fetters and handcuffs and put them on the legs and hands of Cloyce, Easty, Brumidge, and Green. On August 2 Mary Green escaped from Ipswich prison, but was recaptured by William Baker, Constable of Ipswich. On August 23 Mary again escaped from prison and was recaptured the following day by the same constable. In September John Shepard of Rowley was arrested for helping Mary in her escapes. In December Mary Green was one of the signers of the petition from Ipswich Prison. On December 16, Peter Green and James Sanders of Haverhill were allowed to post a recognizance bond for Mary's release after almost 20 weeks in jail. There is no extant court record of her trial. However an account of Peter Green in 1710 says that she was tried. Most likely the trial was during the session of the Superior Court of Judicature in Ipswich on May 9, 1693.

Mary (Johnson) Davis Clarke   **Haverhill**
Married woman, 52   *Charged on August 3, 1692*

Mary Johnson was born in 1638 in Ipswich, daughter of Susannah (mnu) and John Johnson. John Johnson and his wife had come to America on the *James* in 1635 and were taxed in Ipswich in that year. John Johnson is first mentioned in Andover in 1659 when at the age of 50 he was excused from military service. Mary Johnson married Ephraim Davis of Haverhill in 1660. After his death, Mary married again, in 1682. Her new husband was widower Edward Clarke of Haverhill. In 1692, they were living in western part of Haverhill, now the town of Methuen. Mary's sister Hannah Johnson married Samuel Hutchins in 1662; they also were living in western Haverhill.

The other members of the Johnson family were living in Andover. Mary's son Ephraim Davis, Jr. married Mary Ayer of Andover. Mary's brother, Stephen Johnson, Sr. (1640-1688),

married Elizabeth Dane, daughter of the Rev. Francis Dane of
Andover.

Mary's sister Susannah Johnson (1645-1683) married Walter
Wright of Andover in 1667. After Susannah died, Walter
Wright remarried in 1684. His new wife was widow Elizabeth
(Peters) Sadie. John Sadie, son of Elizabeth, became the stepson
of Walter Wright. Mary's brother, Timothy Johnson (1649-1688)
married Rebecca Aslet, daughter of John Aslet, an original
proprietor of Andover.

On August 3 conspirators Robert Swan, Jr. and John Swan filed
a complaint against Mary (Johnson) Davis Clarke for afflicting
Timothy Swan, Ann Putnam, Jr., and Mary Walcott. Mary Clarke
was arrested the next day and examined in Salem. Magistrate
John Hathorne used several arguments, said to be for the good of
her soul, to persuade her to confess, but she firmly refused to
make any admission of guilt.

The Andover conspiracy retaliated by accusing additional
members of the Johnson family. On August 11, Elizabeth Johnson,
Jr. (the daughter of the deceased Stephen Johnson, Sr.) was
imprisoned at Salem. On August 30, Elizabeth (Dane) Johnson,
Abigail Johnson, aged 10, and Stephen Johnson, aged 13 (the
widow, daughter, and son of the deceased Stephen Johnson, Sr.)
were imprisoned.

On September 7, 1692, the widow Rebecca (Aslet) Johnson,
her daughter, Rebecca Johnson, Jr., and John Sadie, Jr., were
arrested at the Andover touch test and imprisoned in Salem.

In the fall Mary Clarke's son, Ephraim Davis, Jr., became a
committed member of the Andover resistance group led by the
Rev. Francis Dane.

Frances (mnu) Hutchins　　　　　　　　　　　**Haverhill**
Widow, 77　　　　　　　　　*Charged on August 18, 1692*

Frances, born about 1615 in England, married, about 1635, John
Hutchins of Haverhill, who died in 1685. In 1692 Frances, about
75, was living in western Haverhill. Frances' daughter,
Elizabeth, was married to Thomas Ayer of Haverhill. Frances'
son Samuel was married to Hannah Johnson of Andover. In 1692,

Samuel Hutchins was elected a Haverhill representative to the General Court.

On August 18, 1692, Timothy Swan, Ann Putnam, Jr., and Mary Walcott filed a complaint against Ruth Wilford and Frances (mnu) Hutchins. On the next day, Frances was imprisoned. On December 21, 1692, the authorities allowed Frances to be released on bail. Samuel Hutchins and John Kingsbury posted the bond. John Kingsbury was her grandson by marriage. No trial records for Frances are extant.

Ruth Wilford   **Haverhill**
Single woman, 20   *Charged on August 18, 1692*

Ruth Wilford was born in 1672 in Bradford, Massachusetts, daughter of Mary (Dow) and Gilbert Wilford. Gilbert died in 1676, and in 1679 his widow, Mary (Dow) Wilford, married widower Matthew Clarke of Haverhill. In 1692 Ruth, aged 20, lived with her mother Mary (Dow) Wilford Clarke, stepfather Matthew Clarke, and eight other children of the Wilford and Clarke families.

After the death of Matthew Clarke's mother, his father Edward Clarke had married widow Mary (Johnson) Davis. On August 2, 1692, John Swan and Robert Swan, Jr. filed a complaint against Mary (Johnson) Davis Clarke of Haverhill.

On August 18, 1692, Timothy Swan, Ann Putnam, Jr., and Mary Walcott filed a complaint against Ruth Wilford and Frances (mnu) Hutchins. On August 19, Frances was arrested, but Ruth Wilford avoided arrest until the following day. There are no trial records extant.

After the witch hunt had ended, Ruth Wilford married Thomas Ayer, Jr. in 1694 in Haverhill. In 1708 the French and Indians attacked Haverhill, burning many buildings and killing about forty residents, among them Ruth (Wilford) Ayer, aged 36, and her daughter, Ruth Ayer, aged 3.

READING

Mary (Dustin) Colson   **Reading**
Widow, 42   *Charged on September 3, 1692*

Mary Dustin was born in 1650 in Reading, daughter of Lydia (mnu) and Josiah Dustin. In 1668 in Reading, Mary Dustin married Adam Colson, who died in 1687. In 1692, Mary, a widow of 42, was living in Reading with her daughter Elizabeth Colson, aged 15, her sister Sarah Dustin, aged 39, and her mother Lydia Dustin in her mid-sixties.

On May 2, 1692, Lydia Dustin was imprisoned and on May 9 Sarah Dustin was imprisoned. On May 14 the Salem Village conspiracy filed a complaint against Elizabeth Colson, but she was able to flee before arrest.

On September 3, 1692, a complaint was filed against Mary (Dustin) Colson, Jane (mnu) Lilly, and Mary (Harrington) Taylor, all of Reading, for afflicting widow Mary (Swayne) Marshall. On September 5 the three accused women were imprisoned in Salem. The afflicted woman, Mary (Swayne) Marshall, was living in Malden. Mary's husband, Edward Marshall, had died on August 3, 1692, aged 50. Prior to her husband's death, Mary (Swayne) Marshall, on May 26, 1692, had claimed that she had been afflicted by Sarah (mnu) Davis Rice of Reading, who was then imprisoned on May 31.

On September 14 Elizabeth Colson was finally captured. Thus, by mid-September 1692, Lydia Dustin, her two daughters, and her granddaughter were all in prison.

On February 1, 1693, Lydia Dustin and her daughter Sarah Dustin were tried by jury at the Superior Court of Judicature at Charlestown. The verdict for both was not guilty. There is no record of the trial of either Lydia's daughter Mary Colson or granddaughter Elizabeth Colson, but, according to Calef, the "daughter and granddaughter were also acquitted." Unable to pay the exorbitant prison fees required for release, Lydia, her two daughters, and her granddaughter were returned to prison. On March 2 Elizabeth Colson was released. On March 10 Lydia Dustin died in Cambridge prison. On March 23, 1693, Sarah Dustin was released. There is no record for Mary Colson.

Jane (mnu) Lilly   **Reading**
Widow, 45   *Charged on September 3, 1692*

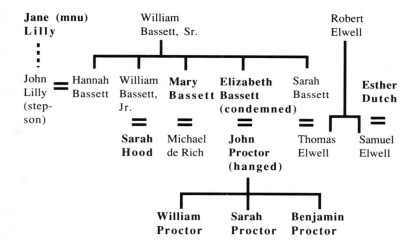

Jane was born about 1647. She married, in 1667 in Reading, widower George Lilly. George was born in 1634 and died in 1691. In 1692 widow Jane Lilly, aged 45, was living in Reading with two sons and a daughter. Her stepson, John Lilly, was married to Hannah Bassett.

A complaint was filed on September 3, 1692, against Jane (mnu) Lilly, Mary (Dustin) Colson, and Mary (Harrington) Taylor, all of Reading for afflicting widow Mary (Swayne) Marshall; the three women were imprisoned in Salem two days later. At her examination, Jane did not confess, saying "if she confessed anything she should deny the truth and wrong her own soul." On December 8, 1692, the authorities allowed Jane to be released on bail. Her sons George and Rueben Lilly together with Capt. John Pearson posted the required recognizance bond. At the same time George Lilly and Capt. Pearson posted a recognizance bond for the release on bail of Pearson's sister, widow Bethia (Pearson) Carter of Woburn, imprisoned on May 9, 1692. On February 3, 1693, at the Superior Court of Judicature at

Charlestown, the Grand Jury cleared Jane (mnu) Lilly by proclamation.

Mary (Harrington) Taylor   **Reading**
Married woman, 40   *Charged on September 3, 1692*

Mary Harrington was born about 1652 in Charlestown, daughter of Elizabeth and Richard Harrington. Mary married, in 1671 in Reading, widower Seabred Taylor, born 1643, son of Elizabeth and Thomas Taylor of Reading. In 1692, Mary, 40, her husband and five children were living in Reading. The youngest child was Thomas, born on May 21, 1692. Seabred's brother, Thomas Taylor, Jr. and his wife, Mary (Hooper) Taylor also lived in Reading,

On September 3, 1692, a complaint was filed against Mary (Harrington) Taylor, Jane (mnu) Lilly, and Mary (Dustin) Colson, all of Reading, for afflicting widow Mary (Swayne) Marshall. On September 5 the three women were imprisoned in Salem.

At Mary's examination, John Hathorne opened by asking Mary (Swayne) Marshall the question, "Mrs. Marshall, do you accuse this woman for hurting you by witchcraft?" Marshall gravely answered, "Yes, she has beat me & came to persuade me to worship her god & told me my god could not save me & she has brought images to me."[436] When Hathorne ordered Taylor to look at her accuser, Marshall fell to the floor. Mary Lacey, Jr., with her spectral sight could see the specter of Taylor sitting upon the prostate body of Marshall. When Marshall could speak again, she said that it was Taylor who struck her down. Marshall meant, of course, that it was the specter of Taylor, because the whole court knew that Taylor had not moved an inch. Hathorne told Taylor that she had a dangerous eye that struck folks down, and this gave him grounds to think she was indeed a witch. As he spoke, Taylor moved her head slightly, and the whole line of afflicted girls fell down like a row of dominos. In the official records it was written that they were struck down by a glance of Taylor.

---

436 Suffolk County, *Court Records*, case 2710, page 43.

Despite this so-called evidence, Taylor would not admit her witchcraft, only saying that "she had in a passion wished bad wishes because Mrs. Marshall had complained of her." Mary Marshall's brother, Major Jeremiah Swayne stepped forward and stated that Taylor "had used threatening words both to his sister and others." The constable reported that, when arrested, Taylor said, "There was a hot pot now & a hotter pot preparing for her [Mary Marshall] here." When the constable had asked Taylor what she meant by the hotter pot, the answer was, "If Mrs. Marshall wronged her, hell would be prepared for her." Relentlessly magistrate John Hathorne kept pounding Mary Taylor with bullying questions. Finally "she in a manner owned" that she had afflicted Mrs. Marshall, and "she said to Mr. Noyes [assistant minister at Salem] and Mr. Keyser the Devil that guides destiny brought her a birch rind which she signed, but she would not own that the Devil baptized her. She owned that she had bent her fist & wished ill to Mrs. Marshall. This is the substance of what Mary Taylor said at her examination."[437] On January 31, 1693, at the Superior Court of Judicature at Charlestown, the Grand Jury indicted Mary (Harrington) Taylor for making her mark on a piece of birch rind. In a trial by jury on February 1, she was found not guilty of witchcraft and was discharged upon payment of fees.

GLOUCESTER

Elizabeth (Austin) Dicer   **Gloucester**
Married woman   *Charged on September 3, 1692*

Elizabeth Austin became the wife of William Dicer, a seaman from Boston. She had lived at Piscataqua in New Hampshire but in 1692 was in Gloucester. Ebenezer Babson of Gloucester made a complaint on September 3, 1692, against both her and widow Margaret (mnu) Prince of Gloucester. They were accused of afflicting widow Eleanor (Hill) Babson and Mary (mnu) Sargent, wife of William Sargent of Gloucester. The two

---

437 Ibid.

accused women were arrested on September 5 and imprisoned in Ipswich. Elizabeth Dicer was one of ten signers of the December petition from Ipswich Prison.

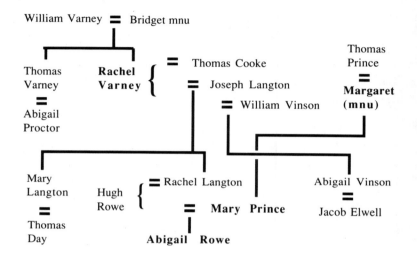

Margaret (mnu) Prince

Gloucester

Widow, 62   *Charged on September 3, 1692*

Margaret was born about 1630 in England. In 1650 she married Thomas Prince of Gloucester. He died in 1690 in Gloucester, aged 71. Their daughter Mary Prince was born in 1658; she married Hugh Rowe in 1674. In 1692, Margaret, aged 62, was living in the Prince house close to Gloucester harbor.

Ebenezer Babson of Gloucester made a complaint on September 3 against both her and Elizabeth (Austin) Dicer, and they were imprisoned on September 5. In early October, Margaret's daughter Mary (Prince) Rowe was imprisoned. On November 5 Margaret's granddaughter, Abigail Rowe, 15, was imprisoned. Margaret Prince was one of the signers of the December petition from Ipswich prison. Widow Margaret (mnu) Prince died at Gloucester in 1706.

Joseph Emons   **Manchester**

Man   *Charged on September 5, 1692*

On September 5 Simon Willard and Elizer Keyser, both of Salem, filed a complaint against Joseph Emons for afflicting Mary Warren. Emons was imprisoned.

Rachel (Varney) Cooke Langton Vinson   **Gloucester**
Widow, 61   *Charged in early October 1692*

Rachel Varney was born about 1631 in England, daughter of Bridget and William Varney, later of Ipswich, Massachusetts. Rachel first married Thomas Cooke, who died in 1650 in Salem. She next married Joseph Langton of Ipswich in 1652. They were divorced in 1660, a rare occurrence in seventeenth-century New England. She then married, in 1661, widower William Vinson of Gloucester, who died in 1690, aged about 80.

Rachel and Joseph Langton's daughter Rachel Langton married Hugh Rowe of Gloucester in 1667; after her death he married Mary Prince. Rachel and Joseph Langton's daughter Mary Langton married Thomas Day in 1673. Rachel and William Vinson's daughter Abigail Vinson, born in 1668, married Jacob Elwell in 1686.

In 1692 Rachel (Varney) Cooke Langton Vinson, a widow, aged 61, was living in Gloucester. Her brother, Thomas Varney of Ipswich was married to Abigail Proctor, sister of John Proctor of Salem. John Proctor was hanged on August 19, 1692. In early October 1692 Rachel (Varney) Cooke Langton Vinson was arrested and imprisoned at Ipswich. Also Mary (Prince) Rowe (Hugh Rowe's second wife) and Phoebe (Wildes) Day (the wife of Thomas Day's brother, Timothy Day) were accused and imprisoned. On November 5 Abigail Rowe, aged 15, (the daughter of Mary (Prince) and Hugh Rowe, Rebecca (Dolliver) Dike, and Esther (Dutch) Elwell were imprisoned. Rachel Vinson was one of the signers of the December petition from Ipswich prison. In 1707 Rachel Vinson died at Gloucester.

Phoebe (Wildes) Day   **Gloucester**
Married woman, 39   *Charged in early October 1692*

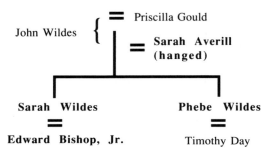

Phoebe Wildes, born about 1653, was the daughter of Priscilla (Gould) and John Wildes of Topsfield. After her mother's death her father married, in 1663, Sarah Averill. Phoebe's father was one of the Topsfield men disliked by the Salem Village accusers. In 1679, Phoebe Wildes married Timothy Day of Gloucester and took up life in that town.

In 1692 Phoebe, 39, her husband, and their six children were living in Gloucester on the westerly side of the Annisquam River. On April 22, 1692, her sister, Sarah (Wildes) Bishop; her brother-in-law, Edward Bishop, Jr.; and her stepmother, Sarah (Averill) Wildes, were imprisoned. On July 19 her stepmother was hanged at Salem. In early October 1692, Phoebe (Wildes) Day was imprisoned at Ipswich prison. Phoebe was one of the signers of the petition from that prison in December. There are no further extant court records. On June 26, 1693, Phoebe's father, John Wildes, married Mary (mnu) Jacobs, widow of George Jacobs, Sr., who had been hanged at Salem on August 19, 1692

Mary (Prince) Rowe   **Gloucester**
Married woman, 34   *Charged in early October, 1692*

Abigail Rowe   **Gloucester**
Single woman, 15   *Charged on November 5, 1692*

Mary Prince was born in 1658 in Gloucester, daughter of Margaret (mnu) and Thomas Prince. In 1674, Mary Prince married widower Hugh Rowe of Gloucester. Their eldest child Abigail Rowe was born in 1677. Hugh Rowe's first wife, Rachel Langton, was the daughter of Rachel (Varney) Cooke Langton Vinson.

Another daughter, Mary Langton, had married Thomas Day of Gloucester.

In 1692 Mary (Prince) Rowe, 34, her husband, and their five children were living in Gloucester. On September 5, Mary's widowed mother, Margaret (mnu) Prince was imprisoned. In early October Mary (Prince) Rowe was imprisoned at Ipswich. Phoebe (Wildes) Day and widow Rachel (Varney) Cooke Langton Vinson, both of Gloucester, were also imprisoned in early October. On November 5, Mary's daughter Abigail Rowe, 15, was imprisoned on a complaint by Lieut. James Stevens, William Stevens, and Nathaniel Coyt, all of Gloucester, for afflicting Mrs. Mary Fitch, the wife of Mr. John Fitch of Gloucester. Mary (Prince) Rowe was one of the signers of the December petition from Ipswich prison. In 1723 Mary (Prince) Rowe, a widow, died in Gloucester.

Rebecca (Dolliver) Dike	**Gloucester**
Married woman, 40	*Charged on November 5, 1692*
James Dike	**Gloucester**
Infant boy	*Imprisoned on November 5, 1692*

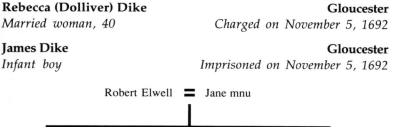

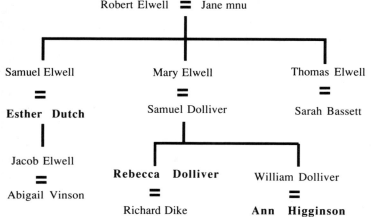

Rebecca Dolliver was born about 1652, daughter of Samuel Dolliver of Gloucester. Rebecca married, in 1667, Richard Dike of Gloucester. In 1692 Rebecca, about 40 years old, her husband,

and children were living on the westerly side of the Annisquam River in Gloucester. On June 6, 1692, Rebecca's sister-in-law, Ann (Higginson) Dolliver was imprisoned. On November 5 Nathaniel Coyt, William Stevens, and Lieut. James Stevens— all of Gloucester—made a complaint against Rebecca (Dolliver) Dike, her aunt Esther (Dutch) Elwell, and Abigail Rowe—all of Gloucester. The three women were imprisoned at Ipswich. Rebecca (Dolliver) Dike took her infant son, James Dike, to prison with her. In the December 1692 petition from Ipswich prison she was the woman prisoner referred to as "giving suck to a child not ten weeks old yet."

Esther (Dutch) Elwell   **Gloucester**
Married woman, 53   *Charged on November 5, 1692*

Esther Dutch was born about 1639 in Newport, Rhode Island, daughter of Grace (Pratt) and Osmund Dutch, later of Gloucester. In 1658 Esther married Samuel Elwell, son of Jane (mnu) and Robert Elwell. Esther (Dutch) and Samuel Elwell had a son Jacob, who in 1685 married Abigail Vinson, daughter of Rachel (Varney) Cooke Langton and William Vinson.

In 1692 Esther (Dutch) Elwell, aged 53, and her husband were living in Gloucester. On June 6 Ann (Higginson) Dolliver, who was Esther's niece, was imprisoned. On November 5 Nathaniel Coyt, William Stevens, and Lieut. James Stevens, all of Gloucester made a complaint against Esther (Dutch) Elwell, her niece Rebecca (Dolliver) Dike, and Abigail Rowe—all of Gloucester—for afflicting Mrs. Mary Fitch, the wife of Mr. John Fitch of Gloucester. The three women were imprisoned at Ipswich. On November 8, "James Stevens testifies and says that Mary Fitch did say that she felt a woman upon the bed, and put forth her hand, and felt the hair and felt the hair of her head and a peg in it; also testifies that she said she was squeezed to pieces, whereas I saw nobody hurt her."[438] In 1721 Esther (Dutch) Elwell, widow, died at Gloucester, aged 82.

---

438 Suffolk County, *Court Records*, case 2689, page 17.

MISCELLANEOUS

Margaret (Stevenson) Scott   **Rowley**
Widow, 71   *Charged about August 5, 1692*

Margaret Stevenson was born about 1621 in England. In 1642 she married widower Benjamin Scott. After living in Cambridge, Massachusetts, they moved to Rowley in 1654. They had six children. Benjamin died at Rowley in 1671. In 1692 Margaret was 71. She was arrested on August 5. On September 15 Philip Nelson and his wife Sarah testified that "for two or three years before Robert Shilleto died we have often heard him complaining of Margaret Scott for hurting of him and often said that she was a witch and so he continued complaining of Margaret Scott saying that he should never be so well as long as Margaret Scott lived & so he complained of Margaret Scott at times until he died." Frances Wycom said "that quickly after the first court at Salem about witchcraft, Margaret Scott, whom I very well knew, or her appearance came to me and did most grievously torment me by choking and almost pressing me to death. And so she did continue afflicting me by times tell the 5th August 1692 being the day of her examination. Also during the time of her examination Margaret Scott did most grievously afflict me, and also several times since, and I believe in my heart that she is a witch."[439] On September 17 Margaret (Stevenson) Scott was condemned by the Court of Oyer and Terminer, and on September 22 was hanged.

Hannah (mnu) Carroll   **Salem**
Woman   *Charged on September 10, 1692*

On September 10 Henry Bragg of Salem filed a complaint against Hannah Carroll, wife of Nathaniel Carroll, wheelwright, and Sarah (Davis) Cole for afflicting his son, William Bragg.

Sarah (Davis) Cole   **Salem**
Married woman, 42   *Charged on September 10, 1692*

---

439 Essex County Archives, *Witchcraft*, 2: 45.

Sarah Davis, born in 1650, married in 1670 Abraham Cole, a tailor of Salem. In 1692, she and her husband were living in Salem. On September 10 Henry Bragg filed a complaint against her and Hannah Carroll for afflicting his son William Bragg. On September 15 Sarah was arrested by deputy sheriff George Herrick. On October 3, 1692, Sarah (Aslet) Cole of Lynn, was imprisoned; she was the wife of Abraham's brother, John Cole. On January 14, 1693, Abraham Cole was allowed to bail out his wife after 17 weeks imprisonment. In May Sarah (Davis) Cole appeared at the Superior Court of Judicature at Ipswich and was cleared by proclamation.

Sarah (Aslet) Cole   **Lynn**
Married woman, 30   *Charged on October 1, 1692*

Sarah Aslet was born in 1662 in Andover, daughter of Rebecca (Ayer) and John Aslet, an original proprietor of Andover. Sarah married, about 1680, widower John Cole of Lynn, a cooper. He was twenty years older than she. His first wife, Mary Knight, whom he married in 1661, had died in 1675.

In 1692 Sarah was living in Lynn with her husband John, his three children, and their two children. About August 15 Sarah Parker, aged 22, of Andover was arrested. Sarah Parker was the first cousin of Sarah Cole. Sarah Parker's mother, Mary (Ayer) Parker, was arrested on September 1 and was hanged on September 22. At the Andover touch test on September 7, Sarah (Aslet) Cole's sister, Rebecca (Aslet) Johnson was arrested. Also arrested at the same time was Rebecca's daughter, Rebecca Johnson, Jr., aged 17. On September 15 Sarah (Davis) Cole of Salem was arrested. She was the wife of Abraham Cole, the brother of John Cole.

On October 1 a complaint was filed against Sarah (Aslet) Cole for afflicting the widow Mary (mnu) Browne of Reading. On October 3 Benjamin Larobe posted a bond for the execution of the complaint on behalf of the widow. Sarah (Aslet) Cole was arrested and imprisoned Salem. Sarah did not confess, but instead gave a lively story. "One night being in bed I was sorely afflicted and saw a ball of fire. The last thing I saw was a dog which I went to strike with a spade and was beat down myself.

The dog went out at a crack in the side of the house. Cole owned that she & some others toyed with a Venus glass and an egg, what trade their sweethearts should be of."[440]

On January 11, 1693, Sarah (Aslet) Cole was indicted for afflicting widow Mary Brown on September 26. At the Superior Court of Judicature at Charlestown on January 31 she was found not guilty in a jury trial. Unable to pay the prison fees required for release, she, together with Lydia Dustin, Sarah Dustin, and Elizabeth Colson, were returned to Cambridge prison. On March 10, 1693 Lydia Dustin died at Cambridge prison, and "Sarah Cole & Sarah Dustin went out of prison the 23rd of said March." John Cole died at Lynn in 1703. In 1741 Sarah (Aslet) Cole, aged 79, died at Bradford at the home of her son, John Cole, Jr.

Henry Somers   **Middlesex County**
Man   *Charged (date unknown)*

According to an account of the sheriff of Middlesex County, Henry Somers was accused of witchcraft and tried at Charlestown in January 1693.

Edward Wooland   **Essex County**
Man   *Charged (date unknown)*

In 1692 Edward Wooland was imprisoned, according to an account of the jail keeper of Salem.

Nicholas Frost   **Piscataqua, New Hampshire**
Man   *Charged (date unknown)*

Thomas Dodd of Marblehead filed a complaint for afflicting his daughter, Joanna Dodd, against Nicholas Frost of Piscataqua.

---

440 Suffolk County, *Court Records*, case 2712, page 49.

CHRONOLOGY OF EVENTS

Date	Event
Date	**Event**
1603	James I ascended English throne
1620	Plymouth Colony settled
1625	Charles I succeeded to the English throne
1626	Roger Conant settled Salem, Massachusetts
1628	John Endicott arrived at Salem as governor
1630	John Winthrop arrived at Boston as governor with the Puritan charter for New England
1637	Pequot Indian War fought "to strike terror into the hearts of the savages"
1637-1638	Anne Hutchinson tried, excommunicated, and driven from Massachusetts
1638	John Wheelwright, banished, founded Exeter, New Hampshire.
1639	First printing press in New England
1649	Charles I beheaded
1649-1660	Puritan Commonwealth in England
1660	Restoration of English crown with Charles II as king.
1656-1663	Persecution of Quakers in Massachusetts
1675-1676	King Philip's Indian War "to destroy the savages"
1684	Puritan charter of New England abolished by the king
1685	James II succeeded to the English throne
1686	Sir Edmond Andros appointed royal governor of Massachusetts by the king
1688	James II deposed in the Glorious Revolution and William III and Mary succeeded to the English throne
1689	Andros imprisoned by the Puritan old guard, who reinstated the old Puritan charter with Simon Bradstreet as governor
1689	Start of King William's War against the French and Indians
1691	King created new royal charter for New England

Year 1692

Mar. 11	Start of arrest phase of Salem Village witch hunt with the arrests of Sarah Good, Sarah Osborne, and Tituba in Salem Village.

Apr. 11	Examination of Sarah Cloyce and Elizabeth Proctor in Salem Town by high ranking Puritan officials, establishing the complicity of the ruling old guard in the witch hunt.
Apr. 1692	Suckling child of Sarah Good died in prison, shortly after prison-keeper John Arnold spent 10 shillings for "two blankets for Sarah Good's child."
May 10	Sarah Osborne died in prison.
May 14	Sir William Phipps, the appointed governor under the new royal charter, arrived from England and displaced Gov. Simon Bradstreet
May 25	A special "Court of Oyer and Terminer" established to try the witchcraft cases.
May 28	Martha (Allen) Carrier arrested, the first one from Andover.
June 2	First meeting (in Salem) of Court of Oyer and Terminer at Salem. Bridget Bishop condemned.
June 10	Bridget Bishop executed.
June 16	Dr. Roger Toothaker died in Boston jail.
June 30	Second meeting (in Salem) of Court of Oyer and Terminer. Rebecca Nurse, Elizabeth Howe, Sarah Good, Sarah Wildes, Susannah Martin condemned.
July 1	End of arrest phase of Salem Village witch hunt with the arrests of Margaret Hawkes and Candy of Salem.
July 15	Start of arrest phase of Andover witch hunt with the arrest of Ann Foster of Andover.
July 19	Rebecca Nurse, Elizabeth Howe, Sarah Good, Sarah Wilds, and Susannah Martin executed.
Aug. 5	Third meeting (in Salem) of Court of Oyer and Terminer. The Rev. George Burroughs, John Proctor, Elizabeth Proctor, John Willard, George Jacobs, Sr., Martha Carrier condemned.
Aug. 19	The Rev. George Burroughs, John Proctor, John Willard, George Jacobs, Sr., and Martha Carrier executed.
Sept. 7	Andover touch test resulting in the arrest of 18 Andover residents.
Sept. 9	Fourth meeting (in Salem) of Court of Oyer and Terminer. Martha Corey, Mary Easty, Alice Parker, Ann Pudeator, Dorcas Hoar, and Mary Bradbury condemned.
Sept. 17	Fifth meeting (in Salem) of Court of Oyer and Terminer. Wilmot Redd, Abigail Hobbs, Margaret Scott, Mary Parker, Abigail Faulkner, Rebecca Eames, Ann Foster, Mary (Foster) Lacey, and Samuel Wardwell condemned.
Sept. 18	Mary Bradbury escaped.
Sept. 19	Giles Corey pressed to death.

Sept. 21	Dorcas Hoar reprieved for making a last-minute confession.
Sept. 22	Martha Corey, Mary Easty, Alice Parker, Ann Pudeator, Margaret Scott, Wilmot Redd, Mary Parker, Samuel Wardwell executed.
Oct. 6-15	Imprisoned children of Andover released on bail.
Oct. 27	John Durrant died in Cambridge prison.
Dec. 3	Ann Foster died in prison.

Year 1693

Jan. 3	First meeting (in Salem) of the Superior Court of Judicature.
Jan. 31	Second meeting (in Charlestown) of the Superior Court of Judicature.
Mar. 10	Lydia Dustin died in prison.
Apr. 25	Third meeting (in Boston) of the Superior Court of Judicature.
May 9	Fourth meeting (in Ipswich) of the Superior Court of Judicature.

CHRONOLOGICAL LIST OF THE ACCUSED, 1692

Charged	Name of accused, Age, Town	Fate after Arrest
November 1691	Martha (Barrett) Sparks, Chelmsford. Committed by Lieut. Gov. Thomas Danforth as a prelude to the Salem witchcraft affair.	Imprisoned more than a year; released on bail December 6, 1692
ARREST PHASE OF SALEM VILLAGE WITCH HUNT		
Feb. 29, 1692	Sarah (Solart) Poole Good, 38, Salem Village	Imprisoned; condemned June 30; executed July 29
Feb. 29	Suckling child of Sarah Good, Salem Village	Died in prison in April 1692 from cold and hunger
Feb. 29	Sarah (Warren) Prince Osborne, 50, Salem Village	Imprisoned 9 weeks; died in prison May 10
Feb. 29	Tituba, Salem Village	Imprisoned 13 months; sold to slavery in 1693
Mar. 19	Martha (mnu) Rich Corey, 65, Salem Village	Imprisoned; condemned Sept. 9; executed Sept. 22
Mar. 23	Rebecca (Towne) Nurse, 70, Salem Village	Imprisoned; condemned June 30, executed July 19
Mar. 23	Dorcas Good, 4, Salem Village	Imprisoned almost 9 months; released on bail Dec. 10
Mar. 29	Rachel (Haffield) Clinton, 63, Salem Village	Imprisoned in Ipswich
Apr. 4	Sarah (Towne) Bridges Cloyce, 51, Salem Village	Imprisoned; cleared Jan. 3, 1693
Apr. 4	Elizabeth (Bassett) Proctor, 41, Salem Farms	Imprisoned; condemned Aug. 5; reprieved for pregnancy; released in 1693

Apr. 11	John Proctor, 60, Salem Farms	Imprisoned; condemned Aug. 5; executed Aug. 19
Apr. 18	Giles Corey, 80, Salem Village	Pressed to death, Sept. 19
Apr. 18	Bridget (Playfer) Wasselbe Oliver Bishop, 60, Salem Town	Imprisoned; condemned June 2; executed June 10
Apr. 18	Abigail Hobbs, 22, Topsfield	Imprisoned; condemned Sept. 17; reprieved; released Apr. 1693 after 12 months imprisonment
Apr. 18	Mary Warren, 20, Salem Village	Briefly imprisoned; released as an afflicted person
Apr. 21	William Hobbs, 50, Topsfield	Released 1693
Apr. 21	Deliverance (mnu) Hobbs	Imprisoned 12 months; Released Apr. 1693
Apr. 21	Nehemiah Abbot, Jr., 29, Topsfield	Released at preliminary examination, the only such case
Apr. 21	Mary (Towne) Easty, 51, Salem Village	Imprisoned; condemned Sept. 9; executed Sept. 22
Apr. 21	Sarah (Averill) Wildes, 65, Topsfield	Imprisoned; condemned June 30; executed July 19
Apr. 21	Edward Bishop, Jr., 44, Salem Village	Imprisoned, escaped
Apr. 21	Sarah (Wildes) Bishop, 41, Salem Village	Imprisoned, escaped
Apr. 21	Mary Black, slave, Salem Village	Imprisoned 8 months; cleared by proclamation Jan. 11
Apr. 21	Mary (Hollingsworth) English, 40, Salem Town	Imprisoned at least 6 weeks; escaped
Apr. 27	Thomas Dyer, Ipswich	Imprisoned
Apr. 28	Samuel Passanauton (an Indian)	Imprisoned
unknown	Female slave of Mrs. Thatcher, Boston	Imprisoned
unknown	Mary Cox	Imprisoned; record of irons ordered for her
Apr. 30	Philip English, 41, Salem Town	Imprisoned but escaped

Apr. 30	Lydia (mnu) Dustin, 65, Reading	Imprisoned; found not guilty Jan. 31, 1693; held in prison for fees; died in prison Mar. 10, 1693
Apr. 30	Susannah (North) Martin, 66, Amesbury	Imprisoned; condemned June 30; executed July 19
Apr. 30	Dorcas (Galley) Hoar, 60, Beverly	Imprisoned; condemned Sept. 9; reprieved; released 1693
Apr. 30	Sarah Morrell, 14, Beverly	Imprisoned 35 weeks; "tried and cleared" Jan. 1693
Apr. 30	Rev. George Burroughs, 41, Wells, Maine	Imprisoned; condemned Aug. 5; executed Aug. 19
May 7	Sarah Dustin, 39, Reading	Imprisoned; found not guilty Feb. 1, 1693; held in prison for fees; released March 23, 1693
May 8	Bethia (Pearson) Carter, 47, Woburn	Imprisoned; released on bail Dec. 8
May 8	Bethia Carter, Jr., 21, Woburn	Fled before arrest
May 8	Ann (mnu) Farrar Sears, 71, Woburn	Imprisoned; released on bail Dec. 3
May 10	George Jacobs, Sr., 76, Salem Town	Imprisoned; condemned Aug. 5; executed Aug. 19
May 10	Margaret Jacobs, 16, Salem Town	Imprisoned; released on bail in December; found not guilty Jan. 3, 1693
May 10	John Willard, 33, Salem Village	Imprisoned; condemned Aug. 5; executed Aug. 19
May 12	Alice (mnu) Parker, Salem Town	Imprisoned; condemned Sept. 9; executed Sept. 22
May 12	Ann (mnu) Greenslade Pudeator, 65, Salem Town	Imprisoned; condemned Sept. 9; executed Sept. 22
May 13	Abigail Somes, 37, Salem Town	Imprisoned; cleared Jan. 6, 1693

May 13	Thomas Hardy, Great Island, NH	
May 14	Daniel Andrew, 48, Salem Village	Fled before arrest
May 14	George Jacobs, Jr., 50, Salem Village	Fled before arrest
May 14	Rebecca (Andrew) Frost Jacobs, 46, Salem Village	Imprisoned 6 months; found not guilty on Jan. 3, 1693
May 14	Sarah (Smith) Buckley, 70, Salem Village	Imprisoned over 8 months; found not guilty on Jan. 4, 1693
May 14	Mary (Buckley) Whittredge, 27, Salem Village	Imprisoned over 8 months; found not guilty on Jan. 4, 1693
May 14	Elizabeth (Hutchinson) Hart, 65, Lynn	Imprisoned 7 months; cleared January 1693
May 14	Thomas Farrar, Sr., 75, Lynn	Imprisoned 7 months; cleared by proclamation Jan. 12, 1693
May 14	Elizabeth Colson, 15, Reading	Fled; captured Sept. 14 and imprisoned
May 15	Mehitabel (Brabrook) Downing, 40, Ipswich	Imprisoned at Ipswich prison
May 18	Dr. Roger Toothaker, 58, Billerica	Imprisoned; died in prison June 16
May 21	Sarah Proctor, 15, Salem Farms	Imprisoned
May 21	Sarah (Hood) Bassett, 35, Lynn	Imprisoned; cleared on Jan. 3, 1693
May 21	Susannah (mnu) Roots, 70, Beverly	Imprisoned
May 23	Benjamin Proctor, 33, Salem Farms	Imprisoned "several months."
May 23	Mary (Bassett) De Rich, 35, Salem Village	Imprisoned about 6 months
May 23	Sarah (mnu) Pease, Salem Town	Imprisoned
May 28	Elizabeth (Walker) Cary, 42, Charlestown	Imprisoned; escaped
May 28	Capt. John Alden Jr., 69, Boston	Imprisoned; house arrest 15 weeks; escaped; cleared by proclamation Apr. 25, 1693
May 28	Capt. John Floyd, 55, Malden	Imprisoned
May 28	Elizabeth (mnu) Betts Fosdick, 32, Malden	Imprisoned

May 28	Wilmot (mnu) Redd, 55, Marblehead	Imprisoned; condemned Sept. 17; executed Sept. 22
May 28	Sarah (mnu) Davis Rice, 61, Reading	Imprisoned
May 28	William Proctor, 17, Salem Farms	Imprisoned; cleared Jan. 1693
May 28	Elizabeth (Jackson) Howe, 54, Topsfield	Imprisoned; condemned June 30; executed July 19
May 28	Arthur Abbot, 53, Topsfield	Imprisoned
May 28	Martha (Allen) Carrier, 38, Andover	Imprisoned; condemned Aug. 5; executed Aug. 19
May 28	Mary (Allen) Toothaker, 47, Billerica	Imprisoned; found not guilty Feb. 1, 1693
May 28	Margaret Toothaker, 9, Billerica	Imprisoned
June 2	Elizabeth (Carrington) Paine, 53, Charlestown	Imprisoned
June 1	Sarah Churchill, 20, Salem Village	Briefly imprisoned; then released as an afflicted person
June 4	Mary (Leach) Ireson, 32, Lynn	Imprisoned
June 4	Job Tookey, 27, Beverly	Imprisoned; found not guilty on Jan. 5, 1693
June 6	Ann (Higginson) Dolliver, 29, Gloucester	Imprisoned
June 28	Mary (Perkins) Bradbury, 75, Salisbury	Imprisoned; condemned Sept. 9; escaped
July 1	Margaret (mnu) Hawkes, Salem Town	Imprisoned
July 1	Candy, female slave, Salem Town	Imprisoned; found not guilty on Jan. 6, 1693
c. July 15	Elizabeth Scargen	Imprisoned
c. July 15	child of Elizabeth Scargen	Imprisoned; died in prison

ARREST PHASE OF ANDOVER WITCH HUNT		
July 15, 1692	Ann (mnu) Foster, 72, Andover	Imprisoned; condemned Sept. 17; reprieved; died in prison Dec. 1692
July 19	Mary (Foster) Lacey, 40, Andover	Imprisoned; condemned Sept. 17; reprieved; pardoned in 1693

July 19	Mary Lacey, Jr., 18, Andover	Imprisoned 10 weeks; released on bail Oct. 6; found not guilty Jan. 13, 1693
July 21	Richard Carrier, 18, Andover	Imprisoned; released on bail mid October
July 21	Andrew Carrier, 15, Andover	Imprisoned; released on bail mid October
July 22	Martha (Toothaker) Emerson, 24, Haverhill	Imprisoned; cleared Jan. 12, 1693
July 28	Mary (Tyler) Post Bridges, 48, Andover	Imprisoned; found not guilty Jan. 12, 1693
July 30	Hannah (mnu) Tyler Brumidge, 60, Haverhill	Imprisoned in Ipswich prison; cleared Jan. 1693
July 30	Mary (Green) Green, 34, Haverhill	Imprisoned in Ipswich prison; released on bail, Dec. 16
c. Aug. 1	Rebecca (Blake) Eames, 51, Boxford	Imprisoned; condemned Sept. 17; reprieved; released Mar. 1693 after 7 months in prison
Aug. 2	Mary Post, 28, Andover	Imprisoned; condemned Jan. 12, 1693; reprieved; released April 1693 after more than 8 months in prison
Aug. 3	Mary (Johnson) Davis Clarke, 53, Haverhill	Imprisoned in Ipswich prison
Aug. 5	Margaret (Stevenson) Scott, 72, Beverly	Imprisoned; condemned Sept. 17; executed Sept. 22
c. Aug. 9	Daniel Eames, 29, Boxford	Imprisoned
c. Aug. 10	Thomas Carrier, Jr., 10, Andover	Imprisoned; Released on bail Oct. 6
c. Aug. 10	Sarah Carrier, 7, Andover	Imprisoned; Released on bail Oct. 6
Aug. 10	Elizabeth Johnson Jr., 22, Andover	Imprisoned; condemned Jan. 12, 1693; reprieved; imprisoned 6 months; released Feb. 1693

Aug. 11	Abigail (Dane) Faulkner, 40, Andover	Imprisoned; condemned Sept. 17; reprieved for pregnancy; released about Dec. 8
c. Aug. 15	Samuel Wardwell, 49, Andover	Imprisoned; condemned Sept. 17; executed Sept. 22
c. Aug. 15	Edward Farrington, 30, Andover	Imprisoned
c. Aug. 15	Sarah Parker, 22, Andover	Imprisoned 17 weeks; released on bail about Dec. 12
Aug. 18	Frances (mnu) Hutchins, 75, Haverhill	Imprisoned; released on bail Dec. 21
Aug. 18	Ruth Wilford, 17, Haverhill	Imprisoned
Aug. 25	Susannah Post, 31, Andover	Imprisoned; found not guilty May 10, 1693
Aug. 25	Hannah Post, 26, Boxford	Imprisoned; found not guilty Jan. 12, 1693
Aug. 25	Sarah Bridges, 17, Andover	Imprisoned 6 weeks; released on bail about October 6; found not guilty Jan. 12, 1693
Aug. 25	Mary Bridges, Jr., 13, Andover	Imprisoned; released on bail October 15; found not guilty May 12, 1693
Aug. 25	Mary Barker, 13, Andover	Imprisoned 6 weeks; released on bail about Oct. 10; found not guilty May 10, 1693
Aug. 25	William Barker, Sr., 46, Andover	Imprisoned; escaped
Aug. 25	Mary (Osgood) Marston, 27, Andover	Imprisoned; released on bail Dec. 20; found not guilty Jan. 12, 1693
Aug. 25	John Jackson, Sr., 50, Rowley	Imprisoned
Aug. 25	John Jackson, Jr., 22, Rowley	Imprisoned
Aug. 25	John Howard, 48, Rowley	Imprisoned
Aug. 29	Elizabeth (Dane) Johnson, 51, Andover	Imprisoned 5 months; found not guilty Jan. 7, 1693
Aug. 29	Abigail Johnson, 10, Andover	Imprisoned 5 weeks; released on bail Oct. 6
Aug. 30	Stephen Johnson, 13, Andover	Imprisoned 5 weeks, released on bail Oct. 6

Sept. 1	William Barker, Jr., 14, Andover	Imprisoned 6 weeks; released on bail about Oct. 10; found not guilty May 10, 1693
Sept. 1	Sarah (Hooper) Hawkes Wardwell, 42, Andover	Imprisoned; condemned Jan. 10, 1693; reprieved; released spring 1693
Sept. 1	Rebecca Wardwell, nearly a year old, Andover	Imprisoned with mother
Sept. 1	Sarah Hawkes, 21, Andover	Imprisoned 5 months; found not guilty Jan. 10, 1693
Sept. 1	Mercy Wardwell, 18, Andover	Imprisoned; found not guilty Jan. 10, 1693
Sept. 1	Mary (Ayer) Parker, 55, Andover	Imprisoned; condemned Sept. 17; executed Sept. 22
Sept. 3	Elizabeth (Austin) Dicer, Gloucester	Imprisoned in Ipswich prison
Sept. 3	Margaret (mnu) Prince, 62, Gloucester	Imprisoned in Ipswich prison
Sept. 5	Mary (Dustin) Colson, 41, Reading	Imprisoned; released Mar. 2, 1693
Sept. 5	Jane (mnu) Lilly, 48, Reading	Imprisoned; released on bail Dec. 8; cleared Feb. 3, 1693
Sept. 5	Mary (Harrington) Taylor, 40, Reading	Imprisoned; found not guilty Feb. 1, 1693
Sept. 5	Joseph Emons, Manchester	Imprisoned
Sept. 5	Nicholas Frost, Portland, N.H.	
Sept. 7	Deliverance (Haseltine) Dane, 37, Andover	Imprisoned 13 weeks; released about Dec. 8
Sept. 7	Rebecca (Aslet) Johnson, 40, Andover	Imprisoned 13 weeks; released on bail about Dec. 8; case dismissed Jan. 7, 1693
Sept. 7	Rebecca Johnson, Jr., 17, Andover	Imprisoned 13 weeks; released on bail about Dec. 8
Sept. 7	Mary (Clement) Osgood, 55, Andover	Imprisoned 15 weeks; released on bail Dec. 20; found not guilty Jan. 12, 1693

Sept. 7	Eunice (Potter) Frye, 51, Andover	Imprisoned 15 weeks; released on bail Dec. 20; found not guilty May 10, 1693
Sept. 7	Sarah (Lord) Wilson, 44, Andover	Imprisoned 15 weeks; released on bail about Dec. 20; cleared May 1693
Sept. 7	Sarah Wilson, Jr., 14, Andover	Imprisoned 6 weeks; released on bail about Oct. 15; cleared May 1693
Sept. 7	Abigail (Wheeler) Barker, 36, Andover	Imprisoned 18 weeks; found not guilty Jan. 6, 1693
Sept. 7	Mary (Lovett) Tyler, 40, Andover	Imprisoned; found not guilty Jan. 7, 1693
Sept. 7	Hannah Tyler, 14, Andover	Imprisoned; released on bail about Oct. 15; found not guilty Jan. 5, 1693
Sept. 7	Joanna Tyler, 11, Andover	Imprisoned; released on bail about Oct. 6; cleared May 1693
Sept. 7	Martha Tyler, 11, Andover	Imprisoned; released on bail about Oct. 6; cleared May 1693
Sept. 7	Abigail Faulkner, Jr., 9, Andover	Imprisoned 1 month; released on bail Oct. 6; cleared by proclamation May 1693
Sept. 7	Dorothy Faulkner, 12, Andover	Imprisoned 1 month; released on bail Oct. 6; cleared by proclamation May 1693
Sept. 7	John Sadie, Jr., 13, Andover	Imprisoned
Sept. 7	Joseph Draper, 21, Andover	Imprisoned
Sept. 7	Henry Salter, 65, Andover	No record of further legal action
Sept. 7	Male slave of Nathaniel Dane, Andover	Imprisoned 8 weeks

ARREST PHASE OF RESIDUAL ACCUSATIONS		
Sept. 10, 1692	Hannah (mnu) Carroll, Salem Town	Imprisoned
Sept. 10	Sarah (Davis) Cole, 42, Salem Town	Imprisoned; released on bail Jan. 14, 1693; cleared May 1693
Sept. 13	Joanna (mnu) Brabrook Penny, 72, Gloucester	Imprisoned in Ipswich
Oct. 1	Sarah (Aslet) Cole, 30, Lynn	Imprisoned; found not guilty Feb. 1, 1693; returned to prison for fees; released Mar. 23, 1693
Early Oct. 1692	Phoebe (Wildes) Day, 39, Gloucester	Imprisoned at Ipswich
Early Oct. 1692	Mary (Prince) Rowe, 34, Gloucester	Imprisoned at Ipswich
Early Oct. 1692	Rachel (Varney) Cooke Langton Vinson, 62, Gloucester	Imprisoned at Ipswich
Nov. 5	Rebecca (Dolliver) Dike, 41, Gloucester	Imprisoned
Nov. 5	James Dike, infant, few weeks old, Gloucester	Imprisoned with mother
Nov. 5	Esther (Dutch) Elwell, 53, Gloucester	Imprisoned
Nov. 5	Abigail Rowe, 15, Gloucester	Imprisoned
Unknown	John Durrant, 44, Billerica	Died in Cambridge prison Oct. 27, 1693
Unknown	Henry Somers	Imprisoned at Cambridge
Unknown	Edward Wooland	Imprisoned at Salem
Unknown	Three or four men	Imprisoned at Ipswich
Unknown	Mary Watkins, a young white woman unable to pay her prison fees	Imprisoned, sold as a slave after August 11, 1693

BIBLIOGRAPHY

Abbot, Abiel, *History of Andover from its Settlement to 1829*, Flagg & Gould, Andover, 1829.

Abbott, Charlotte Helen, Articles from *The Andover Townsman*, Andover Historical Society, Andover, MA, 1895-1910.

Abbott, Charlotte Helen, *Genealogies*, Andover Historical Society, Andover, MA, 1893-1914

Abbott, Katharine M, *Old Paths and Legends of New England*, New York, NY, 1903.

Adams, Charles Francis, *Massachusetts, Its Historians and Its History*, Boston, 1893.

Bailey, Sarah Loring, *Historical Sketches of Andover, Massachusetts*, Houghton, Mifflin & Co., Boston, 1880.

Bishop, George, *New England Judged by the Spirit of the Lord, in two parts, Part First, The year 1656 to the year 1660, Second Part, Continued from Anno 1660 to Anno 1665*, Printed by T. Sowle, London, 1703.

Boguet, Henri, *An Examen of Witches*, Paris, 1603.

Boston Public Library, *Rare Books and Manuscripts*, 1692.

Boyer, Paul, and Stephen Nissenbaum, eds., *The Salem Witchcraft Papers*, 3 vols., New York, 1977.

Boyer, Paul, and Stephen Nissenbaum, *Salem Possessed: The Social Origins of Witchcraft*, Cambridge, MA, 1974.

Bradstreet, Anne, *The Poems of Mrs. Anne Bradstreet, together with her Prose remains*, F. E. Hopkins, ed., New York, 1897.

Bradstreet, Anne, *The Works of Anne Bradstreet in Prose and Verse*, J. H. Ellis, ed., Charlestown, MA, 1867. Facsimile reprint, Gloucester, MA, 1962.

Brattle, Thomas, "Letter of October 8, 1692." Reprinted in Burr, ed., *Narratives of the Witchcraft Cases*, 169-190.

Burr, George Lincoln, ed., *Narratives of the Witchcraft Cases, 1648-1706*, New York, NY, 1914.

Calef, Robert, *More Wonders of the Invisible World, or the Wonders of the Invisible World Displayed in Five Parts*, London, 1700. Reprinted, Salem, MA, 1861.

Chase, George Wingate, *History of Haverhill, Massachusetts*, Haverhill, MA, 1861.

Church, Thomas, *The History of Philip's War, Commonly Called the Great Indian War, of 1675 and 1676. Also of the French and Indian Wars at the Eastward in 1689, 1690, 1692, 1696, and 1704*, Exeter, NH, 1829. Reprint, Heritage Books, Inc., Bowie, MD, 1989.

Colonial Society of Massachusetts, *Architecture in Colonial Massachusetts*, Boston, 1979.

Colonial Society of Massachusetts, *Law in Colonial Massachusetts*, Boston, 1984.

Curtis, Edith, *Anne Hutchinson, A Biography*, Washburn & Thomas, Cambridge, MA, 1930.

Demos, John P, "John Godfrey and His Neighbors: Witchcraft and the Social Web in Colonial Massachusetts" *William and Mary Quarterly*, 33 (April 1976), 242-265.

Dow, George Francis, *History of Topsfield, Massachusetts*, Boston, 1940.

Drake, Samuel G, *Annals of Witchcraft in New England*, Boston, 1869.

Drake, Samuel G, *The Witchcraft Delusion in New England: Its Rise, Progress, and Termination*, 3 vols., New York, NY, 1866.

Earle, Alice Morse, *Customs and Fashions in Old New England*, New York, NY, 1894.

Essex County Archives, *Witchcraft*, Two volumes, Salem, MA, 1692. Copied, 1859.

Essex County, Massachusetts, *Court Records* (includes presentments, orders, depositions, correspondence, deeds, probate, wills, inventories of estates, contracts, correspondence, apprentice indentures, inquests, writs, and executions), 1636-1694.

Essex Institute, *Witchcraft Collection* (includes complaints, arrest warrants, examinations, depositions, indictments, summonses, inquests, mittimuses, and a single death warrant), Salem, MA, 1692.

Felt, Joseph B., *The Annals of Salem*, Salem, 1827.

Fiske, John, *Witchcraft in Salem Village*, Houghton Mifflin Co., Boston, MA, 1902.

Fuess, Claude M., *Andover, Symbol of New England, The Evolution of a Town*, Andover, 1959.

"Further Account of the Trials of the New England Witches, sent in a letter from thence, to a Gentleman in London." Contemporary letter by an unknown writer printed in the 1862 edition of Cotton Mather, *The Wonders of the Invisible World*, 214-217.

Goodell, Abner Cheney, Jr., *Further Notes on the History of Witchcraft in Massachusetts*, Cambridge, MA, 1884.

Greven, Philip J., *Four Generations: Population, Land and Family in Colonial Andover, Massachusetts*, Cornell University Press, Ithaca, NY, 1970.

Hale, John, *A Modest Enquiry into the Nature of Witchcraft*, Boston, 1702. Reprinted in Burr, ed., *Narratives of the Witchcraft Cases*, 399-432.

Hall, David D., *Witch-Hunting*, Boston, 1991.

Hallowell, Richard B., *The Quaker Invasion of Massachusetts*, Houghton, Mifflin & Co., Boston, MA, 1883.

Hawthorne, Julian, *Nathaniel Hawthorne and his Wife, A Biography*, 2 volumes, Boston, 1884.

Hawthorne, Nathaniel, *Alice Doane's Appeal*, 1835.

Hawthorne, Nathaniel, *Edward Fane's Rosebud*, in *Twice Told Tales*, 1837.

Hawthorne, Nathaniel, *Endicott and the Red Cross*, 1838.

Hawthorne, Nathaniel, *John Inglefield's Thanksgiving*, in *The Snow-Image and Other Twice-told Tales*, 1852.

Hawthorne, Nathaniel, *Main-Street*, in *The Snow-Image and Other Twice-told Tales*, 1852.

Hawthorne, Nathaniel, *Mrs. Hutchinson*, 1830.

Hawthorne, Nathaniel, *The Custom-House, Introductory to "The Scarlet Letter,"* Tichnor, Reed, and Fields, Boston, MA, 1850.

Hawthorne, Nathaniel, *The House of the Seven Gables*, Tichnor, Reed, and Fields, Boston, MA, 1851.

Hawthorne, Nathaniel, *The Scarlet Letter*, Tichnor, Reed, and Fields, Boston, MA, 1850.

Hawthorne, Nathaniel, *Young Goodman Brown*, in *Mosses from an Old Manse*, 1846.

Hawthorne, *The Christmas Banquet*, in *Mosses from an Old Manse*, 1846.

Howe, David Wait, *The Puritan Republic*, Bowen-Merrill, Indianapolis, IN, 1899.

Hutchinson, Robert, *Poems of Anne Bradstreet*, Dover Press, New York, NY, 1969.

Hutchinson, Thomas, "The Witchcraft Delusion of 1692, from an Unpublished Manuscript (An early draft of his *History of Massachusetts*)," *New England Historic & Genealogical Register*, 24: 381-414, October 1870.

Hutchinson, Thomas, *The History of the Colony and Province of Massachusetts-Bay*, London, 1768.

James, Henry, Jr. *Hawthorne*, New York, 1880.

Kimball, Henrietta D., *Witchcraft Illustrated*, George A. Kimball, Publisher, Boston, MA, 1892.

Kittredge, George L., *Witchcraft in Old and New England*, Cambridge, Harvard University Press, 1929.

Lawson, Deodat, *A Brief and True Narrative of Some Remarkable Passages Relating to Sundry Persons Afflicted by Witchcraft, at Salem Village Which Happened from the Nineteenth of March to the Fifth of April, 1692*, Boston, 1692. Reprinted in Burr, ed., *Narratives of the Witchcraft Cases*.

Lewis, Alonzo, and James R. Newhall, *History of Lynn, Essex County, Massachusetts,* Boston, 1865. Reprinted, Heritage Books, Inc., Bowie, MD, 1989.

Loggins, Vernon, *The Hawthornes*, New York, NY, 1951.

Marder, Daniel, *Exiles at Home: A Story of Literature in Nineteenth Century America,* Lanham, MD, 1984.

Massachusetts Archives, *Witchcraft*, Boston, MA, 1656-1750.

Massachusetts Historical Society, "Mather-Calef Papers on Witchcraft." 1695, *Proceedings*, 47 (1914), 240-268.

Massachusetts Historical Society, "Recantation of Confessors of Witchcraft."
    Massachusetts Historical Society Collections, 2nd ser., 3, 221-225.

Mather, Cotton, "Diary of Cotton Mather, 1681-1708." *Massachusetts
    Historical Society Collections*, Seventh Series, 7-8, (1911-12).

Mather, Cotton, "Letter of August 5, 1692 to John Cotton." *Massachusetts
    Historical Society Collections*, Seventh Series, 7, (1911).

Mather, Cotton, "Letter of May 31, 1692 to John Richards." *Massachusetts
    Historical Society Collections*, Fourth Series, 8, (1868).

Mather, Cotton, "Letter of September 20, 1692 to Stephen Sewall." Reprinted
    in Upham, *Salem Witchcraft*, 2:487-488.

Mather, Cotton, "The Mather Papers." *Massachusetts Historical Society
    Collections*, Fourth Series, 8, (1868).

Mather, Cotton, *A Discourse on Witchcraft*, A sermon included in Cotton
    Mather, *Memorable Providences Relating to Witchcrafts and
    Possessions*, Boston, 1689.

Mather, Cotton, *Fair Weather*, Boston, 1692.

Mather, Cotton, *Magnalia Christi Americana, or the Ecclesiastical History of
    New England, in Seven Books*, London, 1702. Reprinted in 2 vols.,
    Hartford, 1855.

Mather, Cotton, *Memorable Providences Relating to Witchcrafts and
    Possessions*, Boston, 1689. Reprinted in Burr, ed., *Narratives of the
    Witchcraft Cases*, 93-143.

Mather, Cotton, *The Present State of New England*, Boston, 1690.

Mather, Cotton, *The Return of Several Ministers, June 15, 1692*, Boston,
    1692. Reprinted in the 1862 edition of Cotton Mather, *The Wonders of
    the Invisible World*, 289-291.

Mather, Cotton, *The Wonders of the Invisible World*, Boston, 1692.
    Reprinted with additions, 1862.

Mather, Increase, *An Essay for the Recording of Illustrious Providences*,
    Boston, 1684. Reprinted with title *Remarkable Providences*, London,
    1890.

Mather, Increase, *Cases of Conscience Concerning Evil Spirits Personating
    Men*, Boston, 1692. Reprinted in the 1862 edition of Cotton Mather,
    The Wonders of the Invisible World, 225-284.

Mather, Samuel, *The Life of the Very Reverend and Learned Cotton Mather*,
    Boston, 1729.

McMillen, Persis W., *Currents of Malice: Mary Towne Esty and Her Family in
    Salem Witchcraft*, Portsmouth, N.H., 1990.

Mellow, James R., *Nathaniel Hawthorne in his Times*, Boston, 1980.

Mofford, Juliet Haines, *And Firm Thine Ancient Vow: The History of the
    North Parish Church of North Andover, 1645-1974*, North Andover,
    MA, 1975.

Moore, George H., *Final Notes on Witchcraft in Massachusetts, A Summary
    Vindication of the Laws and Liberties*, New York, NY, 1885.

Morrison, Samuel Eliot, *The Puritan Pronaos: Studies in the Intellectual Life of New England in the Seventeenth Century*, New York, NY and London, 1936.

Murdock, Kenneth B., *Increase Mather: The Foremost American Puritan*, Harvard University Press, Cambridge, 1925.

Murray, Margaret Alice, *The God of the Witches*, New York, 1952.

Nevins, Winfield S., *Witchcraft in Salem Village in 1692*, Salem, 1916.

Noyes, Sybil, Charles Thorton Libby, and Walter Goodwin Davis, *Genealogical Dictionary of Maine and New Hampshire*, Baltimore, 1972.

Otten, Marjorie Wardwell, *Samuel Wardwell of Andover and a Line of his Descendants*, (typescript). 1989.

Otten, Marjorie Wardwell, *The Witch Hunt of 1692*, (typescript). 1990.

Patterson, Bradley Hawkes, *Adam Hawkes, His Life and Times*, Leesburg, VA, 1957.

Perley, M.V.B., *A Short History of the Salem Village Witchcraft Trials illustrated by a Verbatim Report of the Trial of Elizabeth Howe*, M.V.B. Perley, Publishers, Salem, MA, 1911.

Perley, Sidney, *Indian Land Titles of Essex County*, Salem, MA, 1912

Perley, Sidney, *The History of Boxford, Essex County, Massachusetts*, Boxford, MA, 1880.

Perley, Sidney, *The History of Salem, Massachusetts*, 3 vols, Salem, MA, 1924, 1926, 1928.

Phillips, James Duncan, *Salem in the Seventeenth Century*, Boston, 1933.

Phipps, Sir William, "Letter dated at Boston, October 12, 1692," and "Letter dated at Boston, February 21, 1693." Reprinted in Burr, ed., *Narratives of the Witchcraft Cases*.

Quarterly Courts of Essex County, Massachusetts, *Records and Files, 1636–1683*, 8 vols., Salem, MA, 1911-21.

Rice, Charles B., *First Parish at Salem Village, now Danvers*, Boston, MA, 1874.

Robbins, Sarah Stuart, *Old Andover Days*, Boston, MA, 1909.

Robinson, Enders A., and Marjorie Wardwell Otten, *Salem Witchcraft Genealogy*, (typescript). 1987.

Robinson, Enders A., *Genealogy of the Barker Family of Andover, Massachusetts*, (typescript). 1988.

Robinson, Enders A., *Genealogy of the Wardwell Family of Andover, Massachusetts*, (typescript). 1989.

Robinson, Enders A., *The Devil Discovered, Salem Witchcraft 1692*, Hippocrene Books, Inc., NY, 1991.

Robinson, Enders A., *Wardwell and Barker Families of Andover in the Seventeenth Century*, (typescript). 1986.

Savage, James, *A Genealogical Dictionary of the First Settlers of New England*, Boston, 1860. Reprinted, Baltimore, 1990.

Sewall, Samuel, "Diary, 1674-1700," *Massachusetts Historical Society Collections*, Fifth Series, vol. 5.

Silverman, Kenneth, *The Times and Life of Cotton Mather*, New York, NY, 1984.

Smith, Ethel Farrington, *Adam Hawkes of Saugus, Massachusetts, 1605-1672*, 1980.

Starkey, Marion, *The Devil in Massachusetts*, New York, NY, 1949.

Styles, Ezra, *A Report of the Trial of Mrs. Anne Hutchinson*, Boston, 1638.

Suffolk County Archives, *Superior Court of Judicature Records*, 1692-1695. Copied, 1892.

Suffolk County, *Court Records*, Boston, MA, 1692.

Swan, Marshall W. S., "The Bedevilment at Cape Ann (1692)," *Historical Collections of the Essex Institute*, 117 (1981), 153-177.

Sylvester, M., ed., *Reliquiae Baxterianae*, London, 1696.

The Cottage Bible containing the Old and New Testaments, The Rev. William Patton, ed. Two volumes, Hartford, 1844 (An family bible of the Wardwells.)

Trevor-Roper, Hugh R., *The European Witch Craze of the 16th and 17th Centuries*, 1969

United States Government, Works Progress Administration (WPA), *Salem Witchcraft, 1692, A Verbatim Transcript of the Salem Witchcraft Papers*, Three volumes, Salem, MA, 1938.

Upham, Charles W., *Salem Witchcraft*, 2 vols., Boston, 1867.

Walker, Williston, *The Creeds and Platforms of Congregationalism*, New York, NY, 1893.

Wendell, Barrett, *Cotton Mather, the Puritan Priest*, Harvard University Press, Cambridge, 1926

Wendell, Barrett, *Were the Salem Witches Guiltless?*, Salem, 1892.

Whittier, John Greenleaf, *The Complete Poetical Works of John Greenleaf Whittier*, Boston, 1892.

Winthrop, John, *Journal, 1630-1649*, Reprinted, 2 vols., New York, 1908.

Woodward, W. Elliot, *Records of Salem Witchcraft, Copied from the Original Documents*, 2 vols., Roxbury, MA, 1864.

Young, Philip, *Hawthorne's Secret, An Un-told Tale*, Boston, MA, 1984.

Name Index

365

Redd, Wilmot, 163-164, 167, 346-347, 352
Rice, Sarah, 332, 352
Richards, John, 96, 107, 170, 193
Roberts, John, 49
Roberts, T., 49
Roberts, Thomas, 48-49
Robin Hood, 68
Robinson, William, 44
Roger, the Indian, 25
Rogers, John, 103, 280-281
Roots, Susannah, 351
Rowe, Abigail, 336-337, **338**, 339-340, 357
Rowe, Mary, 327, 336-337, **338**, 339, 357
Ruck, John, 66, 69
Ruck, Sarah, 66
Russ, John, 26
Russell, James, 94
Sadie, John, Jr., 159, 222, 267, 274, **299**, 330, 356
Salter, Henry, 159, 173, 222, 233, 242, **325**, 326, 356
Saltonstall, Nathaniel, 96, 107, 109
Scargen, Elizabeth, 352
Scott, Margaret, 163-164, 167, **341**, 346-347, 353
Sears, Ann, 350
Sergeant, Peter, 97, 107, 194
Sewall, Samuel, 94, 97, 107, 169, 193, 201
Shakespeare, 1, 99
Sheldon, Susannah, 88, 280
Small, John, 64
Somers, Henry, **343**, 357
Somes, Abigail, 350
Southwick, Lawrence and Cassandra, 44
Sparks, Martha, 348
Sprague, Martha, 33, 130, 133, 144-146, 148, 220-223, **237**, 238, 241, 243, 252, 256-262, 267-268, 287-288, 292-293, 295, 305, 308, 317-320
Sprague, Phineas, 33, 237
Sprague, Sarah Hasey, 130, 148, 237, 239, 310
Sprague, Sarah, 130, 148, 222, 237, 239, 292, 310, 317

Stacy, William, 111
Stanyel, Anthony, 48
Stevens, Ephraim, 35, 160, **272**
Stevens, James, 339-340
Stevens, John, 26, 33, 35, 272, 322
Stevens, John, Jr., 272
Stevens, Mary, 35, 256, 272
Stevenson, Marmaduke, 44
Stone, Hugh, 115-116
Stoughton, William, 82, 95-96, 131, 169, 193, 200, 202, 246, 251, 296, 306, 311, 313, 322
Suckling child of Sarah Good, 112, 346, 348
Swan, John, 129, 133, 220, 223, **234**, 330-331
Swan, Robert, Jr., 129, 133, 223, **234**, 330-331
Swan, Timothy, 129, 133, 145, 147, 220, 222-223, **234**, 235-236, 238, 251, 284, 304-305, 310, 321, 330-331
Symmes, Zachariah, 171, 175
Taylor, Mary Harrington, 173, 249, 305, 332-333, **334**, 335, 355
Thatcher, Mrs., 349
Thoreau, Henry David, 22
Tituba, 86-89, 107, 112, 119-120, 122, 141, 162, 164, 171-173, 177-178, 201, 345, 348
Tompkins, Mary, 48-49
Tookey, Job, 352
Toothaker, Dr. Roger, 34, 274, **276**, 277-278, 280, 346, 351
Toothaker, Margaret, 101, 274, **276**, 278, 352
Toothaker, Mary, 34, 99-101, 104, 135, 172-173, 175, 182, 184, 274, **276**, 277-279, 352
Towne, William, 91
Trollope, Anthony, 215
Turner, John, 57, 210
Tyler, Hannah, 145, 155, 159, 173, 222, 238, 242, **307**, 308, 356
Tyler, Hopestill, 30, 32, 146, 227-228, 252, 301, 306-308
Tyler, Joanna, 145, 159, 173, 222, 238, 292, **307**, 308, 324, 356
Tyler, Job, 29-32, 228, 232, 237, 301, 307

SUBJECT INDEX

Agawam, 19, 37
Algonquin Indians, 19
ancestral curse, 20-21, 72, 215
Andover conspiracy, 119-120,
    128-132, 147-148, 170, 193,
    217, 232, 256, 287, 307, 330
Andover proprietors, 25
Andover touch test, 35, 120, 150,
    153, 160, 162, 195, 197, 223,
    232-233, 238, 241, 243-244,
    249, 253, 264, 267, 269, 271-
    272, 292, 298-299, 305, 308,
    323-325, 330, 342, 346
Andover witch hunt, 100, 114,
    117, 119-120, 123, 131-132,
    143, 150, 159, 163, 171, 178,
    219, 223, 238, 248, 327, 346,
    352
Antinomian heretics, 47, 208
Arbella, 10, 36
arrest phase, 119-120, 345-346,
    348, 352, 357
Barbados, 44-45, 86
Board of Assistants, 36, 46, 67,
    80
Boston Common, 80
Boston Custom House, 22
Bowdoin College, 21-22
Bunker Hill, 101
cake of rye meal, 87
Calef in Boston, 8
Calvinists, 10
Cases of Conscience, 191
Catholic, 82
chief witch-hunter, 21, 70
Church of England, 10
City upon a Hill, 10
Cochichawick, 23
Council meeting, 97
Court of Oyer and Terminer, 96-
    98, 107, 124, 128, 134, 147,
    150, 162-163, 170, 193-194,

200, 204, 250, 253, 256, 258,
    263, 277, 279, 283, 286, 313,
    341, 346
credible confession, 170, 176-
    177, 179
crowns in Hell, 126
cry out upon these witches, 87
democratic trend, 80
Deuteronomy, 4
Devil's book, 89, 139, 143, 178-
    179, 182, 188, 250, 257-258
devouring fire, 127
devouring lion, 127
disciplinarians, 11
Discourse on Witchcraft, 81
Eagle, 36
eastern land, 68, 213-215
everlasting flames, 127
Exodus, 4
familiar spirits, 4
Fanshawe, 22
fierce land dispute, 91
Frankenstein monster, 192
Gallows Hill, 70-71, 109, 140-
    141, 146, 167, 169, 208, 213-
    214
God will give you blood to drink,
    112
Harvard College, 58, 76-77
hellish rendezvouses, 134, 183
Hooper house, 211
horns and cloven feet, 180
human testimony, 111-112, 122,
    191, 199-200
King Philip's War, 21, 39, 65-67
Kingdom of Satan, 184, 200
kingdom of the Devil, 188
legal complaint document, 128
Leviticus, 4
Macbeth, 99
Main-Street, 140-141, 207
Malleus Maleficarum, 4

373